Connecticut Gridiron

ALSO BY WILLIAM J. RYCZEK
AND FROM MCFARLAND

Blackguards and Red Stockings: A History of Baseball's National Association, 1871–1875 (1992; paperback 1999)

When Johnny Came Sliding Home: The Post–Civil War Baseball Boom, 1865–1870 (1998; paperback 2006)

The Yankees in the Early 1960s (2008)

The Amazin' Mets, 1962–1969 (2008)

Crash of the Titans: The Early Years of the New York Jets and the AFL, rev. ed. (2009)

Baseball's First Inning: A History of the National Pastime Through the Civil War (2009)

Connecticut Gridiron

*Football Minor Leaguers
of the 1960s and 1970s*

WILLIAM J. RYCZEK

McFarland & Company, Inc., Publishers
Jefferson, North Carolina

LIBRARY OF CONGRESS CATALOGUING-IN-PUBLICATION DATA

Ryczek, William J., 1953–
   Connecticut gridiron : football minor leaguers of the 1960s and 1970s / William J. Ryczek.
     p.   cm.
   Includes bibliographical references and index.

   ISBN 978-0-7864-7833-0 (softcover : acid free paper) ∞
   ISBN 978-1-4766-1726-8 (ebook)

   1. Minor league football—Connecticut—History. 2. Football—United States—History. 3. Football players—Connecticut. I. Title.
   GV954.R93 2014
   796.33209746—dc23   2014037050

BRITISH LIBRARY CATALOGUING DATA ARE AVAILABLE

© 2014 William J. Ryczek. All rights reserved

No part of this book may be reproduced or transmitted in any form or by any means, electronic or mechanical, including photocopying or recording, or by any information storage and retrieval system, without permission in writing from the publisher.

On the cover: Hartford Knights quarterback Benny Russell (far left) in a game on October 25, 1969, against the Harrisburg Capitols

Printed in the United States of America

McFarland & Company, Inc., Publishers
Box 611, Jefferson, North Carolina 28640
www.mcfarlandpub.com

To the memory of Dick Bowman, Arnold Dean,
Joe Klimas, Bob Mirabelle and John Skubel,
who shared their memories for this book,
but have sadly left us too soon.

Table of Contents

Acknowledgments ix

Introduction: The Twenty-First Century 1

1. A Minor League Town — 13
2. One Big Step from the NFL — 19
3. That's What They Do in the Fall — 24
4. A Football Crazed Town: The 1962–63 Ansonia Black Knights — 38
5. The 1962 Stamford Golden Bears — 62
6. A Hopeful Beginning and a Rude Awakening: The 1964–65 Hartford Charter Oaks — 70
7. It's Hard to Be a Major League: The 1966–67 Hartford Charter Oaks — 97
8. Two Steps from the Major Leagues: The Meriden Shamrocks and New Britain Bees — 116
9. An Unhappy Relationship: The 1966–67 Waterbury Orbits — 138
10. A New Team in Hartford — 161
11. The Championship Team: The Right Place at the Right Time — 179
12. The Championship Season: The 1968 Hartford Knights — 201
13. The 1969 Hartford Knights — 224
14. The Snow Bowl: The 1970 Hartford Knights — 239
15. Hi Ho, Hi Ho, to Bridgeport We Go: The 1968–70 Bridgeport Jets — 260

16. A Four-Team ACFL: The 1971 Hartford Knights and Bridgeport Jets   287

17. A Perfect Season in an Imperfect League: The 1972 Hartford Knights   302

18. Back in the ACFL: The 1973 Hartford Knights and Bridgeport Jets   320

Epilogue   335

Appendix: Scores and Records by Season   351

Chapter Notes   359

Bibliography   365

Index   367

Acknowledgments

The heart and soul of this book came from the memories of those who played for the teams featured here and those who covered them in the media. Talking to these men and women, whose names are listed in the bibliography, gave me insight into what it was like to be involved in minor league football in the 1960s. It was informative and enjoyable for me, and dredging up memories seemed to bring a lot of pleasure to those on the other end of the phone.

"Never in my life, Bill, did I think I'd be talking again about the Hartford Knights," said Charlie Tiblom.

"Going through all these old programs," said Bob Stohrer, "brings back a lot of great memories."

"It's nice that you remembered us," said John Land. "I put a lot of tough years into football, from Harlem in New York City to Dover, Delaware. It's where my whole life started. It's how I met my wife. I appreciate your call. You make me feel young again."

"You touched a lot of good nerves tonight," said Tim Miller. "I wanted to tell you about the things that made my football life good—and not just football but everything else along the way." Miller recalled the time the Knights had to practice at Colt Park because Dillon Stadium was being used for an Alice Cooper concert. He probably couldn't imagine that forty years later one of the college students attending the concert would be interviewing him about his Knights career, and that he would enjoy it.

Quarterbacks, so actively involved in game strategy, seem to have the clearest memories, able to dredge up minute details of games played long ago. "To this day," said Seiko Murono, "I vividly remember individual plays. They're indelibly etched into my memory."

"I can remember back to the first touchdown I scored in prep school," said Manch Wheeler.

Hearing the voices of Arnold Dean (who unfortunately has since passed away) and Lou Palmer brought me back to Saturday evenings in the late '60s, when they described the exploits of the Hartford Knights for those of us who couldn't get to Dillon Stadium. Both men sounded exactly as they did in 1968. "We just regress," said Palmer. "Every year we get one year younger."

I spent a lot of time in libraries during my research, and would like to thank the reference staff at the Wallingford Public Library; the New Britain Public Library; the Waterbury Public Library; the New York Public Library; the Stamford Public Library; the Ansonia Public Library; Pat Tully, director of Wesleyan University's Olin Library; and especially the staff at the Bridgeport Public Library, where I spent many cozy Saturdays.

Thanks to Joe Williams for inviting me to the Hartford Colonials game and to John Thorn for putting me on the right path, as described in the Introduction. Thanks to Bob Stohrer, Joe Ginnetti and Elaine Savin for providing me with many old game programs; to Bob Anderson for sending copies of articles from his personal scrapbook; to Chris Willis of NFL Films for the copy of the Pottstown Firebirds documentary; and to Seiki Murono for giving me the transcript of his father's testimony before Congress. Thanks once again to my friend Fred Dauch for his careful review of the manuscript and, finally, thanks to my dear wife, Susan, for much-needed grammatical and reference assistance and a concise explanation of the serial comma.

Introduction: The Twenty-First Century

Wallingford, Connecticut, August 29, 2009

Summer had come very late to New England this year and, judging from the chilly wind sweeping through the stands at John J. Richitelli Field, it appeared to be making an early departure. A light drizzle spit rain from time to time, and people arrived carrying umbrellas and wearing sweatshirts. There weren't many spectators, and about fifteen minutes before the scheduled start of the game there were roughly 50 people in the stands. In the bleachers across the field, behind the bench of the visiting Southern Maine Raging Bulls, sat a solitary woman wrapped in a blanket, apparently the only fan who'd accompanied the Raging Bulls from Buxton, Maine. Although the stands were nearly empty, pre-game noise was blasting from speakers atop the press box as if tens of thousands were present.

A woman at the lone entry gate collected the $7 admission fee and made change from an envelope. There were no tickets and she didn't think there were any programs, although she suggested checking at the concession stand, a folding table covered with hot dogs and sodas. She was correct; there weren't any programs.

The small crowd clapped as a stream of players in handsome red and black uniforms ran onto the artificial turf. They were the 6–0 Connecticut Bearcats, probably the best team in the New England Football League. There were about 40 Bearcats, but only 22 Raging Bulls, just enough for two full platoons.

When the game began, it was apparent that the Bearcats were the superior team. Their defense stifled the Raging Bulls and the offense, led by quarterback Ricky Snowden, came through with some big plays. Snowden displayed a quick, shifty running style and a strong arm, heaving one pass 55 yards in the air. The

Bearcats pulled away methodically and won by a final score of 33–2. Without television timeouts, the game moved along quickly, and for the most part the play was quite good. There was hard hitting, a lot of spirit, and some skillful athletic moves. Running plays greatly outnumbered passing plays, which kept the clock moving and created a pace and rhythm that is missing from televised games and their pace-breaking timeouts.

The atmosphere on the sidelines and in the stands was decidedly informal. One of the players left the Bearcat sideline on a couple of occasions to corral his small son, who had escaped from the stands and was running along the track. A very vocal, heavy-set woman, whose conversational context identified her as the mother of quarterback Snowden, maintained a steady stream of humorous and occasionally aggressive remarks toward the officials and opposing players. The mascot of the New Britain Rock Cats (a nearby minor league baseball team) roamed the stands, doing his mime routines and signing autographs. A Southern Maine assistant coach, perched atop the press box filming the game, exchanged good-natured taunts with the fans, extolled the virtues of Maine lobster and took the poor showing of his team with good cheer.

It was good football, and it was entertaining, but to even call it minor league might be a stretch. Most of the spectators were friends or relatives of the players. Walk into a bar in Wallingford and you won't find anyone talking about the Bearcats. If they are sports fans, they probably spent Saturday evening watching major league baseball or exhibition football on television. In the twenty-first century, we have a lot of entertainment options. When you can catch the Jets, Giants, and Patriots in your living room on a 48-inch, high definition television, why go to Richitelli Field on a drizzly night to watch the Connecticut Bearcats?

Hartford, Connecticut, September 19, 2009

Dillon Stadium has changed little over the past 41 years, and sits empty and quiet on this gorgeous, sunny, late summer morning. The stadium now stands in the shadow of the brightly colored Sports and Medical Sciences Academy, and Interstate 91 is within sight to the east. Beyond the highway, on the banks of the Connecticut River, is Charter Oak Landing.

Just beyond the north end zone is an aged tan brick building housing locker rooms and restrooms, while the scoreboard stands to the right of the goal posts in the south end zone. Bleachers rise up on the east and west sides of the field and an antiquated press box sits atop the east side stands. At the Hyshope Avenue entrance in the northwest corner is a cinderblock ticket booth that can accommodate a single person behind its wire grated window. Across Hyshope is a large, unpaved parking lot.

A lot has happened at Dillon Stadium since it was constructed in 1935. The old park has hosted football games, soccer games, and many rock concerts. In 1966, the Rolling Stones played there, a performance that ended abruptly when the crowd became unruly, Mick Jagger threw the mike stand at them, and police rushed onto the stage to protect Jagger and his mates.

On the day I visited Dillon Stadium, however, it was eerily silent and there was virtually no traffic, either on four wheels, two wheels, or two feet. Things were much different forty years ago, especially on Saturday evenings whenever the Hartford Knights were in town. On September 28, 1968, a capacity crowd of over 11,000 rushed onto the field after the Knights defeated the Richmond Roadrunners on a last-second field goal. Two months later, 10,179 fans watched the Knights defeat the Virginia Sailors for the ACFL championship.

Hartford had a myriad of problems in the late 1960s, but its football team was not one of them. According to the Dunkel ratings, the Knights were the best minor league team in America in 1969. Hartford fans flocked to Dillon Stadium and followed their team when it traveled to Lowell, Harrisburg, and especially Pottstown, Pennsylvania, the home of Hartford's most bitter rival. During those turbulent times, people could retreat to the oasis of Dillon Stadium and watch Mel Meeks and Marv Hubbard run the Green Bay power sweep the way Vince Lombardi intended. The Knights weren't going to solve America's problems or even Hartford's, but the people of Hartford cared deeply about their Knights.

"It was huge," said quarterback Manch Wheeler. "Everybody talked about the Knights back then." "Back before talk radio was talk radio," said fullback Don Abbey, "the Hartford radio stations interviewed us and talked about us every morning."

The team's fate was discussed in newspapers, on the radio, and on television, for in that era, local sports mattered. Within just a few years, however, local sports would become far less important. There would be no more Hartford Knights and on most Saturday evenings in the fall, Dillon Stadium would be as empty and lifeless as it is on this sunny Saturday morning.

East Hartford, Connecticut, November 20, 2010

The United Football League came to Connecticut in 2010 in the form of the Hartford Colonials. Like the Continental League of the 1960s, the UFL can't seem to decide whether it is a feeder system for the NFL or a competitor.

On this day, the Colonials' best running back, Lorenzo Booker, refused to play in protest of the league's policy requiring NFL teams to pay a UFL club $150,000 if it signed one of their players after the UFL season ended.

There were a number of former NFL players on the field, including 31-year-old Hartford quarterback Josh McCown, who spent eight seasons in the big leagues and was the starting quarterback for the 2004 Arizona Cardinals. The coach of the Colonials was former Browns mentor Chris Palmer, and across the field on the sideline of the Las Vegas Locomotives roamed former New York Giants head coach Jim Fassel.

The facility in which the Colonials play, Rentschler Field, is first class. Ticket and food prices are reasonable and a family can enjoy an afternoon of quality football without a major financial commitment. One thing the crowd of roughly 15,000 would not enjoy on this day, however, was sunshine, at least for very long. The UFL has a television contract with the Versus Network, and in deference to their scheduling, the game began at 3:30. When the sun went down and the wind kicked up, hats and gloves came out and the lines for hot chocolate and coffee became longer than the queue at the beer stands.

The Colonials were several steps above the Bearcats in many respects, one being cheerleading. While Ricky Snowden's mother was more original and spontaneous, the Colonials cheerleaders, numbering about 30, took the prize for pulchritude and sexy outfits. If not all the players were capable of making an NFL roster, every one of the cheerleaders was qualified to shake her pom-poms in a major league stadium. Also along the sidelines was a group of men garbed in Revolutionary War attire, equipped with muskets and cannons that somehow eluded the security screening. After each Colonial score, they fired an ear-splitting, smoke-filled volley. A colonial-themed mascot and another dressed as Betty Boop, whose connection to the American Revolution is unclear, roamed through the stands doing the types of things that mascots do. Perhaps the most unusual aspect of the game was that fact that one of the officials, head linesperson Terri Valente of Palo Alto, California, was a woman.

The Colonials played well, defeating Las Vegas 27–14, and the crowd was genuinely enthusiastic, although there was more artificial noise emanating from the public address system than was generated by human throats and vocal cords. When the announcer urged the crowd to make some noise for the national television audience, the response was satisfyingly lukewarm. When an attractive young brunette tried to start the wave, she got only a few half-hearted raised hands. I was encouraged by such demonstrations of independence, but perhaps it was just getting too cold to move.

For me, the highlight of the afternoon occurred before the opening kickoff.

Prior to a baseball game, a celebrity often throws out the first ball. In football, the equivalent is the presentation of the ball to the officials. From across the field, in a stiff-legged gait that is the product of too many leg whips from defensive linemen, walked former New York Jet lineman Nick DeFelice who, in the late 1960s, was probably the best offensive tackle in the Atlantic Coast Football League.

The Colonials are the best professional football team in Connecticut since DeFelice's Hartford Knights, and Nick is a living link to the old Knights and the evenings at Dillon Stadium when 10,000 or more fans, unassisted by annoying exhortations from the public address system, roared their approval of the 1968 ACFL champions.

The Colonials are supposed to be Hartford's team, but they play in East Hartford, in a luxurious modern stadium built for the University of Connecticut. The national television contract is at least as important as the support of local fans, and the roster is populated by players from all over the United States. The Colonials wear Hartford uniforms, but they are not Hartford's team in the way that the 1968 Knights were Hartford's team or the 1962 Black Knights were Ansonia's team. They are participants in a televised event that could be staged in Las Vegas, Nashville, or any city with an adequate stadium and solid camera wells. Nick DeFelice and his teammates played at plain old bare bones Dillon Stadium, solely for the benefit of their Hartford fans.

Postscript: A few months later, the Colonials weren't playing for anyone, either in Hartford or on Versus. They lost a sizable amount of money in their first season, and suspended operations prior to the 2011 campaign.

Middletown, Connecticut, April 26, 2012

You don't stumble upon the Cantina Ristorante by accident. You have to look for it. Tucked into the basement beneath the Italian Society on lower Court Street, the Cantina has a small but loyal core of followers who love the authentic, delectable Italian cuisine, appreciate the homey atmosphere, and aren't in a hurry.

Tonight there are about 25 men at the Cantina who are in no hurry whatsoever, for most of them haven't seen each other in 40 years or more. They are, for the most part, large men in their 60s and 70s who at one time played for the Hartford Knights, the Hartford Charter Oaks, or the Ansonia Black Knights. Many live in Connecticut, but others came from Massachusetts, Florida, Virginia, New Jersey, Illinois, Texas, and California. Former Knight fullback Don Abbey, now a successful California real estate developer, took off from Long

Beach in his company plane, stopped in Houston to pick up guard Charley Tiblom, and then in Charlottesville to gather up quarterback Tom Sherman. It is probably the first time in the Cantina's history that people from three far-flung states arrived at the establishment by private plane.

I am the reason they are together tonight, for in the course of researching this book I have found them all and, on this evening, re-connected them to a common past. Nick DeFelice is the reason none of them will pay for their meal as Nick, taking his captainship duties seriously, is our host.

Seeing old friends after several decades is bound to produce a few surprises. Everyone agreed that Norm Davidson was the most youthful looking, but Norm was just a kicker. He had never experienced the hand-to-hand combat of the trenches that will age a man beyond his years. Some of the once powerful, robust linemen are now unsteady old men. Dick Bowman, the former Syracuse star, was transported to the Cantina from the rehabilitation center where he was recovering from a serious operation. He weighed 150 pounds less than when I'd seen him a year ago. Fran Mallick, former Pittsburgh Steeler lineman and Knight defensive captain, leaned on a metal cane for support. Linebacker Bill Lesinski, who during his playing days wore a special helmet because of his numerous concussions, was struggling with the effects of memory loss.

Reunions tend to have dual themes: What are you doing now and do you remember when? After the initial catching up, the old stories began to fly across the long table. Remember the time Gene Gollarney took the microphone and announced that the plane was about to crash? Remember the time Gollarney took Tommy Rowland out to show him how a real man drank? Or how about the time he spiked broadcaster Arnold Dean's coffee when Dean was doing play by play? Unfortunately only memories of Gollarney were with us, for he passed away from a heart attack several years ago. Fred Wallner, the intense coach of the Knights, has also passed away, but nearly everyone had a few stories about Fred. And who really started that brawl in Harrisburg?

I looked at the men sitting around the table and thought of the pictures I'd seen of them when they were playing football. Some would be easily recognizable from the old photos, while others were not. But whether or not they looked the same, they were the same men inside, men with intensity and drive that caused them play a violent, physical game for relatively little pay. I had interviewed each of them and asked why they did what they did so many years ago. From the answers they'd given me I knew I was in the midst of a unique group of men, unlike the more random combinations you find at a meeting of the Rotary Club or at the weekly golf league. Much in the way that war binds soldiers together, playing the violent game of football created a special bond that has endured over four decades, a bond strong enough to bring some of them clear across the country.

Bloomfield, Connecticut, September 7, 2012

Elaine Savin is old enough to a have a grandson who attends the nearby University of Hartford, but she is trim and tan and moves with the fluidity and grace of a much younger woman. It is not Mrs. Savin's appearance, however, that is most striking. It is her manner, for she came of age during an era when manners and social graces were essential ingredients for a society woman. She is friendly, dignified, and has a knack for making visitors comfortable.

I was at the home of Elaine Savin, widow of Hartford Knights owner Pete Savin, because she had agreed to share her memories of the days when the Knights were the most important part of their lives. It was a wonderful time. The Knights almost always beat the opposition, Pete nervously paced the sidelines, Elaine cheered from the stands, and two of their teenage daughters led the cheerleading squad. "I just remember it as being pure joy," Elaine said. "Every

Hartford Knights owner Pete Savin and his wife Elaine leave the field after a 1969 win at Bridgeport (photograph from Hartford Knights program).

bit of it. The whole thing. Whoever was coaching. Whoever was cheering. Whoever was playing. It was just a great time."

Her husband was even more passionate. "As excited as I was," Elaine said, "he was ten times more excited. He loved being involved. He loved getting them new suits or costumes or whatever they're called. He loved doing it, and he was sad when it ceased to exist."

I brought a pile of old programs to refresh Mrs. Savin's memory, and she delighted in thumbing through them and seeing pictures of the Hartford Knights of 40 or more years ago. Something would catch her eye, and she leapt back in time. "Oh, there he is," she said on spotting cornerback Tom Rowland, a particular favorite. "Look at Tommy! How *cute* he was! He had a lovely wife."

Lovely is one of Mrs. Savin's favorite words. Donna Rowland was lovely. So were team physician Dr. Vincent Turco and quarterback Manch Wheeler. Elaine is probably the only person to ever describe intense, hard-nosed Fred Wallner as lovely. Even I was lovely. Then suddenly, in the midst of a reverie, Mrs. Savin would remember she was supposed to be an interview subject. "Ask away," she would say, looking up from the programs. "Ask away."

I nearly lost Mrs. Savin for good when she spotted a picture of the cheerleaders, who included her daughters Stacy and Nina and some of their friends. "I can't *believe* this," she exclaimed. "These girls look *exactly* the same now. They really do. They're in their fifties now, but they look damned good."

Mrs. Savin brought out some props of her own, including a picture of her son (who was four or five years old) playing on the Dillon Stadium sideline with the young son of quarterback Hank Washington, who died tragically at the age of 25.

We were seated on a couch in a very large room a level down from the entrance. "This is where we had the parties," Elaine said. For minor league football players in their early or mid–20s, attending a Savin party was a surreal experience, a fleeting glimpse of how the beautiful people lived, for the Savins and their friends were wealthy and well-connected. Pete was active in politics, and most prominent Connecticut Democrats, including U.S. Representative Emilio Daddario, Senator Abe Ribicoff, and longtime party boss John Bailey, were his friends.

The combination of football players, society people, businessmen, and politicians mingled and all enjoyed the unique company of the others. And if that wasn't sufficient diversity, there was one more group. "I was very involved at the time with the Hartford Ballet," Elaine recalled, "so the ballerinas would come. Everybody seemed to get a kick out of the other groups. Everybody got a kick out of the boys and the boys got a kick out of the ballet dancers and the politicians. The ballerinas thought the players were great." She paused for a moment. "I don't know if the players' wives thought the ballerinas were great, because they were usually unaccompanied."

A lot of wealthy Hartford people had politicians, businessmen, and maybe even ballerinas at their parties, but only the Savins had a whole team of professional football players. During the years from 1968 to 1973, it was the men who played for the Hartford Knights that made the Savins' lives special. "They were just lovely young men," Elaine said, "just lovely. They were always so polite to me, and when they were here it was just—it was just *cool*."

Watching a couple of games, spending an evening with former players renewing acquaintances after four decades, and spending an afternoon with Elaine Savin provided strong evidence that minor league football in the 1960s was much more than a bunch of big, sweaty guys beating the hell out of each other on Saturday nights.

Minor league football is for men who are told at 22 they aren't good enough to do what they've wanted to do all their lives. It's for men who are 30 and learn the NFL doesn't want them anymore. It's a way for a man to postpone adulthood for a few years and keep pursuing a dream, even when he knows deep in his heart it will never become reality. For a man like Pete Savin, who loved football and desperately wanted a major league franchise, it was an opportunity to live his own dream.

Men don't play minor league football for the money. They play because they have been playing the game since they were small boys and can't get it out of their blood. Even when they can't play anymore, it's still part of them. "I'm 75 years old," said former NFL quarterback Lee Grosscup, who played for the Hartford Charter Oaks in 1965, "and I still wake up in the morning and dream of going to training camp."

"Whenever I hear the 'Star-Spangled Banner,'" said former Knights linebacker Ralph Tiner, "I start to get psyched up. I feel the adrenaline start going in my system. It doesn't matter what the event is. You start getting revved up and ready to go. It's been 40 years, but whenever I hear the 'Star-Spangled Banner' on television I get this rush through my system."

In many ways, the story of minor league football is one of failure. Most players didn't make it to the NFL and most teams eventually went broke. Entire leagues collapsed. Yet the failures made the successes so much more precious. Only a handful of players, like Bob Tucker, Nick DeFelice, Jack Dolbin, Lou Piccone, and Marv Hubbard, were fortunate enough to land a spot in the NFL or AFL, and when they did, they still cherished their minor league days. "I would have been less of a player," said Tucker, "had I gone straight to the NFL and not had that experience."

"Without the minor leagues," said Piccone, "there wouldn't have been anything for me. My whole life would have been entirely different, and I don't know where I would have ended up. Without the minors, I was done."

Dolbin went from the Pottstown Firebirds to the Schuylkill County Coal Crackers to the World Football League and finally won a spot with the Denver Broncos, with whom he played in Super Bowl XII. "It was more than a dream come true," he told NFL Films. "It was a miracle come true." When he went to his first training camp with the Broncos, one of the players made a foolish mistake, and a coach yelled derisively, "Where do you think you're playing, Pottstown?" "Coach," Dolbin said, "we didn't do that stuff back in Pottstown. We played the game right back there."

A number of Connecticut cities hosted minor league teams during the 1960s and early 1970s. There were big cities like Hartford, Bridgeport, and Stamford, and smaller ones like Meriden and Ansonia. Some teams had names that reflected the space age '60s, like the Rockets, Jets, and Orbits, while other names, like Knights and Charter Oaks, were evocative of older times.

All teams had one thing in common. They lost money. The 1960s were the decade during which television ownership became virtually universal and live entertainment, be it theater, music or sports, was hard-pressed to compete. Minor league football, which had always been a tenuous enterprise, became even more so in the television era.

The story of Connecticut minor league football is not just the tale of yards gained or championships won, nor of money lost. It is the story of the men who played in Hartford, Stamford, Ansonia, and Waterbury, and competed against men from Pottstown, Providence, and Chambersburg who were pursuing the same dream. It wasn't the NFL, but it was professional football and there is a certain pride in doing something well enough to be paid for it. The stadiums weren't always the best, but there were eleven players to a side and the competition was as fierce at Ceppa Field in Meriden as it was at Lambeau Field or the Cotton Bowl. "It was as real as it was anywhere else," said Knights tackle Dennis Fitzgibbons. "This was our NFL Sunday."

My interest in minor league football began in 1968 at the age of 14 when I discovered the Hartford Knights. For the next two years, my Saturday evenings in the fall were spent listening to Arnold Dean and Lou Palmer describe the exploits of the Knights on WTIC. Hartford had a terrific team, winning the ACFL championship in 1968 and reaching the title game in each of the next three years. For most of that period, my favorite NFL team, the New York Giants, was abysmal, and it was a lot more exciting to be a Knights fan.

In 2000, I published a history of the New York Titans of the old AFL. During my research, I conducted interviews with nearly every living former Titan. A number of them had played in the minor leagues, and their stories of playing for the Boston Sweepers and the Hartford Charter Oaks were nearly as entertaining as those of their time in New York. Hearing the stories rekindled my interest in the minor leagues.

Personal interest is a very weak justification for writing a book. Publishers' offices are littered with unusable manuscripts recounting favorite childhood television shows or hagiographies extolling the virtues of cherished relatives. A readable book requires much more than a nostalgic personal interest.

After combing through old newspapers, interviewing a number of former players and drafting a few chapters, I sat down with John Thorn, the official historian of Major League Baseball and a gifted and insightful writer. I told him what I was doing and asked for his advice. "What does it all mean?" John asked rhetorically. "If you can't tell us what it means, all you've got is a collection of interesting stories from a group of people no one has ever heard of." He suggested reading *Friday Night Lights* and *On Any Given Sunday* for further insight.

What *does* it all mean? Minor league football in the 1960s meant quite a bit to the men who played it. The story of most minor leaguers is one of near misses. An injury, an overloaded roster, or a quirk of fate placed them at Nolan Field in Ansonia instead of playing at Shea Stadium before fifty thousand people. Why did they continue on? Perhaps Nick DeFelice put it best. "It's hard to give up the game," he said. "If I could just do it over—run out through that tunnel just one more time."

DeFelice has been very successful in business and speaks proudly of the accomplishments of his company. Yet, his most animated conversation is about football and his office is filled with football memorabilia. His business card features a picture of his New York Jets helmet.

Minor league football also meant a lot to fans of the Bridgeport Jets, the Hartford Knights, and the other Connecticut teams. "[H]aving a home team to root for which is in contention for a league title," wrote Emmett Spillane in the *Bridgeport Post-Telegram*, "surpasses the thrill of having a local playhouse or symphony, and is much more of a conversation piece than theatrical endeavors."[1]

There weren't a lot of sporting events on television in those days, and most fans focused on their local team, be it high school, college, or semipro. Small Pennsylvania towns like Pottstown and Chambersburg turned out in force to cheer their underdog heroes, men who worked at the local construction company during the week and stopped by the diner on Sunday morning to talk football.

Joan Benedetto, sister of Bridgeport Jet owner Frank D'Addario, attended nearly every home game. "We yelled," she said. "We screamed our heads off, and we ate food that we shouldn't have been eating, but we had such fun. It made me feel young again, like when we used to cheer for the high school team."

Hartford journalist Jerry Trecker wrote, "Hartford's Knights are valuable and vital to this region. Whether they win or lose isn't as important as the fact that more than 5,000 people, on an average Saturday night, look to Atlantic Coast Football League play as one highlight of their week. They don't patronize, perhaps, other recreational opportunities in the area, but they do love the Knights. For them, it's a vital part of urban life."[2] "Our fans were fabulous," said former Knight Dick Bowman. "Hundreds of them would gather for a party before the game; and they would cheer. It was fun. I don't think you see that anymore."

The 1960s were a time of tremendous societal turbulence, a decade during which it sometimes seemed the entire social fabric of the United States was being torn apart. The placid America of Ward and June Cleaver had become the violent America of Eldridge Cleaver. Horrific riots ravaged American cities, tradition was desecrated, and values cherished for generations were questioned. Men wore their hair long and women wore their skirts short. Few men complained about that, but many didn't like the fact that women were no longer content to cook, clean, and take care of them.

Amidst the chaos stood the comforting structure of sports, where ten yards still made a first down and the team with the most points at the end was the winner. Violation of the rules was penalized and, almost without exception, players conformed to the rules. Joe Namath might sport his fur coat and Fu Manchu mustache, but for the most part sports heroes still represented traditional American values. Minor league football had a few characters like quarterback Jim (King) Corcoran, but Corcoran's main vices were womanizing and an overweening vanity, hardly revolutionary qualities in the world of sports.

The story of minor league football in the 1960s is that of underdog players fighting for a place in the NFL against great odds, bouncing back from one setback after another, wondering about what might have been, and enjoying the friendship of their teammates. They had fans who cheered them when they won and second guessed them when they lost, but in any event cared deeply about their fate. Under the lights of Dillon Stadium, Nolan Field, and Municipal Stadium, men who'd been told they weren't good enough for the NFL played for themselves, their teammates, and their fans.

1

A Minor League Town

Historian John Hogrogian, author of a narrative on the 1926 Hartford Blues, wrote, "Hartford, Connecticut, is one of those cities that somehow got lost in the shuffle of medium-sized East Coast metropolises that ring New York like static electrons. There haven't been any popular songs written about Hartford. Broadway plays traditionally open for previews downstate in New Haven.... Likewise, all of Hartford's ventures into big-league sports have ended in frustration."[1]

In 1970, Lou Palmer, who did color commentary for the Hartford Knights, wrote, "In my opinion, the greater Hartford area suffers from a complex; the chief symptom of which is a reluctance to accept anything local as being good.... The [Hartford area] may be a bad one for sports because we may have convinced ourselves of that."[2]

"Hartford is a minor league town," Palmer said recently. "It always has been, going back to the days when Lou Gehrig played baseball here. Here we are between the megalopolises of New York and Boston and we're lost. We're just a little town and we've got a little stadium. To this day, the major event is UConn basketball. It is now and it was back then."

If Hartford is a minor league town, certainly so are Ansonia, Waterbury, and Meriden. In fact, Connecticut, without a landmark city within its borders, is a minor league state, and one of the principal functions of its southwest keystone is to serve as a bedroom community for New York City.

Not every state, city, or town can be major league, and there's nothing wrong with that. There are some damn good minor league towns around the United States. The bad ones are those that bemoan their fate and are embarrassingly eager and desperate to move up the ladder.

At one time, Connecticut was a player in the sporting world. In 1874, Hartford's Dark Blues entered baseball's National Association, the only major league that operated during the first half of the 1870s. Middletown and New Haven also had clubs in the National Association, the former in 1872 and New Haven in 1875. The latter franchises played poorly, suffered financial reverses, and neither lasted more than one season.

When the National League was formed in 1876, Hartford was invited to join and their president, Morgan Bulkeley, was elected the first president of the new league. The Dark Blues played well in that Centennial year, finishing second with a 47–21 mark. Attendance was disappointing, however, and while retaining the Hartford name, the club played all its 1877 home games in Brooklyn.

The Dark Blues left the National League after the season, and Hartford never again had a major league baseball team. It had a number of minor league clubs, and Hall of Famers Lou Gehrig and Warren Spahn honed their skills at Bulkeley Stadium as members of the Hartford Chiefs. From 1886, when the Dark Blues joined the Eastern League, until 1952, when the Chiefs folded their teepee, there were Hartford Bluebirds, Blues, Chiefs, Indians, Wooden Nutmegs, Senators, Bees, and Laurels in the Eastern League, Connecticut League, Atlantic League, Northeastern League, Colonial League, and Atlantic Association. There were brief stretches when there was no Hartford entry in organized baseball, but in nearly every season for 67 years, Connecticut's capital city fielded a professional club.

Several other Connecticut cities have hosted minor league baseball. Legendary Athletics manager Connie Mack played in Meriden, and there were teams in Waterbury, Stamford, New Haven, Bridgeport, New London, and other towns. Norwich served as the Eastern League affiliate of the Yankees for several years beginning in the 1990s, and Bridgeport has had an independent league team for many seasons.

Probably the most successful sports franchise in Connecticut today is the New Britain Rock Cats, the Double-A affiliate of the Minnesota Twins. The Rock Cats have perfected the minor league model, providing affordable family entertainment and good baseball. They accept their market for what it is—minor league.

There were only two major league franchises in Connecticut during the twentieth century. Most Connecticut residents know about the Hartford Whalers, a member of the World Hockey League from 1972 to 1979 and a National Hockey League franchise from 1980 until the club was moved to Greensboro, North Carolina, in 1997.

Very few people, however, know that the Hartford Blues were a member of the National Football League in 1926.[3] The NFL, then in only its seventh year, lagged far behind major league baseball in terms of organization, sophistication, and finances. The pro game of the 1920s ran a distant second to college football in popularity, and franchises came and went with troubling regularity.

1. A Minor League Town

Players jumped from team to team, as owners ignored existing contracts and leapt at the chance to sign a premier gate attraction. There was no set schedule; the number of games played by each club varied. Teams made arrangements as their pecuniary interests dictated, and they frequently interrupted the NFL schedule for exhibitions.

The team that eventually became the Hartford Blues began in Waterbury, under the auspices of promoter George Mulligan. Mulligan was born in England in 1880 and arrived in Waterbury as a young boy five years later. By the 1920s, he was promoting boxing matches, bicycle races, and professional football. In 1924, his Waterbury Blues were the best semi-pro team in the state. The following year, Mulligan made a bold move and signed Harry Stuhldreher, one of Notre Dame's famous Four Horsemen. Stuhldreher had begun the season with the Providence Steamroller, but after playing one exhibition game, asked the club for an increase in pay. When they refused, he accepted Mulligan's offer of a $7,500 salary and a $500 bonus. In October, Mulligan added a second Horseman, Jim Crowley, who played just one game for Waterbury before returning to his fulltime job as assistant coach at the University of Georgia.

On October 18, the Blues upset the NFL's Rochester Jeffersons 7–6. Two weeks later, the Hartford West Enders, another semi-pro club, disbanded, leaving the city's Clarkin Field empty. Mulligan, flush with optimism after the win over Rochester and sensing opportunity in Hartford, picked up the lease and re-named his eleven the Hartford Blues. Guard Steve Owen, future coach of the New York Giants, joined the team, as did yet a third Notre Dame Horseman, halfback Don Miller. With its star-studded lineup, the Blues easily defeated New Britain 28–7 and claimed the championship of the State of Connecticut.

Prior to the 1926 season, Mulligan's application for an NFL franchise was approved and the Blues became one of 22 clubs in an oversized league. Mulligan signed a lease for the 8,000 seat Velodrome, a facility in East Hartford that had a football field surrounded by a bicycle racing oval. Jack Keough, an assistant at the University of Pennsylvania, was signed as head coach, with permission to return to Philadelphia three days each week to maintain his dental practice. While the head coach drilled molars, assistant coach Ernie McCann drilled the Blues.

Although Hartford was playing big time football, its roster was strictly small time. The Four Horsemen had galloped into the sunset, Steve Owen left town with Cleveland, and the replacements Mulligan signed were mostly local semi-pros. Precious few had any NFL experience.

Hartford's first NFL game was at the Velodrome against the New York Giants, who beat them 21–0. After four games, the Blues had neither a victory nor a point, having been shut out twice by the Frankford Yellow Jackets and once by the Brooklyn Lions. Finally, on October 24, Hartford gained its first NFL win, a 16–6 triumph over the Lions.

The team's poor performance, coupled with abysmal weather, led to disappointing attendance. Even the appearance of the Canton Bulldogs, featuring 38-year-old Jim Thorpe, was fraught with difficulties. The Bulldogs' bus got caught in Armistice Day parade traffic and arrived fifteen minutes after the scheduled starting time. Thorpe didn't play because of an injured shoulder. A fight broke out between the fans and a Canton player. Late in the game, darkness came and the lights proved inadequate. Hartford won 16–7, and the unfulfilled promise of an appearance by Thorpe drew a good crowd of 4,000. An indication of the NFL's weakness was the fact that a much bigger crowd (6,000) showed up on November 28 to see the Blues defeat the All-New Britain team in an exhibition game.

Hartford finished the season with a 3–7 record and a 13th place finish. When the NFL decided to reduce the number of teams to 12 for the 1927 season, Hartford was not one of them, and its tenure as a major league football city was over.

By the 1960s, there were no major league teams in Connecticut. There were football teams in the Atlantic Coast and Continental Leagues and Waterbury had a baseball team in the Eastern League. The Hartford Capitols and New Haven Elms played in the Eastern Basketball League.

Probably the most exciting sporting events in the state during that decade were UConn basketball games. Long before the arrival of Hall of Fame coach Jim Calhoun and his national championship clubs, the Huskies were big news. In those days, one didn't need to say UConn *Men's* basketball, for the women's game was several years in the future. The role of UConn females was that of cheerleader, and in the 1960s they cheered for Husky stars like Toby Kimball and Wes Bialosuknia. Kimball led the nation in rebounding his senior year and Bialosuknia finished second in scoring during *his* senior year, with an average of 28 points per game.

For major league sports, Connecticut residents had to look to New York or Boston. The Yankee-Red Sox rivalry was not as heated in the 1960s as it had been in the late 1940s or as it would become in the mid–1970s. When the Yankees dominated the American League in the 1950s and early 1960s, the Red Sox were a perennial resident of the second division and when the Red Sox won the pennant during the Impossible Dream season of 1967, the Yankees were a ninth place team.

The Giants were the favorite football team of most Connecticut residents and they, like the Yankees, had fallen on hard times. The Jets had one magical season, and the charisma of Joe Namath drew many young fans, especially females, to his team. The Boston Patriots had little charisma and a limited following.

The Patriots had never been welcomed in Boston and were always an inviting target for cities looking to attract a major league team. They played at Fenway Park, Boston College, Boston University, and Harvard Stadium, all of which had limited seating capacity. A new stadium for the Red Sox and Patriots was proposed on several occasions and voted down, and both teams hinted that if a new facility was not available by 1970, they would consider moving. In that year, the Patriots would become part of the merged NFL, and league rules mandated that every team must play in a stadium with a capacity of at least 50,000.

In early 1970, it appeared that the Patriots had no future in Boston. Plans for a new stadium had again been stymied, and the colleges expressed reluctance to lease their facilities to a professional club. Patriot owner Billy Sullivan was forced to solicit interest from other cities, for he had just six weeks to meet the mandate.

Hartford Knights owner Pete Savin was one of those interested in the Patriots. "Everybody thought he was going to get it," said Knights defensive back Tom Rowland, "[Coach] Fred Wallner was saying 'Hey, guys, Pete's going to be an NFL owner if things go right.' A lot of the guys were real excited—thinking that if the Patriots came here and Pete's the owner, we might have a real shot at making the team."

Before the Patriots moved anywhere, however, a new stadium in Foxboro was approved and funded, and any chance of a move to Hartford evaporated. Nearly three decades later, in 1998, Connecticut governor John Rowland made another proposal to entice the Patriots to move to Hartford. It turned out that New England owner Robert Kraft was only using the Connecticut offer to sweeten his deal in Foxboro, and again Hartford came up short.

Today, even without major league sports in their state, Connecticut fans have the opportunity to watch numerous games from the comfort of their homes. I write this on a fall Saturday on which there is a television menu of 26 college football games, two college basketball games, and four NBA games, with countless others on radio. In the 1960s, Connecticut sports fans had limited options. On October 6, 1968, for example, Connecticut television offered World Series Game Four between the Cardinals and Tigers on NBC at 12:45. The only other televised sporting event was the Washington-Oregon State football game on ABC at 4:15. On the radio one could listen to the Connecticut-New Hampshire, Bowdoin-Wesleyan, or Bates-Trinity football games. The latter two were available, however, only to those with FM radio reception. The only other sports event on the radio that day was the game between the Westchester Bulls and

Hartford Knights, which went on the air at 7:50 p.m., long after all other broadcasted events had ended.

On Saturdays in the fall, there was generally one national or regional college football telecast on ABC, plus radio broadcasts of local college games in the afternoon. Night college games were rare, and the Knights generally had the evening broadcast hours to themselves.

Even with limited competition, it was hard for a professional franchise to succeed. The Knights were successful at first, but they eventually folded, and the Whalers left town when the city wouldn't build them a new arena. If Hartford, Connecticut's capital, couldn't support a major league franchise, it was inconceivable that the state's lesser cities could do so. They were minor league towns in a minor league state.

2

One Big Step from the NFL

Minor league baseball has been in existence since the late 1800s, and since the 1930s has operated under the general supervision of organized baseball. A number of minor leagues, such as the Pacific Coast League, the International League, and the Eastern League, have survived for many decades with relative stability. For more than 70 years, most minor league teams have been part of a major league farm system, providing an organized flow of talent to their parent clubs.

In contrast to baseball, minor league football has been characterized by an almost total lack of formal organization. With the NFL in such turmoil in its early years, it is little wonder it failed to develop a smoothly functioning farm system. But even by the 1960s, after commissioners Bert Bell and Pete Rozelle made pro football the most popular American sport, the NFL saw no need to establish an effective system for player development. College football provided more than enough players to fill NFL rosters at no cost to the professionals.

Every year colleges turned out new young talent and in the late 1950s, with only twelve teams in the NFL, there were far more players than could be accommodated on their rosters. Top teams might take three or four rookies each year while poorer teams might add a half dozen. Even after the American Football League's eight teams joined the fray in 1960, there was a surplus of talent. Those who didn't make it went to the Canadian League or played sandlot ball. The NFL wasn't that interested where they went, for the next year the colleges would turn out another crop of seniors. In baseball, nearly all players come through the minor league system. In football, they rarely do. Occasionally a player emerged from the semipro ranks to make it to the NFL (John Unitas was the most prominent example) but they were few and far between.

The lifestyle of minor league football players was vastly different from that of their baseball counterparts. Baseball is played almost every day, and with half the games taking place on the road, it isn't possible for players to hold jobs during the season. Football is played just once a week, and it is quite feasible for players to work during the week, practice a couple of evenings, and play on Friday or Saturday night. A twelve game season meant just six road trips, and most football minor leagues were geographically concentrated so that a road game was just a bus ride away.

During the 1950s, minor league football was a very loosely organized affair. Some teams were part of a league, while others free-lanced, scheduling games on an *ad hoc* basis. Most players weren't paid. By the early 1960s, perhaps fired by the success of the AFL, leagues began to spring up around the United States. The most prominent was the United Football League, organized for the 1961 season and featuring teams in the Midwestern states of Ohio, Michigan, Kentucky, and Indiana.

The UFL's inaugural season was relatively successful and five of the six clubs returned in 1962. Only Akron, which finished 0–10 and averaged just 2500 fans per game, failed to survive. For the next three years, teams came and went, sometimes not lasting the season. In 1962, Columbus won six of its first eight games, then lost three in a row and disbanded, forfeiting its final two games. Louisville also forfeited its final two contests after losing star quarterback Harold (Hayseed) Stephens to the New York Titans of the AFL.

The stars of the UFL were either former AFL and NFL players or journeyman minor leaguers. The top quarterbacks were Bob Brodhead, a former Duke star who'd played briefly with the Buffalo Bills, Tom Kennedy, who would eventually play with the New York Giants, and Ed Chlebek, who played several seasons in the minors but never made it in the NFL. Former New York Titan Leon Burton was the UFL's most explosive running back and kick returner. In a 1961 game for Grand Rapids, Burton carried the ball just twice but gained 148 yards and scored two touchdowns. For the season, he gained 737 yards and averaged 8.0 yards per carry. In baseball's minor leagues, such a remarkable performance would earn him a shot in the majors. Burton earned another season in Grand Rapids.

Lured by their large populations, minor loops set up shop in cities like Philadelphia and Chicago, but the franchises were unsuccessful. However, in small and medium sized cities throughout the United States, minor league football teams generated hometown pride and star players became local cult heroes. In 1968, *Sports Illustrated* ran a feature article on the Ohio Valley Ironmen of Wheeling, West Virginia. The city loved its Ironmen, claimed *SI*, just as much as Green Bay loved its Packers. Nearly a thousand residents owned stock in the club and it was not uncommon for an equal number to come out to watch a mere practice. Wheeling didn't have a large population, but was a good venue for minor league sports because there was little else to do there.

2. One Big Step from the NFL

From 1962 through 1964 the Ironmen were the strongest club in the UFL. They won the 1962 title with an 8–4 regular season record and a 30–21 win over Grand Rapids in the championship game. The following year, Wheeling won 12 of 13 regular season contests and defeated Toledo by the same 30–21 score for the UFL title. The Ironmen led the league in attendance both years.

Quarterback Chlebek was a local celebrity, as were several of the other players. The team provided many of them with jobs, and they became members of the community, toiling for a daily wage like everyone else in town. Most college stars shunned towns like Wheeling. If they had to play in the minor leagues, they preferred sunny Orlando or metropolitan Philadelphia, which gave the Wheeling folks an "us against the world" chip on its collective shoulder and engendered a fierce loyalty to those players who elected to come there.

In 1965, the Ironmen joined the Continental League and suffered through a two year 18-game losing streak, but win or lose, they were Wheeling's team, a focus of civic pride in a hardscrabble town that got little respect from the outside world.

By the time the *SI* article appeared, the glory days of the early '60s were long gone, but the Ironmen still drew crowds of seven or eight thousand. They may have been losers, but they were Wheeling's losers, and the town stood firmly behind them. Financial existence was precarious, but the team endured for nine years, a prodigious feat for a minor league franchise. Teams from Philadelphia, Orlando, and Providence failed while Wheeling, under the tenacious leadership of President Mike Valan, survived. A few Ironmen got a shot in the NFL, but the rest had to be content with the adulation of the local residents and the satisfaction of being a big fish in a very small pond. "[T]he people here are real friendly," said Chlebek. "It's a good place to live."[1]

Following the 1964 season, UFL owners divided into two camps. One faction wanted to try to improve the quality of the league while the other advocated reducing costs and operating as a low budget minor circuit. On January 17, 1965, f William Barron, governor of West Virginia, replaced Commissioner George Gareff, a Columbus attorney who'd run the league since its inception. Barron's reign lasted less than a month, for on February 6 five UFL clubs elected to join the new Continental League, which had aspirations of becoming a third major league. The three remaining teams joined the new Pro Football League of America.

The rest of the Continental League teams were taken from the Atlantic Coast Football League, which was organized in March 1962. The ACFL fielded six teams during its inaugural season, all but one of which had operated as independent semi-pro teams in 1961. Two of the entries, the Stamford Golden Bears and the Ansonia Black Knights, were based in Connecticut.

Stamford was a big city and close to the huge population base of New York City. Ansonia, although it was not geographically isolated like Wheeling, had many of the same characteristics as the West Virginia town. It was a solid blue collar community with a voracious appetite for football; it appeared to be ripe for a professional franchise.

For twelve years, from 1962 to 1973, Connecticut had at least one professional football team. The first two faded quickly. Stamford lasted just a year, and Ansonia but two, both drowning in a sea of red ink. The Ansonia franchise was transferred to Hartford and during the 1964 season the Charter Oaks played in the ACFL. The following season, they made the jump to the Continental League, where they spent the next three years. In 1966 and 1967, Connecticut had entries in both the ACFL and CFL, as the Waterbury Orbits played in the former circuit.

By the end of the 1967 campaign, the Brewer family, which had operated the Charter Oaks since the club's inception, had run out of money. They cancelled the final two games of the season, and although they announced their intention to revive the team in 1968, it never happened. The Brewers and their Charter Oaks had reached the end of the line.

The Charter Oaks were supplanted in Hartford by construction magnate Pete Savin and his Hartford Knights, who returned the city to the ACFL after a three year absence. Savin had the capital the Brewers lacked, and the willingness to spend it to build a championship team. The same year that Savin formed the Knights, fellow contractor Frank D'Addario relocated the Orbits to Bridgeport, where as the Jets his club developed a natural rivalry with the Knights.

While the Continental League and the Atlantic Coast League operated in the northeast, circuits were also active in other regions of the country. The Southern Football League operated from 1963 through 1965 with teams in Florida, Alabama, Georgia, and Tennessee. The North American League lasted just two seasons (1964 and 1965) plagued by a combination of low attendance and highly paid talent, including many ex-NFL and AFL players.

The Pro Football League of America, consisting initially of the UFL teams that chose not to upgrade to the Continental League, operated primarily in the Midwest from 1965 to 1967. The Texas League was formed in 1966 and lasted until 1971, playing in 1969 as a division of the ill-fated Continental League.

There were also a number of lesser circuits, including the New England Football League, which included Connecticut franchises in Meriden and Milford and the North American League, which included the New Britain Bees and failed to survive its initial season.

Most minor leagues operated on a regional basis, and there was little cross-pollination of players, who generally stayed in their own area. All leagues had

2. One Big Step from the NFL

one thing in common—they faced a financial struggle from the day they were formed. Some achieved a relative degree of prosperity for a time, but all eventually succumbed to fiscal pressure. While leagues such as the ACFL survived for a number of years, their membership was fluid, for the identity of the teams within a league changed from year to year as some failed and others sprung to life.

Leagues that lasted generally had compact geographical footprints, thus minimizing travel costs, and kept salaries low. After a couple of years of operating in this manner, however, it was inevitable that some of the owners would become consumed by delusions of grandeur. If only better players could be obtained and the territory expanded, the league could move up in status and perhaps even challenge the major leagues. Increasing travel and salary costs was a surefire recipe for disaster, for no league seemed capable of generating sufficient revenue to sustain a first class operation without a television contract, and no minor league was able to secure a contract.

The keys to a surviving (none could be considered thriving) team were a suitable stadium and an owner willing to subsidize losses. The one element that seems elementary to the success of a football team—acquiring skilled players—was never a problem. There were quality football players everywhere, players who loved the game so much they were eager to play under almost any circumstances.

3

That's What They Do in the Fall

Many professional sports leagues have been established during the past century and a half, and most have failed. They fail because attendance is too low, they fail because expenses are too high, and they fail because they can't convince television networks to broadcast their games. No league has ever failed because it couldn't find enough players.

There have always been plenty of football players ready to play for a nominal salary or, in many cases, for nothing but pride, which is inexplicable to many people. They understand playing baseball and basketball for fun, but why would grown men with families play a grueling, physically punishing game like football and jeopardize their well-being for a as little as $25 a night? Why would they play with a cast on their broken hand or in a post-concussion daze? Why would they work all day, drive as far as two hundred miles round trip to practice, and let a fanatic coach like Fred Wallner scream at them? Why did they play with the hope of making an NFL roster when hardly any did?

Even if they succeeded, glory was fleeting. NFL journeymen are soon forgotten and even the very good players of the 1960s are little remembered today. Former Knight Don Abbey said, "I thought football was the most important thing I was ever going to do in my life. But I remember going to a Super Bowl several years ago and they introduced the first twenty-five or thirty MVPs, or however many there were at the time. I had a hard time remembering most of their names. I probably got five or six of them but, boy, over half the guys—I didn't even know who the hell they were, and they were the MVPs of the *Super Bowl*. I was thinking, my god, that idol I'd worshipped for such a long time really wasn't that lasting. This thing that I thought was the most important thing in the world—that I struggled so much to release from my life—I realized in retrospect how important it wasn't."

Hundreds of men played in the minor leagues in pursuit of that fleeting glory. "Everybody has a little bit of a dream," said Joe Klimas. "If you don't give it a try you'll never know if you might have made it." After a couple of years as a quarterback with the Ansonia Black Knights and one with the Meriden Shamrocks, Klimas had his answer. "You realize that you're not going to make the big time and you realize the years are starting to catch up with you and you're not as quick as you used to be. After a while you think it's time to concentrate on trying to build a career because it isn't going to be football."

Playing minor league football, unlike baseball, wasn't a mutually exclusive choice. Minor league footballers could pursue simultaneous careers in teaching, business, or other fields. Their lives unfolded in parallel lines, and when one predominated, the other was eclipsed. When a full time career or family life conflicted with football, the playing career ended. If the NFL beckoned, the other career was placed on hold.

For nearly all former players, the football portion of their lives is a treasured memory, even for those whose careers ended in frustration. Quarterback Harry Theofiledes made it to the NFL for one year with the Washington Redskins, then was cut, and despite excellent play in the minors and some good showings in NFL camps, never made it back. The main reason was that coaches thought he was too short. "It was all good for me," he said. "Was I disappointed that I didn't make it to the big time? Yeah, a little bit. But I have all good memories."

Banging heads with large, muscular men does not seem pleasurable, but the word used most frequently by former players to describe their careers was "fun." "It wasn't like work," said Bob Stohrer. "It was fun. In my opinion it was the greatest job anyone could ever have. My wife and I talk about it constantly. It was the best part of our lives—the camaraderie, the parties, the friends, the emotions you go through on a weekly basis, the excitement of the game. There was nothing better."

And for Stohrer, football has been the best part of a very good life. After his playing career ended, he built a large and successful tire and service station business that earned him a very comfortable living. But selling tires just doesn't match the excitement of running under a pass from Benny Russell or springing Mel Meeks loose with a block, or going out with the guys to talk about it afterward over a sandwich and a beer.

"I just loved the game of football," added Larry McHugh, another ex-player who has gone on to a prominent and very public career. "It was something to do with your buddies. You're not going to get rich and you've got a chance to get pretty banged up, but you never thought about that. Practice was fun. The games were fun. I don't know anyone who played that did not enjoy their experience. Some guys wanted a shot at the pros, but 90 percent of them just wanted to play football. They didn't care about anything else."

"I had a great time," Abbey said of his season with the Knights. "I enjoyed the hell out of it. It was the first time in my life where I really, really enjoyed the game because there was no pressure. Guys were playing the game because it was fun."

They also played because it was their pre-determined destiny. "You were there," Abbey said, "because you were a football player and you were going to play football whether you got ten cents or two hundred bucks. For these guys, football was part of their life and who they were and that's what they did in the fall."

"It was something I had done since seventh grade," said Ralph Tiner, who joined the Knights while pursuing a graduate degree at UConn. "It was kind of a normal thing for me that when the weather got cool you think, hey, this is football weather and I should be playing football. Just to be a regular student didn't seem right."

"You fall in love with the game," said Waide Robinson. "You play in high school and then you play in college and it gets in your blood. It's in your system. I couldn't get it out of my system until my first born came along and my wife said, 'It's time to get serious.'"

Dave Bennett, the backup quarterback for the Knights for several years, said, "I loved the game. I loved practice. A lot of guys hated practice but I loved practice. I would go early, stop in the offices, and watch films. I wasn't just going down to pick up my paycheck. It was a pain in the neck coming down from Massachusetts. I taught. I coached. I had a wife and two little kids. But I loved doing it. I wish I could still do it."

For many, their primary identity was as a football player; it was the role in which they achieved notoriety and the one that bolstered their self-esteem. "It was the comma after my name," said Lee Grosscup. "I was Lee Grosscup, quarterback." "I grew up in Ohio," said Mark Proskine, "in a small town where sports was the main emphasis in everybody's life. That's what I was proud of—being a football player."

"Football made me feel good about myself," said Tim Miller. "When I was growing up in Pittsburgh, I was big and fat. I was six feet tall and 300 pounds and people used to make fun of me. But there was one thing I was good at and that was football. Since it made me feel good about myself, I got better at it. There was a team I wanted to try out for, but we didn't have the money for equipment. My dad worked at the incinerator where they burned garbage and he found me a suspended helmet. He shined it up for me and my mother got some foam rubber and made me some knee pads, thigh pads, and hip pads. Those were the first football pants I ever had."

"I don't know if I ever would have gotten through college if I didn't have to think about playing football and staying eligible," said Pete Anderson.

"Football was one thing I was able to excel in and it kind of made me who I was."

For those who graduated from college and didn't make it to the NFL, playing in the minor leagues was a way to postpone the inevitable. Ken Blasser was cut from a Canadian League team after his graduation from Central Connecticut. "I just didn't know what to do with myself when I got home," he said. "I didn't have a job and I said, 'What am I doing with my life?' I was just conditioned to always play football." He signed with the Knights.

Mike Mosolf joined the Hartford Charter Oaks after being cut by the Dallas Cowboys. "There was a lot going on in the 1960s," he said, "Vietnam and all that. I think people were just adrift. I didn't see any other options—anything in my life that was worth doing. I had a degree in education, but I didn't want to get into teaching right off the bat. Playing football and not having a steady job was kind of my lifestyle of choice."

But eventually, all football careers end. Long Island Bulls quarterback Seiki Murono's decision to concentrate on his banking career came suddenly and with great clarity. "We were playing the Bridgeport Jets," he recalled, "and a huge defensive end came in unblocked. In the film I saw him cock his arm and just knock my lower jaw into my upper jaw. I didn't have a mouthpiece in at the time and he knocked me out. I regained consciousness in the hospital and could feel pieces of my teeth loose in my mouth, which was no fun. I had stitches in my chin and said, 'It's time to hang them up.'"

In 1971, while vacationing with his family on Long Beach Island, New Jersey, Bob Stohrer received a call from Pete Savin indicating that players' salaries would have to be cut to make ends come a little closer to meeting. Stohrer was 27 years old, and after he'd been cut in training camp by the Redskins in 1968, realized he wasn't going to get another chance. "I saw a lot of guys in the Atlantic Coast Football League," he said, "who were around for a long time and weren't going anywhere. They'd had their chance but they'd keep trying for seven or eight years. I didn't want to be one of those guys. I hated to give it up but I decided to accept an offer from the Shell Oil Company."

For some players, it was hard to accept that the end was near. Lee Grosscup had been the first round draft pick of the New York Giants and played four seasons in the NFL and AFL, but when he joined the Charter Oaks in 1965, he hadn't played a major league game in almost three years. At 29, his chances of returning to the big leagues were slim.

"I think a lot of it was ego," he said in retrospect. "I was always thinking I was going to get back to my glory days, and I was going to be that guy again, and when I walked onto the field the magic was going to come back. I had always felt that when I entered a game something really important was going to happen, because I had a lot of confidence in my passing ability. And then there was the camaraderie. There was so much that was attractive, but now, looking back, it seems like it was just *stupid*. Why did I stay as long as I did, because I took a real pounding."

Two years later, Grosscup was working as a color commentator for NBC when Coach John Rauch of the Raiders called and said he might need an extra quarterback. "For a minute, I thought, yeah, I've got to get to camp. It *is* hard to give up the game."

When one's identity is based upon football, it is very difficult to accept the fact that the football phase of life will end at a relatively young age. We've all seen athletes in their prime stating that no one will have to tell them when to retire; they will be the first to know when they can't do it anymore. Then a few years later we see the same athlete, struggling mightily but insisting they are merely in a slump, or trying to correct a mechanical problem, when everybody but them realizes it is over. No matter what the game, it is, as DeFelice and Grosscup said, hard to give it up.

"It was really tough," said Tim Miller. "It was hard to watch and not think about playing." Many players, including Miller, turned to coaching as an outlet, experiencing vicariously what they could no longer do physically.

What did they love about the game, why was it such fun, and why was it so hard to give up? Retired baseball players will tell you they loved the challenge of competition and the camaraderie. For many football players there was an additional element—the love of physical contact, the opportunity to express themselves by hitting others in a violent but legitimate way. "You could go out on the field and hit someone as hard as you want and you wouldn't go to jail," said DeFelice.

"I *loved* to hit people," said Abbey. "I really, really enjoyed the art of the hit to the point where you try to have somebody *explode* when you hit them. The controlled mayhem was like an endorphin rush to me. I really loved the contact."

Ken Blasser had a difficult relationship with his father and used football as an outlet for his pent-up aggression. "I would just go out and take my aggressions out on the field," he said. "I had a lot of rage and that's where I got my release. I loved the contact." Others weren't as introspective. "It was the hitting," said linebacker Bill Richter. "I loved to hit people. It was exciting. I just loved it."

"Even as a kid," said Pete Anderson, "I'd wonder why some of my buddies didn't want to stay on the team. I said, 'This is great. You're getting to hit people. You're getting to tackle people and you're not getting into trouble.'"

When they weren't trying to make other players explode, they enjoyed their company and reveled in the camaraderie. Those who commuted long distances went straight home after practice, but usually a large group would repair to a nearby bar for beer and pizza or sandwiches. "We'd go to the Polish National Home," said Dick Bowman, "or the VFW and have a couple of beers and shoot the breeze. Beers were twenty five cents and we'd just sit around and talk and reminisce. That was the best part of it. You became friends with people because you learned about their lives by shooting the breeze after practice. It's something you can't describe. I really wanted both my kids to play football, even though they're smaller, because you learn something about teamwork that you can't learn any other way. Football is a sport where you can't be an individual, at least not for long, or you'd better look out. Somebody's not going to block for you or something's going to happen to you. I didn't want to see my kids get hurt but there's a lesson you learn by helping each other that I don't think you get in any other sport." He laughed. "And now I'm working on my grandkids."

Camaraderie and teamwork are a little different however, in the minor leagues, where the coveted goal of an NFL spot is determined by individual performance rather than team success. "They say there's no 'I' in team," said Lou Piccone, "but I say 'I' is the only thing in team, because if *I* ain't there, *it* don't matter." When asked about individual performance, players almost invariably say that the team's winning is the only thing that matters. But are they really happier when the team wins, they fumble three times and get cut, or when the team loses, but they score three touchdowns and get promoted to the NFL?

Still, being part of a team is special. "It's the notion that you've got 40 players on a team," said Seiki Murono, "and everyone has a role to play and everybody has to execute his responsibility in order for the team to succeed. It was that whole notion of a collaborative effort to succeed that I liked. I never played any individual sports growing up. I just played football, baseball, and basketball. I liked being part of a team and hopefully a leader on that team, coordinating everyone's efforts and inspiring them. I carried that attitude to the business world and tried to pattern my leadership skills in business after what I did on the athletic field."

Tom Sherman made a similar connection between success on the football field and in the business world. "You've got responsibility. You've got teammates who are depending on you and you're depending on them. If you're a lineman, you've got to rely on the guy to the left of you and the guy to the right of you. You learn so many things without even realizing it, and anybody who plays football has great drive and commitment if he's going to be any good. Here at the University of Virginia [where Sherman was an administrator in the athletic department] when businesses come to campus to interview our students, if they have a regular student and an athlete who are about the same, they're going to take the athlete because he made the commitment of time and responsibility."

"It's the thrill of playing with a bunch of guys," said DeFelice. "It's the camaraderie. It's meeting the families after the game. It's having a beer with the guys. It's almost like going to war. You know how when those guys go to Afghanistan, sometimes they can't wait to get back there because they form a family. That's what we had. We loved each other. We played our balls off for each other."

John Willard, who served in the military, felt his football bonds were stronger. "The military is so huge," he said. "A team is closer because of the numbers involved. It isn't thousands. It's a 40-man roster so the team is much more close-knit than it is in the service."

John Dockery was one of the few minor leaguers who made it in a big way, playing in Super Bowl III as a member of the Jets. "We went through the same thing together," he said of the Super Bowl champs. "We're always bound together, and that's special. You can't take that away from us. No one else can understand the moments we went through."

"If one of those guys that I played with and was close to," said Joe Ginnetti, "called me now, 40 years later, at two o'clock in the morning and said, 'Joe, I'm in trouble, I need your help,' my response would be, 'Where are you and what's wrong? I'll be there in five minutes.'"

Minor league salaries varied considerably. Before the Stamford Golden Bears joined the ACFL, their players weren't paid at all. "Maybe we slipped [star players] like Allan Webb or Johnny Counts ten bucks or twenty bucks after the game," said coach Al Shanen, "but nobody else made any money."

When Bill Richter played with the Connecticut Giants, he made five dollars a game. On teams like the Ansonia Black Knights, it was rare for a player to make more than $35 or $40 a game, and most made $20 or $25. The Hartford Charter Oaks, trying to compete in the tough Continental League, raised the ante in 1966, and Commissioner Sol Rosen stated that annual salary budgets for the CFL ranged from $125,000 to $150,000 for the 35-man roster. By 1968, after some difficult times, the league had established a maximum salary of $200 per game, with a $5,000 limit per game for each team. In the early years of the Knights, Pete Savin paid most of his players $150 to $350 per game. When attendance dwindled in subsequent years, game checks were as low as $50.

Some players claimed to make $500-$750 per game, and many said they were the highest paid on their team or in the league. With multiple claimants, it was hard to say what the highest salaries might have been. Quarterbacks usually got top dollar; Tom Kennedy made between $400 and $800 per game during his career and it is likely that Harry Theofiledes made about $1,000 a game playing for the Bridgeport Jets.

3. That's What They Do in the Fall

When the Knights began to reduce salaries, DeFelice had a particularly difficult negotiating session with Manch Wheeler, the former quarterback who became the club's general manager. DeFelice had been an all-league tackle, the Knights had won the division title, and he expected a nice increase in pay. But Wheeler told him times were tough and salaries had to be lowered. "I'd been protecting his ass as an offensive lineman," DeFelice said, "and now he's coming to negotiate with me."

When Wheeler and DeFelice reached an impasse, Pete Savin entered the negotiation. He explained that he had just paid for an expansion of Dillon Stadium and that money was tight. "Nick," he said, "you've got to help me out."

"Pete," DeFelice replied, "let me ask you a question. When I'm on the football field and I've got a guy who weighs 270 or 280 in front of me and he's beating my head into the ground, do I look to the sideline and say, 'Pete, you've got to help me out?'" "Give him what he wants," Savin told Wheeler.

The war between the AFL and NFL ended with the peace agreement of 1966, and the end of open competition brought the upward salary spiral to a halt. A man with a decent full time job who made $250 a week playing minor league football could make as much or more than an NFL player.

"If I had made the Packer team in '68 I would have made $12,000," said Tom Rowland. "A lot of guys weren't interested in playing in the NFL because of the money situation. If they had a good job, they weren't interested in going on. They were making extra money and had a good thing going." When Bill Tobin played for the Orlando Panthers in 1966 and held a full-time teaching job, he made more than he did as a starting running back with the Houston Oilers three years earlier.

Lou Piccone graduated from the Bridgeport Jets to the New York Jets and earned $12,900 after a 1975 holdout. "People were glad to see me back," he said. "They could identify with me. After all, I was making less than your average garbage collector."[1]

DeFelice played one full season and part of another with the Jets prior to re-joining the Charter Oaks in 1967. "If I had a shot to go back up I would have," he said, "but I was starting to get settled down. I had a job teaching school. I made money playing football and in other part time jobs. I had a new house. I had four kids. In the NFL you weren't making any money. I think it would have been difficult for me to give all that up and go back and play for fifteen grand."

Don Jonas, the best quarterback in the Continental League, once turned down an opportunity to go to camp with the Denver Broncos. If he gave up his teaching job, he would have had to take a cut in pay if he made the Denver roster.

In the heyday of the mid-to-late '60s, minor league money wasn't bad.

Roger Milici made more as a Bridgeport Jet than the $4,900 a year he earned as a teacher. Jim Murphy made $7,000 a year as a teacher, $250 a game playing for the Knights, and more money in the summer working as a cement finisher for Pete Savin.

For John Willard, who attended law school while playing for the Charter Oaks, his salary was a great incentive. "For two nights of practice and playing on Saturday night," said Willard, "$400 a week was good pay for a guy in law school."

For others, the money was irrelevant. Seiki Murono had an MBA in international finance and worked for Chase Manhattan Bank while playing in the CFL and ACFL. "I just did it for the fun," he said. "I enjoyed playing football. Money wasn't the issue. I realized that was probably going to be the pinnacle of my football career, and I was going to play as long as I could, while dedicating most of my energy and attention to my banking career." He would play until his jaws were re-configured by a Bridgeport defensive end.

Nearly all players worked while playing in the minors. "I had jobs all the time," said John Land. "I never just played football. Football supplemented my income but it wasn't my main source of income." Many players were scholastic coaches, which could prove problematic on days they were scheduled to coach in the afternoon and play in the evening. Pete Savin sometimes flew players on private planes and even the Meriden Shamrocks once chartered a plane when quarterback Larry Marsh and a couple of other players had to coach their high school teams.

Some companies resented the fact that their employees played football, concerned about absence from the job or the possibility of a serious injury. "They didn't like it," said Bill Richter. "They liked me but they didn't like me playing. They kept saying, 'Don't get hurt. Don't get hurt.' But it was my own time so they couldn't really do anything about it." Bob Shemeth, who held a marketing position with Clairol in New York, didn't talk about his football career around the office, for fear that it would count against him.

Stohrer worked for a while in the personnel department of Connecticut Light and Power. "The only heat I got when I was hired by CL&P," he said, "was that they were concerned about my ability to both play football and work for them. So sure enough I break my collarbone." Having told the company that football would not present a problem, Stohrer was determined to show that he could work with a minor injury like a broken collarbone.

When he walked into the office Monday morning with his arm in a sling, his boss asked him what he was doing there. "I'm here to work," Stohrer announced. "I couldn't move my hands on the desk," he said recently. "I couldn't raise my hands to write." But he wouldn't go home, and his supervisor proved

3. That's What They Do in the Fall

equally stubborn. "He let me work the whole day and all I could do was sit there and pretend I was working. As I was leaving he said, 'Don't come in tomorrow. Take a couple of days off.' But he let me suffer through the day to teach me a lesson."

Some employers liked having football players on staff. "When I worked at Travelers," said Dennis Fitzgibbons, "I won't say they bent over backwards to be supportive but they were not at all opposed to me playing. Some people would go to the games, and I'd hear a lot of water cooler talk Monday and Tuesday."

"They loved it," said Murono. "They put articles in the Chase newsletter. I worked on the same floor with the person who eventually became president of the bank, and every Monday morning he'd say, 'Well, how did we do this weekend?' They liked the fact that I was a professional at the bank and playing professional football at the same time."

Playing dual roles made for a grueling schedule. When he was in graduate school in Washington, D.C., Murono flew to New York each week to play for the Westchester Bulls. Shemeth and Bob Mirabelle of the Knights worked in New York City, and after a long train ride from Manhattan, car pooled to Hartford for practice three nights a week. "It was a full plate," Shemeth said. "After a game you're hurting. We played on Saturday night and by Monday you're still hurting, but you've got to go to work. It was difficult trying to balance the pain and trying to look professional."

In order to recruit a prospect, it was often necessary to include a job in the package. Nick Cutro, who coached a number of teams, sent letters to prospective players and promised that if they made the roster, he would find them housing and a job. When Cutro coached a team whose owner had a substantial business, finding jobs was easy, but if not, he had to establish relationships with boosters in the area who would hire his players and others who would provide free rent.

Pete Savin was always willing to offer employment that provided steady pay and sometimes required only minimal work. "If a kid needed extra money," said his wife Elaine, "he would find them a job. If some of the Cornell football players were here for the summer he'd give them jobs on the road building crew. They loved it because they could work out and get paid for it."

Several players who taught during the school year spent their summers on Savin construction crews. "It was a great summer job and you didn't have to work too hard," said Joe Murphy. "We made pretty good money," said Tom Rowland, "because they were union jobs. I made a lot more money working for Jet Lines [a Savin company] than I made playing football."

"A lot of us worked for Savin," said Charlie Tiblom. "We would never do anything. The most we did was paint some of those things the cranes go in. Sometimes they'd give us something to do but we were basically paid to sit around the back yard. We thought we were doing a good job if we could find someplace to hide." Once they were sent to clean Herb Savin's pool.

"Basically, it was clock in, go to breakfast, nap, go to lunch, nap, paint construction equipment for an hour or so and then clock out," Bill Fisher told an interviewer years later.

If a player was interested in a career, however, Savin found them more serious employment. Tom Sherman worked for one of the Savin companies as a bookkeeper. "I put in a good day's work," he said. "I wasn't just sitting there drawing a check." Stohrer joined the Savin organization and likewise held down a responsible position, one where he couldn't be criticized for showing up with an injury.

Injuries have always been a part of football, and not only did players of the 1960s suffer broken bones and torn ligaments, they faced a greater risk of permanent damage than today's players, in part because no one was aware of the potential long term effects of concussions. One frequently heard announcers say of an injured player, "It was nothing serious. He just got his bell rung." "There was no such thing as a concussion then," said Bowman. "You just had a headache and they said to get back in there."

"They gave you smelling salts," said Larry McHugh, "and you'd shake your head and get back in there. It was wrong but that was the mentality. Every one of us who played football in that era was knocked out. Today you'd be out for weeks or months, but it was a different time."

"I was never diagnosed with a concussion," said Tom Rowland, "and the main reason was that in college we never even had a team physician. Later, I taught health at Illinois College and learned about the symptoms of a concussion, and I know I had at least three or four of them. One time I had a coach who said I got hit really hard and told me to have my roommate wake me up at two in the morning and give him a call. I did and told him I had a headache and he told me not to go back to sleep. But that was the only time. It was stupid on my part, but you were afraid they wouldn't let you back in the game, so I never went and got it checked out."

In a 1971 game, Knights quarterback Tom Sherman suffered a concussion late in the first half and was dizzy and somewhat confused for most of the last two quarters. Today, his condition would call for a week or two on the sidelines. Then, his addled state dictated a simpler offense, less passing, and more running, as Sherman continued gamely on instinct. Afterwards, Coach Wallner lauded his courage for returning to action.

"They'd hold up a couple of fingers," recalled Joe Klimas, "and ask, 'How many fingers? What's your name? Where are we?' If you were able to answer you went back in the game."

Charlie Tiblom recalled a concussion suffered in college. While the trainer was walking onto the field, Tiblom asked his teammates the score, the place, and answers to all the other questions he knew he'd be asked. When he gave the right answers, they let him stay in the game.

Modern medical knowledge has also altered attitudes toward hydration. In the 1960s, it was believed that drinking fluids led to cramping; asking for water was also considered unmanly. "When I was at Maine," said Pete Quackenbush, "we had guys dropping on the practice field from dehydration. You never drank water because you were too tough. It was a sign of weakness."

Toughness was a major part of a football player's constitution, and playing hurt was a test of his manhood. "All of us just did it back then," said McHugh. "You played with separated shoulders. You played with serious injuries. You played with semi-serious injuries. Would you do it today? No. But back then it was just part of the mystique of playing football. People prided themselves on being able to play when they didn't know where they were."

In the minor leagues, injuries sometimes came about in unusual ways, such as when Nick Cutro took his team to Atlanta in 1964. "We're on the goal line defending," he said, "and all of a sudden John McMullan's screaming. Somebody on the other team had a razor blade and cut his arm. There was blood spurting all over the place and the officials kicked the guy out of the game."

The lasting effects of playing football are evident in many ex-players today. "Oh, my god," said Quackenbush, "I'm a physical wreck. I've had my knee operation. I had a hip replacement. My left shoulder isn't bad but my right one is pretty much shot. I've had both shoulders operated on—one of them twice. I've had a lot of orthopedic problems and I attribute most of them to football."

"We didn't wear face masks," Bob Kelso said of his college days, "so consequently I had all my teeth knocked out. Not all at once, but one here, one there. And I had my nose broken." "I had two total knee replacements," said Tim Miller, "shoulder surgery, four back surgeries and I have a pain pump in my stomach that releases narcotics every six hours. I went through a lot."

"In 2002," said Rowland, "I started having real bad neck problems, so I went to an orthopedist. He said, 'You played a lot of football, didn't you? You have what we call "spear tacklers' syndrome." Did you ever lead with your head?' Well, that's all I ever did. That's how they taught you to tackle. That's the only way they taught you. Jam your head in there. I had all these little bone spurs coming off my spine and they gave me a six cervical vertebrae fusion."

"I've had three knee operations," said Joe Klimas, "and an operation on my back. I've had a broken nose, a broken hand, and some other stuff, but I'll tell you what. I wouldn't trade that experience for anything."

Charlie Tiblom would. "I wish I'd never played football," he said. "I've had a total shoulder replacement. I'm wracked with arthritis. I can't turn my neck all the way around to see when I'm backing my car up. I played with a lot of good players and really enjoyed it, but why we play, I don't know. If somebody said you would be in a car accident by the end of the day, would you drive?"

Don Abbey quit playing football when he couldn't walk, let alone run. "It got to the point," he said, "where I literally couldn't walk. My ankle was frozen in a flexed position for years. If I had played even one more season I would have had a different life orthopedically. I've had twelve knee operations and I'm going in for my thirteenth, which will be a total replacement of the right one. I've already had the left one done. I'm so thankful I gave up the game when I did. God does wonderful things. He acts in very strange ways. I think if I had a better relationship with Coach Paterno or if I hadn't threatened to sue the Dallas Cowboys because of the way they negotiated with me I would have had a different football career. If I'd had a long career, I'd be Jimmy Otto [a former Oakland center who had horrific knees and experienced major health problems after his career ended]."

The treatment for injuries was often steroid-based. "If you would get hurt," said Rowland, "they would give you steroids right away to repair your muscle fiber. Nobody thought anything about taking or giving steroids because it was going to heal you faster. And I remember some of the guys I played with took Benzedrine—bennies. I never took them but a lot of guys did. You've got to remember. You're working all day, you get home, and then you've got to practice from 7 to 9. You're tired. People just did what they had to do and nobody thought anything of it."

"One year some of my roommates were taking them and we never went to bed before three or four in the morning because—hell—they *couldn't* go to bed. They were so jacked up. We would wait for the *Hartford Courant* to hit the newsstand at about three in the morning. I wasn't taking anything but I couldn't go to bed because my damn roommates were all jacked up."

Bob Shemeth recalled a game that was cancelled due to bad weather. "We were all in the locker room," he said, "and people were taking what they needed to keep them stimulated. We were all taped up and ready to go when they came in and said the game was cancelled. Anybody who was taking the stimulants was starting to come down. It was quite an interesting night, to say the least. You can only imagine the things that went on that night."

Amphetamines were freely dispensed on most teams. "If you wanted a shot after the games," said one player, "you could get one. They said it was vitamin B-12 but who knows what the hell I was getting shot up with." The players joked about getting the B-12 shots to make them more virile for their wives after the game.

"I never took a shot of Novocain when I was playing," said Dick Bowman, "because that scared me a little bit. If you play with something and you don't have any feeling, you're going to be feeling something pretty soon. I never took uppers in college, but in the pros I did. You'd take a greenie instead of working out. That's so stupid. It doesn't make you any better but you think you're better. And then you don't sleep for another day."

Pete Anderson thought his retirement at any early age might have been a blessing in disguise. "Steroids were just starting to come into the game," he said, "and being a crazy 22-year-old, maybe it was a good decision to go out when I did. The people who were doing those things have long since passed away. I hope for their sake [today's players] don't enhance themselves too much, because I don't know how some of these guys are going to do once they get into their 50s and 60s."

Football is much different today than it was in the 1960s, but certain aspects are timeless. Camaraderie, competition, and desire have always been part of the game. The men who played for the Hartford Knights, Bridgeport Jets, and Long Island Bulls played because they wanted to make a little money, or because they thought they had a shot at the NFL, but most of all they played because they'd been playing all their lives and loved the game. The travel, the pain, and the struggle were all worth it come Saturday night.

4

A Football Crazed Town: The 1962–63 Ansonia Black Knights

Ansonia was founded on stubbornness. In the late 1830s, an industrialist named Anson G. Phelps, founder of the Phelps-Dodge mining company, had visions of a manufacturing center on the western bank of the Naugatuck River, in the town of Derby. He acquired several parcels of land, and needed just one more to complete the puzzle. A man named Stephen Booth got wind of Phelps' plan and purchased a farm in the midst of the planned development for $5,000. Phelps needed the last piece of land and Booth knew it. He kept raising his asking price until it reached $30,000. Exasperated and angered at the manner in which Booth had negotiated, Phelps decided in 1844 to abandon his plans for the west side of the river and move to the hills on the east bank. He immodestly called his new village Ansonia.

Ansonia remained part of Derby until 1889, when it became the 168th of Connecticut's 169 towns and cities (only West Haven, established in 1921, came later). A number of prominent people hailed from the little town of Ansonia. It was the birthplace of David Humphreys, who accepted the surrendered sword of General Cornwallis at Yorktown. Vincent R. Impellitteri, elected mayor of New York City in 1950, was an Ansonia native. Luther Powell, father of former Secretary of State Colin Powell, worked at the American Brass Company during World War I.

The economy of Ansonia, from its establishment by Anson Phelps, was based on manufacturing. Many immigrants arrived during the early years of the twentieth century and found employment in the town's factories; the main ethnic groups were Italian, Ukrainian, Polish, and Irish. After an initial surge, however, the population of Ansonia stabilized at 19,800 in 1930 and remained at that level in 1960. One of the reasons for the lack of growth was that the town encompassed just six square miles, with a river on the west and steep hills to the east. There was no room to expand.

In 1955, Ansonia was hit by a devastating flood that destroyed the town's three bridges, left many people homeless, and caused millions of dollars of property damage. Soon the local economy was suffering, with unemployment more than doubling from 310 in 1957 to 760 the following year. Mayor Joseph Doyle, who served the city on a part-time basis, was laid off from his full-time job at B.F. Goodrich.

Sam Impellitteri, brother of Vincent and operator of a local restaurant and bar, analyzed the downturn. "When the whisky drinkers switch to beer," he said, "we are having a recession. When the whisky and beer drinkers cut out all their drinking, we are having a depression. Right now we are having a recession. Since the first of the year I've been selling 40 per cent more beer than last year."[1]

Economic stagnation, the deterioration of older downtown buildings, and a lack of parking led to a strategy proposed by nearly all aging factory towns in the late 1950s—urban renewal with federal funding. In 1957, Ansonia adopted a master plan and applied for a grant. The results were disappointingly similar to those achieved by other towns. Neighborhoods were dismantled, a lot of money was made by contractors and, in the end, master planning proved no more successful in America than it had in the Soviet Union. Still, in the early '60s, Ansonia's industrial base, although reduced from the halcyon days of the '40s and '50s, provided a relatively stable source of employment. The biggest manufacturers were the American Brass Company and the Farrel-Birmingham Company, builder of the world's largest sugar mills.

The stubbornness that led Anson Phelps to establish the original village was reflected in Ansonia's residents who, although not wealthy, were proud and self-reliant. Community leaders were a reflection of the populace. Andrew Nolan, who served as mayor from 1936 to 1945, and for whom the Nolan Field complex is named, was a blue collar worker and long-time foreman at the Farrel Foundry and Machine Company.

"It was a middle class, working class town," said former Ansonia sportswriter Harry Katzman. "And mostly everybody worked. You couldn't get checks like you do today." Ansonia would never be a metropolis like New Haven or Hartford, or a wealthy suburb like Greenwich or New Canaan. It was a blue-collar Naugatuck Valley town that loved its football.

Ansonia was commonly known as the Copper City, but it could just as readily been called the Pigskin City. Naugatuck Valley towns follow their football teams with as much fervor and enthusiasm as those in the hotbeds of Pennsylvania, Texas, and Alabama. High school games in Ansonia, Seymour, Derby, and Naugatuck generate far more passion than the games of the Giants, Jets, or Patriots.

In the early 1960s, before the advent of cable television, the focus on local teams was even more pronounced, and the devotion of Valley fans was legendary. Matthew J. Shortell, Jr., better known as "Pop," attended 578 consecutive Ansonia High School football games over a 55-year period. In 1987, he was acclaimed America's number one sports nut in a marketing contest run by a nut company and the same year was inducted into the Connecticut High School Coaches Hall of Fame, the first inductee who had neither coached nor played high school sports.[2]

Rich Marazzi was born in Ansonia in 1943, briefly played football at Ansonia High School, and has lived in the town all his life. He has hosted a talk show on ESPN Radio, has written books about baseball, and is so expert in baseball rules that he is employed as a consultant by a number of major league teams. Marazzi knows sports and he knows his home town. "When you're a young kid in Ansonia," he said, "you're almost given a football from the time you're in a cradle. Anything involving football in Ansonia is *huge*. It's a football crazed town. It has been, it still is, and it probably always will be." Marazzi remembers going to his uncle's house for family gatherings where the main entertainment was showing 16 millimeter films of Ansonia High School games on a bed sheet hung on the wall.

A number of Ansonia boys made it big in pro football, including Allan Webb, a defensive back for the New York Giants, Nick Pietrosante, fullback of the Detroit Lions, and Bob Skoronski, captain and offensive tackle of the NFL champion Packers. During the off season, these men came back to Ansonia and spoke to church groups and civic clubs, often for free. They were a great source of local pride and an inspiration to chubby youngsters who thought they could be the next Bob Skoronski. Bill Richter, who grew up in the Valley and played for the Black Knights, said, "We all had our heroes." Richter's idols were Webb and Ansonia High quarterback Vinnie Drake.

Another local hero normally wore a cassock instead of shoulder pads and a helmet. He was Reverend Arnold Fenton, the famous Punting Parson who was nationally renowned as a teacher of the art of kicking a football. Fenton, stationed at Christ Episcopal Church in Ansonia, was profiled in *Time* magazine and had a number of famous pupils, including NFL star Charley Trippi. For many years, he tutored Dartmouth College punters, and also spent time at Yale and the University of Connecticut.

"He'd be down at the Yale Bowl standing on the sideline in his parson outfit," Marazzi recalled. "It all added to the special aura of football in Ansonia. Back in the '30s and '40s they used to have two hundred people watching the high school team *practice*. It's a football crazy town. But if you really want to know about sports in Ansonia, you need to talk to Harry Katzman."

4. A Football Crazed Town

Harry (Lime) Katzman wrote for the *Evening Sentinel*, which covered the towns of the Naugatuck Valley, for 43 years, serving as sports editor for the last 30. To read the light, breezy style of "Limelites," Katzman's weekly column, is to take a journey back to a bygone era of sports journalism. Like many of his colleagues, Katzman favored repetitive alliteration—the more, the better. Quarterbacks used their "passing paws" to create a "passing party" or handed the ball to the "leather-luggers." Athletes "flashed" in college, they had "pro flings" and if they had a "fractured flipper" they joined the "casualty corps." And in Lime Katzman's world, seldom was heard a discouraging word about the Valley sporting scene.

I called Harry and asked if he would be willing to speak with me on the phone about the Black Knights. He would do better than that, and invited me to visit him and spend an afternoon talking football. Katzman lives in the southern part of Ansonia, near Orange, and I wasn't sure I was in the right neighborhood until I pulled up in front of a house with two cars parked in the driveway. One had a vanity plate that read "Lime" and the other had one that read "Katzman." This was the place.

Entering the Katzman residence, a baby boomer will feel like they are visiting their parents. The interior of the neat white ranch is decorated in a dark-paneled, 1970s motif and the walls, shelves, and tables are covered with pictures of children and grandchildren. When we entered the den, however, it was obvious that this house was not like the home of my parents, for interspersed among the family pictures were many photos of Katzman and the sports celebrities he met over the years.

When he was five years old, Harry Katzman lost much of his right arm in a meat machine at his father's grocery store. With his left arm, he became a basketball player for the semi-pro Ansonia Norwoods, a team that included NBA player Worthy Patterson and Katzman's friend Bill Spivey, a seven-foot center from Kentucky who was kept out of the NBA after being implicated in a college point shaving scandal.

On one occasion, Katzman's team played an exhibition against a squad that included Wilt Chamberlain. "I played about one minute of that game," he recalled, "but I played." Katzman played basketball and softball into his 60s, all the while writing about local sports for the *Evening Sentinel*. He echoed Marazzi's comments on the exalted role of football in the Valley, and then we talked about the Ansonia Black Knights.

The driving force behind the formation of the Black Knights in 1962 was Frank Berlinger, a long time local umpire and Commissioner of the Valley Softball League. Why did he choose to call his club the Black Knights? Marazzi thinks the name was chosen to honor Bob Kyasky, an Ansonia high school legend of the 1950s who went on to play at West Point for the Black Knights of the Hudson. The Ansonia team wore uniforms very similar to those of Army and Marazzi believes it was because of Kyasky that the Ansonia eleven acquired its name.

Berlinger, an employee of Pratt and Whitney, was not a wealthy man. He needed financial backers, and enlisted Clint Hennessey, Clifford Downer, and Pat Mainolfi as his partners. Downer was his brother-in-law, a colorful character with a penchant for gambling. Mainolfi, who owned a company that produced rubber specialty products, had the deep pocket.

Berlinger had the enthusiasm. "He was into everything," said his son Bob. "He was always an optimist. But it was a surprise to all of us when he started a football team. They just decided they wanted to start a team and that was it."

The Black Knights' coach was Gene Casey, a tough but mild-mannered ex–Marine and former line coach at the University of Illinois and Southern Connecticut State College. Casey also coached baseball at Southern and became acquainted with Berlinger when the latter umpired a number of his team's games.

"He was a classic football coach," said quarterback Pudge Henkel. "I don't think there was anything terribly subtle about him. He was just a solid football coach." "He was never a hollerer or a screamer," said Joe Klimas, another Ansonia signal caller, "and he never tore anybody down in front of the whole team. If he had something to say to you he would call you aside, unlike some other coaches."

Casey was quiet, he was calm, and he inspired great loyalty among his players, many of whom followed him from team to team over the next several years. "You'd just die for the guy," said guard Larry McHugh.

Not surprisingly, the Ansonia roster was liberally sprinkled with Southern Connecticut products. "You go with your coach," said linebacker Bob Kelso. "All the Southern guys went there." Southern had a very good football program, but it was a small college that got little respect beyond the New Haven area. "Southern had a better football team, measured by comparative scores, than UConn," said McHugh. "If you went to Southern, you always had a chip on your shoulder."

Kelso was a typical Black Knight—undersized, a step slow, but a vicious hitter. "He was a tough son of a gun," said Tony Pontillo, who played with him in Meriden. "He'd hit everything that moved. You had to watch out or he'd hit *you*." Kelso came hard and usually helmet first. "He was an unbelievably tough guy," said McHugh, "but he got knocked out every freakin' game he played."

Most minor league clubs had a handful of veterans who'd played in the NFL or AFL and some players who'd starred in major college programs. The Black Knights had neither. Nine players from the 1962 roster had never attended college, and several others played just a year or two before leaving school. A few had brief looks in AFL or NFL camps, but none had played in a regular season game in either league.

Several Knights, including linebacker Bill Richter, were veterans of the semi-pro Connecticut Giants. Richter was a mediocre player in high school who weighed just 130 pounds when he graduated. No colleges were interested in 130-pound linebackers, so he went into the service for four years. Richter eventually filled out and, when he was discharged, joined the Giants and then the Black Knights.

Although the Ansonia squad was light on experience, it included some talented athletes. The best lineman, and probably the best player, was offensive tackle Nick DeFelice, whom I interviewed at the headquarters of his company, Oxford Industries. As I stood in the reception area I knew immediately, from the 40-year-old newspaper photos I'd seen, that the tall, 70-year-old man walking toward me was the former captain of the Black Knights. The thick curly hair was white, the body not as chiseled as it was 40 years ago, and he walked with a slight limp, but the face looked the same and DeFelice is only ten pounds over his playing weight. He skis, rides a bicycle, and is as active and fit as a septuagenarian veteran of nearly two decades of football line play can be. He is also a very friendly, charismatic man, and although we'd only met briefly once before, he greeted me warmly.

Offensive tackle Nick DeFelice graduated from the Ansonia Black Knights to the New York Jets, and later served as captain of the Hartford Knights (photograph from Hartford Knights program).

DeFelice grew up in Derby, where every young boy, especially one as big as Nick DeFelice, was expected to play football. His uncles had been star players in the 1940s, and Nick tried out for the high school team expecting to follow in their footsteps.

To his great chagrin, DeFelice was cut. "I was a big kid," he said, "but maybe not as fast as I should have been at that age. All my buddies dressed for the game and I didn't get a jersey. I went up to Coon Hollow Park where they played and hid in the woods because I was so embarrassed that I didn't get a jersey. My buddies were playing in the game and I was watching up in the woods crying."

DeFelice eventually made the team and was good enough to be invited to play for the University of Miami, where he hit the tackling dummies harder than he hit the books. After a year in Florida, DeFelice returned to Connecticut and captained the Southern Connecticut team during his senior season of 1961. When he graduated, DeFelice weighed 230 pounds and, although the New York Giants expressed some interest, they thought he was too small to play tackle. He took a teaching job and signed up to play for the Black Knights on weekends.

DeFelice was joined in late August by McHugh, one of his best friends from Southern, who had just been released by the New York Titans. "There was a special thing between us," DeFelice said recently, "because I knew what he was thinking and he knew what I was thinking."

DeFelice and McHugh had an effective method for dealing with troublesome defensive linemen. If one of them was having a bad time with the man across the line, he would engage his opponent, stand him up, and the other would come from the side and level him. During an Ansonia-Providence game, the pair performed that nifty maneuver on Steamroller defensive lineman Rod MacDonald, a rugged 230-pound Naval Academy graduate. McHugh stood him up and DeFelice enthusiastically knocked him down.

MacDonald got up cursing and vowing revenge. The next play was a sweep where DeFelice's assignment was to pull and lead the blocking, leaving his buddy McHugh alone to deal with the enraged MacDonald. "Larry was furious when I came back to the huddle," DeFelice recalled. "'Hey,' I told him, 'I had to pull.' He wasn't happy."

The Black Knights' biggest problem before the 1962 season was that DeFelice and McHugh did not have an established quarterback to block for. For two months, Berlinger worked the phones trying to get a top flight signal caller. The one he really wanted was former Ansonia High star Vinnie Drake, who played at Fordham and had a trial with the Philadelphia Eagles. Drake was a huge name in Ansonia, having grown up on Elm Street and starred with Allan Webb in high school.

During his senior season, Drake averaged two touchdown passes a game and made the All-State team for the second straight year. In an era when athletes played multiple sports, he also set records in basketball, pitched a no-hitter on the baseball diamond, and competed in the mile run and high jump for the track team.

Despite his formidable talents, Drake faced a monumental obstacle in his quest to play in the National Football League. He was an African American, and the only black man who had played quarterback in the NFL up to that time was the aptly-named Willie Thrower, who played one game for the Chicago Bears in 1953. Drake played semi-pro ball in the U.S., service ball in Europe, and then spent several years in Canada. He was living in Montreal, but Berlinger was willing to fly him in each week for games and allow him to forego practice. Drake wasn't interested.

On August 21, the *Evening Sentinel* reported that "the Knights' GM has been burning up the phones in the hopes of landing a passer of pro caliber and may get his man before tonight rolls around."[3] When the first regular season game came around, however, Berlinger was still burning up the phone lines and his starting quarterback was jack-of-all-trades Joey Landino. Landino was small (5'9" and 180 pounds) and quick, but did not have the arm to lead a top-flight minor league offense.

Pre-season workouts had presented a major problem, as the Knights bounced from one practice facility to another. They began working out at Nolan Field, which would be the site of their home games, but after being relegated to the parking lot, they decided to move to Pine Lot. On August 3, Berlinger announced that he was again changing the practice location, this time to West Rock Park in New Haven. No matter where the club practiced, however, contact work was limited because the team's equipment did not arrive until they had been working out in shorts and T-shirts for several weeks. On August 3, Berlinger announced there would be a scrimmage on Thursday "that is if our equipment finally arrives."[4]

On August 20, the Knights announced that they would play the Wakefield Redskins of the New England Conference for the benefit of the Ansonia Babe Ruth League and Legion baseball. There was indeed a benefit game on August 25th, but the Whitman Townies provided the opposition rather than Wakefield. The latter club played an exhibition against the powerful Providence Steamroller two days before they were scheduled to appear in Ansonia. Apparently, the Steamroller lived up to its nickname and inflicted so many injuries on the Wakefield club that the Redskins called Berlinger and told him they would be unable to keep their engagement. The Townies were a last minute replacement, and the Knights beat them easily, by a score of 45–0.

The opening game of the regular season took place on August 31 against the Frankfort Falcons in Herkimer, New York, a small upstate community just east of Utica. Ansonia's professional football debut was successful, as they beat the Falcons 21–13. Landino, who started at quarterback only because Berlinger couldn't find anyone else, touched off the scoring by throwing an 82-yard touchdown pass to speedy 165-pound halfback Tony Tavares of Bridgeport. Later in the game Tavares ran 45 yards for a second touchdown.

The Ansonia defense limited the Falcons to three pass completions and total offense of just 130 yards, but Landino completed only two passes, and the game, other than Tavares' long runs, was somewhat tedious. Berlinger continued looking for a quarterback.

Tavares, who never attended college, had a tremendous average per carry in 1962, mainly getting the ball on reverses from his wingback position. "He was quick," said Joe Klimas. "He was like greased lightning. Give him a little opening and he was gone."

Tavares was especially dangerous at Nolan Field, with its temporary lighting system. "The lights were on extension ladders," recalled Pudge Henkel, "and the lighting was bad. It was particularly bad in the end zone. Tony wasn't very big, so I'd try to sneak him down the sideline where people couldn't see him. I'd just throw it deep and hope he was there."

Winning was great, but attendance was what mattered, for there was a substantial financial burden associated with operating an ACFL franchise. Before the Whitman exhibition, the *Evening Sentinel* commented, "Tonight will tell if valley fans will support pro football ... many—General Manager Frank Berlinger in particular—feel that the Copper City gridders can make a go of it despite a heavy financial nut."[5] An encouraging total of 4,000 fans watched the Whitman game.

The biggest crowds were expected to be found in Providence, for the Steamroller was probably the most talented team in the ACFL and, like all clubs in the new league save Ansonia, had previously operated as an independent barnstorming club.

If Ansonia had what it took to compete in the ACFL, they would find out early, in grueling back to back matchups against the Steamroller, scheduled for Wednesday, September 5 at City Stadium in Providence and just three days later on Saturday night at Nolan Field. Two games in four days was a difficult test, made even more trying when rain caused a postponement of the first game until Thursday evening and gave the teams just a single day between games.

The Steamroller had a long and storied history, beginning with its formation in 1916 by sportswriters for the *Providence Journal*.[6] The National Football League had not yet been established, and the Steamroller played an *ad hoc* schedule against other independents. They declined to join the league when it was formed in 1920, but after winning three times in six exhibitions against NFL teams in 1924, signed on for the 1925 season.

In 1928, Providence, led by coach and single wing quarterback Jimmy Conzelman, posted an 8–1–2 record and won its first and only NFL championship. That was the pinnacle of the Steamroller saga, for Conzelman soon suffered a knee injury that limited his effectiveness. Star tackle Gus Sonnenburg captured the world wrestling championship and abandoned the Steamroller for the greater profit potential of the "squared circle." The team's record declined, and operations were suspended after the 1931 season. Two years later, with the Great Depression putting a damper on all professional sports, management turned the franchise back to the league. Subsequent versions of the Steamroller appeared beginning in the late '30s, and the 1962 team had been playing for several years.

4. A Football Crazed Town 47

The old Steamroller had played a grueling schedule, staging four games in six days from November 5 to 10, 1929. The game of football had evolved since then, and the quest for gate money had been tempered by common sense and concern for the well-being of players. Two games in three days would have been nothing for the old Steamroller, but in 1962 it was a highly unusual occurrence.

The Thursday night game took place in Providence in front of a live crowd of 8,900 (including an estimated 1,000 who made the trip from Ansonia) and a local television audience. The Steamroller was favored, having won two exhibitions and its opener. "They were loaded," said McHugh. "I always remember the Providence games because they were big, big games for us." "They were tough," Bill Richter added. "They were *always* tough."

And so were their fans. "We're playing up in Providence," recalled DeFelice, "and they hate us. For some reason, they got on Ralph Greco's back. They're yelling, 'Greco, you pig. Greco, you this and you that.' They were just breaking his stones. Finally he takes his helmet off and throws it into the stands. *Throws it into the stands!* The next thing you hear, they're yelling, 'Greco for mayor! Greco for mayor!' He'd become their hero."

The Providence squad was big, with offensive ends that stood 6'7" and 6'5", respectively. Many of their players hailed from well-known college programs, including a number from the Ivy League. One of the tackles was former Harvard captain Bob Shaunessey. Providence also featured Bob Kessler, pro football's first soccer style kicker, who approached the ball from the side two years before Pete Gogolak joined the Buffalo Bills.

The Black Knights were a bit stronger for the Providence game for finally, after all his efforts, Berlinger found a quarterback—sort of. He signed Gary Van Galder, a Stanford grad in his fourth year at the Yale School of Medicine. At 6'1" and 205 pounds, Van Galder was a more impressive physical specimen than Landino, but like Landino, he was not primarily a quarterback. He played the position for two years at Stanford before switching to end for his senior season. At the latter position, he was named to the All West Coast team and invited to play in the East-West game.

In his first game, Van Galder looked like an end trying to play quarterback. He was no match for Providence's Jerry Morgan, a 6'5" Iowa State grad who completed 12 of 21 pass attempts for 266 yards and three touchdowns. Van Galder connected on just 2 of 15 tosses for a total of 15 yards. By the end of the game, Landino was back at quarterback, and the final score was 28–14.

The second game against Providence, a mere two days later, was Ansonia's home opener, and perhaps the club's finest moment. In front of a Nolan Field crowd of 4,500, the Black Knights held the powerful Steamroller to a 0–0 tie. The defensive line play of both teams was ferocious; each limited its opponent to just two net yards rushing. The Knights managed only eight first downs all evening.

Ansonia staged a dramatic goal line stand late in the game, stopping Providence four times from the one yard line. After three smashes into the line gained nothing, Larry McHugh and Bob Dziadik burst through and tackled Bob Adams for a 20-yard loss.

The fact that McHugh was on the field was quite a surprise, for he had been injured during the second quarter and taken to the hospital by ambulance. When what was suspected to be a broken wrist turned out to be just a severe sprain, he was released. With no other means of transportation available, McHugh, still in uniform, jumped in the ambulance and was driven back to Nolan Field. He climbed out and went back into action late in the third quarter. "People still talk about that," he said recently. "The ambulance coming back, me getting out and going in and playing." One person still talking about it is Nick DeFelice. "McHugh was crazy," he said.

It was a sloppy game, but a great moral victory for the Black Knights, holding the league's best team, most powerful offense, and best quarterback scoreless for four quarters. It was, as Coach Casey, master of the cliché, said predictably, "a team effort." He praised his linemen, including McHugh, who, well-rested after his stay in the hospital, played both ways upon his return.

On September 16, the Knights took to the road and lost a heartbreaker to the Stamford Golden Bears. After failing to score in their previous game, Ansonia scored 27 points against Stamford, only to see the Golden Bears rally from a 14-point deficit to gain a 32–27 victory. Tavares broke free for another long touchdown run, this time of 73 yards, but Van Galder and Landino were again ineffective.

For the second time in three games, the Ansonia pass defense proved quite porous, allowing Stamford quarterback Sam Coppola to accumulate 238 yards and two touchdowns. Part of the problem was that the undermanned Knights were usually spent by the fourth quarter. "We were simply exhausted down the stretch," said Casey. "Several of the boys had to go both ways and they were beat the final five minutes."[7] It was clear the club needed more depth, and during the next week, Berlinger announced a rash of signings.

Since neither Van Galder nor Landino was the answer at quarterback, Berlinger signed former UConn player Joe Klimas. Klimas, who had been dropped by Indianapolis of the United Football League, would play quarterback while Van Galder moved back to end.

With a 1–2–1 record, the Knights looked toward a rematch with the one team they'd beaten, the Frankfort Falcons. The Falcons the Knights would face, however, were a different group than the one they'd beaten earlier, for like that of most minor league clubs, the Frankfort roster had evolved as NFL and AFL teams made their cuts.

It was very common for an ACFL franchise to have a core of players from the same college, as Ansonia did with Southern. One man would sign up, tell his friends, and they followed. In 1963, Harrisburg was a haven for ex–Penn Staters and Newark was home to a number of Notre Dame grads. The Falcons were based near Syracuse, New York, and managed to sign several former Syracuse stars, including All-American end Fred Mautino, quarterback Dick Easterly, fullback Gary Fallon, and tackle Ron Luciano, who later achieved fame as a major league umpire and author.[8]

The crew from Southern Connecticut, with their chips planted firmly on their shoulders, beat the big names from Syracuse 7–6, as Kelso blocked Frankfort's extra point try. Landino and Klimas combined for 120 yards in the air and Van Galder, playing much better at end than he had at quarterback, caught 6 passes for 82 yards. The Ansonia offense sealed the victory by maintaining possession of the ball for the last seven minutes of the game.

The joy over the win was tempered by the lack of success at the box office, as only 2,000 fans had paid their way into Nolan Field. Two big high school games in the afternoon and the threat of rain in the evening kept many people away. Sixty five hundred fans in two games would not pay the bills, but Berlinger remained optimistic, hoping for better crowds when Stamford, Portland, and Paterson appeared in Ansonia. "If those three clubs don't pack 'em in," he said, "then it's time to pack it up."[9]

The following week, the Knights traveled to Portland, Maine, and picked up their third win with an exciting, come from behind 20–15 victory. Down 15–13 with less than three minutes left, Klimas drove his club 85 yards for the winning touchdown, hitting Frank Beck in the back of the end zone for the score. Once again Tavares had several long runs, gaining 101 yards on just four carries.

The Knights were in third place following the big win against the Seahawks, two games behind Providence:

Providence	5–0–1
Paterson	3–1–0
Ansonia	3–2–1
Portland	2–3–0
Stamford	2–3–0
Frankfort	0–6–0

For a first year club, the Ansonia eleven had done remarkably well, not only posting a record above .500, but also inflicting the only blemish on the slate of the league-leading Steamroller. With the quarterbacking still suspect, the main strengths of the club had been a rock-ribbed defense and the fancy running of Tavares, who led the league with 293 yards in 29 carries, a remarkable average of more than ten yards per try.

The Knights' next opponent was the Paterson Miners, who had recently dismantled Frankfort 70–0. The Miners were a venerable organization that had been in existence for nearly 30 years. In 1961, they won all 17 of their games and, although not part of an organized league, were generally recognized as the best independent professional team in the country. Quarterback Neal Buckman, a former star at Alabama, threw 40 touchdown passes.

The Black Knights were big underdogs, their roster decimated by injuries. Tavares and two other Knights did not play, and Klimas, Landino, and fullback Maurice Sykes were hurt during the game. Klimas had to go back in with injured ribs after Landino, his replacement, hurt his leg. The Knights did well to hold the margin of defeat to 20–7.

Ansonia had three games left, all at home. Any hope for the championship was gone, and the biggest question was whether there would be enough local support to give the club reason to return in 1963. The first of the three games was against Stamford on October 13. "It could draw more than 5,000 if the weatherman cooperates," said Berlinger. "This is The Game valley fans have been waiting for."[10]

With Klimas injured, Berlinger signed yet another quarterback, 26-year-old Oliver (Pudge) Henkel, who'd been a backup at Yale and was in his second year at Yale Law School. Since he was not fat, people always asked Henkel how he acquired his nickname.

"I was about eleven pounds when I was born," Henkel said. "I was Oliver, Jr., and if you've got that first name there's only Oliver and Ollie and my father had used them both. They were looking for a nickname that might work and apparently I had taken on the characteristics of a ball. I was put on a diet when I was six weeks old. They looked at me and said the only nickname that's apt for this kid is Pudge and it stuck with me ever since."

As a break from his law studies, Henkel had agreed to help coach the Yale freshman team, and became very friendly with fellow coach Gary Van Galder. After practice, Henkel and Van Galder played a lot of pitch and catch and got to know each other well. "Gary suggested," Henkel said, "that I might want to come up and play with the Black Knights. When you get to your second year of law school there's a lot of sameness to it and I was looking for a diversion. I was kind of intrigued and asked him to bring me a playbook. I think Gary was anxious that I go up there because he didn't want to play quarterback anymore."

Van Galder brought the Ansonia playbook to a Yale frosh game on a Friday afternoon, and Henkel agreed to join the team for its game the following evening. "I joined the Black Knights that Saturday," Henkel recalled, "having never met any of the players other than Gary and none of the coaches and having only looked at the playbook. I figured if push comes to shove, well, Gary is in the huddle and he can tell me what to do and if things really get tough I'll just keep throwing to him."

For the upcoming game against Stamford, Henkel would back up Van Galder, who'd been moved back to quarterback after Klimas and Landino were hurt. The Knights now had a quarterbacking contingent consisting of a Yale law student and a Yale medical student. "It was really something," said DeFelice, "for those two guys to come up and play with us slobs, but they were great guys. When we were traveling, the bus would stop in New Haven, and Van Galder would come running out with his stethoscope swinging from his neck and jump on the bus."

Playing in the ACFL was an eye opener for Henkel. "I remember the bus arriving with a visiting team, I think it was the Jersey Giants [in 1963], and the first two guys off the bus were not players. They were traveling with the team, they didn't have jackets on, and they both wore shoulder holsters. It caused me to take a deep breath."

The Stamford game was an artistic success and financial failure. The Knights won convincingly 30–6, and Henkel completed four passes, all to Van Galder. Attendance, however, was less than 2,000, and even the indefatigable Berlinger was discouraged. "We lost a bundle as a result of the poor attendance at the Frankfort and Stamford games," he said, "and if we can't pack 'em in for the Miners and Seahawks, then it's time to pack it up and start looking for another city that will support us."[11] Berlinger was a fixture in the Valley, and it was hard to imagine he would move the franchise far from Ansonia. It was equally difficult to believe that the Knights would draw better in any of the neighboring towns.

The Knights were 4–3–1, a record that was about as good as could have been expected before the season, but apparently not good enough to excite Ansonians. In the next game, against the tough Paterson Miners, the Black Knights played a gritty game but lost 14–7. The offense was helpless against the veteran Miner squad. Ansonia quarterbacks did not complete a single pass in 12 attempts, and the entire team had minus nine yards in total offense and just two first downs.

Baltimore Colt general manager Don Kellett sat in the stands, and according to Berlinger, expressed an interest in establishing an affiliate relationship with the Knights. Unfortunately, there were only about 1,199 other people in attendance. Berlinger said the club would finish the season and then look for a new home for 1963. "When you can't draw with an attraction like the Miners," he lamented, "it's time to move. The valley fans have certainly let us down."[12]

Berlinger switched the final home game to Sunday afternoon, and said that a good final crowd was "a must to keep the Knights in Ansonia."[13] His luck was no better than it had been on Saturday nights, as it rained, causing a postponement to November 25. In the meantime, Berlinger, attempting to generate some additional revenue, scheduled a third game against the Steamroller, the only club that had drawn a decent crowd to Nolan Field. Since the teams had already completed their quota of ACFL games, the third match would be an exhibition. The Knights played surprisingly well but lost a close 22–19 game and drew only 700 fans.

Since he couldn't draw a crowd at Nolan Field, Berlinger elected to shift the final game against the Seahawks to Portland, Maine. The visiting team guarantee would cover travel expenses and player salaries, sparing Berlinger another financial bath.

While Berlinger didn't take a bath, his players did, as the game against the Seahawks was played in a driving mix of rain and snow. The Knights were shorthanded, for the Seahawks had denied their request to postpone the game until the following day. Ansonia dressed only 18 players, and most had to play both offense and defense. Playing against 32 Seahawks, the Knights were exhausted by the end of the fourth quarter. When quarterback Klimas was injured, assistant coach Joe McHugh suited up and went into action. "His wife had told him she'd divorce him if he ever played again," recalled Larry McHugh. "When we stopped on the way home I was the one who called his wife and told her he played. He was in hot water for quite a while."

There was precious little offense in the rain, but there was a lot of defense, as the Knights dropped Portland quarterback Butch Songin repeatedly into the mud. Songin was a big name in the ACFL, having starred in the Canadian League during the 1950s and having started a number of games for the Patriots and Titans of the AFL. But at 38, he was immobile and an easy target for the Ansonia defensive line.

The Seahawks and Black Knights managed only 12 first downs the entire game. Portland's first touchdown came on a 45-yard run with an intercepted Klimas pass, which gave them a 7–0 lead at halftime. The Portland players came out for the second half in fresh, dry jerseys while the 18 Black Knights played in the same soggy outfits for the entire game. The score remained 7–0 until late in the fourth quarter, when Songin completed a long pass for a second touchdown. It was another moral victory but a loss in the record book.

The Black Knights' final record was 4–5–1, not bad for a club making its professional debut, placing them fourth in the six-team league:

Paterson	8–1–0
Providence	8–1–1
Portland	5–5–0

Ansonia	4–5–1
Stamford	2–7–0
Frankfort	1–9–0

DeFelice and Larry McHugh were named to the all-league team and Casey was voted coach of the year. Tavares was third in the league in rushing with 322 yards and had an average of 8.7 yards per carry. He led the ACFL in kickoff return yardage.

The ACFL championship playoff between the Miners and the Steamroller, who tied for first place, was a classic. The game was played indoors at the Atlantic City Convention Hall, and after four quarters the score was tied at 14. The only other time a professional football game had gone into overtime was the epic 1958 NFL championship contest between the Giants and Colts. The Giants and Colts settled the issue relatively early in the first overtime period, but after 15 minutes of additional play, Providence and Paterson remained tied. For a while it appeared the two teams would need a seventh period, but with two minutes left in the sixth, Neal Buckman of Paterson booted a 33-yard field goal to give his club the title.

Despite Berlinger's threats to relocate, the Black Knights returned to Ansonia for the 1963 season. The ACFL, flush from the success of its initial season (for a minor league, survival was considered success), expanded to 12 teams, split into two six team divisions and the schedule was increased from ten to twelve games.

While 1962 had been an artistic success and financial failure for the Knights, 1963 was disappointing in all respects. Coach of the year Casey returned for a second season, as did all-league linemen DeFelice and McHugh. The line was bolstered by the addition of John Skubel, a scrappy, undersized, 205-pound all-ACFL guard who played with Stamford in 1962. Skubel had been teaching in Stamford, but in the summer of 1963, he enrolled in graduate school in Bridgeport. One day in July, Bill Richter spotted him at a Black Knights practice. "What are you doing here?" he asked. "Watching," Skubel replied. "No you're not," Richter said. "You're going to play."

Another talented newcomer was fullback Jim Gabriel, who'd had a trial with the Minnesota Vikings. Gabriel was big, fast, and tough, and Casey put him into the starting lineup immediately. "We expect a lot from Gabriel this season," he said. "He hits hard and keeps digging and comes back with a smile, even after gang-tackled. Jim fits in our style real nice."[14] Gabriel seemed to have the size and potential to play in the NFL, and pro scouts who watched Ansonia games kept an eye on him.

As in 1962, the Black Knights won their opener, defeating the Seahawks 36–19. The win was encouraging, as was the attendance of 5,000, which included the mayors of Derby and Ansonia. The second game of the year was not so encouraging, and commenced a pattern that was to trouble Ansonia all season. They could move the ball, but rarely were they able to get it across the goal line. Providence marched down the field in methodical fashion while the Black Knights were stymied at the Providence 4, 11, and 17. The Steamroller was a good drawing card, bringing 6,000 fans to Nolan Field, but if the home team didn't play better, the fans wouldn't come back.

After three weeks of regular season play, league attendance was encouraging. The Boston Sweepers, a new team that had yet to win a game, had drawn a total of 21,000 for two home dates. Several other clubs averaged between 6,000 and 9,000. Good attendance in August was a positive sign, for the quality of play would improve when NFL and AFL clubs made their final cuts and more talent found its way to the ACFL.

On September 15, the Knights lost to the unbeaten Jersey City Giants at Nolan Field. Again, the home team missed several scoring opportunities, and a key fumble by Gabriel led to one of the Jersey City scores. The announced attendance of 3,500 did not include five police officers and three robbery victims who waited outside the Ansonia dressing room.

On September 4, two of the officers had spotted Gabriel on Dixwell Avenue in Hamden driving a car that matched the description of a vehicle used in two holdups in the New Haven area. Lt. Clarence Drumm of the Hamden Detective Bureau was skeptical, for it made no sense that Gabriel would hold up a gas station. He was a college graduate, an engineer at the Sikorsky plant in Stratford, had no prior criminal record, and was a star player for the Black Knights. But when the lieutenant showed Gabriel's photo to the victims they all said he appeared to be the man.

When Drumm heard that Gabriel might be planning to leave the area for his native California, he decided to act. On game night, the detective and four other officers brought the three victims to Nolan Field and waited outside the Ansonia dressing room. When they saw Gabriel walk past them, all three said he was the man who had robbed them.

Since the officers were in plainclothes, they waited, fearing that if they moved in too quickly the Ansonia players might think they were a gang attacking Gabriel and that a fight might ensue. When Gabriel finally left the locker room with Pudge Henkel, the police took him into custody.

"Jim was a very good football player," Henkel said recently. "I thought he was the best player on the team. He was also articulate and bright and seemed to be a very upbeat person. We were walking out of the field house together and were maybe fifteen paces or so from it when we were surrounded by Connecticut State Police [sic]. That's very disconcerting, especially if you are a third year law student. They arrested him and took him off to jail. I had no idea why they were doing it. I found out the next day when I visited him in jail."

Four days after his arrest, Gabriel pleaded guilty to seven armed robberies of gas stations and liquor stores, and a month later was sentenced to eight to ten years in state prison. His wife, who had flown in from California, sat in the courtroom and wept.

Henkel, with his legal background, tried to help, for he was certain Gabriel was suffering from mental illness. In the few days before the trial, he spent a great deal of time putting together psychiatric evidence he hoped could be used to mitigate Gabriel's sentence, but the judge was not interested.

"I don't want to be a pop psychologist," Henkel said, "but I think holding up filling stations on the Boston Post Road at rush hour leads to the conclusion that he wanted to be caught." Gabriel was a talented artist, and a number of very dark paintings were found in his Bridgeport apartment.

Gabriel was a model prisoner. Henkel, who was practicing law in Cleveland, returned to Connecticut to represent him at his parole hearings. "The warden and I would talk," Henkel said, "and he told me Jim was the very best prisoner he'd ever had in his prison."

Gabriel was active in the Catholic Church, coached the prison athletic teams, taught design drafting to inmates in the evenings, and designed an award winning sports car chassis. "I shuddered a bit," said Henkel, "because I knew that what he needed was psychiatric assistance and he didn't get one minute of it while he was there."

Gabriel's football career was not over. A few years later, Coach Fred Wallner took his Hartford team to scrimmage against a group of prison inmates, whose star player was Jim Gabriel. In 1969, after his release, Gabriel played for the Meriden Falcons and the next year he was a player-coach for the Southington Gems. Then the trail grew cold.

Henkel has made several attempts to find his old friend, but they have been fruitless. Contemporary newspaper accounts said Gabriel was 32 when he played for the Black Knights, which would make him over 80 today were he still alive, and it is quite possible that Henkel is chasing a ghost.

Meanwhile, Gabriel's former Ansonia teammates continued their quest for the ACFL playoffs. Although the Black Knights had played poorly, they were fortunate in that they were in the weak Northern Division. The strength of the league was concentrated in the Southern Division, where three teams were 4–0. In the North, the Springfield Acorns and Mohawk Valley Falcons were tied for first place with 2–2 records. At 1–3, Ansonia was just a game behind.

On September 22, Ansonia upset the previously unbeaten Westchester

Crusaders 35–33. Each team scored five touchdowns, but Bill Brown, the Knights' new kicker, converted all five extra point attempts while his counterpart missed two. It was a stirring victory, with Ansonia overcoming a two touchdown deficit on two different occasions. With the win, the Black Knights remained just a game out of first place.

Northern Division				Southern Division			
Mohawk Valley	3	2	0	Newark	5	0	0
Ansonia	2	3	0	Jersey City	5	0	0
Springfield	2	3	0	Westchester	4	1	0
Portland	2	4	0	Harrisburg	2	2	1
Providence	2	4	0	Pittsburgh	2	3	0
Boston	0	4	1	Baltimore	1	4	0

Providence had gotten off to a rough start, and Boston's appearance at the bottom of the standings was surprising to their fans and a source of bitter frustration to owner Ted Barron. Barron had not expected his team to be winless after five games, and was not happy with Coach Chuck Fuccillo.

Barron was an intense, combative, driven man who began his business career as a junk and scrap collector and eventually made a fortune in waste receptacles and sweeping units. He had attempted to purchase the New York Titans of the American Football League when they filed for bankruptcy following the 1962 season.

In 1962, the Sweepers had been 10–1–1 as an independent team. They'd begun the season as a member of the New England Football Conference, but were expelled after compiling a 7–0 record. In contravention of league rules, Barron had been paying his players. The Sweepers finished the year with five exhibitions against ACFL clubs, winning three and tying one. Now that they were part of the league, they were in the basement.

Some big names appeared on ACFL rosters in 1963. The most famous was Heisman Trophy winner Joe Bellino of Navy. Upon his graduation in 1961, Bellino, like all Academy grads, had to fulfill his service commitment. By 1963, he was stationed at the Newport Naval Base in Rhode Island and was granted permission to play for the Steamroller on weekends. Bellino was a premier gate attraction, but it was not certain how long Providence would have the benefit of his services, for he was scheduled to be transferred shortly to a permanent assignment in Charleston, SC.[15]

A second prominent player was Springfield quarterback Jim Traficant, an all–American from Pittsburgh. Traficant was talented, he was boastful, and he had a tendency to get into trouble. During his senior year at Pitt, he'd gotten into a shouting match with an assistant coach that attracted national attention.

Traficant had been cut by the Oakland Raiders and played a couple of games with Daytona of the Florida State League before joining the Acorns. He did not have a Heisman like Bellino, but he would become much more notorious a few decades later, when he carved out an unenviable reputation as a rogue Congressman.

In 1983, while serving as a sheriff, Traficant was charged with accepting bribes. He beat the rap, was elected to the U.S. House of Representatives, and was re-elected eight times. Traficant's trademarks were a bombastic, aggressive style, an outrageous toupee, and an egregious disregard for the law. In 2002, he was convicted on bribery, racketeering, and tax evasion charges and served seven years in prison.

In Ansonia, Berlinger finally got his own gate attraction, the quarterback he had coveted for a year and a half. At last, Vinnie Drake agreed to return home to play for the Black Knights. Drake could still pass, he could run, and he was an excellent ball handler, due in large part to a pair of enormous hands.

Lime Katzman invariably described Drake as "Ham Hands," using the adjective in virtually every article in which the quarterback's name appeared. "I remember when I first met him and shook his hand," said end Bob Shemeth. "It was about twice the size of mine. He was truly a magician with the football. When he made a fake, you just didn't know who had the ball." "He had huge hands," said Henkel. "He could wrap his whole hand around the football."

Drake's debut was a spectacular success. He watched from the sidelines as Westchester built a 14–0 halftime lead and increased it to 20–7 in the third quarter. Finally, with four minutes left in the third period, Casey sent Drake into action. In the final 19 minutes of the game, he led the Black Knights to 27 points and a 34–20 upset victory. "He didn't drill with us," said John Skubel. "He didn't know the offense. He was just going on talent."

Drake ran for two scores and Chick Henry, Ansonia's leading rusher, scored twice more, forging a win that kept the club within one game of the division lead. Ansonians were thrilled to have the old high school hero back in town, and probably the most excited was his ex-wife, who lived right next to Nolan Field.

Drake hadn't been making his child support payments, but was safe as long as he stayed in Canada. In Ansonia, old "Ham Hands" was subject to the long arm of the law. At halftime, Katzman sidled up to Drake and told him he was going to be arrested after the game. Drake told the reporter he knew but there was nothing he could do about it. Following his terrific second half performance, the Black Knights' new quarterback was served with a warrant, in what was getting to be a depressingly familiar scenario.

Drake lost his touch the following week, as he and Klimas combined for just 4 completions in 25 attempts in a loss to Pittsburgh. A week later, the Black Knights encountered trouble of a different kind. Prior to the game against the Baltimore Broncos, eight Ansonia players, including offensive captain DeFelice and leading rusher Henry, staged a walkout after the release of defensive captain Joe Bucci following an argument with one of the Ansonia directors.

The main reason for the players' dissatisfaction was that they weren't being paid on a regular basis. Bob Shemeth has just one piece of memorabilia from his days in Ansonia, a bounced $25 game check. Bill Richter was owed $65 when the season ended, and is still waiting for it.

A couple of weeks before the strike, Henkel had been recruited to meet with Mainolfi and try to negotiate the payment of past due salaries. "About a third of the way through the season," he recalled, "we had not been paid for the previous game. Because I was going to law school the team thought I should become the spokesperson to negotiate with the owner to make sure we got paid regularly."

Henkel went to Maniolfi's office and talked to him but still the players were not paid. "We went out for warm-ups," Henkel said, "and then went back to that little field house. The team refused to go out and play until the owner agreed to pay us. We finally got a commitment out of him, but I think the game started a little late."

This time the players had taken things a step further and staged an actual walkout. Berlinger said that whoever did not return would be suspended, and insisted the game against the Broncos would go on. He brought back a number of players released earlier in the season to replace the strikers and said Drake would bring a couple of men from Montreal.

"We plan to finish the season in the Atlantic Coast Football League," Berlinger said, "and hope to keep the franchise in Ansonia next year.... There has been only a handful of players who have been causing us trouble and stirring up dissension among other players." He insisted that everyone had been paid up to date.

"They had a couple of guys come in," said Bob Kelso, probably referring to Drake, "and they gave them quite a bit of money. We got ticked off about the inequity of pay because we played just as hard." Unequal pay was even more galling when it wasn't delivered.

DeFelice stated recently that the players merely wanted to scare Berlinger and had no intention of following through on their threat not to play. The brief job action came to an end and the game went off as planned. Even with the returning strikers, the Black Knights were short-handed, with just 28 players making the trip. Some went both ways and others played unfamiliar positions. Fortunately, Baltimore had won only one game all year, and the Knights were able to defeat them 26–19.

Henry, who'd been one of the strikers, put on a terrific performance. He ran for a 71-yard touchdown on the first play from scrimmage and scored the winning touchdown on a one yard run in the fourth quarter, gaining a total of 147 yards on 18 carries.

"Chick was a tough kid," said Kelso. "He had good moves and he was a hard-nosed kid." "I think he could have had a shot at the pros," said Larry McHugh, "but he was married with kids. Back then you had a lot of guys who got married right out of high school."

Ansonia was just a game and a half behind division-leading Providence with two games left as they headed for Hazleton, Pennsylvania for a neutral site rematch with the Broncos. As it had so many times during the 1963 season, disaster befell the Black Knights.

Although it was only the first week in November, there was snow in Hazleton. Drake's original flight from Montreal was cancelled and he ended up stranded in New York. Joe Klimas, expecting that Drake would start, did not make the trip, and the Knights dressed only 23 players. Larry Klimas, who had never played the position before, agreed to take over as the starting quarterback. Joe McHugh was still an assistant coach, but apparently his wife had instilled sufficient fear in him to prevent him from suiting up. Klimas threw five interceptions in the snow and his teammates fumbled four times. It was a sloppy, one-sided 26–0 loss, eliminating the Black Knights from contention.

The final game of the season was at Nolan Field against the Sweepers, who had just one win all season. Owner Barron finally lost his patience with Coach Fuccillo and fired him. For the game against the Black Knights, he decided to coach the team himself, stating that he couldn't do any worse than Fuccillo had done. In fact, he did much better, as the Sweepers beat Ansonia 38–7. Less than 1,000 spectators watched the finale.

The Black Knights finished with a disappointing 4–8 record, good for fourth place in the six-team Northern Division. Four wins, two arrests and a continuing sea of red ink boded poorly for the future of professional football in Ansonia. No Black Knight made the all-star team, although Henry finished third in rushing with 684 yards and a 5.0 average.

Shortly after Newark defeated Springfield 23–6 in the championship game, the ACFL announced it would field 14 teams in 1964. One of the applicants for a new franchise was Hartford. Berlinger indicated he would invoke the rule that gave an existing club veto power over any prospective franchise within 50 miles, but it was an impotent gesture. The Black Knights were the product of Berlinger's energy and enthusiasm and Pat Mainolfi's money. By the end of the 1963 season, Berlinger's enthusiasm was waning and Mainolfi had lost about as much money as he intended to lose.

"After two years," said Katzman, "they got tired of putting in their money and that was it." "I don't think they realized," said Bob Berlinger, "all the stuff they had to go through to get into the league—the coach—the players—how much they were going to pay the players. It was overwhelming. It was fun for a couple of years but I don't think they realized they were getting in over their heads."

Why didn't Ansonia, which was so crazy about its high school team, turn out in greater numbers to watch the Black Knights? "The first games they played," said Rich Marazzi, "they drew well because it was an attraction. But once they began to lose a few games, the year wore on and the nights got cooler, the crowds dwindled." Unfortunately, as the nights got colder, the Knights got colder as well, staggering to the finish line in each of their two seasons.

"For the first two or three games," said Bob Berlinger, "people came to see what was going on, but for some reason, the attendance at each game was less and less. We had the product on the field. I don't know why the people stopped coming. That's the thing that bugs me and that's the thing my dad couldn't understand." "They did their best," said Katzman. "The people just didn't go. I don't know why. They had good players and the other teams had good players."

The fans that did come to the games were enthusiastic, nearly as rabid as those who followed the high school team. Bill Richter's mother-in-law was among the loudest. "She brought this big old cowbell to every game," Richter said, "and if you were sitting below her you got your ears rung off." Perhaps that was why people stopped coming.

People who are fanatic about local sports are often parochial, and while a number of the Black Knights were local products, the majority was not. Gary Van Galder was a big name at Stanford, but who in Ansonia had heard of him? Even Southern Connecticut State, located less than ten miles from Ansonia, was in another football orbit.

Another consideration was the Black Knights' record. The 4–5–1 mark in 1962 was admirable for a first year team playing against established clubs like the Steamroller and Miners, but one of the reasons the high school teams were so popular is that they almost always won. A sub-.500 record was unheard of.

Marazzi had another hypothesis. "I think the lack of offense had something to do with the crowds dwindling," he said. "I remember going to the games and there wasn't much going on offensively." In two years, the Black Knights never had a top quarterback, other than the 19 minutes of excitement provided by Vinnie Drake. The NFL learned in the 1930s that 0–0 ties don't attract big crowds, and changed the rules to encourage passing and scoring.

"They had some of the better local talent," Marazzi said, "and there was good talent on the teams they played against, but to have any kind of a rhythmic offense over a period of time you have to practice a lot. You have to have timing. I think one of the reasons the defense dominated was because the offense didn't have much time to practice. Even when they did practice, twice a week, I'll guarantee there wasn't full attendance because these guys were working."

Henkel and Drake stepped into the quarterback position without a minute of practice time. Planning on the fly, the Black Knights and most other teams were limited to very simple offensive patterns. "We made up plays on the sidelines," said Stamford coach Al Shanen, "because our practice time was so limited. I'd grab the halfback and tell him to run down ten yards and do a square out."

Defense, mostly a function of aggressiveness and pursuit, can be polished much more easily than offense. The Black Knights' shining moment, the 0–0 tie with Providence, was a combination of hard hitting and turnovers.

Yet another factor in Ansonia's difficulties was the specter so greatly feared by minor league baseball—television. NFL games could be viewed from the comfort of one's living room, and while the Black Knights did not play on Sunday afternoons, many fans had their fill of football between the high school games on Saturday afternoon and an NFL contest on Sunday. Saturday night was not the traditional time for football in Ansonia, as evidenced by the fact that Berlinger had to bring in temporary lights.

At an ACFL meeting at the Hotel New Yorker the first weekend of February, league officials decided that if they could have only one team within a 50 mile radius, they would rather it be in Hartford. The Black Knights' franchise was revoked and Hartford was admitted. The financial problems, the spotty attendance, and the chaos of 1963 sealed the fate of professional football in the Naugatuck Valley.

Berlinger said he planned to field a team in the New England League, and perhaps re-enter the ACFL at some future date, but it was just hopeful talk. The league had heard the last of Berlinger, and the two year story of the Ansonia Black Knights came to an inglorious end.

5

The 1962 Stamford Golden Bears

Unlike the Ansonia Black Knights, the Stamford Golden Bears had been in existence for several years before joining the ACFL. Previous incarnations of the team played as early as 1940, and for the six years prior to 1962, the most recent version operated independently or played in loose confederations.

The Golden Bears had been resurrected in the mid–1950s by a Stamford native named Dennis (Whitey) Behunick. After leaving the Marine Corps in 1954, Behunick went down to New Jersey to watch a friend play semi-pro football for the Franklin Miners. He became so enthused that he joined the Miners as their quarterback and played several games before he was injured. In the fall of 1956, Behunick decided that if Franklin could have a team, so could Stamford. He convinced his friend Mike Potenza to join him in forming a new version of the Golden Bears.

Behunick was a friend of New York Giants defensive end Andy Robustelli, and convinced Robustelli to co-sign a note that provided the Golden Bears with the funds to purchase uniforms and cover start up expenses. Robustelli also gave Behunick a Cleveland Browns playbook that became the basis for the Stamford offense.

The Bears quickly became a powerhouse in the New York metropolitan area, playing against the likes of the New Haven Annex Rams, the Astoria Regalmen and the St. Alfonso Boys' Club of Port Chester. In 1958 they won the championship of the loosely organized New York-Connecticut League, finishing the season undefeated and outscoring their opponents 215–23. One of the victories was an upset of the Flushing Vets that snapped a 35-game winning streak. After a couple of seasons, Behunick and Potenza were ready to shut down operations, but coach Al Shanen wanted to continue and took over the management of the club.

While the social structure of the 1950s tended toward rigidity and conformity, minor league football played during that decade followed the permissive, independent and freedom-loving ways of the 1960s. Schedules were developed in a haphazard manner, and if teams were undermanned or depleted by injuries they often cancelled a scheduled game and took the week off to regroup. Players came and went from one team to another with relative freedom, and sometimes groups of players got together and played as informal all star combinations. Crowds were fairly small, with a reported record gathering of 2,500 for a 1958 game between the Golden Bears and the St. Alfonso Boys' Club. Teams survived because the players were paid little, if at all, and travel expenses, with clubs located in close proximity to each other, were minimal.

Two great individual success stories arose from Shanen's Golden Bears. The first involved Allan Webb, an Ansonia native who played at Arnold College with Robustelli. After leaving Arnold, Webb spent two years in the Navy and then played in the Canadian League and with the Golden Bears. Robustelli had gotten him a tryout with the Rams but, despite some impressive performances in the preseason, Webb didn't make the team.

When Robustelli was traded to New York, he got Webb a 1961 audition with the Giants. Webb told the Giants he was 23, seven years younger than his actual age, and nearly nine years after his final college game, made the Giants squad as an offensive back. He was eventually shifted to defense, and remained with the club through the 1965 season, playing in three NFL championship games. Webb later coached in the ACFL, became an NFL assistant coach, and held administrative positions with the Cleveland Browns and San Francisco 49ers before retiring in 1995.

The second Stamford star to get an opportunity in the NFL was Johnny Counts, a fleet University of Illinois dropout who starred as a halfback with the Golden Bears in 1961. In the summer of 1962, as the Golden Bears prepared for their first season in the ACFL, Counts was eighteen miles to the east at the New York Giants camp at Fairfield University. He made the team and spent two years in New York.

When Joe Rosentover formed the ACFL in March 1962, the Golden Bears, having conquered their limited world, decided to join, not fully appreciating how playing in a relatively formal organization would differ from the anarchic manner in which they were accustomed to operating. Shanen said he believed that the Bears had taken "the highest step ever attempted by a southern Connecticut franchise in football," and praised the new league as a bold venture, well beyond the Eastern Professional Football League.

"It was a conference," he said recently, "rather than a helter-skelter program. People wanted to know what kind of team we were. Were we just getting guys out of the bars to play on Friday night? We tried to bring it up to a semi-pro level and make it a filtering process for some kids to get a tryout with the professional teams."

Shanen had recently become head coach at Stamford's newly-opened Rippowam High School and stepped down as coach of the Golden Bears. He would serve the team only as an informal advisor, while the head coaching duties were assumed by Sam Coppola, the Bears' veteran quarterback.

Coppola was a local legend, born and raised in Stamford. He starred in several sports in high school, lettering in baseball, football, basketball, and track, and excelling as an amateur boxer. At 15, he had a tryout at Ebbets Field with the Brooklyn Dodgers and two years later got a look from the Philadelphia Athletics.

Coppola chose to attend Fordham University rather than play professional baseball, but instead of playing quarterback, as he had in high school, Coppola was a halfback. He never asked why. "I couldn't tell coach [Lou] DeFillippo I was a quarterback because it just wasn't the mindset," Coppola said years later. "Today you would transfer if they didn't give you the position. I was the silent quarterback."[1]

After graduation in 1953, Sam joined the Marines, where he played quarterback and suffered a serious knee injury that would plague him for the rest of his career. When he was discharged from the service in 1956, Coppola still had dreams of an NFL career, but there was little interest in someone who was 26, had not played quarterback in college, and had a damaged knee.

With no NFL prospects, Sam returned to Stamford and went to work with his father and brother at Stamford Tile, the business his father founded several years earlier. His cousin, Mike Potenza, convinced him to join the Golden Bears.

For the next few years, Sam Coppola was a very busy man. He played quarterback for the Golden Bears and semi-pro baseball for the Stamford Tilers. In September, when the seasons overlapped, he occasionally played nine innings of baseball with the Tilers in the afternoon and four quarters of football with the Golden Bears in the evening. He became CEO of Stamford Tile after his father's sudden death in 1961. He invested in real estate. He married, divorced and remarried. He had an unsuccessful tryout with the New York Giants in 1958.

"Sam had the athleticism," said Shanen, "the quick release, the stature, the durability, and the strength to make it in the pros, but he just never got the right opportunity." "As long as he was protected," said Stamford fullback Bruno Amato, "Sam Coppola was lethal throwing the football ... if we gave Sam time to throw he'd cut the other teams to ribbons with his passing.... Sam was a great quarterback as long as he had time to throw the ball."[2] By 1962, Coppola had played six years with the Golden Bears and was 32 years old. He planned to be a non-playing coach, with former Canadian Leaguer Red Jackson taking over at quarterback.

Fullback Amato was also a Bear veteran and a local favorite. "They loved Bruno in Stamford," said guard John Skubel. "All the girls loved him. They'd chant Bru-no, Bru-no." Amato had been in camp with the New York Titans in the summer of 1962 but was released without even being allowed to participate in any contact work. With Counts gone, he was the best running back on the Golden Bear roster, and the chief protector of Coppola and his vulnerable knee.

"Bruno was a tough, tough kid from the east side of Stamford," Shanen said. "He only knew one way to run and that was straight ahead, like a bowling ball going down the alley knocking people over. He was tough, tough as nails, a classic pro fullback who could put that block on the end. He never lifted a weight, but he was strong as could be."

Amato had gotten much of his strength working in his family's monument business, lifting heavy stones from the time he was ten years old. After he graduated from high school, teammates Amato, Shanen, and Fred Dugan, an end who later played with the Redskins, earned scholarships to Dayton University. About two weeks into their freshman year, Shanen went to Amato's room to pick him up to go out for pizza and a beer. "We went down looking for Bruno," he recalled, "and the room was empty. He went home. He gave up his scholarship to go back and work in his family's business."

The only 1962 Stamford all-star was Skubel, a recent graduate of Central Connecticut State. Skubel had been a star at Central, but at 205 pounds, he wasn't about to play offensive guard in the NFL or AFL. He did, however, receive an invitation to a Boston Patriot tryout camp and, even though he knew he had little chance of making the team, Skubel was curious to see how he stacked up. He left his Meriden, Connecticut, home one summer evening and headed for Boston in his beat-up old Ford, with a two-by-four propping his seat back upright. He had to stop about every 20 miles and bang the board back into place with a hammer.

Arriving late at night, Skubel slept in his car outside Nickerson Field, where he'd been told the tryout would be held. He woke up to learn that the site had been changed, so he banged his seat into place and caught up. After two days of workouts, Patriots coach Mike Holovak called each man into his office. "You're not big enough," he told Skubel, "you're not fast enough, and you're not strong enough." Skubel took a teaching job in Stamford and joined the Golden Bears.

After one exhibition game, a 12–10 loss to the independent Baltimore Broncos, the Golden Bears prepared for their opening game against the Providence Steamroller at Michael Boyle Stadium in Stamford. There was one minor problem. The game was scheduled for Sunday night, August 26, and as of August

20, the club had not been granted the right to use the field, despite the fact that they had played there in 1961.

The Golden Bears practiced in the parking lot of St. Cecilia's Church, the only available lighted surface in the area, and needed the stadium only on game nights. Boyle Stadium, named after Stamford High School's legendary coach and athletic director, was constructed under the auspices of the Works Progress Administration and opened in 1937. It was the best facility in the city and the Bears joined the ACFL under the assumption they would play there. Some members of the city's education administration, however, thought otherwise. Superintendent of Schools Joseph Franchina delegated the decision to the school board and left for vacation, not to return until after the scheduled game with Providence.

Those who opposed the Golden Bears' use of the facility claimed that, during the prior season, the team had left the field in poor condition, but the real issue was whether the Bears were a profit making entity and, if they were, should they be allowed to use a city-owned facility?

"There were rumors going around," said Shanen, "that everybody was making a lot of money, when actually, *nobody* was making *any* money." Although anyone could have assured the board that no one in their right mind would start a minor league team with the intention of making a profit, the board hired the accounting firm of Price, Waterhouse and Company to make the determination.

The accountants' biggest problem was verifying income and expenses, for documentation was often lacking or vague. The players' traveling expenses were paid in cash, to save the trouble of writing individual checks, and many receipts were missing. The accountants did their best, verified what they could, and were able to conclude, "It's quite obvious from the results to date that it's not making any profit." The board then voted 5–2, with each Democrat in favor and each Republican opposed, to allow the Golden Bears to use Boyle Stadium in 1962.

With only four days to prepare, the first game was a logistical nightmare. Since Boyle did not have permanent lights, temporary lighting had to be brought in and set up. Unfortunately, the generator failed twice during the first quarter, and for interludes of twenty five and thirty five minutes, fans and players waited in darkness until the generators were restarted.

"Everything went black," said Shanen, "and we all rushed over to the generator in the semi trailer truck. The guy we'd rented the lights from was pounding away, doing this and changing that but he couldn't get them going. There was a former football player named Jake DiLeo who had a contracting business. Jake came over and said, 'Let me in there.' He switched a few wires and pounded a few things and he got the lights going."

Perhaps the interruptions bothered the heavily favored Steamroller, for the

Providence club barely defeated the Golden Bears 10–7. Attendance was only 3,500, including 1,200 youngsters who were admitted free.

For their second game, the Golden Bears took to the road and lost 14–0 to the Maine Seahawks in Portland. After watching his team score just seven points in two games, Coach Coppola put himself into the lineup to replace Jackson, who'd arrived with a big reputation but played poorly.

After just two weeks in the ACFL, the Stamford club had reached a critical juncture. They had two losses, poor attendance in their one home game, no offense, and a failed lighting system. Their best runner, Amato, and their best receiver, Bill Meade, were injured and their starting quarterback had been ineffective.

"In the space of eight days," said the *Advocate,* "the success of the Stamford Golden Bears football wise, and at the gate, will be determined in two big home games."[3] In accordance with the order of Commissioner Rostover, a backup generator was obtained to prevent power failures. To boost attendance, the Bears planned a halftime fashion show and announced they would admit women and children free if accompanied by an adult male.

The first of the two games was against Frankfort and the second was against Ansonia. The Bears hoped that the intrastate rivalry would spark fan interest and that Ansonia would bus a number of fans down from the Valley.

The Bears beat Frankfort 14–0, with Coppola at quarterback, and posted an exciting come-from-behind 32–26 win against the Black Knights. Unfortunately, just 2,000 fans watched the Frankfort game and, despite being bolstered by the Ansonia visitors, the crowd for the game with the Black Knights was only 2,300. With the added expense of operating in the ACFL, the Golden Bears wouldn't survive if they couldn't attract more than a couple of thousand per game.

There was football fever in Stamford, but most of it was channeled to the high schools and the New York Giants. Robustelli was a local hero, as were Webb, Counts, and Dugan. Many of the Giants made their off season home in Stamford and were well known to the residents. The Golden Bears had done well as a barnstorming combination, but as a fully salaried professional club operating in a formal league, they faced heavy odds. Ansonia was the type of small town that was often successful in the minor leagues. There were few diversions, and the citizens rallied around their team with the fierce enthusiasm reserved for small town underdogs. There were too many other attractions in Stamford.

One possibility for survival was to play some home games at a neutral site, where the novelty might attract larger crowds. The Golden Bears talked about playing half their 1963 home games in Mount Vernon, New York, and as a test scheduled an exhibition game in that city against the Plainfield (NJ) Giants. The *Advocate* had its doubts, reminding its readers that when Mount Vernon had its own team, they couldn't draw more than a few hundred fans, despite having Johnny Counts in the backfield. Could the Golden Bears do any better? They could not, attracting just 300 to watch an easy Stamford win. Mount Vernon was out.

The following week, the Golden Bears learned the difference between their past existence and life in the ACFL. They were scheduled to play in Providence on Friday, September 28, but Stamford officials tried to get the game shifted to Saturday to accommodate the work schedules of some of their players. Such things were not done in the ACFL. Fortunately, heavy rain and wind caused a natural postponement to Sunday afternoon, delaying the 49–0 thrashing the Bears suffered at the hands of the first place Providence club. The loss to the Steamroller was the start of a five game losing streak that dropped the Golden Bears from a 2–2 mark to a final record of 2–7 and a fifth place finish in the six team circuit.

In mid–October, the *Advocate* reported the club's modest aspirations. "The members of the Stamford Golden Bear football squad, realizing that there has been a drastic financial and playing slump in recent weeks, reiterated their determination to complete the Atlantic Coast Football League season this week."[4]

On the first weekend in November, a scheduled game with the league leading Paterson Miners was postponed due to rain. The Golden Bears wanted to play the makeup game later in the month, but the Miners insisted on playing the following Wednesday night. Paterson won 31–0. Four days later, the Bears lost badly again, 47–6 at Portland.

If Coppola's pass protection appeared to be defective against the Seahawks, there was a legitimate reason, for one of his guards was operating under a severe handicap. League rules required that each team dress at least 22 players for each game or face a fine. The bus to Maine made several stops along the way, and when they stopped for the 22nd player, he wasn't there and no one knew where he was.

Shanen was traveling with the team and slipped on the extra uniform, with the intention of standing on the sideline to fill out the roster and avoid the fine. He had pants, a shirt, shoulder pads, and a helmet, but he didn't have hip pads and he didn't have spikes. Below his trousers he wore black socks and black patent leather shoes. At least he would be comfortable on the sideline.

Unfortunately, Shanen wasn't on the sideline for long. One of the Golden Bears' guards was injured and Shanen had to take his place. "I got the crap beat out of me," he said. "It was a slippery field and I was wearing patent leather shoes. Every time Sam dropped back to pass, they pushed me back toward him like I was on roller skates. Sam was getting pissed off at me, and I said, 'Sam, do a rollout so maybe I can get a body block on the guy.' Then I got a cracked rib and played the rest of the game with that. I could not walk for a week."

With the team in disarray, and no money left in the till, the Bears cancelled the final game of the season, as the *Advocate* said, "calling it an end to a dismal season artistically and financially."[5] "The insurance costs," said Shanen, "were getting to be astronomical, and things were just disintegrating financially. When you talk about going to Baltimore and Portland, those are big trips. You might have to go the day before and stay overnight. The expenses were killing us. I figured that was it and that we ought to pack up the store and call it a day."

By failing to complete their schedule, the Golden Bears virtually assured their expulsion from the ACFL and forfeiture of the surety bond they posted prior to the season. When the league held a meeting in early December, the club was formally dropped, to be replaced in 1963 by the Boston Sweepers. There would be no Golden Bears in 1963, even on an independent basis. It was an ignominious end for a team that had so many fine seasons and produced Allan Webb and Johnny Counts. The Atlantic Coast League was a bit too fast for an organization that operated by the seat of its collective pants and on a financial shoestring. After just a single season of organized football, the career of the Stamford Golden Bears was over.

6

A Hopeful Beginning and a Rude Awakening: The 1964–65 Hartford Charter Oaks

When the Ansonia Black Knights ran out of gas at the end of the 1963 season, the ACFL was eager to replace them with a Hartford franchise that had fresh capital and access to a larger population base. The capital was supplied by Don and Ned Brewer, owners of the Brewer Machine Company and former players with the semipro West Hartford Spartans. The Brewers thought the atmosphere in Hartford was ripe for a new team. "We've had nothing around here for 15 years," Don said, "and we feel people are ready to support a pro football club."[1] He and Ned possessed the two attributes required for minor league ownership, naïve enthusiasm and a little cash. Most minor league operators had a greater supply of the former than the latter, but the Brewers said they were willing to invest $100,000.

Don Brewer was more active than Ned in the operation of the team, but very few of the old Charter Oaks have vivid recollections of him. "Unlike Pete Savin," said Bob Stohrer, "he wasn't the type of guy that got close to you. He was around the practices but I never really got to know him." Center John Willard remembered Brewer's father as being a fine gentleman who was very knowledgeable about football, but he didn't have many memories of Don or Ned.

The key to a successful Hartford franchise was obtaining the use of Dillon Stadium, located in the southeast section of the city and used primarily for high school games. Dillon was the best facility in the area but, like Nolan Field and Boyle Stadium, had no permanent lights. Ansonia and Stamford brought in temporary lighting, which was inferior and, in the case of Stamford, unreliable. The Brewers wanted a better solution, and had the support of Thomas Corrigan, a young attorney and chairman of Hartford's recreation committee. Corrigan recommended a $100,000 bond issue to put lights in Dillon Stadium.

The cost of the project was critical, for any bond of more than $100,000

6. A Hopeful Beginning and a Rude Awakening 71

Bill Brewer (center) with sons Ned (left) and Don (photograph from Hartford Charter Oaks program).

required a referendum. Nearly all Hartford voters were taxpayers but not all were football fans. Further, a referendum would take time, and only days remained until February 1, the date the Brewers planned to apply for membership in the ACFL.

Without a guaranteed place to play, and without lights in the place he wanted to play, Brewer went to the league meeting in New York and filed his application. The ACFL quickly and unanimously agreed to grant Hartford a franchise, subject to signing a lease for the use of Dillon Stadium and putting up permanent lighting.

Confident that the city would acquiesce, a committee, formed by the Brewers and chaired by Mayor William Glynn, decreed that the name of the new club would be the Charter Oaks. "The name Charter Oaks has a connotation of strength, sturdiness, and an ability to bend with the wind," said Glynn.[2] Deciduous oaks did not require artificial light to survive, of course, something Brewer's football-playing Charter Oaks needed desperately.

One of the members of the naming committee was Bill Lee, longtime sports editor of the *Hartford Courant*. Lee was a big booster of Hartford sports, and had grandiose notions as to the city's potential, notions he felt were neither appreciated nor shared by local politicians. With the impending probability of professional football in Dillon Stadium, he wrote, "The City of Hartford, snoozing these many years where sports are concerned, is stirring."[3]

It did not stir quickly enough for Lee, however, and he would become a painful thorn in Don Brewer's side during the next four years. While he deemed the Charter Oaks a welcome addition to the sports scene, Lee couldn't foresee anything very exciting happening in Dillon Stadium. "Dillon Stadium isn't much," he wrote. "It is, in fact, not a stadium at all but just a playing field with bleachers and an entirely inadequate press box. Still, the present Dillon Stadium is better than nothing. It is a small beginning. In a city with the meager history of Hartford in such matters, I suppose even a small beginning should be gratefully accepted."[4]

The Brewers had a franchise, a name, and probably a stadium with lights. All they needed was a coach, 36 players, and fans. The first need was the easiest to fill, for there was always an abundance of qualified men seeking to coach a professional football team. The Brewers found a good one in Fred Wallner, an intense, chain-smoking former Notre Dame and NFL lineman.

Wallner was a native of Greenfield, Massachusetts, who had been one of the best high school fullbacks in the state in the 1940s. At nearly 200 pounds, he was bigger than most linemen, and was a terror running out of the backfield. In 1945, his junior year, the *Fitchburg Sentinel* described him as "a lightning, lethal, lumbering hulk of gridiron greatness" and compared him to Bronco Nagurski.[5]

After a stellar career at Notre Dame, Wallner played four years for the Chicago Cardinals, earning a Pro Bowl berth in 1955. In 1960, he came out of retirement at the age of 32 to serve as player-coach for the Houston Oilers. By 1963, he was an assistant coach at Tulane University.

Wallner still had relatives in the northeast, including his brother Carl, who told Fred about the Charter Oaks. Fred, who wanted to return home, settle down and raise his young family, contacted the Brewers, and on February 19 he was introduced as the first coach of the Hartford Charter Oaks.

Fred Wallner (photograph from Hartford Knights program).

6. A Hopeful Beginning and a Rude Awakening

Just a few days later, the City Council approved the bond issue and the Brewers had a lighted place to play. The only remaining task was to find 36 players capable of competing in the Atlantic Coast League. Other than Richmond and Atlanta, which were admitted to the league along with Hartford, all of the other teams were holdovers from 1963. The Charter Oaks were given the rights to all players of the defunct Ansonia franchise, but otherwise had to start from scratch. "We're two years behind," Wallner said.[6]

Several of the old Black Knights signed with Hartford, including tackle Nick DeFelice, running back Chick Henry, defensive end Bob Shemeth, defensive back Joe Bucci, and veteran end and punter Bill Boehle. To fill out the remaining roster spots Don Brewer, who acted as general manager, began contacting professional teams in the United States and Canada looking to establish relationships for leads and referrals. The Portland Seahawks, who had an arrangement with the Montreal Alouettes of the Canadian League, were the only ACFL franchise in the league to have a formal affiliation with a club at a higher level. The Steelers sent some players to the Pittsburgh Valley Ironmen and the Bears sent some to Springfield, while the rest recruited on an *ad hoc* basis.

The Oaks held an open tryout July 5, and began signing players. One of the stumbling blocks for the Brewers was their difficulty in finding full time employment for the players. Most locals already had jobs, but it was hard to recruit a player from beyond the Hartford area unless the club could help him find a full time job. Later, when Pete Savin operated the Hartford Knights, he employed many players in his numerous business enterprises, but apparently the Brewer Machine Company had no room on its payroll for football players.

The first time the Oaks took the field was on August 8 for an exhibition against the Springfield Acorns. They did so without their new lighting system. Two days before the game, no one was sure where the lights were. The only thing the manufacturer could tell the Brewers was that they were somewhere between Red Wing, Minnesota and Hartford. The order had been preempted and delayed by a priority order for the Cape Kennedy space center, and then the company lost track of the shipment after it left the factory. They put a tracer on the poles and the Brewers put in an order to New Jersey for temporary lights. For the opener, Dillon Stadium would look a lot like Nolan Field in Ansonia.

Bill Lee was disgusted. "It has been a public disgrace these many years," he wrote, "that the proud city of Hartford should be years behind other cities in the matter of facilities for spectator sports both indoors and out."[7]

The new Charter Oaks shone brightly under the temporary fixtures, although they lost 14–11. The Oaks played a competitive, exciting game, dominating play during the second half. The best news of all was that the stands were crammed with 7,622 people, and more had to be turned away because there was no room. The New York Giant-Minnesota Viking exhibition game was on television that evening, and the fact that the Oaks drew so well was a good portent for the fall, when they would have Saturday evenings to themselves.

Many of the fans who were unable to get in parked on the nearby highway in order to watch for free, and had to be chased away by the police. To add to the confusion, there was a false alarm in the vicinity of the stadium that brought fire engines roaring into the densely packed neighborhood.

The crowd was not only large; it was vocal and enthusiastic. "When I played with Houston in the American League," Wallner said afterward, "we never had a crowd on hand that responded with the enthusiasm that this one did."[8] Even Lee was impressed. "If you weren't there," he wrote the following Monday, "you missed something. If you did not see the Charter Oak football team's opener at Dillon Stadium Saturday night, give yourself a good swift kick and make up your mind not to stay away from the next one."[9]

Many people apparently heeded Lee's advice, for the phones lit up at the Oaks' Pearl Street office from the time it opened on Monday. On Thursday, the city council voted to add seating that would increase capacity to 9,000 and commissioned an investigation of area traffic patterns to alleviate some of the tie-ups that occurred the previous Saturday. The next day, radio station WPOP announced that it would broadcast every regular season game. All in all, it was a good first week.

While off the field good news continued unabated, Wallner was concerned with what might occur on the field the following weekend in Portland, Maine when the Oaks opened the regular season. The Hartford defense had played better than Wallner expected against Springfield, and the running game, with former Black Knights Chick Henry and Maurice Sykes, had controlled the action in the second half.

On the negative side of the ledger, quarterback was a problem. Starter Bob Barrows separated a shoulder against Springfield and was lost for at least a month, and backup Jerry Johnson, a halfback at Montana State, had played the last three quarters. Johnson could run, but was not much of a passer.

As expected, the opening game was a battle between the running game of the Oaks and the passing attack of the Seahawks, fueled by quarterback Manchester (Manch) Wheeler, a former Maine star cut loose by the Boston Patriots the previous week. Wheeler liked to put the ball in the air, and would set records with 33 completions in 73 attempts during a Seahawk game later in the season.

Wheeler threw a mere 46 passes against the Charter Oaks, completing 22 for 233 yards. Six foot five inch end Hugh Rohrschneider caught 11 of them. The previous year, Rohrschneider had been the favorite receiver of record setting quarterback George Bork on the Northern Illinois University undefeated national small college champions.

Bork was the first collegian to throw for more than 3,000 yards in a season, and Rohrschneider established a college division single season record with 76 receptions his junior year and caught 75 more his senior season. In 1964, his first professional season, Rohrschneider caught an astounding 106 passes for the Seahawks.

The Knights completed just four passes for 37 yards, but rushed for 357 yards and won the game 27–21. Sykes gained 133 yards, Henry 99, and quarterback Johnson 83 on just five carries. Henry scored the winning touchdown on a 58-yard run.

The home opener the following week was a smashing success, despite a cold and rainy night. The lights had finally arrived and the crowd of 8,200 surpassed the sellout gathering of two weeks earlier, thanks to the additional seating. "Man and boy," Lee gushed afterward, "I've worked in this town longer than I will admit except under oath, but I cannot remember a more excited or better-pleased crowd of spectators leaving a Hartford game of any kind."[10]

The Oaks gave the fans a good show. The highlight of the Ansonia Black Knights' 1962 season had been a 0–0 tie against the heavily-favored Providence Steamroller, and perhaps the finest hour of the 1964 Charter Oaks was their decisive 38–21 victory over the Steamroller on opening night. Sykes ran for four touchdowns and Henry for two more, as the Oaks shredded the veteran Providence defense for 248 rushing yards. Johnson didn't do much passing, but it didn't matter, nor did the fact that Hartford managed to convert just two of six extra point attempts.

After two weeks, the Oaks were undefeated and even the skeptical Lee was ready to dream. "The Oaks haven't won the ACFL title," he said in the afterglow of the Providence win, "but may be on their way, at that, incredible as this seems."[11]

It seemed a little less incredible a week later after Hartford upset the undefeated Boston Sweepers on the latter's home grounds. The Sweepers featured players like quarterback Don Allard, a former Canadian League star who played briefly with the Titans and Patriots, kicker Booth Lusteg, who would later kick in the AFL and NFL, and former Titan halfback Rick Sapienza.

Sapienza played just two games with the Titans and had been a minor leaguer since 1960. In his final AFL appearance, Sapienza was sent in to punt with seven seconds left in the game and the Titans leading the Patriots 24–21. He fumbled the snap and the Patriots recovered and scored the winning touchdown as time expired. Sapienza was cut the following week and never played another game of major league football.

In the second quarter of the game against Hartford, with the score tied 7–7, Sapienza, punting from deep in his own territory, bobbled the pass from center and was tackled in his own end zone for a safety. The Sweepers regained the lead with a touchdown in the third quarter, but Johnson led the Oaks on a game winning drive that culminated with an 11-yard pass to Sonny Dennis, Hartford's first passing touchdown of the season.

Johnson was in the game to direct the final drive because Jim Parker, who had been signed after Barrow's injury and was the Oaks' best passer, dislocated his shoulder during the third period. With Barrow and Parker both out, the Oaks were in desperate need of a quarterback who could throw the ball. The formidable running game wouldn't be very effective once opponents realized they could ignore the threat of a pass.

Before the following week's game, the Oaks signed Mike Mosolf, a graduate of the University of Idaho who'd had a tryout with the Dallas Cowboys in 1962 and later played with the Indianapolis Warriors of the United League and the Saskatchewan Rough Riders of the Canadian League.

Mosolf had been around a bit. He'd been in the service for two years, then went to junior college and finally to Idaho. He played a number of positions in college, and went to the Dallas camp as a defensive back. "They put the stopwatch on me," he recalled, "and said, 'that's it.' Tom Landry called me into his office and said, 'son, you like to hit 'em but you can't catch 'em.'" Mosolf could pass better than Johnson could, but he was, like Johnson, primarily a running quarterback.

The Oaks' unblemished record was blemished badly on September 5 by the Newark Bears, winners of the 1963 ACFL championship. Against the Bears, the Oaks could neither run nor pass, and suffered an inglorious 37–10 defeat. The home club's best offensive weapon was the safety; they had two of them.

Quarterback continued to be a problem, as Johnson was flattened on the third play of the game and lay prone on the field for a long time. The newly-arrived Mosolf sat on the Hartford bench holding a towel to his face, for just before the clubs took the field, he suffered a nosebleed. "I didn't know what the heck was wrong with me," he said recently. "I'd just gotten off a plane and I thought maybe it was from that." With Mosolf *hors de combat*, Johnson was revived by the trainer, helped to his feet, and ordered not to run with the ball.

Despite their quarterback troubles, following a 16–6 win over Springfield on September 12, the Oaks held sole possession of first place.

Northern Division			Southern Division		
Hartford	4	1	Newark	4	0
Boston	3	1	Pittsburgh	4	1

6. A Hopeful Beginning and a Rude Awakening

Springfield	2	2		Jersey City	3	1
Mohawk Valley	1	3		Harrisburg	2	3
Portland	1	3		Richmond	2	3
Westchester	1	4		Hazleton	1	4
				Atlanta	0	4

The Hartford offense wasn't overwhelming against Springfield, but the Oaks managed yet another safety, their fifth of the young season, a remarkable total for an entire year, let alone just five games. A ferocious pass rush and tight secondary defense held Springfield to minus ten yards passing. The Acorns' Mel Meeks, probably the best runner in the ACFL, was able to gain just 24 yards.

The win over the Acorns was the high water mark of the Hartford season. The following week, they played poorly and had to mount a last minute comeback to tie the lowly Westchester Crusaders 28–28. The Oaks fumbled nine times, and both teams complained about the poor condition of Dillon Stadium. The new lights had made the field quite popular for high school football and soccer games and the heavy usage had taken a toll on the turf. The grass was worn thin and every play generated a major dust storm, nearly obscuring the players from view.

Tying the game was an adventure. Al Freiheit kicked the first point after touchdown before breaking his ankle, an injury that would sideline him for the season. End Frank Beck kicked the conversion after the second score and Bill Boehle kicked the third. After the Oaks closed to 28–27 on a pass from Johnson to Boehle with 25 seconds remaining in the game, Wallner had to decide who would attempt to tie the game. He chose Boehle, whose first try had been shaky. "Again," wrote Jerry Trecker, "the ball climbed slowly toward the crossbar. Again it barely cleared the height."[12]

The following week, Hartford traveled to Providence for a rematch with the Steamroller. Like all minor league teams, the Oaks and the Steamroller had drastically overhauled their rosters since the first game between them in late August. The most important addition to the Steamroller was talented quarterback Tom Kennedy, a Los Angeles State grad who'd played for the Wheeling Ironmen of the United League the previous two seasons. Kennedy and Jerry Morgan split the quarterbacking chores for Providence and combined for more than 200 yards passing in a 28–24 Steamroller win.

The Steamroller had always drawn well and anticipated a crowd of about 10,000. Unfortunately, the turnout was only about half that, a disappointing occurrence that had become painfully familiar in the ACFL. Tom Granatelli, owner of the champion Newark Bears, said he might have to relocate if his team didn't get better support. The Westchester Crusaders played in a stadium that held just 5,500, and it was nearly impossible for them to cover expenses even if they sold out every game. It was absolutely impossible when they drew 2,000, as they did when they entertained the Oaks.

The poor attendance led to a predictable result. During the first week of November, Commissioner Rosentover revoked the franchise of the Atlanta Spartans for failure to meet their financial obligations. In addition to the usual difficulties attendant to minor league football, Atlanta, as the outlying franchise, incurred crippling travel expenses.

The Spartans had missed their last payroll and the players had been paid by the league. Two days after the commissioner pulled their franchise, the Spartans raised enough money to satisfy the arrearages and were readmitted. The action came too late, however, to prevent cancellation of the game against the Pittsburgh Valley Ironmen. The Spartans were replaced on the Ironmen's schedule by the independent Washington Sharks, a game that would count on Pittsburgh Valley's ACFL record.

But Hartford was winning, and the fans were coming. The Brewers didn't always release official attendance figures, but it appeared that more fans were flocking to Dillon Stadium than were attending games in other ACFL cities. A crowd of 9,143 had watched the loss to Newark, giving the Oaks an average of about 8,700 for two games, while road games at Portland, Boston (the Sweepers actually played in Everett, Massachusetts, about four miles north of Boston) and Springfield drew an average of about 6,200. The Brewers had to make their money at the gate for, unlike most ACFL owners, they did not share in concession income.

Following the Providence game, the Oaks were in third place behind the Sweepers and Steamroller, and their shortcomings had become obvious. They'd gained 1451 of their 1925 yards of offense via the ground route, and while the defensive line was formidable, the secondary came up short, literally. Cornerbacks Tom Calabrese and Ken Luciani were just 5'8" and 5'9" respectively, and it was difficult for them to cover receivers like 6'7" Curt Lucas of Providence and 6'5" Hugh Rohrschneider of Portland.

Injuries had also begun to take their toll on the thin Hartford roster. Henry was out with a rib injury, leaving Sykes to bear the brunt of the rushing burden. Johnson suffered a concussion in the Providence game, and followed Barrows and Parker to the sidelines. Starting guard Ernie Colquette suffered an ankle injury and defensive back Joe Bucci hurt his shoulder.

The depleted offense was helpless against Westchester, which defeated the Oaks 19–2, the only Hartford points coming on their favorite scoring weapon, the sixth safety of the season. Two weeks later, the Oaks virtually eliminated themselves from championship contention by losing to Springfield. With a 5–4–1 record, Hartford was in fourth place, well in arrears of the Sweepers, who were 8–1.

6. A Hopeful Beginning and a Rude Awakening

Although they had virtually no chance for postseason play, the Oaks finished their first season in impressive fashion, winning three of their last four games, despite a continuing wave of injuries. The club was especially thin at quarterback, where they had only Mosolf. Johnson had been moved to safety to plug up the holes in the secondary created when Calabrese suffered a season-ending neck injury and Luciani hurt his knee. Linebacker John Geraghty shifted to cornerback. "We put a linebacker and a flanker back in the secondary against Atlanta," said Wallner, "and held our breaths."[13]

On October 31, the Oaks defeated the first place Sweepers for the second time, snapping a seven game Boston winning streak. The one-sided 28–10 score was even more shocking considering that Sykes, the Oaks' biggest offensive threat, suffered broken ribs on the second half kickoff and missed the rest of the game. Mario Mendez, a running back who'd played one game earlier in the season for the San Diego Chargers, scored twice and Mosolf threw two touchdown passes.

Hartford finished their first ACFL season with an 8–5–1 mark, tied for third place in the Northern Division with the veteran Providence eleven. It was an excellent professional debut and much better than anyone had expected. Operating in a small stadium, the club had drawn well, better than the champion Sweepers. The Brewers were happy, Wallner was happy, and even Bill Lee was happy. They all looked forward to challenging for the championship in 1965.

Wallner led his team to a league championship in 1965, but that team was not the Hartford Charter Oaks and the league was not the ACFL. For the Oaks, who started the season with high hopes, 1965 was a miserable year, ending with a battered, demoralized last place team that played under three different head coaches.

In early January 1965, there were rumors of a possible merger between the ACFL and the United Football League, which had been in existence since 1961. Mike Valan, president of the UFL Wheeling Ironmen, told the *Wheeling Intelligencer* that the two leagues had been holding weekly meetings since mid-November with the intention of combining the financially strapped organizations. All eight UFL clubs lost money in 1964, as had most ACFL teams. Valan said the Ironmen, probably the most "profitable" UFL franchise, lost a total of $35,000 over the previous three years.

At first blush, combining two floundering leagues and increasing travel costs by spreading the clubs halfway across the country did not seem to be a formula for success. The magnates, however, had a grand vision. In early February, they announced the formation of the Continental Football League, which was not to be a minor league, but a third major league that would compete with the National and American Leagues for players, fans, and television contracts.

The CFL believed that a television contract was the solution to the financial riddle of minor league football. The Oaks had filled or nearly filled Dillon Stadium on several occasions in 1964, but even a packed house didn't guaranty profitability. Television fueled the professional football boom of the early 1960s and if the CFL could supplement gate revenue with broadcast income perhaps it too could achieve the level of profit being made by the NFL and beginning to be realized by the five-year-old AFL.

In early March, the CFL owners hired 66-year-old Kentucky politician and former major league baseball commissioner Albert B. ("Happy") Chandler as commissioner under a three year contract that was variously reported as paying him thirty, forty or fifty thousand per year. Chandler had a somewhat stormy reign as baseball commissioner. He was in office when Jackie Robinson broke baseball's unwritten color line, and his support of Robinson was the high point of his baseball career, an admirable accomplishment for a man who lived his entire life in the South.[14] Chandler's tenure in office, however, was not a pleasant one. He was an egotistical, extroverted, strong-willed, independent man who quickly learned that baseball owners did not want a strong leader looking out for the interests of baseball as much as they desired a compliant figurehead who would not interfere with their self-interested course. In 1951, the owners found such a man in Ford Frick and declined to renew Chandler's contract.

Chandler knew football. He'd been a quarterback at Transylvania College and had coached at Centre College. When Chandler was baseball commissioner he was fond of drawling, "Ah loves baseball." The transition to "Ah loves football" was an easy and natural one, and Chandler quickly took to the stump on behalf of the Continental League. "We won't become feeders or farm clubs," he said. "That's what destroyed minor league baseball."[15] Continental League contracts contained a reserve clause, binding players not only for that season, but effectively controlling them until they played out their option.

The new league had ten franchises for its first season, split into two divisions:

Eastern Division	Western Division
Newark	Charleston
Norfolk	Fort Wayne
Philadelphia	Hartford
Toronto	Rhode Island
Wheeling	Richmond

Why were Hartford and Rhode Island, much farther east than Toronto and Wheeling, in the Western Division? A more important question was whether the teams would be able to absorb the increased travel costs inherent

6. A Hopeful Beginning and a Rude Awakening

in the geographically dispersed league. Virtually all of the Atlantic Coast League cities could be reached from Hartford by bus, while CFL trips were almost always by air. Baseball had had minor leagues since the nineteenth century, and one of the keys to their survival was a geographically compact circuit. There was nothing compact about the new Continental League.

Increased travel costs would not be a problem if the CFL was truly a major league. NFL teams traveled from coast to coast and made money. But as was pointed out by many cynics, it took more than Chandler's bombastic pronouncements to make a major league. "Talk, television and Happy Chandler won't amount to Beans," Bill Lee pointed out, "if Brewer cannot sign up top flight operatives."[16] Regarding the CFL's claim to be a major league, Lee said, "It seemed like bloated overreaching."[17]

There were others who doubted the ability of the Continental League to be a "major" league. Dick Beddoes of the *Toronto Globe and Mail* wrote, "The [Toronto] Rifles play in something called the Continental Professional Football League, a ten-team alliance containing such two-bit towns as Wheeling, Fort Wayne and Hartford."[18]

During the spring, Don Brewer made a great effort to re-sign the players that had taken his club to a third place finish in its initial season. "It just sort of came together in 1964," said Mosolf, "and most of those guys were coming back. So they were optimistic about the next season."

Lee asked the obvious question. If, as Brewer claimed, the Continental League was "the strongest minor league in the United States (apparently he had not heard Chandler's statement that the CFL was not a minor league)," how did he expect to win a championship with the same players who'd finished third in a much inferior league? Shouldn't he be signing better players?

Chandler's league might not be a farm system, but until they signed a major television pact they did not have the money to sign top flight players, and the notion that anyone capable of playing in the NFL or AFL would sign with a CFL team was a long stretch.

There would be no television contract in 1965, although there was a possibility that some teams might have a few of their games telecast to a local audience. The best the Charter Oaks could do was to have some games shown on subscription channel 18 in Hartford. Brewer had ACFL players, minimal broadcast revenue, a high school stadium, increased travel costs, tougher competition, and heightened expectations. It was a problematic combination.

The Oaks began the 1965 season the same way they ended the previous one—with a quarterback problem. In January, Mosolf signed an ACFL Charter Oak contract, which became null and void when Hartford joined the Continental League. Therefore he signed a Hartford CFL contract. In late April,

Mosolf signed a third contract, this one with the Holyoke Bombers of the Atlantic Coast League, a team owned by Springfield contractors Socrates Babacas and John Gentile. The offer included the promise of a job as an oiler on one of Babacas' construction crews, a step up from Mosolf's Hartford job driving a beer truck.

Babacas was a unique character who appeared to have quite a bit of money and clearly had a lot of moxie. "Babacas was a Greek guy," said Dick Bowman, "and you've never seen anything like this guy's operation. He would recruit people by bringing them up and partying. It was unbelievable. They tried to put this team together with somewhat questionable business ethics."

"I didn't know if the [Hartford] contracts were binding," said Mosolf. "I was a guy from rural Idaho and east coast culture was a real eye-opener for me. I wasn't too bright at the time and [Babacas] signed me even though I already had a contract."

Hartford went to court to enforce their contract. The Charter Oak pact had been signed first, and the judge ruled that Mosolf would play with Hartford or not at all. A few days after practice began, he reported to the Charter Oaks. "I didn't have a lawyer," he said. "I didn't go to court. I just went along with whatever the Brewers wanted. I went back to the Charter Oaks and everything settled down pretty fast."

Other Continental League teams boasted talented quarterbacks like Bob Brodhead of Philadelphia, Dan Jonas of Newark, Tom Kennedy of Rhode Island, and Dan Henning of Norfolk. Brodhead played briefly with the Buffalo Bills and had thrown a total of 75 TD passes during three years in the UFL. Kennedy would be starting for the New York Giants within a year. Jonas would set many CFL records before becoming a star in Canada and Henning, a future NFL head coach with the Falcons and Chargers, had spent time as a backup with the Chargers.

The Oaks had Mosolf and they clung to him, even though he didn't really want to be there, because he was the best quarterback they had. Jerry Johnson had been switched to defensive back and then released in training camp. Another quarterback candidate was Rich King, a two-way performer from Syracuse. King was a better defender than quarterback (although Don Brewer would later take issue with his defensive skills), and since the Syracuse attack relied upon the running of Floyd Little, King didn't get to do much passing.

Just before the start of camp, the Oaks signed Ron Fletcher, a pint-sized 5'7", 142-pound signal caller from Oklahoma who'd thrown a 55-yard touchdown pass in the 1963 Orange Bowl and a record 95-yarder in the following year's Gator Bowl. With such impressive accomplishments, Fletcher's signing was greeted with great fanfare.

Unfortunately, the two touchdown passes were the entirety of Fletcher's college career. He was a classic overachiever who walked on as a sophomore after selling hot dogs at the concession stand as a freshman.[19] Fletcher made the team as the fifth string quarterback and had been inserted into the Orange Bowl for just the one play. Since the Sooners almost never passed, Fletcher took the Alabama team completely by surprise. Prior to his Gator Bowl heroics the following season, he had thrown exactly two passes all year. One was incomplete and the other was intercepted.

Like so many small men attempting to make good in a big man's game, Fletcher compensated for his lack of size with hustle and noise. *Courant* reporter Frank Keyes described him as "the tiniest tot in the play-for-pay ranks, and also the most talkative."[20] Once, after completing a pass during a scrimmage, he let out a bloodcurdling Rebel yell that reverberated throughout Colt Park.

Whenever an unlikely looking athlete appears on the scene, he is invariably compared to others with similar shortcomings that have been successful. Thus, Fletcher was compared to Eddie LeBaron, a 5'7" quarterback who had eleven good years in the NFL. As it turned out, the main similarity between Fletcher and LeBaron was that both were 5'7". Fletcher had much more in common with the overwhelming majority of short men who spend Sunday afternoons in front of their televisions watching strapping 6'3" athletes play quarterback. After some unimpressive work in exhibitions, Fletcher went back to Georgia to begin a coaching career.

King injured his shoulder and the Oaks were once again left with only Mosolf, who was not a prototype pocket passer. "[Coach] Lowell Lander told me I had the worst footwork he'd ever seen in a quarterback," Mosolf recalled. "He was talking about a dropback quarterback, and being an option guy, it was probably true."

Following a 10–3 loss to Newark in the final exhibition game, Keyes wrote, "[T]here are jobs open at the 64 Pearl Street office for two experienced quarterbacks able to do two things—throw the ball accurately from the pocket on drop back plays, and handle the ball efficiently."[21]

During the next three weeks, the Oaks found their two quarterbacks. On August 11, they obtained Manch Wheeler in a trade with the Norfolk Neptunes. A 1962 graduate of the University of Maine, Wheeler led the Black Bears to an undefeated season his senior year, and was signed as a free agent by the Buffalo Bills.

Typical of the haphazard scouting methods of the era, Buffalo came upon Wheeler by accident. The Bills had been scouting Maine end Dave Cloutier, and while looking at films, Buffalo coach Lou Saban saw Wheeler throw a 75-yard touchdown pass and decided to sign him as well.

There were seven quarterbacks in the Bills camp, but while there was quantity, there was little quality. From their inception in 1960, Buffalo had a hole at the quarterback position that would not be filled until Jack Kemp arrived late in the 1962 season. "When I got to camp," said Wheeler, "I realized that none of them could throw. They didn't have professional football arms. Fortunately I did, so right away I showed off my arm and within a week we were down to three quarterbacks." Wheeler was one of them and began the season on the taxi squad.

Wheeler was activated late in the season and played in four games. When the Bills acquired Kemp on waivers, however, Wheeler went back to the cab squad. In 1963, Buffalo drafted Daryle Lamonica of Notre Dame and, with two Pro Bowl quarterbacks ahead of him, Wheeler was relegated to the taxi squad for another year. The following season, he had a tryout with the Patriots, but had little chance to make an impression, for he spent most training camp sessions quarterbacking the second team offense against the first string defense.

"I was the quarterback for the rookies," he said, "and I was playing against Houston Antwine, Larry Eisenhauer, Bob Dee, and Jim Hunt. I was on my back most of the time in every scrimmage, so you really couldn't show anything." Wheeler was cut and played with the Portland Sea Dogs of the ACFL, where he threw for 18 touchdowns and more than 3,000 yards.

Two weeks after signing Wheeler, the Brewers announced that Lee Grosscup would join the Charter Oaks. Grosscup was a big name. He had been an all-American quarterback at the University of Utah and the 1959 number one draft choice of the New York Giants.

While at Utah, Grosscup often used the "shovel pass" and several decades later on *Monday Night Football* was credited with inventing the maneuver. "I did not invent it," Grosscup said recently, "contrary to what Al Michaels may have said. I get way too much credit for it. It became famous because we used it three times against Army and set up three touchdowns. The following week Navy stole the play and used it against Army and the announcers referred to it as the 'Utah pass.'"

In New York, two obstacles blocked Grosscup's anticipated rise to stardom. One was the presence of star quarterbacks Charley Conerly and Y.A. Tittle. The second was Grosscup's non-conformist nature. "I think I was the only English major in the NFL when I came up," he said. "I was an English major and I was—and still am—passionate about classical music, so I think they automatically figured I was a flake, a beatnik."

When Grosscup was in college, he teamed with writer Murray Olderman to produce a series of journal entries that were published in *Sports Illustrated*. While they contained nothing terribly controversial or offensive by today's stan-

6. A Hopeful Beginning and a Rude Awakening

dards, Grosscup expressed feelings and emotions, something football players of the 1950s did not do.

When he arrived at his first Giants training camp, Grosscup, like most rookies, was treated roughly by the veterans, a situation he spoke about with Howard Tuckner of the *New York Times*. Tuckner published an article titled *The Lonely Life of a Rookie Quarterback*, which lowered Grosscup's popularity among the veterans even more. His tenure with the Giants, which lasted three years, was not a happy one, for he played very little and not very well. "It's an unresolved time," Grosscup said years later. "It's kind of a disappointing time. I really wanted to make it. I think I was trying too hard and I think I stayed too long."

In 1962, Grosscup was released by the Giants, picked up by the Minnesota Vikings and cut again just before the start of the season. A few days before the opening game, he was signed by the New York Titans of the AFL, who were desperately in need of a quarterback.

Grosscup joined the Titans in Oakland and, with only a couple of days of practice, had the best game of his professional career. On his first AFL play, Grosscup, whose primary asset was his strong right arm, threw an 80-yard touchdown pass to Art Powell. On his second, he threw a 19-yard touchdown pass. For the day, Grosscup had five completions in just eight attempts, for 186 yards and three touchdowns. The Titans won 28–10.

The Oakland game was the high point of Grosscup's season. The next week in San Diego, the Titans lost 40–14 and Grosscup spent the afternoon being battered by Charger defensive end Ron Nery. A few weeks later he suffered a severe knee injury and limped through the rest of the season.

It was assumed that, restored to health, Grosscup would be the Jets' starting quarterback in 1963, but he was cut at the end of the exhibition season. He played briefly in Canada and then spent 1964 on the taxi squad of the Oakland Raiders. The Raiders, with their non-conformist image, seemed a perfect fit for the iconoclastic quarterback. "It's easy to feel at home on this club," he said. "Coach Al Davis takes only clubhouse lawyers, rejects and undesirables."[22]

Grosscup met Don Brewer on Memorial Day weekend in 1965 and promised him that if he did not make the Oakland squad that summer, he would play for the Charter Oaks. "I'd read about the Continental League," Grosscup said, "and I wanted to have a backup plan in case I got cut again. I still wanted to play some football."

The Raiders' third preseason game was in Salt Lake City, which was a bad omen for Grosscup. "I kept going back to Salt Lake City," he recalled, "playing in the old stadium and getting cut. That happened three different times, once with the Giants, once with the Vikings, and once with the Raiders." Although

Lee Grosscup with New York Giants circa 1960 (courtesy Lee Grosscup).

he was offered a second season on the Raider taxi squad, Grosscup declined and embarked for Hartford to serve as player-coach.

The 28-year-old quarterback had continued his literary efforts since his college days, having published a full-length diary of his 1962 season with the Titans, titled *Fourth and One*. The book received good reviews and sold out a first run of ten thousand copies, but a planned serialization in the *Saturday Evening Post*, which would have generated invaluable publicity, was cancelled. The *Post* had recently been sued for libel by University of Georgia coach Wally Butts and was hesitant to publish what some considered controversial material, although Grosscup's book is decidedly tame by today's standards.

While in Hartford, Grosscup intended to write a novel about professional football, but the book was never published. "Now I can see why," he said recently. "It was really poorly written, which had a lot to do with the fact that I was really progressing with my drinking. I was probably in the middle stages of alcoholism at that time.[23] I was trying to write something like *Catch–22*, which I was really enamored with at that time. I got some colorful rejection notices but never came close to having it published." The only writing Grosscup produced during his Charter Oak days was a piece for the *New York Times* called "The Joe Namath of the Continental League," describing his experiences in Hartford.

The handsome quarterback was also interested in television and movies. He sought bit parts in Hollywood and while he was in Hartford hosted a fifteen minute weekly sports show on Channel 18. Grosscup made $400 a week for playing and $200 for broadcasting, a very nice living in the world of minor league football and far more than he would have earned as an Oakland taxi squadder.

Looks and brains were nice, but Fred Wallner was interested in Grosscup's powerful right arm, and believed that with Grosscup and Wheeler he finally had two men capable of mounting a professional passing attack. With runners like Maurice Sykes and newly-acquired halfback Mike Haffner, Hartford appeared to have a much more balanced offense than the run-oriented club of 1964.

Grosscup, with his strong arm, loved to throw the ball, and was especially fond of the long pass. Wallner, on the other hand, preferred the power sweep, run early and often. In one of Grosscup's first games, with the Charter Oaks trailing and a key third down situation looming, Wallner sent in a play from the sideline.

"It was Red 8 46 Power, because Fred ran that five out of ten plays anyway," recalled end Bill Boehle. "That was an off tackle where we had a double team with the tight end and a kick out with the fullback. It was just power—here we come and try to stop us. But in the huddle Lee said, 'They're expecting that play. Johnny [Wardlaw], go down and do a square out and go. I'm going to hit you with a bomb and we're going to win this game right here.' He missed him by five or six yards, we wound up having to punt, and Gross got on Fred's crap list that night."

Haffner was not as big a name as Grosscup, but he was a high profile player from a big time football program, a former UCLA single wing tailback who'd played in the 1962 Rose Bowl. Haffner's versatility was perhaps his curse, for he'd played tailback, halfback, and receiver in college and never spent enough time at one position to convince professional scouts he could play in the NFL. Further, he'd already had knee surgery.

Haffner was not selected in the 1965 draft, "which shocked the hell out of me," he said, and signed with Los Angeles as a free agent. The Rams seemed a good choice, for they were a local team, and their best receiver from 1964, Bucky Pope, had been seriously injured in a car accident.

The Rams, however, had drafted Jack Snow, a talented receiver from Notre Dame who would be a star for them for several years, and traded for all-pro Tommy McDonald. There was no room for Mike Haffner. "Harland Svare was the head coach of the Rams," Haffner recalled, "and he called me in one day and told me to bring my playbook. He said, 'Mike, you can't play at this level. Go back to school and get your master's.' Then he turned his back and sat down at his desk. Well, that pissed me off."

Haffner spoke with Elroy Hirsch, the former star receiver who was then the Rams' head of player personnel, and told him he thought he could play. Hirsch referred him to Jim Dawson, a former UCLA assistant, who told Haffner the club had some connections with the Charter Oaks, and that if he still wanted to play he could hook him up in Hartford.

Haffner thought he would get another shot at the NFL because he had the one element that so many marginal players lacked: speed. "I was always the fastest guy at UCLA and when I got to the Rams camp there wasn't anybody faster. I was really disillusioned that I didn't stick, and I was bound and determined to get even."

The Oaks won their opening game without Wheeler, Grosscup, or Haffner, which was a very encouraging sign. On a mid–August night in Richmond during which the temperature on the field reached nearly one hundred degrees, Hartford parlayed tough defense and conservative offense into a 17-10 win over the Rebels. Mosolf threw two long touchdowns passes and the Hartford defensive front held Richmond to minus six yards rushing. If they could win with Mosolf, what would the Oaks do with Wheeler and Grosscup?

Misfortune struck the Oaks before their second game even began when Wheeler, holding the ball for pregame field goal practice, suffered a split finger on his throwing hand. He played sporadically and ineffectively as the Toronto Rifles ruined the Oaks' CFL home debut by crushing them 39–16. Mosolf couldn't move the team and the run defense, which had been impregnable against Richmond, was shredded by the Rifles' Ron McCauley and Joe Williams.

The optimism that followed the opening win completely vanished after just a single defeat. "[T]he future is bleak," wrote Frank Keyes. "The Hartford Charter Oaks have become a reclamation project." It was apparent, wrote Keyes, that the old UFL clubs were stronger than the old ACFL teams (former UFL teams won their first six games against former ACFL opponents), yet the Oaks were no better than they had been a year ago. The defensive secondary, decimated by injury, was still a weak link, and the offensive line, weakened by the loss of tackle Nick DeFelice, who'd moved up to the New York Jets, was thin.

Bill Lee, who always lauded the Brewers' noble intentions but rarely praised their results, published two letters from readers. One chided Lee for being so critical of the team, while the second, signed "Bald Eagle," claimed the Brewers were too cheap and unwilling to pay for the talent needed to compete in the new league.

Don Brewer responded angrily to the second letter. He stated that the Hartford operating budget was as high as that of any CFL team and that even if his club sold out Dillon Stadium for every game he would not turn a profit. "Perhaps the Bald Eagle would like to invest some of his earnings in the Oaks," Brewer suggested.

Between the time of Lee's column and the publication of Brewer's rebuttal, the Oaks lost two games and their coach. On September 4, they lost 27–21 to Richmond when the Rebels scored 17 points in a second quarter rally during which the Richmond quarterbacks exploited gaping holes in the Hartford secondary. On one occasion Brewer, standing on the Charter Oak sideline, blistered defensive back Rich King when he came to the bench after being burned by a Rebel receiver.

It was not the first time Brewer had been critical of his players. It was the owner's custom to stand on the sideline and, since he paid the bills, Brewer thought it was his prerogative to shout advice and criticize his players' performance.

The King incident was the final straw for Fred Wallner, and on Tuesday, September 7, he announced his resignation. The *Courant* reported that Wallner, who admitted earlier he had been approached by the Holyoke Bombers, had applied for the head coaching position with the Meriden Shamrocks of the New England Football League. The report was quickly denied. There was no new job; Wallner was simply fed up with Brewer's interference. "Internal problems," he said, "involving management and the team, problems over which I have no control, have forced my decision to resign as head coach."[24]

Lee, a big Wallner fan with little love for the sometimes abrasive Brewer, immediately jumped into the fray and excoriated the owner for his sideline conduct. "The Brewer family were amateurs," he wrote, "when they came into professional football promotion here. For a season of learning the ropes, they had solid support at every turn. Management in the second season of operation has not been completely professional. Complaints have mounted."[25]

The players were solidly in Wallner's corner, and the entire incident was an embarrassment to the club. Wallner was well-respected in the football fraternity and his departure was a great blow to the club's prospects and reputation.

At the same time Wallner resigned, there was a rumor that the Charter Oaks would be sold, possibly to the owners of the Shamrocks. Brewer denied the rumors and insisted that the club was not for sale and would not be moved. He appointed Grosscup as interim head coach.[26] King, whose play had initiated the sorry sequence of events, was released.

In his first week as coach, Grosscup cut five players, which left the club with only 33 sound bodies to face the Newark Bears. "They told me we had to pare down," Grosscup remembered. "We had this big offensive lineman. When I cut him he started crying. This poor guy was saying that he couldn't feed his family. It was just a horrible thing and all of a sudden I'm on the other end of it. Instead of getting cut myself I'm cutting someone else and it just felt horrible. I thought, oh my god, what have I done? I just wanted to get away from it as quickly as possible."

Grosscup's first game as head coach was as bad as might have been expected under the circumstances. The Oaks were clobbered 43–0 in a sloppy game marred by numerous skirmishes. Wheeler started at quarterback. "The Newark Bears were really tough," he said, "so Grosscup started me. I said thanks a lot. I can get my brains beat out while you stand on the sideline."

Wheeler and Grosscup combined to throw 43 passes and gain just 133 yards. Newark quarterback Dan Jonas, on the other hand, decimated the Hartford secondary for a record 445 yards. Apparently King had not been the problem. A number of Oaks were injured, including publicity director Jack Murray, who was hospitalized upon his return to Hartford with a badly pinched nerve in his side.

With Murray sidelined, Grosscup, with his writing background, added interim public relations director to his interim head coach title. "I experienced great anxiety in those days," he recalled, "and often flashed on death. On my tombstone, it read 'Lee Grosscup, interim corpse.'"

On September 16, one of Grosscup's interim titles was removed when Newark assistant Lowell Lander was named head coach. Apparently watching the 43–0 debacle a few days earlier had not discouraged the 32-year-old former

6. A Hopeful Beginning and a Rude Awakening

Chicago Cardinal. After a one game NFL career that was ended by a severe knee injury, Lander began coaching in 1962 with the Cleveland Bulldogs of the United League. For the past three years he had been the top assistant at Newark.

Lander was much less intense than Wallner, brought a more relaxed style to the Charter Oaks, and was well-liked by the players. He was a charismatic, somewhat flamboyant man who the following spring would marry a glamorous former New York model named Carol Lee Lucas. "Lowell was a piece of work, man," said Grosscup. "That guy was a character." For the remainder of the 1965 season, Lander's life was somewhat hectic, as he shuttled between Hartford and his home in New Jersey, where he worked as a recreation director.

Lander's first game was no more successful than Grosscup's, as the Oaks lost to Norfolk 44–6. Neptune quarterback Dan Henning again torched the Hartford secondary, and Wheeler and Grosscup continued to be ineffective. By the end of the game, Mosolf was directing the Charter Oak attack. The pass blocking was terrible and it was better to have the scrambling Mosolf in there to dodge onrushing linemen.

With a porous secondary, a weak offensive line, an ineffective passing game, a new coach, and a revolving roster, it was apparent the Oaks were in for a rough season. "There is no way of blinking from sight," wrote Lee, "the evidence that misery continues to stalk the Hartford Charter Oaks football team."[27] Fullback Maurice Sykes and tight end Tom Krzemienski, known as "Ski," were among the few bright spots.

Sykes, the former Ansonia Black Knight, was one of the CFL's leading rushers. He was a powerful man, a strong blocker who could run inside and outside and catch passes. Sykes was a quiet, mysterious type, and there were rumors that he had served time, but few of his teammates knew much about him.

"[Krzemienski]," wrote Bill Lee, "has more guts in his makeup and glue on his fingers than any man in the league."[28] The tight end grew up in Beaver Falls, Pennsylvania with 16 brothers and sisters in a house designed for fewer, for there was only a single bathroom. "The girls got to go first," Krzemienski remembered, "and we just had to stand outside and hold it until there was an opening."

At Beaver Falls High School, Krzemienski was the favorite receiver of Joe Namath, and a local reporter referred to them as "The Hungarian Howitzer and the Polish Picker."[29] The Howitzer went to the University of Alabama and the picker went to Michigan State, where coach Duffy Daugherty assured him his club would throw the ball. The Spartans threw the ball according to Big Ten standards of the early 1960s, which wasn't much. "Primarily I was a blocker," Krzemienski said. "I was another tackle, because passing wasn't in our game plan. Our game plan was to run, run and run."

After he graduated, Krzemienski had a free agent tryout with the Jets, but was cut in late August. He called his mother to tell her the bad news, and she told him she already knew, for a man from the Hartford Charter Oaks had called looking for him.

Krzemienski suffered from the twin curses of most top minor league receivers, a lack of size and insufficient speed. He had great hands, good moves, and the courage to catch the ball in traffic, but he simply couldn't run fast enough to get the attention of major league scouts. And at 200 pounds, he wasn't big enough to be an NFL tight end.

"I wasn't fast," he said, "but I was quick off the line and I was a very, very good blocker because that's what I had to learn to do at Michigan State. And I had no problem catching the ball. It was just kind of a natural ability."

"Too bad he didn't have a body," said Mike Haffner, "because Tommy could *play*. He was too small to play tight end and not fast enough to play out wide. He was one of those 'tweeners' and it was *such* a shame because the guy was a hell of a football player. He could catch it."

Krzemienski's hustle and desire made him a great favorite with the fans, the media, and his teammates. "I *loved* that guy," Grosscup said. "He was a guy you really like to have as a teammate because you know he's going to give you everything he's got for the full 60 minutes. I told Al Davis, 'I think he's too small and too slow, but if you want to take a shot with a guy who'll do anything to catch the football, this is a guy you want to have on your team.'" Apparently, Davis stopped listening when he heard too small and too slow, for he never gave Krzemienski a shot with the Raiders.

"He was *really* competitive," Grosscup said. "I loved throwing the ball to him. One time he ran a slant out and up where he went out to the flat and then turned up the field. I threw the ball out there and didn't think he was even going to come close to it. He did a full dive and came down with the ball and I remember thinking it was one of the best catches I'd ever seen."

"It was a flag pattern to the left corner of the end zone," said Krzemienski. "Grosscup threw it to my right and all I could do was turn around with my back to the ball and it fell into my hands for a touchdown. That was pretty impressive. I was very happy about that catch."

The turnover continued, and by the third week of September only nine holdovers remained from the 1964 club. Some players came and went in mysterious fashion. Lou Holland, a back who'd played for Wisconsin in the 1963 Rose Bowl, left the team because he missed his wife. Cloyd Webb, a 6'5" former Iowa end, flew into Hartford and signed a contract. When he called his mother to tell her about it, she told him about some personal issues that required his presence in St. Louis. He left on the next plane. Webb returned a few days later,

6. A Hopeful Beginning and a Rude Awakening

was soon injured, and then released after a total of about three weeks in Hartford.

"The turnover of that roster was amazing," said Mosolf. "I ran into guys I'd played with in Canada, guys I'd played with in Indianapolis, on the West Coast, and at Idaho. Some guys from Oregon. They were coming and going like it was a Greyhound bus station."

There were, however, some quality players on the roster, including Dave Pivec, a linebacker from Notre Dame who went on to play three years with the Rams and one with the Broncos as a tight end. Minor leaguers with NFL aspirations had to be versatile, and one of Pivec's great skills was as a long snapper.

"He was the best long snapper I've ever seen in my life," said Haffner, who was the holder in Denver. "He came up to me and said, 'Mike, where do you want the laces?' I told him I liked to catch them on my right hand so all I had to do was put the ball down. I'll be damned if he didn't snap it back with the laces in the same place *every damned time*."

The string of embarrassing Charter Oak defeats continued. The Wheeling Ironmen were winless before beating Hartford 34–14. The Oaks were hindered when their bus got lost twice en route and they arrived just before game time.

The first place Philadelphia Bulldogs won 62–22 at Dillon and the Fort Wayne Warriors won 49–13 in their rinky-dink high school stadium. With a 1–8 record and an eight game losing streak, the Oaks, suffering from an epidemic of injuries, faced a game with the Charleston Rockets, who were 9–0 and in first place in the Western Division. If the Hartford club was 36 points worse than Fort Wayne, how badly would they lose to undefeated Charleston?

The answer, surprisingly, was by three points. Prior to the game, Hartford signed defensive back Jim Ward and defensive end Ron Nery, the former San Diego Charger who had ruined Grosscup's second game with the Titans by spending most of the day slinging him around the New York backfield. Grosscup contacted Nery in California and convinced him to quit his construction job and come east. "I don't like you at all because of what you did to me," Grosscup told him, "but I want you on my side."

The Charleston game was the beleaguered Hartford club's finest hour of 1965. They held a team that had never scored less than 20 points in a game to just three field goals. Although they lost 9–6, it was a moral victory. As he had done in San Diego three years earlier, Nery spent the entire game in the opposing backfield. The Rockets' potent passing game could muster just 74 yards, a far cry from what quarterbacks had been doing to Hartford all season.

If the quarterback didn't have time to throw, he couldn't exploit the Oaks' vulnerable secondary. And that secondary was less vulnerable with the addition of Ward, who played an excellent game. If kicker Bill Shockley had been a little more accurate, the Oaks might have won. Shockley was a former AFL player who was in the Continental League because his strong leg was not always true. Against the Rockets, he connected on two short field goals but misfired three times from the 44 yard line.

The Oaks also might have won if Grosscup had completed more than 10 of 34 pass attempts. They might have won if Sykes, their principal running threat, had not torn a leg muscle in the first half. The Oaks had no one to replace him, so he finished the game, but was limited to blocking and serving as a decoy. Haffner, Hartford's second best runner, was also injured and forced out of action.

Grosscup, with his big reputation, had been a disappointment. For the season, he completed just 39 percent of his passes and was the tenth ranked passer in the CFL. Some of the failure was not his fault, for his receivers displayed a great penchant for dropping passes. "I had more passes dropped that year," he recalled. "I bet I had ten to fifteen touchdown passes dropped. We had guys that could get down the field but they couldn't catch the ball." When Lander talked about moving Haffner from running back to flanker, someone asked why. "He catches the ball. It's that simple," Lander replied.

One of the receivers who had a hard time catching the ball was John Wardlaw. "Nobody could stay with him," Grosscup said, "but he couldn't hold onto the ball. He had the speed, he had the juke-ability, but he didn't have the sure hands. If you could have combined him and Krzemienski you would have had an all-pro wide receiver."

In addition to receivers who couldn't catch, the Charter Oak quarterbacks suffered from linemen who couldn't protect them. "We had a very small, weak offensive line," said Grosscup, "and I got sacked a lot. After about two weeks I was saying, 'What am I doing here?' I called Al Davis and asked if there was any way I could come back. He said I had a contract and I had to stay. I've always said about the quarterback position that if you've got the right coach and the right supporting cast it's the greatest position in the world. If you have the wrong coach and the wrong supporting cast it's a true nightmare."

A week after the Charleston game, the Oaks broke their long losing streak with a 20–2 win over the Rhode Island Indians and their star quarterback, Tom Kennedy. Nery even provided some offense by intercepting a pass and carrying it 49 yards for a touchdown. The Oaks carried Lander from the field as if they had won an NFL championship.

The victory over Rhode Island was the final win of the 1965 season. After holding Charleston and Rhode Island without a touchdown, the Oak defense surrendered 55 points to Fort Wayne and 41 to Charleston while losing their final three games. The remaining weeks were a succession of losses, injuries, and continuing roster shuffles. Even Lander got hurt, suffering a compound fracture of his finger at practice one evening. It was a rough year for the rookie coach, who also got a speeding ticket on newly-opened Route 91 while returning from Newark.

As the quality of the team became evident, the fans stopped coming. "Let's face it," Grosscup said. "All football fans are the same. They love a winner and they hate a loser. We were not only not winning but we were not looking that great either." Grosscup's reputation, charm, and articulate manner gave him an aura and created high expectations. The Hartford fans, having been led to believe he would be the savior of the franchise, were so disappointed they even came out to boo Grosscup in practice.

"I was the principal object of their animosity," he recalled. "That's part of playing quarterback. You get way too much credit when things are going good and way too much blame when things are going bad."

His old Giant teammate Charley Conerly had always told Grosscup he didn't mind people booing if they paid their money to get into the park. The fans who booed him in practice hadn't even paid. And when they did pay their way into Dillon Stadium, the fans got their money's worth. "Dixie cups were wadded up and thrown at us," Grosscup said. "One guy got pelted with an egg. We wore our helmets all the time and I felt like wearing mine even when I spoke at banquets."

It was a tough season for Grosscup, and perhaps the best thing that happened to him in Hartford was meeting a lovely French girl who he squired around the city for most of the season. Grosscup and Haffner, the West Coast boys with much in common, palled around together, and met two French *au pairs* (a pair of *au pairs*) who happened to work for a big supporter of the Charter Oaks and were apparently willing to overlook the twelve losses.

"I played football," Haffner said, "chased the ladies and drank a little too much." What did he think of Hartford? "I don't remember too much about Hartford except for the French girl I met." Grosscup, Haffner, and two other players shared a house, and one afternoon one of the other two walked in to find Grosscup in the bathtub with two Swedish flight attendants. With one extra attendant afloat, Grosscup invited his roommate to join him, but the latter, who had a girlfriend back home, declined.

The Continental League had proven much tougher than the ACFL, and the Oaks finished their first season in the league in last place in the Western Division. After winning the opener, they lost 12 of their final 13 games. The Brewers re-hired Lander for the 1966 season, and by offering a full-time salary, convinced him to re-locate to the Hartford area.

While the Charter Oaks had a bad season on the field, all of the CFL teams had poor years financially. The owners could take solace in the fact that all the teams of the American Football League, now on the verge of merging with the NFL, lost money in their first season. The AFL losses in 1960, ranging from $175,000 for Buffalo to $900,000 for the Los Angeles Chargers, were in fact much greater than the CFL deficits. The AFL, however, had a national television contract before it played a game and the stadiums, while not comparable to NFL facilities, were certainly superior to virtually all the CFL parks. Most importantly, the AFL had owners like Lamar Hunt and Barron Hilton, who could shoulder losses for an indefinite period. There weren't many Hunts or Hiltons among the CFL owners. As the league prepared for its second season, Happy Chandler continued to speak bravely of major league status, but his owners had other ideas.

7

It's Hard to Be a Major League: The 1966–67 Hartford Charter Oaks

In minor league football, the offseason is often more eventful than the playing season. Just a few weeks after the 1965 CFL campaign ended, the controversy over accepting optioned players from the NFL and AFL threatened to sever the relationship between the owners and their commissioner, who apparently had not learned the lesson major league baseball owners gave him 15 years earlier. "As long as I am commissioner," Chandler said in early January, "our league will never have an optioned player."[1] If the league wanted to use optioned players, he would "go home to mamma in Kentucky."

Chandler cited the state of baseball's minor leagues, which had declined from 59 when he was commissioner to 20. That was due, he said, to their being vassals of the major leagues. "We like to think of ourselves as the third major league," he said. "There are no options—the players' contracts belong to us."[2] He declared that Charleston, the CFL's best team in 1965, could have beaten any AFL team and that soon his league would be the equal of the NFL and AFL in terms of "talent, television money and national prestige."[3] He issued an ultimatum that each CFL team must have a stadium seating at least 20,000 by 1967, or it would be tossed from the circuit.

While Chandler clung to his hope of being a third major league, CFL owners, having suffered through a bath of red ink in their first season, were less enthusiastic. A year of drawing about 10,000 fans per game had not convinced them they were on the verge of becoming the equal of either the AFL or NFL, and using taxi squad players, whose salaries were paid by the major league clubs, would ease some of their financial pain.

"[T]he Continental League need not apologize for being minor," Bill Lee wrote. "With, or without, the use of players optioned to it by the National and

American Leagues, the Continental is not 'a third major league.' It was silly when Chandler first made this claim and even more pointless now. Perhaps it would make more sense for Hartford and other Continental League cities to set their sights on a target that can be hit. The people who pay three or four dollars a seat for Continental League games never believed they were watching a 'third major league' and these are the most important people concerned with the future."[4]

Lee's colleague, Frank Keyes, was gentler. "Is the Continental a minor or a major professional football league?" he asked rhetorically. "The truth be known," he answered, "it isn't either. It will attain its directional orbit in the next two or three years."[5] If the CFL made arrangements with the two established leagues and accepted optioned players, Keyes said, it was a minor league by means of its relationship. If it remained independent, it would probably grow, but Keyes thought it was unlikely it would ever be a viable competitor to the NFL and AFL.

Even the undefeated Charleston Rockets had been unable to make money. CFL salaries were high by minor league standards and travel expenses, with a far-flung footprint, were a burden. Most trips were made by charter flight, and the distance between some of the league cities necessitated overnight stays.

On January 14, after the CFL trustees voted 8–1 to consider using optioned players, Chandler resigned, absolving the league of all his future salary obligations. Apparently he did not "loves football" any more, at least not the kind contemplated by Continental League owners. Sid Rosen, general manager of the Newark Bears, assumed the commissionership on an interim basis. Rosen was not a big name but, unlike Chandler, he had a solid background operating a minor league franchise and harbored no delusions of grandeur. Don Brewer and Tom Granatelli of the Newark Bears were commissioned to seek a "name" leader and, during the next few weeks, former Giant star Kyle Rote emerged as the leading candidate.

Rather than worry about competing with the AFL and NFL, Rosen had more immediate and pressing concerns, like getting at least eight solvent teams on the gridiron for the 1966 season. The reliable Wheeling Ironmen, despite their isolated location, stagnant economy, and a scraggly depression era field, would return for the 1966 season. Rhode Island dropped out, leaving in its wake star quarterback Tom Kennedy. Washington was granted the right to assume the Rhode Island franchise, contingent upon finding a suitable playing site. They intended to ask the city to allow them to play in D.C. Stadium, home of Redskins, and their chances were slim. Fort Wayne talked about moving, but then purchased the stands from the World Fair Singer Bowl and declared their intention to stay. Charleston's directors were also thinking about moving.

7. It's Hard to Be a Major League

On February 10, the CFL held a meeting in New York at which Rosen was named acting commissioner for one year. It was also announced that Granatelli, who said he lost $150,000 in 1965 and $250,000 over four years, was moving his team to Orlando. When, as expected, Washington was unable to acquire a playing field, the league replaced Providence with a New York franchise granted to Fred F. Finklehoff, a 54-year-old producer of television and stage shows.

Finklehoff planned to call his club the Stars, promised to bring show business to the Continental League, and vowed to have his games televised. He wanted either Charley Conerly or Y.A. Tittle as his coach and, in order to get some players, acquired the right to negotiate with the league for the Providence contracts.

Finklehoff had more flash and sizzle than staying power. About a month after he was granted the New York franchise, he offered $105,000 for the Charleston club, which declined. Charleston president Vic Green said Finklehoff wanted his team because he had previously sold his New York franchise to a group from Montreal. Apparently, the sequence of events left Charleston in Charleston, but where did it leave New York? And where did it leave Perry Moss, former coach of the Rockets, who'd signed a ten-year contract at $50,000 a year to coach Finklehoff's new team?

On April 1, the curtain came down on Finklehoff's football career when the league announced that it had repurchased the New York franchise from him for an undisclosed sum because the producer had motion picture commitments that would prevent him from devoting sufficient attention to football. On the surface, the parting was amicable, and no mention was made of the mysterious Montreal investors.

Rosen indicated that there were two groups of investors interested in the New York team. One supposedly would install former New York Yankee announcer Mel Allen as general manager. The other would move the franchise to Washington, D.C., and wanted to hire legendary Oklahoma coach Bud Wilkinson to run the team as coach and general manager.

One needed a scorecard and an eraser to keep track of the frenetic movements of Continental League teams, for shortly thereafter, Montreal investors announced that they had acquired the Charleston Rockets. The franchise would go to Montreal and the Charleston players would go to New York. The day after the announcement, the Charleston shareholders shocked the rest of the league by voting to retain their franchise and send it to neither New York nor Montreal.

Montreal eventually ended up with a team after all. Fort Wayne's Al Savill, the third owner in four years, found operating a minor league team as unfulfilling as his two predecessors and sold the franchise to a Montreal group. The new owners, John Newman and Russ Scrim, appeared to have capital, and owned several construction companies that operated in Canada, Africa, and Asia. Their team would be known as the Beavers, or *Les Castors*. The big draw of a Montreal franchise was that the Expo 67 exhibition, then in the planning stages, included a 25,000 seat stadium, which *Les Castors* hoped to occupy.

On April 30, the Brooklyn Dodgers were announced as the tenth Continental club, with rights to the Rhode Island players, including the coveted Tom Kennedy. They didn't have Tittle or Conerly, but they did have former Giant star Andy Robustelli as coach. The general manager was an even greater celebrity. There were few bigger names in sports than Jackie Robinson, who became the "first Negro to become general manager of a top flight integrated professional team."[6] The announcement of Robinson's appointment as general manager was about the last mention of his name in connection with the club, for he continued working for Governor Rockefeller on civil rights issues and retained his various business interests.

The Dodgers had a famous name, a famous coach, and a famous general manager, but not many players and only a second rate stadium. The club would play its games on Randall's Island, located in the middle of the East River. As the *Courant* pointed out, "It is fairly difficult of access."[7] The big hope was that Brooklyn would build a new 30,000 seat stadium the following year, but in the meantime the Dodgers were sentenced to Randall's Island, nearly as hard to get into as the prison at nearby Riker's Island was to get out of.

The Charter Oaks planned to move, but not in 1966. On April 11, at the Terrace Room at Bradley Field, the Brewers announced plans for a $12 million real estate project in Windsor Locks (about 12 miles north of Hartford) on a 143-acre parcel located alongside the access road to the airport. The development would include a shopping center, at least one and possibly two theaters, a gas station, a motel, various commercial establishments, and a $3 million stadium that would seat 30,000. The latter facility would be completed in time for the 1967 season. The stadium was designed so that it could be easily expanded to 45,000–50,000 seats if the Oaks outgrew the initial capacity. Two things were needed to make the project a reality. The first was a zoning change and the second was $12 million.

After the dust had cleared, the CFL again found itself with ten teams, with Orlando, Montreal, and Brooklyn replacing Fort Wayne, Rhode Island, and Newark. Hartford was moved from the Western Division to the East.

Lowell Lander returned for his first full season as coach, and hoped it would be better than the previous year. The 1966 team would be his to mold from the first day of training camp which, unlike 1964 and 1965, was a real training camp. During the previous two years, pre-season practices had been held at

Dillon Stadium and Colt Park, just as they were during the regular season. In 1966, the Brewers secured accommodations at Westminster School in Simsbury, where the players were housed and practices held daily, just like at a real professional football training camp.

"That was the closest thing to being in the NFL that I experienced," said Bob Shemeth. "I almost lost my job. We were there for two weeks and I took one week of vacation. I don't remember what I did for the second week but I pulled something off."

The Oaks had been caught short in their first CFL season, learning too late that ACFL holdovers were not talented enough to compete against the former UFL teams. The 1966 squad would be different. Lee Grosscup retired to take a public relations job with the Oakland Raiders and serve as color commentator for AFL games on NBC. Manch Wheeler was not re-signed. As their starting quarterback, the Oaks signed John Torok, who was second in the nation in total offense at Arizona State and who'd had a 1965 tryout with the New York Giants. After the Giants cut him, he led the Mobile team to the North American Football League championship game.

Maurice Sykes, who'd never fully recovered from his severe leg injury, was traded to Norfolk and replaced by Bobby Gaiters, a New Mexico State product who'd had a great rookie season with the New York Giants in 1961. Gaiters gained 462 yards rushing, displayed breakaway ability on kickoff returns, and was named the Giants' rookie of the year. His principal shortcoming, which proved his eventual undoing, was an inability to hold onto the ball. He fumbled eleven times and played very little in the championship game against the Packers. Two games into the following season, he was gone, and after short stints with the 49ers and Broncos, disappeared from the major league scene.

Gaiters played for the Newark Bears in 1965, when Lander was an assistant. When the Newark franchise relocated to Orlando, many players who had jobs and families in New Jersey decided not to go. The same was true of the Fort Wayne to Montreal move. The league accommodated several players by arranging trades, one of which brought Gaiters to Hartford.

A large contingent of players came to Hartford from California. Before he decided to retire, Grosscup had been active in recruiting a number of them, as had new linebacker Mickey Caruso. Caruso didn't have the size or talent to play in the NFL, but he was a fanatic hitter. "Pound for pound," said Grosscup, "he was one of the toughest guys I've ever seen. Lowell Lander loved the guy." "He was small for a middle linebacker," said Shemeth, "but boy, was he a hitter."[8]

One of the best players to come from the west was Bill Leeka, a handsome All-American tackle from UCLA. Leeka was named to the UCLA all-century team and coach Red Sanders called him the best offensive lineman he'd ever coached. He was a late draft choice of the Steelers, but never played in the NFL.

"Bill Leeka was probably the most memorable of all the Charter Oaks or Knights," said Shemeth. "He was one of the best-looking guys you'd want to meet and he was one crazy guy on the football field. He was in-sane." Leeka drove around Hartford in a pickup truck souped-up in the style that was popular on the West Coast during the Beach Boys era.

In California, Leeka pursued an acting career and became one of the pioneers of beach volleyball. During the mid–'60s, the beach volleyball scene drew UCLA basketball stars like Keith Erickson, Greg Lee and John Vallely and pro footballers like Leeka, Grosscup, and Mike Haffner.

Linebacker Frank Goldberg from Central Michigan was not as mellow as the California contingent. "They didn't come any crazier than this guy," said Shemeth. "He either had to be on drugs or he had a death wish. He would go down on the suicide squad and throw his body at the four blockers that were in the wedge and level all four of them. He was probably a good guy off the field but he was a complete football lunatic." "He got knocked out a lot," added Bob Stohrer.

In 1966, as they had the previous year, the Charter Oaks won their opening game. This time, it was a big upset, a 36–31 victory over the Philadelphia Bulldogs, who'd finished 10–4 the previous year and beaten the Oaks 62–22. Philadelphia's most dangerous weapon was quarterback Bob Brodhead, the 1965 CFL MVP. "Brodhead was one of those guys who would just pick you apart," said Grosscup, "he'd carve you up."

Brodhead was a quarterback who set records year after year in the minors but never got another shot in the majors. One of the reasons was his body. Brodhead roomed with Sonny Jurgensen at Duke and had a physique similar to that of the pot-bellied Redskin quarterback. He looked more like the accountant he was during the off-season than a professional football player.

Some of the records Brodhead established were less than stellar, such as the time he dropped back to pass against Charleston in 1965 and kept retreating until he fell down for a 51-yard sack. Most of his marks were of a positive nature, however, such as the 3,778 passing yards he gained in 1965, more than any quarterback in the history of U.S. professional football. He also threw for 33 touchdowns, only three less than Y.A. Tittle's NFL record.

Brodhead made mincemeat of the 1965 Oaks, but the 1966 Hartford team was more resilient. Jim Whitmore intercepted three of Brodhead's passes and the Oaks capitalized on a number of Bulldog turnovers to score 33 points in the first half. Two fumble recoveries gave them a 14–0 lead with only six minutes elapsed in the game. A total of only 10 points were scored in the second half, as

Lander used his ground game to kill the clock and keep the explosive Philadelphia offense off the field.

The Oaks' offense was better than it had been in 1965, but the defense continued to be leaky and wound up giving up more yards than any other team in the league. Lander's specialty was offense, and if assistant John Dell Isola's defense was going to give up points, Lander's offense would simply have to score more.

Hartford traveled to Toronto for its second game and lost badly 35–14, as the Rifles rushed for 346 yards. Toronto had the two best runners in the CFL in Joe Williams and Bob Blakely, and Hartford was unable to stop them. Lander even tried a five man line without success. Blakely gained 151 yards and Williams had 115, as the Oaks, who trailed 28–0 at halftime, were never in the game.

As major league teams made their final cuts, the Oaks beefed up their roster. Perhaps the best addition was defensive end Fran Mallick, a 6'3" 250-pounder who, despite never having played in high school or college, spent the entire 1965 season with the Pittsburgh Steelers. Another Californian, Andy Von Sonn, a linebacker from UCLA who'd started seven games for the 1964 Rams, arrived from the Atlanta Falcons camp.

"Oaks Eight Weeks Ahead of Last Fall's CFL Pace," read the *Courant* headline after Hartford defeated the Brooklyn Dodgers 24–14 at Dillon Stadium.[9] Three of the Oaks' points came when Bill Shockley kicked a league record 48-yard field goal, a mark that was broken twice the next day.

The game was a rough one, a contest that teetered one incident away from a brawl. Finally, with the game nearly over, a Brooklyn player kicked a prone Charter Oak and was ejected. Rather than go to the locker room, the player remained on the sideline and became the object of a great deal of booing and taunting from the crowd. The fans had been rough on the visitors all night long, and when the game ended some of them came down from the stands and started trading punches with the Dodgers. From all accounts, the fans got the worst of the exchange, since most of the players were still wearing their helmets and pads and many of the fans were fueled by alcohol and had more courage than agility. The police tried to break up the fracas, but were badly outnumbered and one fan, a fiftyish man with a brace on his leg, was injured.

Don Brewer went to the Brooklyn locker room to apologize to coach Andy Robustelli, and Commissioner Rosen, who was present, said he deeply regretted the incident. "Things like this can happen," he said, "in a stadium as intimate as Dillon. When the spectators sit this close to the action and the players hear every word of abuse thrown at them, tempers are sure to flare."[10]

Salvatore Pistorio, president of the Metropolitan Hartford Sports Club, sent a letter of apology to Robustelli. Bill Lee suggested Rosen institute a rule that all players had to leave the field immediately after the end of a game. He also castigated the fans that started the ruckus. "People who must get stiff, bagged, half drunk or crocked on Saturday nights should do their drinking in saloons, or in the privacy of their game rooms at home. Football players who insist on hanging around after the last gun to have it out with jeering spectators should be run right out of the Continental Football League."[11]

The win over Brooklyn was the first of three straight, and after five weeks the Oaks were tied with Toronto for first place in the Eastern Division with a 4–1 mark. The pass defense continued to be shaky, but the Oaks were scoring points and playing exciting football.

The Oaks' winning streak was broken at Montreal, when the offense couldn't make up for the defensive shortcomings and Hartford went down to a 31–7 defeat. Still, the club remained tied for first.

Eastern Division			Western Division		
Hartford	4	2	Orlando	6	0
Toronto	4	2	Charleston	4	2
Norfolk	4	2	Montreal	3	3
Philadelphia	2	4	Richmond	1	5
Brooklyn	2	4	Wheeling	0	6

Brooklyn was not only in last place in the Eastern Division; it was essentially bankrupt, and many of the stockholders wanted out. From the middle of September through the end of the season, the Dodgers' operating expenses were paid by the league. Unable to draw at Randall's Island, they moved their final two home games to Hartford and Mount Vernon, New York.

After a loss to Norfolk dropped them out of a first place tie, the Oaks paid a visit to Wheeling, home of the Western Division's worst team. The Ironmen hadn't won a game, but at least they were solvent, and they were one of the toughest, if not *the* toughest, team in the CFL. After a game against Wheeling, the other team might be victorious, but they knew they had been in a battle.

The Ironmen's coach and general manager was Bob Snyder, one of the first T-formation quarterbacks for the Chicago Bears in the 1930s and '40s. One year he served as backfield coach at Notre Dame during the week, helping to install the T-formation, while playing for the Bears on Sundays. Snyder had been coaching at the college, NFL, and minor league levels for many years, and looked the part. He was portly, about 270 pounds, with a fleshy face and the tough-talking clichés one would expect of a man coaching a team from West Virginia. The *Courant's* Frank Keyes described Snyder as a "big, bulky, boisterous, blustery, blatant, blathering, blasphemous bull."[12]

7. It's Hard to Be a Major League

Snyder didn't have much money to work with, and the facilities were awful, but he had molded the Wheeling squad in his own tough image. In addition to their bruising linemen, the Ironmen had recently acquired talented quarterback Benji Dial from the Pittsburgh Steelers.

Wheeling was unpleasant under normal circumstances, and when the Charter Oaks visited there on October 9, it was raining heavily, a downpour that turned the barren field into a sea of mud. Only 3,521 spectators braved the storm and made their way to the island.

Neither team was able to muster much of an offensive attack. The Oaks were leading 17–13 with less than five minutes left in the game when Dial led his team down the field toward a potential winning score. He threw a pass intended for big end Bob Dunlevy at the Hartford 10. Defensive back Ray Woitkowski, a youngster from Pittsfield, Massachusetts who'd been discovered in a tryout camp, stepped in front of Dunlevy, picked off the pass and ran 90 yards for the touchdown that sealed a 24–13 win.

The Hartford quarterback for the Wheeling game was young Ken Lucas from the University of Pittsburgh. Torok, who'd thrown well early in the season, suffered a separated shoulder and was out of action for several weeks. Lucas was elevated to the starting role, and the Oaks signed veteran Butch Songin as his backup.

Songin was a crotchety veteran whose opinionated nature was a major reason for his long career as a minor league wanderer. When he was released by the New York Titans in 1962, he leveled a virulent blast against owner Harry Wismer and coach Bulldog Turner. "I'm happy to be the hell out of here," he said. "I can say that I have never seen an organization as fouled up as this one." And it was unlikely he said "fouled."

"Butch was a little cocky at times," said Roger Ellis, a Titan teammate and longtime friend. "He rubbed some people the wrong way. He would just say what was on his mind. He meant well, but sometimes Butch would say things when he probably should have kept his mouth shut." Songin had been bouncing around the minors for a long time, and listed his age as 37. According to most sources, he was 42.

Following the victory at Wheeling, the Oaks lost badly to the resurgent Philadelphia Bulldogs and then beat Wheeling at Hartford by the identical 24–13 margin by which they had won at Wheeling. Songin started and went virtually all the way, passing for 220 yards. At 6–4, the Oaks were one game behind Toronto, which was scheduled to play at Hartford on October 29. It was one of the biggest games in the history of Hartford professional football, and a full house was expected at Dillon Stadium.

Even though the evening was chilly and windy, nearly 11,000 fans showed up and saw a game that was both exciting and heart-breaking. The Oaks held a 14–10 lead with less than three minutes remaining when they punted to the Rifles. Wayne Crow's punt into the stiff breeze rolled dead on the Toronto 22 and the Rifle offense, which had done little all evening, faced the difficult task of having to take the ball 78 yards down the field to win the game.

They did just that. After two incomplete passes, quarterback Tom Wilkinson hit Bob Blakely with a screen pass that the halfback carried all the way to the Hartford 29. On the next play, flanker Bob Morgan went in motion and linebacker Andy Von Sonn followed. When Morgan began to run downfield, Von Sonn took a shot at him and whiffed. There was no one behind Von Sonn, and Morgan was wide open in the end zone. Wilkinson hit him with the game winning pass and the championship hopes of the Charter Oaks were, for all intents and purposes, dead. They had a 6–5 record and were two games behind the Rifles with just three to play.

The last three games were not pretty, and the season that had begun with such promise staggered to a close. The Oaks lost to the Dodgers 20–6, as Tom Kennedy again shredded their vulnerable pass defense. The game against Orlando, the final home contest of the year, promised to be a mismatch, for the 10–2 Panthers, with the highest payroll in the league, featured star quarterback Don Jonas and his fleet of talented receivers.

Jonas was probably the top minor leaguer of the 1960s, certainly the best who never made it to the NFL. He won four MVP titles in the U.S. and one more while finishing his career in Canada. Jonas first came to the ACFL as a receiver with Harrisburg in 1963, but switched to quarterback when the Capitols were beset by injuries. He was also a kicker, and scored 135 points in his first season. In 1967, playing for Orlando, he threw 41 touchdown passes.

With nothing to lose, Lander gambled repeatedly. He tried an onside kick on the first play of the game—and failed. With just 32 seconds elapsed, the Oaks were behind 7–0. They tried for a first down on fourth and one at their own 21 and failed again, leading to another touchdown. Later, the Oaks tried a reverse on a kickoff and lost the ball on their own four when the handoff was flubbed. The final score was 40–7. It might have been closer had Lander played conservatively, but what was the difference between losing 24–7 and 40–7. At least he gave the home fans a good show.

The last game of the year was a 31–24 defeat in Charleston, with the winning score coming when Songin's pass was intercepted and returned for a touchdown. The highlight of the evening was a remarkable performance by Hartford safety Wayne Crow. Crow, who'd been a starting running back and punter for the Oakland Raiders and Buffalo Bills, announced before the game that it would be his last. In the first quarter, he intercepted a pass and returned it 54 yards for a touchdown. In the third quarter, he picked off another pass under the goalposts and ran it back 100 yards, the longest interception runback in the two-year history of the league. It was not enough to save the Charter Oaks from their fourth consecutive loss, and they returned home with a disappointing 6–8 record.

Some players went directly home after the game, and one took a very circuitous route. Andy Von Sonn got permission to drive to Charleston rather than take the bus, so that he could depart directly for California. Rather than drive to Charleston, West Virginia, however, Von Sonn mistakenly went to Charleston, South Carolina, about 390 miles away. He drove to Atlanta, took a plane to West Virginia, flew back to Atlanta after the game, and then drove home to California.

The final statistics found some of the Oaks among the league leaders, including Gaiters, with 688 rushing yards, and fullback Chuck Munford, close behind with 523. Shockley tied for the lead with 15 field goals and was fourth in scoring with 77 points. Tight end Tom Krzemienski had 63 receptions for 748 yards.

About two weeks after the final game, the Oaks generated more news coverage than they had received for anything they did on the playing field. On November 30, Don Brewer asked Lander to come to his office for a meeting, which the latter assumed would be to discuss contract terms for the following season. The Oaks had won four more games than in the previous year and there had been no morale problems. Instead of offering Lander a new contract, however, Brewer fired him. "I can sum up my feelings in one word," Lander said afterward, "SHOCKED! I am really just SHOCKED!"[13]

Lander quickly recovered from his shock and hurled a vicious diatribe at Brewer. He said he had been told by several people that Brewer criticized his coaching from the press box during the 17–14 loss to Toronto. Lander ignored the issue until the owner came to him one day on the practice field and asked what was bothering him. "I told him exactly what was bothering me," Lander said, "and he admitted to me at that time that it was true."[14] He had suggested Brewer fire him and hire himself as head coach and pointed out that Fred Wallner had quit his coaching job because he wouldn't tolerate Brewer's meddling.

Further, Lander said, he had pitiful resources and had to perform most of Brewer's duties as general manager. "I had to be head coach, general manager, director of player personnel, public relations director and just about everything else connected with the operation of a pro-football team," he said. Lander had only Dell Isola as an assistant, while other CFL clubs had five to seven aides. As a further indignity, Lander and Dell Isola had been assigned to work in the Brewers' unheated garage on South Quaker Lane. Eventually, the coaches decided to use the Wethersfield apartment they shared as the Charter Oak coaching headquarters.

Lander said that the Brewers' shallow pockets hindered his ability to produce a winning team. In mid-season, he wanted to sign running back Charley Leigh, but Brewer wasn't willing to meet Leigh's price. Two weeks later, after Leigh gained 185 yards and made two long touchdown runs against the Oaks, Lander walked up to Brewer on the sideline and said, "That's the kid we couldn't afford."[15]

As they had with Wallner, the players lined up on their coach's side. Captain John Willard appeared at a press conference organized by Lander and said, "I am not authorized to speak for the players, but I think they would agree with everything Lowell has said."[16] Willard added that the players had no idea there was trouble between the coach and the owner, and felt that Lander had done a good job. "I felt he was getting as much as he could out of the ballclub," Willard said recently, "and he was a good guy. I thought he deserved a shot, so I supported him." Several players said they would not play for another coach, but Lander urged them to stay and give their best for his successor.

Commissioner Rosen backed Brewer and said cryptically that the Hartford owner had no choice but to fire Lander, and had he been in the same situation he would have done the same thing. Rosen, who had known Lander when the latter was an assistant at Newark, had referred him to Brewer. "Lowell," Rosen said, "has a wonderful football mind, he's an outstanding coach, and he's got a great future in football coaching. But he's got some personal problems to settle or outgrow first."[17] He said that, contrary to Lander's claim that the Brewers wouldn't spend money on players, Hartford had the second highest payroll (behind Orlando) in the league.

Bill Lee initially came down on Lander's side, stating that the Charter Oaks had embarrassed themselves by losing two excellent coaches and that the club was back where it had started three years ago. A few days later, Jack Murray, former public relations director of the Charter Oaks, wrote a letter to Lee refuting Lander's claims. He said the decision to fire the coach had been a wrenching one for Brewer and had nothing to do with Lander's coaching ability. "I am not in a position to go into the reasons for Lowell being fired," he wrote.[18]

Frank Keyes also came to Brewer's defense. He said he was in the press box during the Toronto game, and every other game that season, and had never heard the owner criticize Lander's strategy. Apparently Keyes felt he was the one Lander had said told him about Brewer and he was angry about it. Name names, he challenged the coach. Keyes said he knew the reason Lander had been fired, "since I've read conclusive documented evidence in the company of a *Hartford Courant* executive. There's no doubt in my mind. I'm not at liberty to reveal the details, but the letter I read was dated in October, quite a few weeks before the end of the season."[19]

What was in the letter, and what were the personal problems Rosen referred to? And why was Brewer so silent? The answer came on January 3, 1967, when Lander was arrested by Detective Dale Peterson of the Wethersfield Police Department on two counts of receiving money under false pretenses. An anonymous caller who identified himself only as a "sports fan" called the Police Department and said he saw Lander at an Asylum Avenue hotel. Peterson went to the hotel, saw Lander, and hollered, "Hey, coach." Lander, who must have realized Peterson wasn't looking for his autograph, denied being Lowell Lander. Finally, when asked for identification, he admitted he was the man Peterson was seeking. He was taken to the police station, booked, and released on bail. In a statement after his release, Lander said he was innocent of all charges and planned to sue Brewer and the Charter Oaks, as well as an unnamed Hartford bank.

When the facts came out, the Brewers and the Hartford police looked foolish. The charges were dropped in mid–January and it was revealed that the entire matter involved only $100 and was the result of a couple of innocent mistakes. Lander had cashed two $50 checks, one on an account that had been closed by the bank without his knowledge and the other intended to be drawn on an account with sufficient funds but mistakenly written from the wrong checkbook. Unfortunately for Lander, his arrest was trumpeted in bold headlines and his exoneration buried so deeply that, if it appeared in the *Courant*, I couldn't find it.

The interlude between the 1966 and 1967 CFL seasons was, like the prior winter and spring, very eventful. As always, the new year began with optimism, with applicants for new franchises and talk of expansion. In early January, a week before the inaugural Super Bowl game, Commissioner Rosen announced that groups from Chicago, Milwaukee, and Little Rock were interested in joining the league.

At the other end of the spectrum, Wheeling, Charleston, and Richmond were tottering. In addition, some resolution was needed for the Brooklyn Dodgers, who'd been operated by the league since the second month of the 1966 season. Montreal appeared to be solvent, but they had a stadium problem. *Les Castors* had been promised seven dates at the Expo 67 site, but wound up with only five, all late in the season when the Canadian weather generally turned bitter. The club tried to obtain some dates at McGill University but was unsuccessful.

At the same time Rosen made the announcement about the interest in Milwaukee, Little Rock, and Chicago, he stated that the Pacific League, an eight team circuit with clubs in California, Oregon, and Canada, would be added as the Golden West Division of the Continental League. The old CFL clubs would continue to have Eastern and Western Divisions, the Golden West clubs would play among themselves, and the Golden West champion would play the winner of a game between the Eastern and Western Divisions for the CFL title.

In May, Rosen raised the possibility of yet another division, a Central Division consisting of the teams of the Professional Football League of America. The merger with the PFLA never materialized and, like their counterparts in the east, the Golden West Division of the CFL gained, lost, and relocated franchises before settling on seven locations. The combination was a loose one, and the Golden West Division operated in a parallel universe. They didn't play the eastern teams, and the eastern press didn't report much about them. The *Courant*, which gave the Oaks consistently good coverage, never mentioned the teams in the Golden West Division nor did they publish their standings.[20]

Gradually, the uncertainty surrounding the CFL was resolved. Robustelli wanted to buy the Brooklyn club, but couldn't raise the money and, as in 1957, the Brooklyn Dodgers left town. The franchise was transferred to Akron, Ohio, into the hands of contractor Frank Hurn. Hurn came in with a big splash, naming former NFL quarterback Tobin Rote as his general manager and Hall of Fame halfback Doak Walker as coach.

The citizens of Wheeling were much more successful than those in Brooklyn, as a "Save the Ironmen" campaign netted $182,000, paying off the team's debt and leaving $25,000 in the coffer for the upcoming season. In another part of West Virginia, the Charleston Rockets declared themselves ready for the 1967 season. One of the key ingredients for the survival of a minor league football franchise is a wealthy investor with deep pockets. The Rockets had the deepest of pockets in 29-year-old John D. (Jay) Rockefeller IV, a stockholder who pledged $76,000 to keep the team afloat. Richmond had neither the small town pride of Wheeling nor a Rockefeller, and surrendered its franchise.

Richmond finished the 1966 season with a 4–10 record and lackluster support, and few were surprised when they ran up the white flag. The other CFL casualty, however, was a shocker. At the end of May, the Philadelphia Bulldogs, champions of the league in 1966, announced they would not field a team in 1967. It was possible, the Philadelphia backers said, that the club might resume operations in 1968 in either Tampa or Charlotte, but there would definitely be no Philadelphia entry in 1967.

There was little doubt that the Hartford franchise would survive, and they focused on two priorities during the spring of 1967. The first was finding a coach to replace Lander. The second was selling enough season tickets to convince potential financiers of the new Windsor Locks stadium that the venture was viable.

7. It's Hard to Be a Major League

Finding a coach was much easier than selling tickets. In early January, Ken Carpenter, a former Cleveland Brown and Canadian League running back, resigned as head coach of the Charleston Rockets because he wasn't sure they would have a team in 1967. When the Brewers went looking for Lander's replacement, Carpenter was an obvious candidate, for he was experienced, respected, well-liked, and unemployed. He signed with the Oaks in early April.

Carpenter was a number one draft choice of the Browns and played in NFL championship games in each of his four years in Cleveland. He then played six seasons in Canada. But a very good player does not necessarily make an inspirational leader. Under Carpenter, the Oaks would play to the level of their ability, and in 1967 a mediocre Hartford team achieved mediocre results.

Most successful professional football coaches are maladjusted individuals who are intense, focused, obsessed, and generally have few interests beyond football. Vince Lombardi was the most successful coach of the 1960s, but if the world was filled with Vince Lombardis, it would be a very difficult place to live.

Fred Wallner was the best coach Hartford ever had, and was as focused and intense as Lombardi, George Allen, or any of the other great coaches of his era. In 1964, Wallner took a modestly talented team and nearly led them to the championship. Later, when Pete Savin gave him the best players money could buy, Wallner's teams dominated the Atlantic Coast League.

Carpenter, 41, was calm and laid-back. "He operates on a low key according to his own timetable," wrote Frank Keyes. "Drills never last more than an hour and a half.... He's all business, yet he'll never be accused of over coaching or slave driving."[21] "The Oregonian—and he's a big, rugged one—is a relaxed, orthodox mentor. He's been described as a coach who plays football according to the book. But he's not ultra conservative, nor is he an innovator or long shot gambler on the gridiron."[22]

Keyes wasn't sure Carpenter's calm demeanor was good for the Oaks. "Coach Ken Carpenter," he wrote a month into the season, "has made nervous Nellies out of many Hartford rooters because of his even temperament and low key approach."[23]

Earlier, following a one-sided loss to Norfolk, Keyes had taken the coach to task. "Take off those kid gloves. You never wore any when you were learning to play this game in a lumber camp out in eastern Oregon." After such a poor performance, Keyes wrote, the antidote was three straight days of scrimmaging. "At least we could determine," he wrote, "who wants to play football and who doesn't."[24]

The effort to sell tickets was named Project 11,000, the number of season passes the Oaks needed to sell to demonstrate to the Winston-Muss Development Corporation of New York that they could put enough bodies in the stadium to pay the rent. The main effort was concentrated on Hartford area businesses and social organizations, who were encouraged to buy blocks of tickets and donate them for the use of underprivileged or handicapped children. The Kiwanis Club pledged its support, as did the Elks, the Jaycees, the Metropolitan Hartford Sports Club, and the Hartford Electric Light Company. The latter organization bought 100 seats, paid for the campaign posters, and agreed that its Men's Club would buy additional tickets. By the end of May, the Oaks had reached 20 percent of their goal.

From that point, however, the effort stagnated, and it became apparent that the Brewers were not going to sell anywhere near 11,000 season tickets. Bill Lee said that the Oaks had not shown the locals enough to justify their support. He lamented the fact that they had traded their leading rusher, Bob Gaiters, to Anaheim and that they were rather lackadaisical about generating publicity. "Whereas other teams in all professional leagues have sent to this desk a stream of pertinent information about training camps and exhibition schedules, the Oaks have offered nothing in that direction. Are they going into a pre-season camp this summer?"[25]

The Oaks did have a pre-season camp, once again at Westminster School, but in deference to Carpenter's relaxed attitude, it started later than that of most clubs and didn't last long. The sprint car session commenced July 28 and culminated with two exhibition games in five days beginning August 12. Carpenter's Oaks lost both games and a cornerback.

Thirty eight players took the charter flight to Montreal for the game against the Beavers, but only 37 came back. The missing one was Chris Mitchell, a quiet youngster from South Carolina State College who was trying to make the Oaks' roster as a defensive back.

When the plane landed in Montreal, Mitchell ate with the team, took the bus to the Beavers' stadium in Verdun, and then disappeared. The last anyone knew of him was that he was overheard asking directions to the Montreal suburb of LaSalle. The police were notified, but after several days there was no inkling as to his whereabouts.

There was trouble in the CFL before the regular season even started. On August 21, Akron owner Frank Hurn fired general manager Tobin Rote and coach Doak Walker. He said the two men weren't giving him adequate performance for the money they were being paid. Rote countered that he hadn't been paid at all and neither had most of the club's creditors. He said Hurn had put just $2,000 of his own funds into the operation.

One of the aggrieved creditors was the Continental Football League, which had not been paid the $50,000 due for the purchase price of the Brooklyn franchise. Since there was no one in the wings waiting to take Hurn's place, however, the other owners were loath to jettison Akron, which would leave the league with an uneven number of teams.

Toronto was also experiencing financial difficulty, and either disbanded or was suspended, depending on whose version was accepted, on September 6. Five days later, at a league meeting in Wheeling, the Toronto franchise was reinstated. The club would play all its games on the road and be supported by the league until Rosen could find a new ownership group. In the interim, the Rifles missed a game with Wheeling, enabling the Ironmen, who'd finished 0–14 in 1966, to gain a win by forfeit.

After playing one game under league auspices, the Rifles went down for the count. The worry about an unbalanced league proved groundless, for Akron was dismissed the same day. The divisions were re-aligned and the schedule redone. Both Toronto and Akron had been in the Northern Division, so Norfolk was moved from the South to create two three team divisions. The league, which had encompassed ten clubs in 1966, was down to six, not counting the teams on the West Coast. The Toronto and Akron players were distributed to the remaining teams in a dispersal draft.

By the time Akron and Toronto folded, the Oaks had gotten off to a good start. They defeated Wheeling in the opening game, lost decisively to Norfolk, and managed to garner wins against the reeling Akron and Toronto clubs before they bit the dust. After four games, Hartford had a two game lead over their three competitors in the Northern Division. Unfortunately, the transfer of Norfolk dropped them into a tie with the Neptunes, who were also 3–1.

The Oaks had a very different roster in 1967 than they had the previous year. Torok returned at quarterback, backed up by former Purdue star and minor league veteran Ron DiGravio and Vidal Carlin, a rookie from North Texas State. Carlin was one of three players sent to Hartford on option by the St. Louis Cardinals.

The top running back was Harry Blackney from Long Island, who was just 19 years old when the season began. Blackney was considered one of the best NFL prospects on the Hartford roster, and Frank Keyes went so far as to say he would risk the family jewels that Blackney would get to an NFL camp before any of a number of Ivy League stars, including Brian Dowling and Calvin Hill.

Fleet Terry Best, returning for a third season, was Hartford's top receiver. Bob Stohrer, another holdover, had a great opening game, catching six passes for 124 yards before fracturing a collarbone, which put him out for the season. Krzemienski, Hartford's best receiver in 1966, was hampered all season by an ankle injury.

The Oaks' good start was a bit deceiving. The opening win was over Wheeling, which hadn't won a game in 1966. The victory was achieved in exciting, come from behind fashion, and even Lee allowed himself to get carried away. "Hartford's Charter Oaks had Dillon Stadium jumping Saturday night," he wrote. "If Charter Oak touchdowns follow the pattern of Saturday night, the City of Hartford had better reinforce the Dillon Stadium bleachers." In a cautionary note he added, "There may be tougher teams in the Continental League than Wheeling."[26]

There were indeed tougher teams than Wheeling—and Toronto and Akron—and when the Oaks played them, they lost—five times in a row. By late October the club was 3–6 and out of contention for the division title. Norfolk, the transferee to the Northern Division, was well out in front with an 8–1 mark.

Lee abandoned his earlier optimism. "There is no fun watching a chronic loser," he whined in the aftermath of the streak. "Even the pass holders begin to yowl when their team has been knocked off five straight."[27]

The roster experienced tremendous turnover. Torok was released, as was star defensive lineman Clem Smarra. Smarra said it was a matter of ridding the team of two hefty salaries, which Don Brewer denied. Stohrer announced that his collarbone had healed and was released. He also claimed the Brewers didn't want to pay him. Running back Cornell Champion was released for what many believed to be the same reason.

In the middle of the week following the fifth consecutive loss, the Oaks did something very unusual for a professional team. Carpenter held a 45-minute scrimmage, which became so lively that a couple of linemen squared off against each other and had to be separated by their teammates. That was just what Keyes had suggested back in the summer when he worried about Carpenter's placid temperament.

Sure enough, the Oaks proceeded to beat Montreal 38–14 in their next game, and Keyes wasted no time making the connection. "Honed by a hard-hitting, head-knocking scrimmage as recently as Thursday," he wrote, "the Oaks finally put one together in which both the offense and defense did a first class job."[28]

The next week, the Oaks posted the first shutout in their three years in the CFL, upsetting the Charleston Rockets, 17–0. Hartford had never beaten the Rockets before, and the previous week Charleston had demolished Wheeling by the score of 75–0, setting a number of league records in the process. How did the Oaks accomplish such an amazing feat? "The resurgence, or the resuscitation," Keyes wrote, "clearly is dated Thursday, October 28. That would be the night ... that the battle of blame was fought with blocks and tackles instead of epithets and scorn."[29] The 28th, of course, was the evening of the fateful scrimmage.

The following week, the effect of the scrimmage had apparently worn off, as division leading Norfolk defeated the Oaks 43–21. The loss was discouraging, but even more daunting was the size of the crowd, which numbered just 4,500, nowhere near the 11,000 needed to prime the pump for the new stadium. The mini-winning streak had not caught the fancy of the Hartford fans, and the meager gathering was about the same as the club had drawn for the previous two games.

The loss to Norfolk was the final game in the history of the Charter Oaks. Although there were two games left on the schedule, both against Montreal, the Oaks and Beavers received permission from the league to cancel them. "Since neither Oak-Beaver game can affect the standings," Sol Rosen said in a formal statement, "both teams were granted permission to close out the season after the Nov. 12 game and begin preparations for 1968."[30]

The most important preparation for the following year was to save the salary and travel expenses that would be incurred by playing the final two games. Despite the optimistic pre-season projections, 1967 had been another difficult year for the Continental League. A few optioned players from the NFL had helped, but not enough. Toronto and Akron had collapsed shortly after the start of the season, and as more evidence was uncovered, it appeared that the Akron owners should never have been admitted in the first place.

Shortly after the franchise was revoked, Summit County prosecutor James Barbuto announced that he planned to summon a grand jury to investigate the Vulcans' collapse. Hurn owed about $85,000 to a number of entities, including Kent State University, where the team conducted its preseason camp, and several hotels. Barbuto wanted to know how much due diligence the league performed before granting Hurn a franchise and how deeply they were involved in the Vulcans' finances.

After the Oaks and Beavers cancelled their final two games, the eastern wing of the CFL was left with just four teams to finish the season. While there was a lot of brave talk about the league coming back stronger than ever in 1968, it was hard to see how that was going to be accomplished. For the Oaks, after a season of disappointing attendance, the prospect of a spanking new stadium in Windsor Locks was a distant dream. And soon, they would even be evicted from tired old Dillon Stadium.

8

Two Steps from the Major Leagues: The Meriden Shamrocks and New Britain Bees

Hartford wanted to be Boston or New York, and on its best days, Meriden thought it could be Hartford. In 1965, Meriden was a blue collar manufacturing city, with a population of just over 50,000. It was strategically located midway between New Haven and Hartford and bisected by Interstate 91, the major highway that would eventually run from New Haven north to the Canadian border. A new thoroughfare, Route 6A, running east to west, opened on October 27, 1965, and would allow motorists to get through Meriden much more quickly, although police hoped not as quickly as the 78 miles per hour registered by Salvatore Cretella of New Haven. Cretella had the honor of earning the first speeding ticket on the new highway ten minutes after the ribbon was cut.

From its beginnings until 1806, Meriden was a section of neighboring Wallingford, and by the twentieth century, it was a melting pot of southern and eastern Europeans and African Americans. The first major wave of immigrants was the Irish, driven to American by the great potato famine of the mid-nineteenth century. By 1910, Italians formed the largest ethnic group, and there were also large numbers of Germans and Poles, all looking for work in Meriden's factories. Following World War II, many African Americans arrived from the south. As in so many northern cities, the arrival of blacks was greeted with apprehension, and in the early 1980s, Meriden acquired unwanted notoriety when the Ku Klux Klan chose the city as the site of some of its most prominent rallies.

In the 1950s, Meriden's major employers were International Silver and New Departure, a division of General Motors. International Silver's business plummeted in the latter part of the decade, when cheaper stainless steel imports increased their market share from 4 percent to 82 percent. President Eisenhower failed to support tariff protection, and Meriden mayor Henry Altobello, on behalf of the 6,500 International Silver employees, sent the president a critical letter. In January 1965, General Motors announced its intention to close the New Departure plant, jeopardizing 1,650 jobs. The decline in employment spurred an exodus to the suburbs.

Meriden was in many ways like Ansonia, a city spun off from a neighboring town whose manufacturing base attracted a diverse population. Meriden did not have Ansonia's mania for football, but the city took parochial pride in its high school sports, and supported a number of minor league baseball teams.

By the 1960s, Meriden was ready for minor league football. The ACFL was a stretch, but there were other possibilities. One of them was the New England Football League which, in 1964, consisted of six Massachusetts and two New Hampshire clubs.

Leagues like the NEFL were closer to the semi-pro circuits that operated in the 1950s than they were to leagues like the Continental that aspired to major league status. The players were mostly local, they were paid very little, often about $25 a game, and the caliber of play was not up to the level of the ACFL and CFL.

End Roger Milici explained the difference between the NEFL and the ACFL. "I think it was the consistency," he said. "There were some good football players in [the NEFL], but there were some weak positions. I could've caught 30 passes a game if they'd thrown to me enough, because the backs couldn't cover me. The Atlantic Coast League was more challenging."

For the 1965 season, the NEFL granted new franchises to three Connecticut cities, Meriden, Ansonia, and Stratford. The franchise that was supposed to be in Stratford eventually wound up in Milford, and the Ansonia team never materialized.

In Meriden, realtor and insurance man Thomas Kelly and his partner, John Matcheski, a former policeman, raised capital, hired Phil Vece as coach, and began to sign players for a team known as the Shamrocks. The prize catch was tight end Tom Rychlec, a Meriden native and a graduate of American International College. Rychlec played with the Detroit Lions in 1958, but was cut in 1959. Coming back to his hometown after a year in the NFL was a humbling experience, and Rychlec wasn't ready for the real world. "I really wasn't interested in a job," he said. "You feel you're superior to everybody. You're in the limelight."

When the AFL was formed in 1960, Rychlec got a second chance. He was the starting tight end for the Buffalo Bills from 1960 to 1962 and caught 84 passes in three years, including a team-leading 45 in 1960. After a few games with the Denver Broncos in 1963, Rychlec was released again at the age of 29.

After he received news of his release, Rychlec was sitting in his hotel room, waiting to clear waivers. He was three games short of qualifying for a pension, and hoped to hook on with some club long enough to get in his time. The phone rang and he jumped to answer it. To his disappointment, the caller was from the Hartford Charter Oaks. Rychlec said he was looking to play in the NFL or AFL and wasn't interested. The man said he would call back later.

An hour passed, and the persistent Charter Oak representative called again; this time Rychlec said yes. He played for Hartford in 1964, but with an opportunity to go back to his hometown, signed with the Shamrocks for 1965.

The quarterback of the Shamrocks was young Larry Marsh, a recent graduate of Norwich University in Vermont and an English teacher at Newington High School. The fullback was 5'10", 228-pound Tony Pontillo, a Bridgeport native who'd starred at Garden City Junior College in Kansas and Panhandle A&M University in Oklahoma. In his first year at Garden City, Pontillo broke the school's single season rushing record despite playing in just five games. The next year he gained 1,250 yards, scored 96 points, and was named to the National Junior College All-American team. In his senior year at Panhandle A&M, he averaged 117 rushing yards per game, again scored 96 points, and was named an honorable mention NAIA All-American.

After his graduation in 1962, Pontillo had a tryout with the Denver Broncos, but at a stumpy 5'10" and without great speed, he wasn't the type of back the pros were looking for. Pontillo's forte was running over people and it was harder to run over big AFL linemen like Ernie Ladd and Earl Faison than it was to run through the defenders in the Frontier Conference. He tried out with Indianapolis of the United League, but had knee problems and returned to school to finish his degree. Then the Shamrocks were formed. "I was coaching at Shelton High School," he said, "but I felt I wasn't done yet."

Pontillo didn't look like a football player. "He looked," said a teammate, "like a fat, out-of-shape guy because he'd had surgery that affected his stomach muscles. He looked kind of like a big-bellied old guy." Coach Gene Casey called him the Dancing Bear.

On the field, however, Pontillo looked every bit the football player. "He was a bull," said teammate John Skubel. "He would just run over people and he had deceptive speed." "He was built like a beer keg," added Bob Kelso. "But when he'd come at you—he could *hit*. He was compact, he was deceiving, and he was damn good. He had good balance and good speed, although to look at him you wouldn't think so."

A number of old Ansonia Black Knights joined the Shamrocks, including Skubel, fleet halfback Tony Tavares, and linebackers Kelso and Bill Richter. The Hartford Charter Oaks had stepped up to the Continental League for the 1965 season, and a few players who couldn't make the grade joined the Shamrocks, including running back Chick Henry.

8. Two Steps from the Major Leagues

Finding players was the easy part of the equation. The challenge for minor league teams was finding enough paying fans to cover expenses. Kelly courted his business associates and hired enthusiastic young Mike O'Connor as public relations director. O'Connor, 21, had just completed his junior year at Central Connecticut State College and had been a part time sportswriter for the *Meriden Record* since his high school days. He was full of fire and he came cheaply.

The Shamrocks encountered a problem as soon as practice began in late June. Regular season games would be played at Ceppa Field, but the grass at Ceppa had recently been seeded and the team was not allowed to practice there. The Shamrocks tried to practice at Washington Park, but stopped after two players were injured on the treacherous surface. Finally, after extensive negotiations with city officials, the Shamrocks received permission to practice on the portions of Ceppa Field where the grass had taken hold. Fans were invited to watch, but Kelly pointed out that they would need to stay off the new grass.

On September 8, the Shamrocks signed defensive back and linebacker Dick Connors. Connors had a glowing football resume, having spent time in the training camp of the New York Giants that summer. He said Giant coach Allie Sherman told him to stay in shape, and if there were injuries in the defensive backfield, he might call him back.

When the *Morning Record* reported on Connors' background, it failed to mention that he had been part of another organization, for which he wore number 20231, a rather high number for a defensive back. The organization was the Connecticut state prison system. Connors spent 15 months at Cheshire Reformatory and 37 months in Wethersfield State Penitentiary.

Born to an absent father and an indifferent mother, Connors was raised by relatives and spent some time in a school for orphans and unruly boys. By the age of twelve, he had become an excellent athlete. After an outstanding freshman season in both football and basketball at Bullard-Havens Technical School in Bridgeport, Connors was thrown off the basketball team, and quit school early in his sophomore year. At the age of 16, he began playing semi-pro football against top clubs like the Franklin Miners and basketball against some of the top high school players in the area.

When he wasn't playing sports, however, Connors was getting into trouble. He hung around street corners and pool halls and discovered heroin. It was love at first sight. Connors began getting high every day, even once before a football game. Needless to say, he didn't play well in the first half, but crashed at halftime and played the second half with a vengeance.

Connors soon began committing crimes to support his habit. In the morning, he and his friends stole copper pipe from construction sites and in the evenings they robbed gas stations. He had excelled at almost everything else in his life, and became a skilled criminal, admired by his peers. "I was still the star of the game," he said later, "but now it was a different game." Connors said that it wasn't hard to avoid criminal prosecution for heroin use, because the drug was so rare the police didn't know what it was.

During one robbery, Connors' accomplice was caught and implicated him. He was sentenced to 18 months to five years in the Cheshire Reformatory. Connors was 19, and his weight, after all the heroin use, was down to 162 pounds. He put his time in Cheshire to good use, earning his high school diploma, gaining 20 pounds, excelling in prison sports, and kicking his heroin habit cold turkey.

Released from prison, Connors got a construction job, started playing semi-pro football again, and moved in with his mother and her new husband. The husband didn't like the idea of having his wife's ex-convict son in the house, and one night crushed up some antihistamine pills, put them in tinfoil next to the sleeping Connors' bed, and called the police. The police said it was the purest heroin they'd ever seen and packed Connors off to a Hartford jail, where he remained for 30 days until laboratory tests revealed the true contents of the foil package.

Even though Connors had been exonerated, no one believed him. He lost his construction job, went back to heroin and was arrested a dozen times. Sent to a federal drug program at a Lexington, Kentucky prison, he was declared cured, but shot up twenty feet beyond the prison wall after his release. Arrested for larceny in 1961, he was declared a hopeless drug addict and sent to the Wethersfield State Penitentiary.

At Wethersfield, Connors decided to turn his life around. He lifted weights, played basketball and football, and became the best athlete in the prison. He also began to read and think deeply about his life. Connors became a prison celebrity, completing his image with a beautiful blond girlfriend who arrived nearly every visiting day.

Connors never used drugs after he was released from prison in 1963. He got a job as a sheetrocker and worked himself into top condition. One day in July 1965, he left work early and drove to the training camp of the New York Giants in Fairfield. Leaping over the restraining ropes separating the spectators from the players, he approached coach Allie Sherman and asked for a tryout. He said he was 23 years old and had played at the University of Miami. Things were different in 1965, and rather than call security, Sherman looked at Connors' fit build and told him to suit up.

Connors impressed the Giants with his athleticism, but was hampered by his lack of knowledge. He had, after all, acquired virtually all of his football experience on prison teams. Connors survived the first two cuts, but as time went on, he noticed the veterans were avoiding him. He suspected they had

8. Two Steps from the Major Leagues

learned of his past. Connors didn't survive the third cut, and joined the Hartford Charter Oaks. After a couple of games, he left and arrived in Meriden to play for the Shamrocks.

Phil Vece had been fired the day before Connors was signed. Vece had been irritated by what he deemed to be interference on the part of the owners, claiming they came up to him on the sidelines during games with substitution suggestions. "We just didn't see eye to eye," he said.[1]

Ironically, Fred Wallner had resigned as head coach of the Hartford Charter Oaks the same day Vece was fired, also over resentment about owner interference. There were rumors that Wallner would be the next Shamrock mentor, but Kelly selected injured linebacker Bob Kelso to succeed Vece.

There was a lot going on during the second week of September. The Shamrocks fired their coach, the Charter Oak coach quit, and attorney Alan Solomon, one of the members of the Meriden ownership syndicate, sent a telegram to Don Brewer offering to buy the Charter Oaks for $50,000. Solomon said he and his partners had been so encouraged by Meriden's support of the Shamrocks that they were ready to expand their horizons. If the offer was accepted, the syndicate would operate both clubs, and might use the Shamrocks as a farm club for the Charter Oaks. Brewer did not respond.

Despite the distractions, the Shamrocks were doing very well on the field. Kelso made a victorious debut, as his club beat the South Boston Chippewas 41–14 before an encouraging crowd of 4,100 at Ceppa Field. After five games, the Shamrocks were right in the middle of the NEFL race.

Portland	5	1
Meriden	4	1
Nashua	3	1
Milford	3	2
Brockton	3	3
South Boston	1	5
Whitman	0	6

The next two weeks would be critical, as the Shamrocks faced back to back games against Nashua, the first in Meriden and the second in Nashua. The Shamrocks predicted a crowd of more than 6,000 in Meriden and the Colts expected 8,000–9,000 at Nashua's Holman Stadium. Nashua's high powered offense was the most explosive in the NEFL, averaging nearly seven touchdowns a game. At the helm was former Syracuse quarterback Dave Sarette, who led the Orangemen to the Orange and Liberty Bowls.

At Meriden, the attendance of 5,400 was close to the predicted crowd, and the Shamrocks came close to defeating the Colts, losing a hard-fought 32–30 battle. The game featured the punishing running attack of the Colts against the passing of Marsh and Jerry Johnson, the former Charter Oak quarterback who'd been signed two weeks earlier.

Late in the third quarter, with the Colts holding a 32–14 lead, Marsh passed his club down the field and hit Rychlec with a 12-yard touchdown pass, and again for the two-point conversion to narrow the gap to 32–22. With four minutes left in the game, Marsh hit Rychlec with a 31-yard scoring pass, and once again for the two-point conversion to make the score 32–30, a field goal away from victory.

The Shamrock defense held, and Marsh got the ball back on the Meriden 41 with 1:30 remaining. He completed two passes, the second to Rychlec at the Nashua 41. The tight end attempted to lateral to a teammate, but his fumble was recovered by Nashua and the last Shamrock hope was extinguished. Still, it had been an exciting game before a big crowd, "one of the most spectacular football shows ever staged at Ceppa Field"[2] according to the *Morning Record,* one which would hopefully whet the fans' appetite for more Shamrock football.

There had been an unsettling aspect to the large crowd, however. In addition to whetting their appetites, the fans had been wetting their whistles. No alcohol was sold at Ceppa, but many people brought their own supply and some consumed far too much of it. Others complained and the Meriden Recreation Department ordered the Shamrocks to put a stop to the imbibing.

The following week, Nashua again beat Meriden, this time by a 43–33 margin. After the second defeat, the Shamrocks were two games behind Nashua and Portland, each of which had a 6–1 mark to Meriden's 4–3, with just five games left in the season.

Despite drawing good crowds, the Shamrocks were experiencing financial problems. For the eighth game of the season, the players volunteered to waive their salaries and spare the club the $2,500 weekly burden. Playing for free didn't impact the quality of the team's performance, as they beat the Whitman Townies easily, 42–20. The following week, however, the Shamrocks lost to quarterback Sam Coppola and the Milford Rockets 32–21, seemingly putting an end to their championship aspirations. The top two teams qualified for the playoffs and the 5–4 Shamrocks were in fourth place.

Portland	8	1
Nashua	7	3
Milford	6	3
Meriden	5	4
Brockton	5	4
South Boston	2	9
Whitman	0	9

For the remaining three games of the season, the Shamrocks hired Fred Wallner as an "advisor" to assist coach Kelso and consult with the club on business matters. Kelly denied that Wallner would coach the team in 1966, stating that the former Hartford coach had "bigger things in mind for himself."

Apparently, Wallner gave the Shamrocks good advice, for they won their final three games, which placed them in a tie with second place Nashua for the final playoff berth. One of the wins was over the Brockton Pros by the convincing margin of 55–13 before a very sparse crowd in Eldon B. Keith Field. "It was the bowels of the football world," said John Skubel. "There wasn't a blade of grass on the field and there were maybe two or three toilets that worked. We were so pissed off that we just killed them. Tony Pontillo ran wild."

The Shamrocks would play Nashua in Meriden to determine which team would face Portland for the NEFL title, and they would do so without head coach Bob Kelso. Kelso had become increasingly annoyed with Wallner, and during the final game of the regular season, as he stood seething on the sidelines, Kelso made up his mind to quit. Wallner, he said, had usurped his authority, completely taken over the defense, and was making substitutions without Kelso's knowledge or consent.

Wallner and the Shamrock owners expressed surprise and regret. "I am very surprised," Wallner said. "I never suspected that anything was wrong between us and never intended such to be the case."[3] Public Relations Director O'Connor said the club would talk to Kelso and try to convince him to revoke his resignation.

Kelso, who hadn't really wanted to coach in the first place, held firm. "He was very aggressive," Kelso said recently of Wallner, "so I said the hell with it. I let it go. For the money I was making it wasn't worth the aggravation. I didn't need confrontation of that kind. I didn't need somebody who was supposed to be my assistant taking over."

As expected, Wallner was named head coach. At Kelly's request, Captain Skubel made a public statement supporting the new coach. "I tried to be fair to both sides," he said. "What I was trying to do was keep the team together. Otherwise we were going to break apart and there wouldn't be a team."

NEFL rosters had been frozen, but before the regular season finale with Milford, the Shamrocks reached agreement with the Rockets to allow Milford to use newly-acquired fullback Bill Strumpke while the Meriden club added linebacker Bill Lesinski, who'd played for Wallner with the Charter Oaks. For the playoff game, Nashua agreed to let the Shamrocks use Lesinski and Rich King, the defensive back whose tongue-lashing at the hands of Hartford owner Don Brewer had led to Wallner's resignation. In return, Nashua would also add two players not previously on their roster.

Even without formal negotiations, NEFL rosters were often fluid, and occasionally men played under assumed names. Dick Bowman, then playing with the Charter Oaks, remembered going to a game in Meriden to watch his buddy Gus Giardi play for Nashua.

"My wife and I went down to watch the game," he said, "and I'm having a beer in the stands and I got really excited. I had a few beers and then at halftime I went down to see if I could suit up. I suited up and played the second half for Nashua in a uniform that didn't fit. That was crazy. You can get hurt like that. But it was fun."

The Shamrocks defeated the Colts 24–12, as Pontillo thundered for 205 yards. He broke the 1,000 yard barrier with a 73-yard touchdown ramble during the second period. Two of the Meriden points came when Lesinski blocked a punt out of the end zone for a safety.

The win set up a title game between the underdog Shamrocks and the Portland Mustangs at Ceppa Field on November 21. It was a great night for the Shamrocks, the only disappointment being a crowd which numbered just 3,800. Wallner's swarming defense harassed Portland quarterback Ron DiGravio all night and the only Mustang touchdown came after they recovered a fumble on the Meriden 10 yard line. Meriden native Bill Boehle, a former Charter Oak playing his only Shamrock game, caught a touchdown pass, as did Rychlec.[4]

Pontillo scored on a 50-yard run and defensive back Jerry Johnson returned a fumble 49 yards for a fourth touchdown. The Shamrocks had a 28–6 victory and an NEFL championship in their first season. "That was a great game," said Pontillo. "When we beat them they were sick. They were literally sick. They were good sports but they never thought we would beat them."

It was not certain the Shamrocks would be around to defend their title in 1966. If they did, it would be without Wallner, for in early January, he signed to coach the newly-minted ACFL franchise in New Haven. It would also be without the previous year's owners, for on January 26 Matcheski, speaking on behalf of the investor group, announced that the team was for sale. It took a lot of money and time to operate the franchise, Matcheski said, and the owners hadn't enough of either.

On March 11, Kelly announced that the effort to sell the club had failed and the franchise was dropping out of the NEFL. Less than three weeks later, however, the Shamrocks were back, as Matcheski acquired a 100 percent interest in the team and stated his intention of rejoining the league. He invited all members of the 1965 squad to a meeting at the Broadview Restaurant at which he described his plans for the coming season. To replace Wallner, Matcheski hired Gene Casey, ACFL coach of the year with the 1962 Ansonia Black Knights.

Whitman and Brockton dropped out, and the NEFL fielded just five teams in 1966: Meriden, Bridgeport, Nashua, South Boston, and Portland. The schedule was reduced to eight games. The Shamrocks, determined to remedy the attendance and consequent financial problems of 1965, accelerated their marketing efforts. They formed a Shamrock Booster Club and at the first exhibition game gave away a Honda motorbike, two bicycles, and two autographed footballs, all donated by members of the Booster Club.

The Shamrocks began the regular season by winning their first three games, without a close call. They scored 101 points and held their opponents to just 22. Marsh and Pontillo sparkled on offense, as did Warren Miller, a swift halfback from Southern Connecticut whose speed complemented the power of Pontillo. The defense, led by Dick Connors, was virtually impregnable. What more could a Shamrock fan want?

They must have wanted something, for not enough were trekking to Ceppa Field to allow Matcheski to pay the bills. Only 1,300 had attended the recent Milford game. On September 10, sports editor Cliff Burton wrote an article in the *Morning Record* headlined "Shamrocks 'Hurting' at Gate."[5]

"Help Wanted," the piece began, "3,500 males and females to gather within the confines of Ceppa Field tonight to make the Shamrocks football game with the Maine Mustangs a financial success. The crowds at the first four games have indicated that there just aren't enough interested fans here and in neighboring Wallingford to make the Shamrocks a financial success.... If the people don't turn out to see tonight's final home game of September ... then it certainly seems that the city of Meriden sadly, but truly neither wants nor deserves a football team of the Shamrocks caliber."

Burton rattled off potential objections to attending a Shamrock game and countered them all. The price was reasonable, cheaper than that charged by the Hartford Charter Oaks or Waterbury Orbits. Yes, some fans were offended by the drinking habits of other patrons, but that was nothing unusual at sporting events. Finally, Burton defended the caliber of play in the NEFL, and extolled the talent on the local club.

The week after Burton's article appeared, the Shamrocks had another disappointing crowd. On September 20, Meriden public relations director Don Fass appeared on Dick Bertel's Americana show on WTIC radio and said the Shamrocks could soon become "a team without a city."[6] Matcheski said that the fate and future of his club would be determined by the support received for the game against Nashua on October 8. "We can't afford to keep going," he said, "with the small crowds we have drawn to date."[7]

Nearly every game included a special promotion, including Bridgeport Night, when the Shamrocks from that city were honored and Bridgeport residents were encouraged to attend. The game against the Milford Rockets was designated Middletown night, and captain John Skubel, a native of that city, was honored by Middletown mayor Kenneth Dooley. Another evening was Wallingford Night, honoring the Wallingford players and featuring Miss Wallingford of 1966. If Miss Wallingford couldn't attract male football fans, perhaps they didn't deserve the Shamrocks.

In the two weeks prior to the Nashua game, the Shamrocks saw their winning streak ended by the Rockets, who beat them 41–13, and then traveled to Portland, where they were pre-ordained to suffer a financial loss no matter what the outcome on the field. All the Shamrocks would receive would be the $500 minimum guarantee, which would not come close to covering salaries and the cost of the long bus ride to Maine. In addition to the cost of the bus, the club incurred the expense of a chartered plane to transport five players who had high school coaching duties in the afternoon.

Nashua, a strong club in 1965, was even better in 1966. The New Bedford Sweepers of the Atlantic Coast League had disbanded, and a number of its players signed with South Boston and Nashua. The Colts were undefeated when they came to Meriden to play the Shamrocks.

They left on the short end of a 25–21 score, as Pontillo led a Meriden ground attack that gained nearly 200 yards. With a 4–1 record, the Shamrocks moved in front of Nashua, which was 3–1. Attendance was 3,500, a little more than what the Shamrocks had been averaging, but not encouraging for a game against the best team in the league.

The Shamrocks lost their next game, falling to the Colts by a 21–13 score at Nashua. Going into the last weekend in October, the Shamrocks were 4–2, a game behind the 5–1 Colts. As in 1965, the top two teams would meet in the title game, and Meriden clinched a playoff spot with an easy 34–6 win over South Boston. The Shamrocks' final game, against Portland, was won by forfeit. Mustang coach Dan Mahoney called Matcheski early in the week and told him the Portland squad was down to just 18 players and could not make a representative showing.

Nashua could tie Meriden with a win in its final game, while a loss would place them in a second place tie with Bridgeport and necessitate a playoff between the latter two clubs for the right to play the Shamrocks for the championship.

Nashua beat South Boston 27–13 and the title game was scheduled for Saturday, November 12 at Ceppa Field. At stake was $400 for the winners and $300 to the losers—for the entire team. The two clubs had fought evenly over the past two years and the matchup seemed to be a good one. Casey went on the local ABC and NBC affiliates to promote the game. "[T]onight's crowd," the *Record* predicted with its usual optimism, "should be the best of the season at the Harrison Street battlegrounds."[8]

8. Two Steps from the Major Leagues

The crowd, 3,000 strong, was not the best of the season, but the game was a dilly. Early in the second quarter, Nashua had a 14–0 lead. The Shamrocks drove down the field and reached the Colts' nine-yard line, from which Marsh hit end Tom Morgan with a touchdown pass. Al Freiheit's conversion was partially blocked and the score was 14–6.

Early in the third quarter, Meriden halfback Warren Miller ran 15 yards for a score, but a two-point conversion attempt failed and the Shamrocks trailed by two, 14–12. After Nashua scored and converted once more, Herb Sutton ran the ensuing kickoff back 97 yards to make the score 21–19. The Shamrock defense held and an 18-yard punt gave them the ball in good field position.

Marsh hit Rychlec with two passes that brought the ball to the Nashua 24, where the drive stalled with five minutes to go in the game. Freiheit came on the field to attempt a field goal that, if successful, would give the Shamrocks the lead. Ceppa was a high school field and the goal posts were at the back of the end zone, so the attempt was from 41 yards. Freiheit hit the ball solidly and it sailed toward the goal posts. Referee Walter Bell started to raise his arms, hesitated, and then indicated that the ball had sailed to the left of the uprights. The fans booed and the Shamrocks were furious, but the call stood and the Colts ran out the clock. The Shamrocks had to settle for second place and the $300 loser's share.

Miller led the league in rushing with 423 yards and a 6.6 average, and was named rookie of the year. He didn't make the all star team, but eight Shamrocks did, including Pontillo, Connors, Skubel, Rychlec, defensive end Joe Genovese, defensive tackle George Bauman, and defensive backs Lennie Tremaglio and Jerry Johnson.

There was no professional football in Meriden in 1967. Shortly after the championship game, it was announced that Matcheski had sold the franchise to a group from New Britain that would field a team in the North American Football League.

New teams like the New Britain Bees kept popping up because there never seemed to be a shortage of men who thought they could operate a professional football franchise. A flag bearer was shot down and bloodied, and there was always someone willing to pick up the standard and carry it forward. Professional football struggled in its first year in Meriden, but John Matcheski took over for Tom Kelly in 1966. After a second year of losses, Matcheski wanted out and up stepped Charles Koenig, a former advertising executive and vice president of sales at a Newington car dealership.

Koenig's group included Jerry Goeke, who was also affiliated with the dealership, and attorney Mitchell Gardner. Fresh and full of innocent enthusiasm, they obtained the use of Willow Brook Park, scraped together enough money to get started, and launched their team with a flourish. In early June, the Bees hosted a kickoff luncheon attended by more than one hundred people and featuring an appearance by Linda Santa Cruz of Arkansas, an 18-year-old beauty crowned Miss Honey Bee by the American Federation of Beekeepers. Several less pulchritudinous football types, the most prominent of whom was New York Giant quarterback Gary Wood, also attended as the undefeated Bees, their coffers full, predicted great things for their maiden season.

In the 1920s, New Britain had quite a formidable semi-pro club, and teams featuring stars like Jim Thorpe, Red Grange, and Notre Dame's Four Horsemen appeared in the Hardware City. The New York Giants, the New York Yankees, the Providence Steamroller, and others brought their teams to New Britain, but when the NFL became more structured, the visits stopped, and there had been no professional football in the city for 40 years.

The North Atlantic Football League had no Thorpes or Granges, or even Gary Woods. It was a brand new five-team circuit, operating under the leadership of Commissioner James Westhaver of Stamford. The New Hampshire Colts, based in Nashua, and the Bridgeport Rockets (FKA the Milford Rockets and the Connecticut Rockets) had been members of the now defunct NEFL, while the other NAFL teams were the Jersey Generals, Hudson Valley Vikings (sometimes referred to as the New York Vikings), and the Bees. The Vikings appeared to be the strongest team in the league. They hired former Eagle great Steve Van Buren as coach and signed a number of ex–Continental League players.

Many familiar names appeared on the Bees' roster. The coach was former Charter Oak and Waterbury Orbit mentor Fred Wallner. Quarterback Larry Marsh, who'd set a number of passing records in Meriden, agreed to follow the franchise to New Britain. He was joined by a number of former Shamrocks, including tight end Tom Rychlec, fullback Tony Pontillo, halfback Warren Miller, kicker Al Freiheit, and defensive back Jerry Johnson. Running back Tommy Morris of the University of Idaho came from the Waterbury Orbits, as did defensive lineman Dick Bowman. Just before the opening game, the Bees were strengthened by the addition of 6'5" former Central Connecticut tight end John Mulligan, who had been in camp with the New York Giants.

Meanwhile, Koenig attempted to drum up local support, making the rounds of civic clubs and hosting a press conference that was covered by WTIC television and all the local papers. The Bees were the beneficiaries of a supportive press, with the *New Britain Herald* leading the way. The *Herald* provided frequent coverage, urged the fans to go to the games, and predicted great results and robust attendance.

The Bees justified the *Herald's* confidence by winning both of their exhibition games, the first a surprising victory over the 1966 NEFL champion New

Hampshire Colts. Unfortunately, an element beyond the control of Koenig rained on his parade. Both games were at home, and both were played in terrible, rainy weather. Only 1,500 braved the elements for the New Hampshire game, which the *Herald* declared "one of the most exciting grid battles seen here in a long time."[9] "Certainly," it continued, "if that is the brand of ball the Bees are to play this season, capacity crowds will turn out to see them." But they wouldn't turn out if it continued to rain.

The Bees' first regular season game was on the road against the New Jersey Generals at Asbury Park, New Jersey on August 10. The Generals were coached and quarterbacked by 43-year-old former AFL signal caller Butch Songin, the same Butch Songin who had declared himself retired after his final game with the Hartford Charter Oaks in 1966. Like the Vikings, the Generals had a number of former Continental League players and had been organized several months before the New Britain club.

The Bees upset the Generals 10–7. Mulligan caught six of Marsh's passes for 91 yards and Al Freiheit's 31-yard field goal in the third quarter was the winning margin. Wallner's club had surprised everyone, including Robin Spencer of the *Herald,* who took the four-hour bus ride to Asbury Park to cover the game. "From watching the Bees play against Butch Songin and his boys," Spencer said, "one would never guess these fellows have only been playing together for a few short weeks."[10]

The Bees' home opener was also a success, as they beat the Rockets 14–3 before approximately 5,000 fans. The spectators had difficulty following the action, for someone had broken into the New Britain locker room before the game and stolen all of the club's home uniforms. The Bees played in their road uniforms, while the Rockets wore their red and white home outfits. The numbers of the home and road uniforms were different and the program had the wrong numbers.

Both natural and man-made disasters plagued the second home game, in which the Bees beat New Hampshire. Rain caused the game to be postponed until Sunday evening, and the start on Sunday was delayed due to a failure of a portion of the lighting system. Once, after the game was started with limited illumination, the ball had to be moved to the opposite side of the field to enable New Britain punter Bill Boehle to see the pass from center.

The Bees split their next two games, losing 36–21 to New Jersey and beating Bridgeport 3–0 on Freiheit's field goal. Freiheit, a Glastonbury police officer and a veteran of the Charter Oaks and Shamrocks, didn't have much range, but a kicker who was reliable on extra points and short field goals was a valuable man on a minor league roster.

Freiheit played two years of football at Denver University, but when the

Al Freiheit puts his old-fashioned square-toed kicking shoe into the ball (photograph from Hartford Charter Oaks program).

school terminated the program, he transferred to West Virginia University and played soccer. Despite his soccer background, Freiheit kicked a football in straight-on, conventional style. "It's very hard to kick a football soccer-style in the pros," he said. "In college you can tee the ball up and get more height. In the pros you have to kick the ball from the ground. It's very hard to get the ball up high enough to get over the rushing linemen only seven yards away from you. Besides, it takes a different set of muscles and different coordination."

In the Bridgeport game, the Bees also received a great effort from linebacker Bob Risley, who blocked two field goals and anchored a ferocious New Britain defense. In the third quarter, Risley took a hard shot to the head and had to be helped to the sidelines. He sat on the ground, clearly dazed, in a moment captured by the *Herald* photographer. Today, he would have been taken to a hospital for post-concussion evaluation. It was 1967, however, and Risley went back into action and blocked his second field goal attempt of the evening.

The win over Bridgeport set up a confrontation between the New York Vikings (4–0) and the Bees (4–1) that would decide first place in the NAFL. The New Yorkers had a tremendous size advantage over the Bees, with a defensive front that averaged 300 pounds. Bob Van Nasse weighed 335 and teammate Jerry James 325. Across the line, Bee center Ted Jartos weighed 215.

"Fans who turn out to root for New Britain's Bees against the New York Vikings Saturday night at Willow Brook Park," the *Herald* cautioned, "might be advised not to stand too close to the sidelines.... If one of those Viking monsters accidentally fell on an ordinary citizen it might add up to quite a few lost work hours ... did you happen to catch some of the weights of those gorillas announced in yesterday's *Herald*?"[11]

In addition to being big, the Viking players were highly credentialed for a league like the NAFL. Many of them came from the Continental League, some had played in Canada and tackle Carmen Cavalli played the entire 1960 season with the Oakland Raiders. Halfback Mike Hagler had starred in the Rose Bowl, in Canada, the ACFL, and the Continental League. Quarterback Seiki Murono had backed up Bob Brodhead with the 1966 Continental League champion Philadelphia Bulldogs.

Murono, a 23-year-old Japanese American, had an interesting background for a professional football player. Anyone of Japanese heritage born in 1944 is likely to have a noteworthy story, and that of Murono is chilling.[12] Seiki's father, Ginzo Murono, was born in Kyoto, Japan and moved to Peru to join his uncle, who'd started a business specializing in the unlikely combination of office supplies and sporting goods. The uncle died, and Ginzo, along with a partner, acquired the business.

On January 6, 1943, Ginzo, his wife, and his two children spent the afternoon at the shore with his partner's family. At around 7 p.m. they drove to the latter's home and found two Peruvian policemen waiting for them. The police told Murono's partner they were taking him into custody by order of the United States government. An hour later they returned and took Murono as well.

When Murono arrived at the police station, he was placed in a basement with about 60 other Japanese, who had been rounded up on the premise that they were a threat to the security of the United States. The next morning, the prisoners were loaded into three trucks and driven for two days, without food, to the port of Talara, where they boarded the American ship *Frederic C. Johnson*.

The journey to San Francisco took three weeks, during which conditions were miserable and the passengers were given little food. When Murono arrived in the United States, he was asked two questions. Was he an American citizen? He was not. Did he have a visa to enter the United States? When he said he did not, he was arrested as an illegal alien. After a few days in San Francisco, the prisoners were sent to the Kennedy Internment Camp in Texas, where Murono spent six months before being transferred to Crystal City Camp in Crystal City, Texas.

Murono's family had no knowledge of his whereabouts until he was allowed to send a letter to his wife six months later. Ginzo told her he was safe, and that she had two options. She could wait for his return, or in six months, when the United States sent a ship for the prisoners' families, she could join him. Mrs. Murono packed two suitcases and, with her two small children in tow, abandoned the business, five thousand acres of land, and the life she had known in Peru for an unknown future in a hostile America.

Seiki Murono at Franklin and Marshall College (courtesy Seiki Murono).

The Muronos reunited in Crystal City and it was there that Seiki, their second son, was born. When the war ended, the Murono family accepted a U.S. government offer to settle in Seabrook, New Jersey, with the prospect of jobs at Seabrook Farms Frozen Foods. It was a giant step down from Ginzo's life as a prosperous Peruvian businessman, but a significant step up from that of prisoner.

Seiki (who did not speak any Japanese) and his

8. Two Steps from the Major Leagues

older brother quickly acclimated to life in New Jersey and both played high school football well enough to be recruited by Franklin and Marshall College, a small Division III school in Lancaster, Pennsylvania. Seiki captained the football and baseball teams and in football was twice chosen Most Valuable Player of the Middle Atlantic Football Conference. As a relatively unpolished quarterback from a small school, however, he received no offers from the NFL or AFL. He took a job with Chase Manhattan Bank in New York and commuted to Philadelphia to play for the Bulldogs on weekends. When the Philadelphia team disbanded during the offseason, Murono signed with the Vikings.

During the week before the Viking game, Wallner added a quarterback of his own, veteran Manch Wheeler, who'd played for him in Waterbury the previous year and had just been released by the Orbits. Marsh had been hampered by an injury, and the possibility of him ending up under a 335-pounder sent Wallner scurrying for an experienced backup.

The luster of the confrontation between the league's two best teams was tarnished by a mid-week announcement that the Bees were experiencing financial difficulties, and that they were not the only NAFL team short of cash. Koenig supposedly had incurred a deficit of $31,000 and it was reported that the Vikings had a shortfall of $40,000; apparently feeding those 300-pounders was expensive.

There were a number of rumors about the Bees' financial status. One of the false ones, Koenig claimed, was the size of the loss. The $31,000 represented total expenditures, he said, and the net loss was only $11,000. He also denied that (i) the club had unpaid bills; (ii) the local high schools would be unable to play night games because the Bees had not paid their lighting bills; and (iii) the club's insurance policy had been cancelled for non-payment.

The New Britain owner said it had been suggested to him that the club would be profitable if it either moved back to Meriden or joined the ACFL. He said he planned to do neither and was determined to stick it out in New Britain with the NAFL. The two upcoming games with the Vikings (by a quirk of the schedule, the Bees had back to back contests against the New Yorkers) would determine the fate of the franchise.

"We're going to play," Koenig vowed, "if I have to ring doorbells and sell the tickets myself."[13] He said he had called the Vikings twice during the week and confirmed they would show up in New Britain on Saturday night. That was encouraging but somewhat unsettling, for that same weekend Green Bay was scheduled to play in Chicago, and George Halas did not announce that he had spoken with Vince Lombardi and been assured the Packers would show up on Sunday.

A couple of days before the big game, Viking coach Van Buren came to

New Britain as living proof that his club intended to play at Willow Brook Park Saturday night. The coach's visit was a public relations coup. He stopped by a local luncheonette to talk football with the patrons, and took in half of the Pulaski-Wilbur Cross high school game.

On Saturday night, the Bees, the Vikings, and a disappointing total of just 3,500 fans showed up at Willow Brook Park. The lure of the Vikings was offset by the uncertainty surrounding the status of the teams and the league. The Bees and their fans had a better time than the Vikings, as the home club was victorious by a convincing 34–17 score. Quarterbacks Marsh and Wheeler threw over and around the 300-pounders, accumulating 298 passing yards, the final New Britain touchdown coming on an 80-yard pass from Wheeler to John Wardlaw. At the end of the evening, the New Britain Bees occupied first place with a 5–1 record.

And there they stayed. On September 25, Gino Quiriconi, president of the Bridgeport Rockets, announced that the NAFL was ceasing operations for the season due to financial problems. "We went up to practice one day," said New Britain defensive back Joel Cooney, "and there was no practice." The league might try to play in 1968, Quiriconi said, but there would be no more games in 1967.

On October 7, the *Herald* ran a short filler piece headlined "Future of Bees Remains a Mystery."[14] The next mention of the club was the announcement later that month that John Matcheski was suing Koenig and his associates for failure to pay the remainder of the purchase price of the Shamrock franchise. There would be no more professional football in New Britain.

With New Britain out of the picture, professional football returned to Meriden in 1968. In late February, Kelly announced the formation of a franchise in another new circuit, the Eastern Football League. He hired Gene Casey as coach and began to sign players.

The 1968 and 1969 seasons were disappointing and devoid of the excitement generated by the champions of 1965 and the runners-up of 1966. The Eastern Football League was a weak organization comprised in 1968 of the Shamrocks and four clubs from the Massachusetts towns of Malden, Marlboro and Dorchester, and the New Hampshire town of Rochester.

Many of the old Shamrocks returned to the fold, including Marsh, Pontillo and fleet split end Tom Morgan. "Tom was about 160 pounds and he could run," said Pontillo. "We'd put him in and tell him to run as fast as he could. Larry would throw the ball 60 yards and then we'd get him out of the game. Tom never wanted to get hit so he'd run like hell. He didn't want to get touched so he'd run faster than everybody."

The biggest name associated with the 1968 Shamrocks was in the broadcast booth. Games were taped and played on WMMW during the daytime (the station went off the air in the evening), with Joe Castiglione, now the radio voice of the Boston Red Sox, doing play by play, color, and engineering.

At the end of the regular season, the Shamrocks were in second place with a 4–3–1 record and qualified to play first place Marlboro for the league title. The tie game, a 12–12 deadlock with the Rochester club, also known as Tri-City, featured a very controversial ending. The Shamrocks were handicapped by the absence of Marsh, who was unable to make the trip, and further hindered by the officials, who marked off 92 yards in penalties against them and only 27 against Tri-City.

The most egregious officiating came after Meriden tied the game 12–12 with 1:30 remaining on a pass from backup quarterback Beau Billingsley to Morgan. The Shamrocks had a very good kicker, soccer stylist Carl Morello, and seemed certain to get the extra point and the victory. A full two seconds before the snap count, a Tri-City lineman burst across the line, leveled Morello and injured him so severely he had to leave the game. Tri-City was penalized for being offside but not for a personal foul. Without a kicker, the Shamrocks had to try for two points, and Pontillo bulled over the goal line for an apparent 14–12 lead. An official, however, claimed that Pontillo's forward progress had been stopped on the one and disallowed the points.

After the game, Casey was livid. "It was pathetic," he said of the officiating. "They stunk up the joint."

Marlboro coach Bob Brennan, whose team had lost in Rochester, concurred. "They're the worst I've ever seen," he said, "real bad. Heck, they penalized Malden 200 yards."[15]

Marlboro, as the regular season champion, had the right to determine the site of the championship game. They wanted to play at home but, since Marlboro had no lights at their field, the Shamrocks preferred to play in Meriden, in the belief that a night game would draw a larger crowd.

Attendance for the year had been disappointing, with crowds much smaller than those of the Shamrocks' first two seasons, and Kelly wasn't enthusiastic about busing his club to Marlboro for another meager payday. Pontillo said he would not play unless the game was at Ceppa Field. "That's how I felt," he said recently, "because I owed something to Meriden. They took me into their arms and treated me like one of their own." When Marlboro refused to come to Connecticut, the Shamrocks' board of directors voted not to play the game and the season ended on a disappointing note.

The 1969 season was even worse. The Meriden club had a new name, the Falcons, and a new coach, Joe Gresko, but they had many of the same players, including Marsh and Pontillo. A second running back, and sometimes quarterback, was Jim Gabriel, the former Ansonia Black Knight who had been released from prison. As in the case of Dick Connors, the press made no mention of Gabriel's past.

Many of the Falcons had high school coaching jobs, and on Saturdays their scholastic commitments often prevented them from playing if the Falcons were on the road. For a game in New Bedford, the team brought just 18 players, and lost 48–30.

The Falcons finished with a losing record, and the crowds were small, just a few hundred for home games. After a 22–20 win over Portland before just 450 fans, the *Record* said, "Those who stayed away missed an exciting hard fought game."[16]

For two years professional football in Meriden had been great fun, with crowds of 3,000 or 4,000, which, although not enough to generate a profit, was probably the best Meriden could do. Those who supported the team loved their Shamrocks. "When we went on the road we've have 10 or 15 cars full of fans following the bus," said Pontillo, who had a sandwich named after him at a local shop. "There wasn't anything we couldn't do in that town."

Despite their financial troubles, Kelly and Matcheski were supportive, generous owners. They were at every game and attended most practices. When Skubel injured his knee in 1966, the owners insisted on paying his salary for the remainder of the year. "They took it out of their own pockets," he said. "They used to have a party after almost every game at Kelly's house, where he had an indoor pool. We were a close team because we got together after the game, not just us but our girlfriends and wives."

The Shamrocks had, in fact, provided Skubel with his wife. After the games, he usually stopped at the concession stand, where he took particular notice of a pretty young blond volunteer. One night he asked if he could give her a ride home, but the young lady said she lived close by and would walk. "I wasn't too quick on my feet," Skubel said. "I didn't realize I could have walked her home." But Skubel was persistent, and they soon began dating and eventually married.

The Falcons were transplanted to Southington for the 1970 season to play as the Southington Gems. Marsh was the quarterback, general manager, and one of five owners. Rich Balducci, an assistant coach at East Catholic, was another owner and served as head coach. Jim Gabriel was the fullback and Balducci's assistant.

The Gems played at Southington High School and, while they said their eventual goal was an ACFL franchise, the level of talent in the Eastern League was nowhere near that of the Atlantic Coast League. There were no former NFL players on the roster, and the players' names were recognizable only to local residents who recalled them from high school glory days.

The Gems got off to a flying start, winning their first six games, but skidded to a dismal finish, losing their last four. The team had undersized linemen, and as the season wore on, they wore down, allowing a total of 133 points in the four losses, which were one-sided defeats of 26–3, 32–2, 41–16 and 34–9. The final EFL standings were as follows:

Malden	9–1
Nashua	7–3
Southington	6–4
Fitchburg	6–4
Rochester (NH)	1–9
Portland (ME)	1–9

After one season, which the *Hartford Courant* charitably described as "successful but disappointing"[17] the Gems disbanded.

9

An Unhappy Relationship: The 1966–67 Waterbury Orbits

In the mid–1960s, Waterbury, Connecticut, was an aging factory city, struggling to retain its population during an era when the middle class was fleeing to the suburbs. The brass industry that had been the backbone of the area's economy for decades was slowly dying, and Waterbury desperately needed something that would infuse new life into the city. That something wasn't likely to be another heavy industry, for all across the United States manufacturing was in the early stage of a long decline.

Mayor Frederick Palomba, like most politicians, was an optimist, and was greatly encouraged by the imminent completion of two major highways, Routes 8 and 84, which would intersect at Waterbury. Since people could now get to his city more easily, Palomba reasoned, he might be able to convince the owner of a professional sports franchise to re-locate to Waterbury. Sports provided fun and entertainment, might spur economic growth, and in any event would enhance the city's image.

The operation of a minor league franchise in any sport is a precarious undertaking, and there is almost always a club in search of a new home. Just as Palomba began looking for prospects, the Eastern League farm team of the San Francisco Giants announced that they intended to relocate from Springfield, Massachusetts, to Bristol, Connecticut.

Henry Wojtusik, the mayor of Bristol, was eager to have the Giants, but others in his city were not. Among the latter group was former Finance Commissioner Thomas O'Brien, who went to court to obtain an injunction that would prevent the city from leasing Muzzy Field to the Giants.

O'Brien muddied the waters sufficiently, and by early March the Giants, feeling unwelcome and pressed for time, began looking for alternatives. Palomba moved quickly, and on March 21 the Giants announced that they would play in the Brass City's Municipal Stadium during the 1966 season. "This is one of the

9. An Unhappy Relationship

biggest things that has ever happened to the city," Palomba said. "It's a wonderful step forward."[1]

A couple of weeks later, Waterbury landed a second team, also fleeing from a city that didn't want them. Like Bristol had spurned the Giants, New Haven had been inhospitable to a football team called the Orbits. In January 1966, the ACFL had granted a franchise to a partnership owned by New Haven area businessmen Dan Adley, Jim Lamberti, C. Newton Schenk, and Israel "Babe" Gordon. Milt Rosner, a former minor league baseball player, manager, and scout, was the general manager.

The New Haven group intended to play in Quigley Stadium in West Haven, but after being rebuffed set their sights on Bowen Field in New Haven. Bowen would need to be lighted in order to be used for minor league football and, unfortunately, people who lived in the neighborhood were strongly opposed.

"There are some very short sighted people down there on the sound," Schenk said, "and they have not given us a fair shake."[2] The New Haven investors met with Palomba, and on April 9 the mayor held a press conference to announce that the Orbits would play their six home games in Waterbury. Municipal Stadium didn't have lights either, but Waterbury agreed to install them and perform other upgrades estimated to cost a total of about $100,000. The renovations included additional bleachers that would increase capacity to about 10,000.

The Waterbury sports community was excited by the prospect of two new teams. Frank Monardo of the *Republican* was relieved that Waterbury was no longer left behind while cities like Bridgeport and New Haven moved forward with urban redevelopment projects. While they were building, Monardo lamented, "Waterbury bickered. It seemed destined to always be last in the race." But that was all changed, he said. "Sports shot Waterbury into the forefront of state conversation."[3] Monardo predicted great things for both the Giants and Orbits.

The new lights went on for the first time on May 16 when the Giants hosted the Pittsfield Red Sox. Attendance was 2,676, not bad for an Eastern League game in May. Monardo was so euphoric about the new club that a few weeks later he wrote a column suggesting that Connecticut should attempt to secure a major league franchise.[4] The attendance on opening night in Waterbury, he said, exceeded that at major league games on some days (generally cold, rainy late September days in Cleveland or Chicago), and Connecticut's population of 2.6 million was more than that of several major league cities.

When Monardo vetted the idea to others in town, they were lukewarm. He sent a copy of his article to Connecticut governor John Dempsey, who wished him well but said he was not an expert on the subject and disinclined to speculate on the success of such a venture. C.C. Johnson Spink, editor of *The Sporting*

News, was more direct. "I really don't think there is much chance for major league baseball in Connecticut," he wrote.[5] After evaluating the feedback, Monardo admitted, "Now that I've listened to many opinions, I'm inclined to agree that big league ball in Connecticut is a risk."[6]

The Orbits were coached by Fred Wallner, who had signed (reportedly for $14,500 and a percentage of the gate) to coach the New Haven franchise in January. Waterbury nearly procured quarterback Glynn Griffing, a former Ole Miss All American and New York Giant, but the $12,000 price tag was too high. They settled for steady minor league veteran Manch Wheeler.

The Orbits also signed a defensive tackle from Phoenix named Wayne Coleman. Coleman was big, standing nearly six foot four and weighing 250 pounds, and tough, having won the heavyweight division of the Phoenix Golden Gloves tournament. He learned to fight while growing up in some tough neighborhoods where, as he said, "You had to fight." His uncle, Herb Coleman, competed in about 70 professional bouts and once fought champion Jim Braddock. Wayne intended to follow in his uncle's footsteps and embark on a professional boxing career after the Orbits' season ended, and travelled to New York four times each week to work with famed trainer Gil Clancy. His boxing career never panned out, but Coleman eventually achieved great renown in a related field (see the Epilogue).

Wallner signed a number of former Charter Oaks, including ex–Syracuse star Dick Bowman, defensive back Ken Luciani, end Bill Boehle, and speedy receiver John Wardlaw. Roger Milici, a Charter Oak in 1964 who played with the Milford Rockets of the NEFL in 1965, would play end opposite Wardlaw. Milici arrived in Waterbury under a cloud, for the Rockets claimed he had signed a contract for 1965 that included an option for 1966, and he was therefore property of the Milford club. The Rockets threatened to take the case to court.

It was ironic that the Rockets fought so hard to retain Milici, for they hadn't really wanted him in the first place. The 1964 Charter Oaks were not much of a passing team and Milici's statistics were unimpressive. The Oaks weren't interested in re-signing him and, as Milici said, "Nobody else came a-knockin."

He showed up at a Milford practice session and practically had to beg for a tryout, but he made the team and became one of the best receivers in the NEFL. Now the team that hadn't wanted him didn't want him to leave. Eventually, the situation was resolved and Milici was cleared to play in Waterbury.

Milici and Wardlaw were a dangerous combination. "I had my best year when Johnny was on the team," said Milici. "He had a lot of talent and he was a lot faster than I was so we worked well together. They couldn't double team either of us."

The Orbits looked good in their exhibitions, beating the Jersey City Jets, the Virginia Sailors, and the Rhode Island Steelers. Each game was played at a different location, the first in Bridgeport, the second in New Haven, and the finale at Nolan Field in Ansonia. Unless they were willing to travel, Waterbury fans' appetite for ACFL play was whetted only by newspaper accounts.

Initially, the Orbits practiced at Nolan Field, former home of the Ansonia Black Knights, for they weren't allowed to use Municipal Field. Even after the season started, the Orbits could only practice behind the right field fence, as the baseball Giants had exclusive use of the playing field. When his club was finally allowed to begin practicing at the stadium, Wallner invited people to come out and watch. Two days later, however, Rosner announced that practice sessions were closed to fans on any day the Giants played at home. For a new team trying to generate interest, it was a difficult situation.

The Orbits lost their opening game 14–6 to the Atlantic City Senators in Atlantic City before a disappointing crowd of only 2,298. The home opener was August 27 against the powerful New Bedford Sweepers. It would be the first professional football game ever played in Waterbury and the Orbits expected a capacity crowd. Miss Connecticut, Carole Ann Gelish, made a ceremonial first kickoff out of the hold of Mayor Palomba, and Republican gubernatorial candidate Clayton Gengras sat in the stands.

The crowd of 5,800 fell well short of the expected 10,000, but the game was an artistic success, a 21–7 Orbit victory. Wheeler connected with Milici for two touchdown passes, one a 58-yarder, and halfback Tom Morris ran for a third score. Monardo, the Orbits' #1 booster, asked fans what they thought of the evening and received a mixed response. Some thought the caliber of play was good, others that it was sloppy. Some thought the ticket prices were too high, others that seven dollars for two choice seats was quite a bargain. What Monardo did not do was survey the 4,200 who had been expected to make up the rest of the sellout and ask them why they hadn't come.

Following the New Bedford game, the Orbits signed quarterback Hank Schichtle, who spent the entire 1964 season with the New York Giants, although he appeared in just one game and did not throw a single pass. Schichtle was cut by the Giants before the 1965 season, sat out a year, and went to the camps of the Atlanta Falcons and San Francisco 49ers in 1966.

Although he was released by both clubs, Y.A. Tittle, the San Francisco quarterback coach, thought Schichtle had NFL potential and urged him to keep playing. Duke Delpo, who'd managed the old Waterbury Indies football team for many years, watched Schichtle and Wheeler in practice and said, "They both looked like NFL quarterbacks. I don't see how the Orbits can ever lose with quarterbacks like these."[7] In addition to Schichtle, the Orbits added running back Jerry Stevenson, on loan from the San Diego Chargers.

The Orbits' next game was also at home, against the Jersey Jets, who featured former New York Jet Bob Schweickert. Schweikert was typical of college stars who became marginal NFL players, a versatile athlete, but not skillful enough in any one aspect of the game to be a professional standout. He was a quarterback who could run but not pass very well, he was not big and strong enough to be a running back, and not fast enough to be a wide receiver.

With the Orbits fresh off the upset win over New Bedford and loaded with new talent, the *Republican* again predicted they would attract a sellout crowd of 10,000. The attendance, at 6,320, was a little better than it had been on opening night, but Schweickert, although not good enough for the Jets, was more than the Orbits could handle. He played both halfback and quarterback, passed for 104 yards, ran for 133 and caught 3 passes for 46 more. The Jets scored 35 points in the second half of a convincing 45–30 win. The Waterbury highlight was the running of Stevenson, who gained 138 yards in his first game. Schichtle's debut was less successful, as his first two passes were intercepted.

After a 17–17 tie with the Rhode Island Steelers at Pawtucket, the Orbits faced the Scranton Miners, whose roster featured eleven players sent to them by the parent Giants. The Giants had one of the worst years in their long, storied history in 1966, finishing 1–12–1, so their castoffs were not of the highest caliber. Still, they were just a notch below the NFL.

In addition to playing a team stocked by an NFL affiliate, the Orbits faced a second formidable obstacle. The bus in which they left Waterbury had two flat tires en route, and the players had to switch to a second bus, which arrived at Scranton just 34 minutes before game time, nine hours after leaving Waterbury.

With barely enough time to dress and no time to warm up, the Orbits quickly fell behind and trailed 13–0 at halftime. Stevenson returned the second half kickoff 85 yards for a touchdown, and scored twice more on short runs. Schichtle replaced Wheeler and threw the ball well, while the Orbit defense held the Miners scoreless in the second half, resulting in a 20–13 win. In his first three games, Stevenson had gained 416 yards and averaged 6.5 yards per carry.

When the season began, there had been five teams in each division, but by the end of September there were just four. Early in the month, the New Bedford Sweepers filed a lawsuit against the Boston Patriots, claiming the latter had reneged on an oral agreement to provide the Sweepers with four to six players at the Patriots' expense. In return, Boston would have the right to sign any member of the Sweepers to an AFL contract. The Sweepers also alleged that several members of their 1965 team had attended the Patriots' 1966 camp and returned "all busted up."

The day after the lawsuit was announced, the Sweepers withdrew from

9. An Unhappy Relationship

the ACFL, claiming that without the players promised by the Patriots, they could not operate. One game was cancelled, but the following week, after a heroic effort by New Bedford mayor Edward Harrington and a group of local businessmen, the Sweepers returned to life and were re-admitted to the league.

The second coming lasted just six days before the Sweepers folded for good. Within a week, the Southern Division was also reduced to four teams when Atlantic City was expelled for failing to post the required $10,000 bond. The schedule was reworked and the remaining teams soldiered on.

The Orbits won their next two games, but during the second, a 51–7 romp over Scranton, Stevenson suffered a knee injury. Even without him, the Orbits gained their fourth straight win, 35–0 at Harrisburg. Their record was 5–2–1 and a showdown on the road against 7–0–1 Lowell on October 15 would determine whether the Orbits would have a shot at the title. Meanwhile, during the week before the Lowell game, another franchise bit the dust, as the Rhode Island Steelers folded and cancelled their final five games. The schedule was re-arranged once more.

The Orbits were all but eliminated from contention when they lost 29–24 at Lowell. A number of Orbits were injured during the game, which boded poorly for the rematch in Waterbury the following week. The Orbits' best hope for a title was that Lowell would follow New Bedford, Atlantic City, and Rhode Island into insolvency. It would take a miracle to beat them on the field.

The Orbits pulled out the second Lowell game with some last minute heroics. Late in the fourth quarter, Wheeler took his club 80 yards in four plays to narrow the margin to 17–13. After a Lowell punt, the Orbits took the ball on their 11. With 1:57 remaining, Waterbury faced a fourth down and ten on their own 46 yard line. Wheeler hit Milici with a 54-yard toss that gave the Orbits a 20–17 victory.

Unfortunately, Lowell won its next game, eliminating the Orbits from contention. They finished strongly, however, winning their final two games to end the season with an 8–3–1 mark, good for second place in the Northern Division. The final standings were as follows:

Northern Division				Southern Division			
Lowell	9	2	1	Virginia	10	1	0
Waterbury	8	3	1	Jersey	8	3	1
Scranton	2	10	0	Wilmington	4	7	1
				Harrisburg	3	8	1

It was an excellent first year for the Orbits (at least on the field) and it had likewise been an outstanding year for Roger Milici and Jerry Stevenson. Milici, who led the ACFL with 13 touchdowns and 1,083 receiving yards, was like many top minor league receivers. He bore the dual curses of coming from a small school (Southern Connecticut) and lacking outstanding speed, but his great moves and sure hands made him an ACFL standout.

"If Roger was two-tenths of a second faster in the 40," said teammate Joe Ginnetti, "he would have made people forget about Del Shofner. He had great hands and he was tough. He wouldn't admit he was tough because he didn't like to block. We had a formation called X-tight, where Roger was the X-receiver and was supposed to shift in next to the tackle. He'd look back but he would never come tight to the line of scrimmage."

"The tackle next to me," said Milici, "was a 300-pound guy who was always complaining. There'd be a 180-pound guy in front of him beating him all the time and he'd say, 'You've got to come in and help me block this guy.' I'd say, 'You're bigger than both of us put together and *you can't block him?*'"

Stevenson led the league in rushing with 942 yards and when the Orbits' season ended, the New York Giants wanted to take a look at both him and Milici. Stevenson's case presented a problem, for he had been sent to Waterbury by the Chargers with the understanding that he would not be sold to another team without San Diego's permission. The Giants obtained the Chargers' permission by agreeing to compensate them if they signed Stevenson.

Stevenson did not perform well for the Giants. "Jerry played like an all-American when he was with us," said Milici. "He was terrific. Then when we went to New York it looked like he was playing football for the first time. He couldn't hit a hole. He couldn't run. He couldn't catch. He couldn't do anything. It was unbelievable. I never saw anybody have such trouble. And this was a guy who was so talented. He was strong, he was fast; he could bowl people over or run around them. But in New York I was almost embarrassed for him because he couldn't do *anything.*"

Despite Stevenson's difficulties, New York offered both players positions on the taxi squad, and Milici obtained a leave of absence from his teaching job. The Giants were decimated by injuries and it appeared that one of the former Orbits might be activated during the final five weeks. Unfortunately, neither was, as the season, mercifully for the Giants, came to an end.

Like Stevenson, Milici learned that he didn't have a future in the NFL. "In New York," he said, "I had a long talk with [Giant coach] Allie Sherman about my lack of speed, the possibility of a career in the NFL, and the fact that I wasn't getting any younger. He wasn't very successful in New York, but he was great with me. We had a real heart-to-heart talk and he opened my eyes. When I left the Giants I no longer aspired to make football a full-time career."

At the end of March 1967, Chick O'Malley, general manager of the Waterbury Giants, announced that the local owners had lost $14,000 during their first season. The news was greeted with disbelief, for the attendance of 80,000 exceeded O'Malley's projected breakeven point of 77,000. One old time local baseball operator estimated that the team made $100,000. Many thought there were more people in the park than was announced as the official attendance. Frank Monardo, who thought Connecticut deserved a major league team, could not believe the figures.

A couple of days later, the Orbits reported a loss of $72,132. Attendance at the final home game, a paltry 2,000, brought the total for the year to 25,000. The largest crowd was just over 6,000, and the sellouts so confidently predicted by the *Republican* never materialized.

"Good god, yes," said Milt Rosner, "we are disappointed." He said that prior to the season the owners thought they might lose $20,000 or $25,000 the first year, but they never expected such a large deficit. Rosner hoped to reduce the loss by the sale of Milici, Stevenson, and Don Gunaldo. The Orbits received an initial payment of $1,000 for each, and would get an additional $4,000 for any of them that made a 40-man roster. But even if all three made it, the proceeds would scarcely make a dent in the large loss.

The financial detail was discouraging, for gross revenue was just $63,000, only slightly more than the salary expense of $60,000. In addition to salaries, there were rental payments for Municipal Stadium, guaranties to visiting teams, travel costs, fees to the ACFL, and other miscellaneous expenses. The average attendance was only about half of that needed to break even.

Faced with such a grim picture, the Orbits considered moving to another city, with New Haven and Bridgeport most prominently mentioned. There was no indication, however, that New Haven had changed its stance on lighting Bowen Field, and the Rockets of the North Atlantic Football League had recently been denied use of Bridgeport's new Kennedy Stadium. Mayor Palomba said he expected the Orbits to stay in Waterbury.

Palomba was correct, as the Orbits returned for a second season. Fred Wallner left to coach the New Britain Bees of the North Atlantic League and was replaced by Nick Cutro, a short, chubby, 31-year-old former running back at Shippensburg College. On the undefeated 1957 Shippensburg team, Cutro averaged an astounding 13.2 yards per rush and in one game carried the ball three times for 154 yards.

He had gaudy statistics and Little All American status, but at 5'7" and 190 pounds, Cutro didn't have a major league body. He also had a damaged knee. Still, there weren't too many backs who'd averaged more than 13 yards per carry, and the Philadelphia Eagles invited him to try out. "I had a bad knee when I went with the Eagles," said Cutro, who'd had surgery just two months earlier. "I shouldn't have gone. I should have stayed out another year. I just didn't have the cuts left in my body."

With his aspirations of an NFL career ended, Cutro embarked on a coaching career that began at Bayonne High School in his home town.[8] He was hired as an assistant, but when he reported for his first day, he was told that his boss had resigned and that he would be the head coach. It was a dubious honor, for the Bayonne team hadn't won a game in three years and hadn't scored a point in two years. "They couldn't beat *anybody*," Cutro said.

In their first game under the new coach, the team achieved a moral victory, scoring a touchdown in a game they lost by about 40 points. Bayonne didn't win any games in Cutro's first year, but they did manage to score regularly. The next year they actually won a game. Then the superintendent of schools decided he would rather have a band than a football team, and the program was abolished.

Cutro was hired by St. Mary's High School in Rutherford, New Jersey where, with some talent to work with, he won two state championships. The young coach was a high energy individual perfectly suited to motivate impressionable high school boys. He made football fun. "I used to race them after practice," Cutro said. "I watched them. I made sure they went to school and their grades were OK. I made it happy for them and they loved it. They didn't want to go home after practice. They wanted to practice all night."

If the players wanted to practice all night, they would have had to do so without their coach, who was moonlighting with the Jersey Giants of the ACFL as a halfback and assistant coach. In one game he scored four touchdowns. "It rained that night," he recalled, "and it was really cold. I just hit the right holes and made the right cuts. My knee had healed and it was strong."

The 1963 season was Cutro's last as an active player. The next year he assumed the Giants' head coaching position and held it for the next three years, posting a 31–8–1 record. The Giants won the Southern Division title in 1965 but lost to New Bedford in the championship game. During his final year in New Jersey, the team was affiliated with the New York Jets, and Cutro got to know Weeb Ewbank, the Jets' coach and general manager. It was Ewbank who wanted Cutro in Waterbury, for during the off-season the Orbits had become an affiliate of the Jets.

The relationship took a long time to come to fruition. During the first week of December 1966, a rumor surfaced that the Orbits would affiliate with either the Packers or Bears. In mid–January Rosner said, "We're very, very close," but would not name the team. By the end of April, speculation centered on the Jets and the rumor gained credence when it was announced that Ewbank would be the featured speaker at a meeting of the Orbits' newly-formed booster club.

9. An Unhappy Relationship

Finally, on June 6, the Orbits made the official announcement that they would be a farm club for the Jets and that Cutro would be their head coach.

The Continental League, at least initially, aspired to be a third major league, and eschewed affiliations. The ACFL harbored no such illusions and longed to be a feeder system. In 1967 each of its teams was affiliated, and Ewbank said he expected to send 15 to 18 players to the Orbits, which would account for nearly half of the 36-man roster. The salaries of the optioned players would be paid by the Jets.

The Orbits' exhibition season began on August 12 and the regular season on August 26, well before the Jets made their final cuts, and the Waterbury roster during the early weeks consisted of holdovers from 1966 and a number of players who been with Cutro in New Jersey.

Schichtle signed with a Canadian League team, leaving Wheeler as the only returning quarterback. Milici was cut by the Giants at the end of July and rejoined the Orbits a few days later. Stevenson was also cut but was sent to the Giants' farm team in Westchester.

In mid-August, the Jets made their first wholesale shipment of players to Waterbury. The biggest names were defensive back Earl Christy, who would later play in Super Bowl III, lineman Gene Bledsoe, an 8th round draft choice from the University of Texas, and linebacker Mike Stromberg, a 14th round choice.

One player still in the Jet camp was coveted by the Orbits. Bob Schweickert, who'd played so well against Waterbury in 1966, didn't appear to have a spot on the Jet roster. Cutro held a place open for him in Waterbury, playing the exhibition season with Wheeler as his only quarterback. He told Wheeler not, under any circumstances, to run with the ball, orders Wheeler ignored. "Every time he carried," Cutro said, "I wanted to run on the field and block for him myself."[9]

Schweickert didn't make the Jet team, but neither did he wind up in Waterbury, leaving Cutro with a vacancy at quarterback. He didn't get just any quarterback; he signed Jimmy Corcoran, who would become the most famous minor league player of the 1960s, mainly as the result of Corcoran's Herculean efforts at self-promotion. He called himself the "King," almost always referred to himself in the third person, and established a reputation as a boastful playboy in the Joe Namath mold.

"I *really* liked the King," said Orbit defensive back John Dockery. "He was one of those glorious characters that you meet in life. The King was just energized like a neon sign rolling down the road in his Lincoln Continental convertible. He was like a character out of Damon Runyon."

Corcoran was a good quarterback who had the ability to be an NFL backup, or maybe a starter for a weak club, but his flamboyant, narcissistic personality

The legendary Jim (King) Corcoran (photograph from Pennsylvania Firebirds program).

was tolerable only if he was a star. "I could do the job," Corcoran said, "but the NFL coaches didn't buy the act."[10]

Corcoran went to camp with the Jets one year, and roomed with Namath, who was his idol. "I am the King," he told Namath, "and you are the Lord." Corcoran went out of his way to attract attention, and he did, but it was not the kind of attention that would earn him an NFL roster spot. At the Jets camp, he drove a car that he said had been owned by former Secretary of Defense Robert McNamara.

Namath liked his women and his late nights, but he had great talent, a big contract, and knew where the line was. He usually didn't cross it, and when he did, such as in the Bachelors III episode, he backtracked before it was too late.

The King made a career of crossing the line, which destined him to the life of a big fish in small ponds like Waterbury, Pottstown and Chambersburg. In an odd way, that was good for Corcoran, who was not cut out to be second string. He had the personality of a celebrity and while he wasn't good enough to be a star in New York or Los Angeles, he could be the center of attention in Pottstown.

Bob Tucker, the long-time Giant tight end, was Corcoran's favorite receiver at Lowell and Pottstown. "He probably had a stronger arm than Fran Tarkenton," Tucker said, "although Tarkenton had a much better grasp of NFL play. Corcoran was a great quarterback and could have played in the NFL, but he was just a little bit too flamboyant for some of the coaches and he drew so much attention to himself that it became a negative. And that was sad because he did have enough ability to play in the NFL. He was better than some of the quarterbacks we had in New York, I can tell you that."

"He would have been great in today's game where you market yourself. After every play you can cheer yourself. You see these guys doing their jig and going through their gyrations. They wouldn't last long in our day but now it's part of the game. And Jimmy was a self-promoter."

"Then," added former Hartford Knight Dennis Fitzgibbons, "sports were athletics and not the marketing and hype they are today, where it's all about me. Then it was all about team and Corcoran was probably one of the first guys to break that mold. He wanted to be the Joe Willie of minor league football."

Despite his massive ego, Corcoran was generally liked by his teammates. "He was a *nice* guy," said former Knight Ken Blasser, who got to know Corcoran in Canada. "He was cocky, but in a good way. He didn't bother anybody." "The guys loved him," said Cutro. "He didn't cause any problems. He showed up for practice and he was a leader on the field. He was a good kid but his mouth kept him out of the NFL. He made enemies of some of the coaches and they said he was a pain in the ass or he disrupted practice. We never had that problem with him. The players liked him."

Born into difficult circumstances in Jersey City, Corcoran always seemed to be trying a bit too hard to compensate for the deprivations of his youth. His father died in 1966, and Corcoran never saw his mother thereafter. He had lived on his own since high school. On a rainy afternoon during a game in his senior year, Corcoran emerged for the second half wearing a clean uniform and sunglasses. Someone yelled from the stands, "Hail to the King," and a legend was born.

Corcoran's ability as a passer earned him a scholarship at the University of Maryland. According to his own account, the King set a number of records at Maryland, including bedding 38 of the 47 members of Kappa Delta. When Corcoran married at 19, he didn't let matrimony interfere with his Olympian sex life.

Corcoran's statistics on the football field were not as dazzling as those accumulated in the sorority house, and he played sparingly, while exasperating Coach Tom Nugent with his extracurricular antics. Perhaps his most memorable performance as a quarterback came in 1961. At that time, freshmen were not allowed to play varsity sports, and in a frosh game against the Naval Academy, Corcoran passed for 322 yards and beat Navy plebe Roger Staubach's team 29–27.

Three years later, in 1964, Maryland's varsity upset Navy and Staubach, the reigning Heisman Trophy winner. In subsequent years Corcoran loved talking about how he beat Staubach that day, but the Terrapins' quarterback was Phil Petry, while Jimmy Corcoran sat on the Maryland bench.[11]

Despite his inexperience in college competition, the King's natural ability to throw a football gained him invitations to several professional training camps over the next few years. His skill earned him an invitation and his behavior got him released. Corcoran wanted to be an NFL quarterback, but not as much as he wanted to be the King.

"Part of his persona," said Dockery, "was the class clown, and I don't know if anyone wanted their backup quarterback to be like that. He was always in character. I'm sure there was another side to him—a serious side—but I don't think he showed that to too many people."

Corcoran came to the Orbits from the camp of the Denver Broncos, where his competitor for the backup spot, Scotty Glacken, wasn't too impressive but supposedly had a three-year, no-cut contract for $150,000. Therefore Glacken stayed and Corcoran went to Waterbury. "Corcoran appears to have the necessary confidence," was reporter Jon Stein's understated opinion upon the King's arrival.[12]

Roger Milici described Corcoran's grand entrance into the Brass City. "He drove up in this black Lincoln Continental," Milici said, "with doors that opened in opposite directions. He had all the windows rolled up and you could see he was rockin' to the tunes. He pulls into a parking space, gets out and he's all sweaty. He kept the windows up because he wanted everybody to think he had air conditioning."

By the time Corcoran reported to the Philadelphia Bell training camp in 1974, he'd polished up his entrance. As he drove in, his sidekick announced over a PA system, "The King has arrived. Lock up your daughters and be sure your wives are in by a decent hour."

With Corcoran on board, Wheeler was cut, which came as somewhat of a surprise, particularly to the *Republican*, which had printed a lengthy and laudatory profile of Wheeler just four days earlier. The same day, the Orbits signed running back Allen Smith, a talented athlete from Findlay College in Ohio who had been selected by the Jets in the sixth round of the 1966 draft. The Detroit Lions of the NFL had also drafted Smith, so the Jets gave him a $10,000 signing bonus. The youngster had never had much money, and $10,000 seemed like an unbelievable fortune. He gave $3,000 to his church, loaned some money to some friends, who never repaid him, made a few bad investments, and soon the entire bonus was gone.

Smith spent the 1966 season on the Jets' taxi squad, and was activated for one game. At the end of training camp in 1967, he was cut. He had no job and only $60 in cash. The season was about to begin and other teams were trying to pare their rosters rather than add players, but Smith managed to get an invitation to try out with the Lions. He gave $50 to his wife to cover her hotel costs, put the remaining $10 in his pocket, and boarded a plane for Detroit. Lion coach Joe Schmidt told Smith that his roster was set and, while he could keep him around for a week or two, there would probably not be a place for him. "It was the lowest point in my life," Smith said.[13]

Smith was about to go back home to Toledo when he got a call from Nick Cutro asking if he wanted to play for the Orbits for $200 a game. For a man with less than ten dollars in his pocket it was an offer he couldn't refuse. "I said to myself," he recalled a few months later, "here I go from the big time down to the dumps. The cellar of football."[14]

The first opponent the Orbits were scheduled to face with Corcoran and Smith was the Wilmington Clippers—or maybe Waller's Renegades, for the Wilmington franchise was in a state of great upheaval. During the week before the game, the sports department of the *Republican* placed a call to their counterparts at the *Wilmington News-Journal* to get some background on the Clippers. They were surprised when Hal Bodley of the *News-Journal* told the *Republican* that the Clippers had folded. Attendance for the first two home games had totaled only 2,100, and the principal shareholder of the Clippers, Edward DuPont of the wealthy DuPont family, decided to cut his losses and withdraw his support.

Bodley said there would be a team in Waterbury to play the Orbits, its expenses paid by the ACFL. There were a couple of potential owners sniffing around and the league wanted to keep the franchise alive for a possible sale. Coach Ron Waller affirmed that the team would play but joked that, since the owner had skedaddled, they might play as Waller's Renegades.

Milt Rosner was apoplectic when he read the story in the *Republican*. He'd called the newspaper earlier and told them to disregard any news they received from the Wilmington press. "What difference does it make what name they come up here under," he said. "The players are what count."[15]

The Wilmington players appeared in Waterbury as advertised. "When the owners left," said Clipper running back John Land, "the players stuck together because we had committed to playing when the team started and we didn't want to stop. We were hoping that a new source of money came in to get us through the season. It would have messed up the whole schedule if we folded."

Uncertainty over the Clippers' status, plus a drizzly night, resulted in attendance of less than 3,000. A few days later, Rosner called a New Haven paper and told them the *Republican* was responsible for the low attendance by printing rumors of Wilmington's demise.

Rosner was supposed to be promoting the team, and feuding with the local paper was not helping. A week later, after the Orbits lost badly to Westchester, the *Republican* wondered whether, since they had reported the defeat, the Orbit general manager would hold them liable if attendance was down the following week.

Before losing to the Bulls, the Orbits had beaten the Clippers/Renegades for their first win, but after a tough loss to Lowell the Orbits were 1–3 and last in the Northern Division. A number of soft spots had been uncovered, one of which was a weak defense. The offensive line was also leaky, which led to sacks and interceptions, for Corcoran frequently unloaded the ball hurriedly and unwisely to avoid the rush. Field goal kicking was also a glaring fault.

There weren't many talented kickers in minor league football. The 1967 ACFL booter with the most potential was Tom Dempsey of Lowell. Dempsey, a former junior college player born with a withered right hand and a stump of a right foot, wrote to a number of teams asking for a tryout, but the Packers were the only one to answer. They told him to go to their farm team in Lowell and see what he could do.

Dempsey made the team on potential. He was not very accurate on field goal attempts, but his kickoffs were breathtaking—high and majestic and often sailing into or beyond the end zone. Even with his physical handicaps, Dempsey played a little defensive end. "I've learned that I have to push off with my left foot," he said, "regardless of which way I want to go—that's the biggest problem."[16]

9. An Unhappy Relationship

All minor leaguers faced long odds, but for Dempsey they were even greater. The NFL was leery of players who were a couple of inches too short or a step too slow. What would they say about a man who was a whole hand and half a foot short?

After Cutro saw Dempsey kick against his team he told the Jets he wanted to bring him to Shea Stadium for a tryout. When Jet assistant Clive Rush saw Dempsey, he wanted to send him home. "How can you put a football player on the field with half an arm and half a foot?" he asked Cutro. "I'm telling you," Cutro replied, "this kid can kick the ball higher on kickoffs than anybody and you won't get any returns."

Finally, Cutro went to Ewbank and convinced him to let Dempsey kick off and try some field goals. "His first kickoff was higher than Shea Stadium," Cutro said. "It was like a punt. Every field goal was perfect. But Clive Rush said, 'Nah, we can't do it.' They let the kid go."

The Orbits could have used Dempsey. In training camp, they had three aspirants for the kicking position, soccer stylists Carl Morello and Alkis Panagoulias and straight-on kicker Tom Shive. Cutro was not enamored of soccer style kickers, who he thought kicked the ball too low and were rattled by the prospect of physical contact. He elected to keep Shive, who made one of two extra points in the opening game, then missed three straight in the win over Wilmington. Two went under the crossbar and one ricocheted off it. No field goals and three of seven extra point attempts wasn't satisfactory, so Shive was cut and Stan Curko was signed.

Curko made two extra points, but missed all three of his field goal attempts, each from 30 yards or less, in the three point loss to Lowell. Therefore Cutro brought back Panagoulias, who in his first game missed an extra point and had another blocked. Exit Panagoulias.

The next candidate was former Buffalo Bills kicker Booth Lusteg, a 28-year-old with a lengthy resume.[17] Lusteg was a graduate of the University of Connecticut who played basketball and baseball in college. After graduation, he bounced around minor league baseball a bit, and after being released four times, took a job as a junior high school math teacher on Long Island. Somewhere along the way he had a bit part in an off–Broadway play called *Six Characters in Search of an Author.*

One day, during a touch football game with his fellow teachers, Lusteg got off a booming punt. Most people would have admired it, felt a glow of pride, and gone back to class. Lusteg took it as a sign he could make the grade as a kicker in professional football. In the spring of 1963, he attended an open tryout conducted by the Jets and showed enough to be invited to training camp, where his greatest notoriety came when he vomited out of a second floor dormitory window. Unfortunately, the vomit carried farther than most of his punts. He tried to make it as a defensive back or wide receiver, but was too slow and had bad hands. His Jet career ended after four days.

Lusteg decided to get some experience in the minor leagues and asked Newark Bears coach Steve Van Buren for a tryout. He told Van Buren he'd played for the Ansonia Black Knights. He hadn't, but didn't think Van Buren would check up on him. Lusteg signed with the Newark club for $35 a game. In the season opener, wracked by nerves, he missed his first two extra point attempts, but rallied to kick a couple of field goals.

The next week, the Bears signed former AFL kicker Bill Shockley and Lusteg was released. He tried out unsuccessfully with the Westchester Crusaders and Hartford Charter Oaks, and decided that he would try one more team. If he didn't make it he would take up a more stable profession. He called Boston Sweeper owner Ted Barron and told him he'd played for the Jets, not mentioning it was just for four days. Barron signed him and Lusteg spent two years kicking for the Sweepers.

Following the second season, Lusteg contacted virtually every NFL and AFL team and sent them his Sweeper statistics. The only club that was interested was the Bills, who'd lost star kicker Pete Gogolak as a free agent to the New York Giants. Lusteg thought that at 27 he was too old for a rookie and told the Bills' scout his name was Wallace Booth Lusteg (Wallace was his younger brother's name), he was 24 years old (Wallace's age), and a graduate of Boston College (Wallace's alma mater).

The Bills' first exhibition game was a nationally televised affair against the Patriots at Boston College. The local papers gave the supposed hometown hero a big buildup, and when the Buffalo bus got lost, his teammates, under the assumption he knew the area well, looked to him for directions. Lusteg, searching frantically for street signs, was finally able to guide them to his "alma mater."

Once the team arrived at the stadium, things went much better. The rookie kicker made four field goals, including a 47-yarder, and added four more in the next game. Just when it looked like Lusteg had a chance to make a major league roster, the Sweepers filed a suit against the Bills for $50,000, claiming Lusteg was under contract to them. The two clubs had previously agreed on $500 as compensation, but the deal was never signed. Eight field goals in two games had increased the price one hundredfold. For years no one had wanted Lusteg; now two teams were fighting over him.

The Sweepers and Bills negotiated a settlement and Lusteg made the 1966 Buffalo roster. The high point of his season was kicking four field goals that provided the margin of victory in a key 33–23 win over the Jets. The nadir came in a game against the Chargers. The Bills trailed 17–3 before backup quarterback

9. An Unhappy Relationship

Daryle Lamonica came in and led them to two touchdowns, then drove them deep into San Diego territory. With six seconds left in the game, Lusteg lined up for a potential 23-yard game winning field goal—and missed it.

As he left the field, the Buffalo fans, never known for their patience, cursed him and tore at his jersey. After he'd dressed, a security guard offered to sneak him out the back, but Lusteg declined. Escorted by three police officers, he made his way through the crowd and, as a form of self-punishment, decided to walk two miles to his apartment. He was so obsessed with his depression that he didn't notice a car pull up beside him. Two men got out and starting running behind him, yelling, "You no-good bum, go back to Boston. We don't need you. You stink." One of the men punched him in the back. "I didn't resist," Lusteg said later. "I just let the one kid hit me. Then he ran back to his car. I didn't even try to get the license number. I felt I deserved what I got."

The Bills won the division title and Lusteg scored 98 points, the most of any AFL kicker. Unfortunately, Buffalo lost to Kansas City 31–7 in the AFL championship game, depriving Lusteg of a chance to play in the first Super Bowl.

After being cut by the Bills in 1967, Lusteg auditioned for the Jets, but was not about to dislodge Pro Bowler Jim Turner. Cutro wanted him to sign with the Orbits, but Lusteg said he was waiting to hear from San Diego about a possible tryout. When nothing concrete developed, Lusteg signed with the Orbits and said he would kick against the Virginia Sailors provided his injured right foot had healed.

Lusteg did not kick against the Sailors, nor did he ever play for the Orbits. He said he had "something in the fire" and his foot still hurt. "The image adds to Lusteg's image of being a kook," wrote Jon Stein. "He sustained [the injury] a month ago catching his foot in a hole while kicking in the dark."[18]

Whatever Lusteg had in the fire apparently didn't catch. "Keep on trying, Booth," Stein wrote.[19] In November, Lusteg signed with the Miami Dolphins and Stein noted sarcastically, "His injured foot must have healed by now."[20] Defensive back John Dockery handled the Orbits' kicking for the rest of the season. He was accurate on short field goals and, unlike his predecessors, able to make extra points.

Dockery was a key acquisition for the Orbits, not for his kicking but for his skill as a defensive back. He was a former Harvard star who was a good enough baseball player to rise as high as the Double-A level in the Red Sox organization. His path to the majors was blocked by the talented young Boston keystone combination of Rico Petrocelli and Mike Andrews and by the fact that he batted just .166. "I loved baseball," he said. "It was my first choice, but I wasn't good enough."

Dockery's football career also appeared to be over when he was cut by the Dolphins in training camp, and he enrolled at Columbia to pursue a master's degree in city planning. George Paterno, brother of Joe and Dockery's high school coach, contacted Weeb Ewbank, who worked Dockery out and urged him to play in Waterbury to get some experience. Dockery played very well for the Orbits and Ewbank signed him for the Jet taxi squad. He practiced with the Jets during the week and played with the Orbits on weekends.

As the season wore on, the Orbits played better and it was evident that running back Allen Smith was their best player. He scored six touchdowns in his first three games and showed ability both as a runner and a receiver. Smith's Achilles heel, at 5'10½" and 195 pounds, was his size. That was a particular problem for Ewbank, for one of the most important jobs of any Jet running back was protecting Joe Namath and his fragile knees. The Jet backs, Matt Snell, Emerson Boozer, Bill Mathis, and Mark Smolinski, were all big men.

In 1965, the Jets cut former Princeton star Cosmo Iacovazzi, nephew and namesake of the future ACFL commissioner. "We're still looking for a big running back," said a Jets spokesman. "It's too bad he wasn't big enough."[21] At 5'11" and 209 pounds, Iacovazzi was taller and heavier than Smith, which boded poorly for the latter's chances.

"They look at people," Roger Milici said, "and they say they're too small. But Allen was as tough a guy for his size as anyone. He was tough and he could give out punishment. He didn't back down from anyone."

Scout Jim Garrett of the BLESTO-V combine watched Smith play and was impressed. "It's a crime Smith is not playing on an NFL team now," he said, but admitted he'd have a hard time selling his employers on a player that small. Smith had good hands, Garrett said, good balance, a great first step, and ran a 4.6 forty yard dash. But he was too small.

Because of the Orbits' arrangement with the Jets, Smith was in an interesting position. He was not on the Jet taxi squad and if a club wanted to sign him after the season, they could negotiate directly with Rosner. Prior to that time, however, the Jets had the right to sign him to a taxi squad contract, which would tie him to New York and prevent him from signing with another club.

With every game, Smith became more valuable. The screen pass from Corcoran to Smith became Waterbury's best weapon. "On a screen pass to him," said lineman Joe Ginnetti, "you just had to touch someone and he was by you in a heartbeat—in a *heartbeat*. He reminded me of Joe Morris, the little back who played for the Giants several years ago." After seven games, Smith had ten touchdowns and by the end of October led the ACFL in rushing, receiving, and scoring.

9. An Unhappy Relationship

The Jets needed a running back, for Snell had been injured all season. When Boozer got hurt in early November, Ewbank summoned Smith to New York to practice with the team, but did not sign him to a contract. One day, when Smith's name was mentioned during a press conference, Ewbank said Smith made a mistake by not playing for the Jersey Jets in 1966, as he had suggested. He admitted that Smith's blocking had gotten better, but said, "He's not Bill Mathis or Mark Smolinski."

Smith missed the Orbits' final game with a minor back injury. A few days later, Ewbank said Smith had lied about his back in order to avoid getting hurt and that the Jets had been ready to sign him to a contract when he abruptly disappeared, telling the team his mother had been in an automobile accident. He said he was unable to get in touch with Smith and that the story was apparently another lie, designed to hide the fact that Smith was working out with the Lions and Steelers.

It was puzzling that Ewbank couldn't reach Smith, for Jon Stein spoke with him at his home in Toledo. Smith told Stein his back injury was legitimate, but he *had* worked out with the Steelers. The Lions had forced him leave the Steeler camp, since they held his NFL rights.

Smith's contract situation was illustrative of the problems faced by minor league players. ACFL contracts were not only binding; most contained an option clause obligating the players for the following season and forcing major league teams to negotiate a sale price with the minor league club. Most teams were unwilling to pay for the rights to a player who might only be needed to fill in for a week or two. Taxi squadders playing in the ACFL under major league contracts were the only ones with a viable chance of moving up.

Smith said he had a week-to-week deal with the Orbits and was thus not bound to them either for the remainder of the 1967 season or for 1968. The Jets had no claim to him since, although they were paying him to practice, they had not signed him to a contract. Smith said that if Rosner tried to prevent him from signing with an NFL team he would sue. That was a second strike against Smith. He was not only small; he was also feisty and problematic.

Finally, just before Christmas, Smith signed with the Chicago Bears for a small bonus. No one protested, and the Bears agreed to give the Lions a draft choice if he made the 40-man roster. He did not, and never played in another NFL or AFL game.

Another difficulty in the Jets' arrangement with the Orbits was illustrated by the case of end Tommy Burnett, one of the famous Burnett brothers. Older brother Bobby starred as a halfback at the University of Arkansas and went on to become the 1966 AFL Rookie of the Year with the Buffalo Bills. Younger brother Billy was a star with the Razorback teams of the late '60s.

Tommy Burnett, unlike his brothers, was an end whose claim to fame at Arkansas was catching the touchdown pass that beat archrival Texas in 1966. In 1967, he was placed on the Jet taxi squad and assigned to the Orbits. Burnett suffered a minor knee injury in early October, and although he was not expected to miss much playing time, the weeks went by and he did not return to active duty. Ewbank said the reason Burnett did not go back to Waterbury was that he was afraid of getting hurt again and missing a potential opportunity with the Jets.

The Orbits had a good second half of the season. After the loss to Lowell dropped them to 1–3 and last place in the Northern Division, they had the good fortune to play the Harrisburg Capitols. The Capitols were in the midst of a horrendous campaign, having recently lost 71–7 to the Virginia Sailors and 42–6 to the Westchester Bulls. In five losses they had scored just 19 points while surrendering 158 to the opposition. They beat their scoring average in the 26–5 loss to the Orbits.

As the season drew to a close, Waterbury was one of the hottest clubs in the ACFL, winning five of seven games to put them at 6–5 entering the final game of the season against the division champion Bulls. Without Smith, absent with his mysterious back injury, they lost to finish 6–6, good for third and last in the Northern Division.

As it did every offseason, the ACFL tried to repair its battered carcass. The team in the most dire straits was Wilmington. When its owner jumped ship, the league covered the players' salaries for a week, after which the players were paid by dividing the gate proceeds. For their first game under the socialist experiment, the Virginia Sailors paid Wilmington's traveling expenses. Former owner DuPont allowed the team to use the equipment he'd purchased, and at home games some of the players' wives took tickets and staffed the concession stands to save money. The league kept the franchise alive with the hope of selling it, with the proceeds to be divided among the players and coaches.

The Clippers, despite their financial woes and the fact that they hadn't gotten a single player from the parent Eagles, were actually a decent team. Ron Waller was a first class coach and, although the Clippers finished 2–7, they played competitively almost every week. Midway through the season, Waller was offered the head coaching job at Harrisburg, where he could draw a paycheck rather than rely on gate receipts. The league asked him to remain in Wilmington to hold the team together and Waller acquiesced, only to see the Clippers fold with three games left in the season.

Harrisburg lasted until the end of the season, a testament to the club's fortitude rather than its ability. They lost all eleven of their games and were outscored 389 to 30, averaging less than a field goal a game. When no buyers appeared for the Wilmington franchise, it was combined with Harrisburg for the 1968 season.

Waterbury's performance on the field, especially in the second half, was respectable, but the results at the box office were abysmal, much worse than in 1966. Even the *Republican* lost some of its optimism. In 1966 the paper confidently predicted crowds of 10,000 that never materialized. In 1967 they predicted 5,000, but even that hope went unrealized.

Rosner blamed the press for the low turnout for the Wilmington game, but that turned out to be one of the best crowds of the season. Only about 2,000 watched the Lowell game in September, and when the Giants came to Waterbury in the cold of November, the announced crowd was just 1,205, including absent season ticket holders.

"It's no big secret," wrote Stein, "that the Waterbury Orbits have taken a beating in attendance this season."[22] Rosner said revenue was about half of what it had been in 1966 and admitted that even the sorry announced crowds had been overstated. "[Attendance]," reported Stein, "averaged somewhere around 2,000 per game although none could be sure of the figures given out, because they were sometimes adjusted by Rosner. One night the Orbits did quite poorly at the gate and he gave out a larger figure because of 'pride.'"[23]

The pride of Waterbury had been injured a few months earlier when the San Francisco Giants decided to move their Eastern League franchise to Amarillo, Texas. Frank Monardo leapt to his city's defense. The problem, he claimed, was the low population of Waterbury, and he presented a chart showing the population of all major league baseball cities and their attendance. Waterbury, he pointed out, was tied for 14th with Washington, each having attendance equal to nearly 80 percent of its population. The Mets and Yankees were well in arrears, having drawn just 25 percent and 14 percent respectively, of New York's 7.8 million citizens. The logic wasn't all that compelling, and no one was talking of moving the Mets or Yankees to Municipal Stadium.

It was apparent that the Orbits would also be leaving, and new *Republican* sports editor Don Harrison delivered the eulogy. "The departure of the Orbits," he wrote, "will end a somewhat unhappy relationship between a club owned by New Haven area businessmen and a city it never really became a part of."[24]

Rosner was the face of the Orbits, but he was an outsider, and often a rather abrasive one when things didn't go his way. Moreover, he was a baseball man, not a football man, and he and Cutro often argued about personnel decisions. "That was one of the worst experiences of my life," Cutro said recently. "Waterbury was probably my worst experience ever in football." The fact that Cutro commuted from New Jersey and was not in town promoting the team also hurt attendance.

In February, the ACFL announced that the Orbits were moving to Bridgeport. The city had a new stadium and was closer to New York, which pleased the Jets. Another plus was the fact that there would be local ownership in Bridgeport. The short, unhappy life of the Waterbury Orbits was over.

10

A New Team in Hartford

Nineteen sixty-eight was one of the most violent, divisive years in the history of the United States. In many ways it was like 1860, when the rupture led to the secession of the southern states and a bloody Civil War. The nineteenth century conflict pitted north against south, while the turmoil of the 1960s was demographic rather than geographic, a conflict between those who were older, wealthier, and had a vested interest in maintaining the status quo and, on the other side, the poor, the young, and those who believed they had been left out of the postwar march to prosperity.

There were many times in the late 1960s when it seemed as though the country might descend into a civil war, but there were so many different factions in rebellion that they rarely moved cohesively. Black militants were perhaps the most violent group, but their numbers were small, and when the violence of the Black Panthers supplanted the non-violence of Dr. Martin Luther King, blacks lost the support of the white middle class. By 1968, as American cities were devastated by deadly riots, arson, gunfire, and wholesale looting, the civil rights movement seemed more threatening than inspiring.

Fear of a black rebellion had been the nightmare of the white South since the days of Nat Turner in the mid-nineteenth century, and to them the race riots in northern cities were a warning that Armageddon was imminent. The activity of young whites, with their drugs and rock music and their rejection of traditional values, was threatening to anyone—north or south—who had a stake in maintaining the status quo.

Hippies and yippies were mostly non-violent. The Students for a Democratic Society blew up a few buildings, but they represented a very small faction. The most visible hippies, Abbie Hoffman and Jerry Rubin, were loud, controversial, and sometimes funny, but their act was more outrageous than threatening. The galvanizing aspect of the youth movement was a vehement opposition to the war in Vietnam and the military draft, which snatched up young men and sent them to Southeast Asia to fight a war they saw as imperialist, morally unjust, and dangerous to their physical well-being.

On August 26, 1968, the national convention of the Democratic Party began in Chicago. By the time it ended three days later, battles between young protestors and the Chicago police had been broadcast to living rooms throughout the country. America hadn't experienced such internal violence since the anarchist riots of the late nineteenth century, and never before had such scenes been seen live by so many. All three major television networks covered the convention and reporters Mike Wallace and Dan Rather gave first-hand accounts of their rough treatment at the hands of the police. While there had been many violent scenes during 1968, those that took place at the convention, more than any other, thrust the conflict into the faces of all Americans.

Connecticut's problems mirrored those of the nation. On the day before the Democratic Convention began in Chicago, there was a gun battle between members of the paramilitary right wing Minutemen and the state police in Voluntown, a tiny community tucked into the northeast corner of the state. A group of 25 to 30 pacifists who called themselves the Committee for Non-Violent Action (CNVA) had established a community on a 40-acre Voluntown farm in 1960. They were committed to the removal of violence from all aspects of life, even to the point of refusing to defend themselves if attacked.

At 2:45 a.m. on August 27, four Minutemen wearing masks and carrying rifles stormed the CNVA house and tied up two women who were posted as lookouts. While the CNVA was caught completely by surprise, the FBI and the Connecticut State Police were not. They had been tipped off to the raid and were lying in wait in the surrounding woods. With parachute flares illuminating the night, the police burst from the woods and initiated a gun battle in which all four Minutemen, a trooper, and a female pacifist were wounded. Among the Minutemen were Frank Barber, chairman of the Norwich George Wallace for President Committee, and 79-year-old George Rood. The most seriously injured Minuteman was 24-year-old Louis Rogers, who was blinded.

The pacifists instituted round-the-clock guard shifts, although it is not certain what they would have done if they encountered someone. Perhaps the intruders would have been subjected to a ferocious barrage of reasoning, for the CNVA stated that they would have interfered with the police raid had they known about it because they had a duty to try to reason with intruders. They also said many of them would refuse to testify against their attackers. Fortunately, there was no need for testimony, as the Minutemen pleaded guilty in November.

Violence and unrest create opportunity for demagogues, and on October 8, one of the leading demagogues of the twentieth century arrived in Connecticut. As American cities burned, atavistic Alabaman George C. Wallace rose from the ashes as a serious contender for the nation's highest office. While it was highly unlikely that Wallace, the candidate of the American Independent Party, would be elected, he might win enough electoral votes in the southern states to throw the election into the House of Representatives.

Wallace spoke to 1,500 people at Bridgeport Airport, where he was cheered by his loyal base and heckled by students. Wallace sparred with the hecklers, asking whether there was a barber strike in the area, and when some raised their hands in the stiff-armed Nazi salute, he reminded them that he fought the Nazis before they were born.

Wallace then went to Stratford's Avco Lycoming plant, where 5,000 came out to hear him, and nearly all of them were enthusiastically in his camp. Wallace railed against professors, students, journalists, and anarchists. "There are more of us than there are of you!" he shouted. Wallace promised "Law and Order," an appealing promise in a time of chaos and confusion.

About ten days later, Democratic nominee Hubert Humphrey came to Connecticut. Humphrey was struggling, his campaign shackled to the unpopular war and the violent image of the convention. Accompanied by Governor John Dempsey and Senator Abe Ribicoff, Humphrey gamely stumped through the state, speaking in Hartford and Waterbury and taking a bad licking at Avco Lycoming.

The *Hartford Courant* didn't like Humphrey or Wallace, and endorsed Richard Nixon. "Mr. Nixon is the man best qualified of those available to lead the country through the trying next four years," it told Connecticut readers. Connecticut didn't listen, giving its eight electoral votes to Humphrey.

Although nearly a half century has passed, Connecticut struggles today with many of the same problems that plagued it in 1968. Then, Senator Thomas Dodd was under investigation for financial improprieties. Forty years later his son, Senator Christopher Dodd, was under investigation for financial improprieties. In 1968, the state legislature was accused of concealing deficits by borrowing money to pay current expenses, just as they were 40 years later. Then, as now, ambitious publicly financed real estate projects designed to revitalize downtown Hartford were stalled. The dates have changed but the issues remain the same, and no less intractable.

Connecticut had a serious budget deficit in 1968. In November, State Comptroller Louis Gladstone announced that the projected shortfall for the fiscal year that would end in June 1969 was $123 million. William Czuckrey, executive director of the Connecticut Municipal Council Number 4 of the American Federation of State, County and Municipal Workers, urged Governor Dempsey to form a council to recommend legalizing every possible form of gambling in Connecticut. Horse racing, a lottery, and casino gambling were mentioned as possibilities, and rarely has vice been advocated with such high-handed moral fervor.

"Are we so pure and perfect," Czuckrey asked rhetorically, "that we can afford to maintain an image of snobbish superiority of moral character of some mysterious undefined fashion and condemn gambling practices that all our neighboring states condone?" Research director John Tarrant of the state tax department countered with statistics indicating that New York's lottery was "a wholesale flop" and that the potential of horse racing was limited due to the proliferation of racing in New York. Lotteries and legalized gambling, Tarrant declared, were not the solution to the state's fiscal woes.

As they are in the twenty-first century, the State Board of Education was seriously concerned about racial imbalance in a number of Connecticut school systems, and proposed a plan under which schools that did not achieve balance would be penalized and those that did would be rewarded. It was estimated that the cost of achieving racial balance would be $25 million over two years.

Racial problems plagued the city of Hartford. Riots took place in the streets and Hartford Knights players were given dashboard passes to allow them to drive to and from practice after curfew. Emergency measures were enacted to counteract violence at Weaver High School and Hartford Public High School, with special security personnel hired to patrol hallways, restrooms, and cafeterias.

Drug use among young people was increasing. Hartford police estimated that at least one in ten students over the age of 13 had experimented with recreational drugs. Heroin use was negligible, but marijuana and pills were readily available. Glue sniffing was another source of kicks, and in late October the Hartford Public Health Council instituted regulations designed to curb that vice.

The Hartford economy was struggling and losing jobs. On June 26, Olivetti Underwood Corp., one of the United States' largest manufacturers of typewriters, announced it was closing its Hartford plant, which had been idled by a strike for two weeks. The company had settled strikes in 1962 and 1965, but rather than compromise once more, it decided to shift production to other states. "This is a terrible blow," said Labor Commissioner Renato Ricciuti of the 2,000 jobs that left with Olivetti. He said he would offer "all the resources of the state" to keep Olivetti in Hartford. The union planned a protest march and asked the NAACP and CORE to join them.

The Hartford Board of Education also had a labor problem, as Hartford teachers voted on October 31 to stage the first strike in the city's history. On Friday, November 1, the schools opened but most teachers either stayed home or walked the picket lines. By the end of the day, all but five of the city's schools closed. The city considered the strike an illegal act, prohibited by Connecticut law, and negotiated in that spirit, threatening teachers with contempt of court citations and seeking to hire substitutes to take their places.

On Monday, Superior Court Judge James McGrath threatened to jail teachers for contempt if they didn't return to their classrooms. That day, the city said that 934 of the approximately 1,500 Hartford teachers showed up for work, although all of the high schools and a number of elementary schools remained closed. On Tuesday, the teachers followed the advice of union president Arthur Brouillet and voted to end the strike.

College campuses were the epicenter of youthful unrest, and the University of Connecticut was the scene of several skirmishes. One began when the Dow Chemical Company sent recruiters to Storrs to interview prospective job candidates and saw them confronted by an angry group of students and faculty members. Twelve protesters refused orders to disperse and were threatened with disciplinary action.

The twelve, along with their supporters, demanded that President Homer D. Babbidge, Jr. grant them amnesty. They occupied Gulley Hall and announced plans to spend the night. Babbidge, anxious to avoid a confrontation that, in the heated atmosphere of 1968, might well have escalated to violence, said no disciplinary action would be taken against the occupiers, since they had not disrupted any university activities. He indicated, however, that he would not grant amnesty to the Dow protestors.

Babbidge was soon faced with another dilemma when a second group of students approached Gulley Hall with the intention of dispossessing the protestors by force. The president convinced the second group to meet with him in a nearby classroom and, after a tense session, they agreed to leave the Gulley occupants in peace.

During the night several faculty members visited the occupants and tried to talk them into leaving. Many inside the building wanted to capitulate, but a hard core group had convinced them to hold out, and seemed intent on provoking a confrontation with the police.

By the following afternoon, the patience of Babbidge and the State of Connecticut had worn thin and 150 state troopers prepared to storm Gulley Hall and empty it by force if necessary. Provost Edward Gant stood in front of the building and read a statement indicating that the police were ready to enter and charge all those inside with trespassing. Faced with armed resistance, the protestors decided that discretion was the better part of valor and left.

About two weeks later, violence finally erupted on the Storrs campus. On this occasion the recruiter was Olin-Mathieson Corporation, which manufactured ammunition for M-14 and M-16 rifles. When students began smashing windows and tearing lattice work from the house in which the company's representatives were working, Babbidge again called in the state police. They arrived in full riot gear and waded into the crowd, dragging the protestors to buses and placing them under arrest. By the end of the melee four people had been injured and twelve were arrested. The Students for a Democratic Society issued a statement promising revenge and including the phrase "blood for blood." Babbidge said it was the saddest day of his life.

With Connecticut and the United States on the brink of civil war, what was the opinion of football players, most of who were of the same generation as the protestors? "Didn't talk about, didn't know about it, didn't care about it," said Bob Stohrer. "It was very apolitical," added Pudge Henkel. "Politically, it was almost agnostic."

"I was involved with my own little life," said Jim Murphy. "I was teaching school. I had a wife and baby. I was playing for the Knights and getting a master's degree. I was kind of in my own cocoon and didn't see much of it." "It was all football," said John Land, who played in the ACFL from 1966 to 1971. "I don't remember having one conversation with anybody about world affairs or U.S. affairs."

"Some of us talked politics," said Knights cornerback Waide Robinson, "and we were trying to mentor kids long before the mentoring programs that are out there today. And then you had guys that partied a lot. And you had some that were just pure athletes—all they wanted to do was get up to the next level."

Some players *were* interested in experiencing the youth culture. Mark Proskine and Pete Quackenbush of the Knights attended the aborted Powder Ridge rock festival in 1970. "There were ambulances," the latter recalled, "and they were hauling people away from drug overdoses." Still, Quackenbush was more curious than involved. "I knew all that stuff was going on," he said, "but Mark had more of a social conscience than I did. He was much more into politics."

Many men in their twenties became politically aware when they were drafted into the armed services, but a number of football players were exempt from military service. Some had chronically bad knees or shoulders. Others were over the maximum weight limits. Some were married, while others were overage.

When Connecticut voters went to the polls in November to elect a president, Hartford ballots included a referendum question that was, according to the sports and political establishment of the city, a choice between economic stagnation and the opportunity to put Hartford on the sports map and assure its financial future. The voters would decide whether they wanted a brand new Civic Center.

In early September, the City Council had voted to approve a $15 million

10. A New Team in Hartford

bond issue to fund construction of a downtown Civic Center, subject to referendum. The proposed project was to be a partnership between the public sector and a private developer. The city would build the arena and the developer would construct contiguous retail and commercial space. In early 1966, a Baltimore consulting group had performed a study projecting that a civic center would probably lose money during the first few years. Two years later, a second analysis projected immediate breakeven results with the potential of a modest surplus. The city leaders accepted the second analysis and forged boldly ahead.

The *Courant's* Bill Lee lined up squarely behind the proposal, telling his readers that if they voted against it, "you may regret it as long as you live." It was "one of the most magnificent plans ever devised to make Hartford a better city in which to live." Lee would vote for the proposal if he could, but like so many boosters of Hartford, Lee lived in the suburbs. "Please don't make a protest about this thing being all right for me because I don't pay taxes in Hartford," he wrote. "It is much bigger than that."[1]

The *Courant's* editorial staff also urged an affirmative vote, citing projections of an immediate increase in annual tax revenue of $200,000 to $250,000 from the center and $1.5 to $2.3 million per year from the surrounding development. What the *Courant* didn't say was that much of the projected increase in taxes would be needed to cover debt service on the bonds, which would be $1 million the first year.

Arthur J. Lumsden, president of the Greater Hartford Chamber of Commerce, estimated that the city's convention business would triple and bring an additional $15 million in revenue to Hartford businesses. He noted that New Haven and Springfield had constructed convention centers, and worried that Hartford would be left behind.[2]

Not everyone was as excited as Lee and the Chamber of Commerce. The Concerned Citizens' Council was upset by the fact that a civic center received priority over educational facilities, and questioned the revenue assumptions that made the project so appealing.

By the time Richard Nixon was elected to the presidency and the Civic Center project was approved (by a 2 to 1 margin), a football team called the Hartford Knights was preparing to take part in the championship game of the Atlantic Coast Football League.

The first public notice of the Knights had come on January 15, 1968, when members of the greater Hartford media received the following announcement: "Peter M. Savin and Herbert C. Savin of the Roger Sherman Rigging Company cordially invites (sic) you to attend a press conference and luncheon concerning an important sports announcement Monday, January 22, 1968 at 12:00 noon, Carlton Room, Hotel America, Hartford, Connecticut. Please reply."[3]

Pete Savin, whose given name was Marvin Steven Savin, was the 38-year-old son of Abraham I. "Butch" Savin, founder of a construction conglomerate and well-known in horse racing circles. Butch's brother, Moses Savin, was mayor of New London, Connecticut. Pete was a graduate of the prestigious Loomis School in Windsor, Connecticut, where he played football and baseball, and a member of the Cornell University Class of 1952. He served as a lieutenant in the U.S. Army for two years immediately following his graduation, and then joined the family business and became a highly visible member of the Hartford community.

Several years earlier, Butch Savin's accountant advised him to find a hobby that could generate a tax loss. The elder Savin decided to breed and race thoroughbred horses, an enterprise that turned out to be very successful. Savin's Mr. Prospector was sire to a number of top thoroughbreds and Royal and Regal ran in the 1973 Kentucky Derby, actually leading for the first few seconds.

"Every time he would pump money into horse racing," said broadcaster Lou Palmer, "he had a string of winners." Pete eventually took over the stable and breeding operation but, as his wife Elaine said, "We found that the racing business is a wonderful hobby but it's a *really* bad business." Eventually, Butch Savin's son found the ultimate tax shelter—owning a minor league football team.

Savin was a big sports fan and had always wanted to own a pro franchise. He was friends with Ralph Wilson, owner of the Buffalo Bills, and Sonny Werblin of the Jets, and at various times was reported to have been interested in acquiring the Patriots, Eagles, and 49ers. Manch Wheeler, who quarterbacked the Hartford Charter Oaks and Waterbury Orbits under Fred Wallner, worked for Savin's rigging company. "I knew from working for Pete," Wheeler said, "that he was very interested in that sort of thing. So I told Fred, 'Go talk to him. See if you can sell him on it.'"

Horse racing had a great deal of glamour, but operating a football team was even better. Savin couldn't invite his horses to parties and show them off to his friends like he did with his football players, and he couldn't befriend the horses the way he could the players. For Savin, operating the Hartford Knights was the highlight of a very interesting life. "He'd always wanted to own part of a football team," said Elaine, "and that was the greatest desire of his whole life."

Before the Savins held their press conference, a story appeared in the *Hartford Courant* stating that the brothers were about to accept a franchise in the Atlantic Coast Football League and attempt to oust the Continental League's Charter Oaks from Dillon Stadium. New ACFL Commissioner Cosmo Iacovazzi refused to confirm or deny the rumors. He would only say that the league was about to hold a meeting at the Roosevelt Hotel in New York to select three new franchises.

10. A New Team in Hartford

When the Savins made their formal announcement, it was exactly what the rumors said it would be. They had obtained an ACFL franchise and would apply to the Hartford City Council for the lease of Dillon Stadium. If they were successful, it would mean the end of the Charter Oaks, since Dillon could not accommodate two teams and there was no other suitable playing site in Hartford.

In early February, the Continental League announced that it had merged with the Professional Football League of America and that there would be 20 teams in the combined circuit. The Charter Oaks would be one of them, if they had a place to play.

Just one day after the formal announcement, the Savins submitted their lease application to the city. They offered $65 per practice session, more than the $41 paid by the Charter Oaks, and $600 per game, a slight increase from the $573 paid by the Oaks. The Savins also offered to post two $100,000 performance bonds, one to guaranty the lease obligations and the second to cover all other expenses. The bonds were a key to the proposal, since the Charter Oaks still owed the city $1,300 due under the 1967 lease.

On March 18, before the city had a chance to make a decision on the Knights' proposal, Don Brewer announced that the Charter Oaks would cease operations. He sent a letter to his stockholders indicating that losses for the past four years had totaled $250,000 and that the prospect of raising additional capital was dim. Brewer took a number of parting shots, blaming Bill Lee for "distortions and inaccuracies" that had hurt the club and its economic prospects. He decried the efforts of the "giant Savin operation" to dispossess him from Dillon Stadium and claimed that extreme political pressure was one of the causes of his exit. In conclusion, Brewer stated that "we must now yield to the onslaught which has battered at our walls these past four years."[4]

"They did a pretty good job with what they had to work with," Dick Bowman said of the Brewers, "but they didn't have deep pockets. Don Brewer was a good guy, but he had no money, and if you don't have money you can't go into something like this or you'll go bankrupt."

Pete Savin had far greater resources than Don Brewer, and operating the club was more joy than struggle. "He absolutely loved what he did with that team," said broadcaster Arnold Dean. "No amount of money was too much. He wanted the best uniforms, the best coaching staff, the best accommodations."

While Brewer blamed the media for his failures, Savin courted them. "He was always very cordial and friendly," said Dennis Randall of the *Hartford Times*. "He would come up and say hello to you at the games or at practice. He was not an aloof guy; he tried to be a regular guy."

Every week during the season, the Knights held a press conference at their office, at which offensive and defensive players of the week were honored and the most recent game was discussed. "Every Tuesday," said Randall, "we'd go to the Knights' offices to rehash the previous week's game. Fred Wallner would spend an hour with us running the film back and forth to demonstrate certain techniques, or what went right and what went wrong." The press always gave the Knights a nice write-up the next day.

The beat writers traveled together, and were friendly and cooperative competitors. Bruce Berlet of the *Courant* and Howie Holcomb of the *Times* worked the Knights' beat in tandem for three years. When one had to file a dispatch to meet a deadline, the other kept an eye on the action, and they always compared notes. "I always said," Berlet related, "we may not be right, but we'll always be the same." And with only two reporters in attendance most nights, that was all that mattered.

WTIC of Hartford, a powerful 50,000 watt station, broadcast almost every game the Knights played, with the veteran Arnold Dean on play-by-play the entire time. His first analyst was Lou Palmer, who in 1978 became the first announcer hired by ESPN. Dean had worked with Palmer on various assignments but never on live game broadcasts.

"Normally," said Dean, "the relationship between the play-by-play man and the analyst is something that grows smooth with time. But with Lou, the first time we did a game together it was like we were a matched set. I would do the play-by-play as concisely as I could and he would come in immediately with a comment that fit the situation perfectly and then get it back to me just in time to get the ball snapped."

Dean and Palmer enjoyed each other's company in a way that few others would. On airplanes, they would quiz each other on the players' numbers. "I'd say 'number 40,'" Dean related, "and he'd say 'Tom Morris.' We knew all of the Knights' numbers, so we would play that game with the other team. I'd throw out a number and he'd say the player. He'd throw out another player and I'd give the number."

When the plane landed, Dean and Palmer often found themselves in challenging surroundings. "I worked with a lot of kids over the years who wanted to get into this business," Dean said, "and I told them, 'Don't get the idea that the bigger the game, the more difficult it is.' The higher you go, the easier it is. At the Super Bowl they do everything but give you a play-by-play sheet before the game is even played. They give you *every* convenience. With the Knights we had to sometimes guess at the yardage markers. Guys would change uniforms at halftime and they wouldn't even tell you. There are tremendous inconveniences."

"One time," he said, "we got out there and they didn't have any markings on the field for the yardage. All they had were placards on the sidelines every

10. A New Team in Hartford

ten yards. But it seemed like every person on the field was standing in front of them. Somebody would break this way and that way or break up the middle and I had no idea where he ended up. I'd have to go back to the 10 yard line, which was the first marker I could see, and count 20–30–40 and say 'OK, he made about a 30 yard pickup on that play.'"

Palmer remembered working with an engineer who was seeing his first football game. "Not only had this guy never seen a football game," Palmer said, "he'd never been at a sporting event. He said he worked at a Christian radio station. He brought us a stand up microphone like you would see Bert Parks use at the Miss America pageant." The commercial breaks were mis-timed, the announcers were cut off in mid-sentence, but it was all part of broadcasting in the ACFL.

The media that followed the Knights became part of the family. "It wasn't my team," said Holcomb, "but it *was* my team. I was there during the week and every Saturday. I knew the guys and cheered with them and was sad with them. I know there's supposed to be no cheering in the press box but that's a load of crap because you can't be with a small town team like that for five years and not think something of them." Dean was a professional broadcaster and never used terms like "we" or "us," but deep in his heart he too was rooting for the Knights.

Every good team needs a mascot and a song, and the Knights had both. Their mascot was a horse named Lancer, ridden by Mrs. Ann Johnson and their song, called "The Knights Are Out to Win," was written by Henry Steiner, II:

> THE KNIGHTS ARE OUT TO WIN
> Down the field, boys!
> The taste of victory will be sweet
> Oh, the Knights are out to win.
> Never yield, boys!
> The black and gold will not be beat
> Oh, the Knights are out to win.
> Win the crown, Knights.
> For Hartford Town, Knights.
> And if you're down Knights, never give in.
> Down the field, boys,
> And doom the others to defeat.
> Oh, the Knights are out to win.

Savin quickly learned that while there was fun to be had as the owner of a football team, players sometimes presented problems he hadn't experienced with his equine investments. Elaine Savin remembered getting a call in the middle of the night from a player who was in a phone booth—naked. He couldn't remember how he got there or how he lost his clothes. "Pete took the call," Mrs. Savin said, "and then turned to me and said, 'You won't believe this.' He wanted Pete to come get him in the middle of the night."

"He always helped them out," said Knights secretary Sandy Rubera. "If they had issues or problems, they would go to him and he'd help them out." She recalled being at a party and talking with a state trooper friend who told her he had just arrested one of the Knights players for a minor offense.

Sure enough, when Rubera arrived at work on Monday, she received a call from the player, who asked if he could speak to Savin. He arrived with the young lady who had been involved in the escapade and met with the Knights owner. "Peter gave him a lecture," Rubera recalled. "He asked him what he was thinking to have done what he did, and in the end everything worked out all right."

If you were going to play minor league football, Hartford was a very good place to do it, for Savin operated his franchise almost like an NFL club. "There was something about the setup in Hartford," said Waide Robinson, "that made you feel like you were there with the big boys." Salaries were higher, travel was first class, and the team always ate its pre-game meal at a nice restaurant. Game programs were top quality and 40 or 50 pages long, filled with ads, photos, stories and statistics, while those of other ACFL clubs were often just a few mimeographed pages.

"It's not like you were going to get rich," said Dick Bowman, "but you were going to make more than most of the other players, you were going to have the best equipment, and you were going to have an organization behind you that really wanted you to do well. I'd been with a lot of teams and that was far and away the best minor league program and organization that I ever had the experience of playing with. There were teams galore and leagues all over the place but it was really minor league football until the Savins came along." "Pete Savin was a major league guy in a minor league situation," said linebacker Mark Proskine.

"We flew to games," recalled Nick DeFelice. "They treated us like we were in the National Football League. I was the athletic director at Hamden Hall Country Day School. We played Saturday afternoons and if the Knights had a Saturday night game they'd pick me up in their private jet and fly me to the game. They treated us royally. We dressed in blazers with the Knights logo on them."

"Peter was first class all the way," said Manch Wheeler, who served as general manager from 1969 to 1971. "I was trying to save money by using buses and he said, 'No, we're not putting the boys on buses. We're going to fly.' I said, 'Peter, it's going to cost a lot more money.' He said, 'I don't care.'"

Many players have forgotten the details of the games they played, but everyone remembers Pete Savin's parties at his spectacular Bloomfield hilltop mansion.

There was a big bash on his birthday, and generally another around the holidays, after the Knights' season was over.

"That's as close to Hollywood as I ever got," said Howie Holcomb. "When you came into the house you were on the top floor and walked down a wrought iron staircase into what was normally the living room. There was a heated marble floor that was used for dancing. There were two bars, plus guys walking around with wine and beer. There were snacks and appetizers and at ten o'clock you sat down to a full course dinner. There were two orchestras and continuous music. It was a nice little addition to covering football."

"The party really wowed me the first time I went there," said lineman Pete Anderson. "My wife still talks about it. It was such a big deal at that time. I don't think it could be any more impressive today if you went to Jerry Jones' house or the Maras' house."

"They had guys parking your car," said Lou Palmer, "and then they drove you up to the house in a golf cart. The minute I walked in with my wife, Elaine Savin met us at the door and asked what we were drinking. I said I'd have a scotch and soda and when we got inside she handed me this *huge* tumbler that was one hundred percent scotch. She said she couldn't find any soda. It was an absolutely wild celebration and just a great time."

"I have great memories of Pete," said lineman John Skladany. "As an owner he was right there with us. He was good to us and he enjoyed being around the players and being around the game. If you needed something, you could go to him and he would try to help you out. If you needed a couple of extra bucks or you needed a job in the off season, he'd try to make it right for you. I don't think he ever cared about making money. He liked going to the games, he liked the competition, and he made it fun."

"Pete Savin was more of a personality than an employer," said Bob Stohrer. "This was *his* team. You often hear about the tough times, the bus rides, the lousy accommodations and all those things, but he made it as easy as possible on us. He was a very unique guy and he and his family loved us. He was just a great man. You didn't feel like you were playing minor league football."

Savin went to nearly every practice and was on the sideline for each game, proudly wearing his football shoes, his black Knights windbreaker and cap, and working the officials hard. "Christ Almighty," said Joe Murphy. "He used words I'd never heard before." Lou Palmer and Arnold Dean said that when he paced the sideline he reminded them of Allie Sherman, the wiry, intense coach of the New York Giants. "He loved it," Dick Bowman said. "He was out there half pretending to coach. He just wanted to be a part of it. Pete would yell and holler and scream."

There was a major difference between Savin and other powerful, egotistical owners of sports franchises. Pete screamed at the officials. He sometimes fought with the other owners. But he never interfered with the way his coach ran the team and never belittled his players in public.

Although both Pete and Herb made the announcement of the Knights formation, it soon became apparent that Pete was the driving force behind the franchise. He was initially assisted by general manager Joe Fenton, a former Cornell football player who was an Academic All-American his senior year. Like many Cornell football players, Fenton worked for the Savin organization during the summer, as a ditch digger. Following graduation, he joined the Navy, where he advanced to Lieutenant junior grade as a UDT-22 frogman. He was discharged in 1965 and had been working for the Savin companies ever since.

The other full time member of the administrative staff was secretary Sandy Rubera, an East Hartford native who'd aspired to a career as a flight attendant. She was working at Pratt and Whitney when a friend, knowing she was a big football fan, told her of the opportunity with the Knights. Rubera was the team's

Coach Fred Wallner (left) and owner Pete Savin on the Hartford sideline.

secretary from the day they began operations until the day they closed the doors in 1973. She was young, pretty, and a little naïve. Once when she pointed out how nice it was that so many of the wives followed their husbands around the league, someone had to explain to her that they weren't wives. The players were very protective of Rubera, treating her like a little sister, and if anyone made unwanted advances they were likely to be confronted by a very large football player.

The Knights trainer was Tom Altieri, who'd acquired his skills during his service in World War II as the trainer for Paul Brown's famous Great Lakes teams. Altieri, who operated a fitness center in Meriden, also remained with the Knights for their entire existence.

At the press conference announcing the acquisition of the franchise, Savin indicated that a coach had not been named, but it was assumed that Wallner, who'd been an advisor, would be the man. The formal announcement of Wallner's appointment was made in March.

Wallner, 40, was still fit and trim, an intense chain smoker with an almost completely bald head that he usually covered with a fedora or baseball cap. Although he worked in a sales capacity for Heublein, an international liquor distributer, Wallner was totally focused on the game of football. "Fred was a piece of work," said Dennis Fitzgibbons, "a crazy man. He was really, really intense. He would just eat, sleep, and drink football. He was as intense a fellow as you'd ever want to meet."

Coaching a minor league team is different than coaching an NFL squad. The NFL coach, with his many assistants, is like a CEO, overseeing the operation and setting the tone, but often having little involvement in one-on-one instruction. A minor league coach, with a smaller staff, usually took a more "hands-on" approach.

A second difference is that minor leaguers are not full time football players. "It wasn't like coaching an NFL team," said Lou Palmer, "where it's an end-all and be-all and that's all you do. Some of these guys had other commitments. But Wallner approached it like he was coaching an NFL team."

"There was no joking with Fred," said Jim Murphy. "It was *business, business, business!* If you made a joke, he'd look at you as if to say, 'What is this guy *saying*? That's not the way we do things around here.'"

"I had a lot of respect for that guy," said former Charter Oak Mike Mosolf, "but at times I was afraid of him. He didn't have a lot of patience and he had an explosive temper. A couple of times I thought he was going to punch me." "I was scared to death of him," added Ken Blasser.

The most common adjective used by Wallner's former players to describe him was "hard-nosed." Perhaps the best description was given by fullback Don

Abbey. "Fred was just a really, really, really kind man, a nice man," Abbey said, "in a violent sort of way. If we were going to war, I would want to be in a trench with Fred, and there weren't many other coaches I would say that about. We all knew what the game was about. It's knocking the other guy on his ass. Fred made it more fun. He didn't have favorites. He busted everybody's butt."

"He reminded me of a guy," said John Sponheimer, "who would run through a wall rather than walk around it. He had a rough, gruff exterior but was a little softer once you got to know him."

"I never met anyone quite like him," said Roger Milici. "I'll always remember him addressing the team in his boxer shorts and fedora. He was very passionate about the game and about winning. He was never a big fan of mine because he didn't think I had enough speed to make the team. But I loved to play for him because he was a winner. Years later when I played against his teams, even though he knew me well he'd tell the guys to jack me up. He would do anything for a win."

"Fred was very dynamic," said Dick Bowman. "He'd get in there and take a shot. The first day I walked in there I'm thinking 'I'm a big time player but they just don't realize it yet.' He gave me a shot in the solar plexus and I couldn't even breathe. I wasn't ready for it. Then I got ready and broke his watch the next time."

"Fred would see something," said Nick DeFelice, "and he'd start walking down the line talking to the offensive linemen. By the time he got to the end you'd see everybody doing the same thing—strapping on their helmet because they knew they were going to get hit. He was going to show you and he was going to hit you."

"You're 22 or 23 years old," said Fitzgibbons, "and as big and strong as you're ever going to be and here's this guy old enough to be your dad and he's demonstrating on you, saying, 'c'mon, bring it, bring it, give me your best shot.'" "He'd give somebody a forearm shiver," said Charlie Tiblom, "and really jolt them and he'd say, 'I should be out there playing. My heart says go but my legs say no.' He used to say, 'Gentlemen, you've got to do what you can with what you've got while you've got it before you lose it.'"

The practice incidents were instructional. On a couple of other occasions, Wallner went after players in anger. "We had a kid from the Patriots named Preston Johnson," said one former player, "and Fred went after him in the locker room. They were trading punches. Fred was twenty years older but he went after him. Johnson was gone the next week."

Wallner could be brutal on certain players. "One of the things you don't like," said Stohrer, "is when you see somebody pick on someone to the point of that person breaking down. He could do that. He could get on a guy so bad that he'd try to break him down. It's character building for some people and for others maybe not. If you didn't have the guts and ability to get the job done or you quit in practice or whatever, he'd beat you up. He'd beat you up pretty good. You had a bad game and you were on the fourth team on Monday."

"He kind of drilled some people," said Tom Rowland. "He could be really harsh to people if they screwed up. Fred could just be merciless. God, you just felt so sorry for the guys he would get on. But maybe he had to be that way. Maybe that's why he was so successful."

Despite his aggressiveness and violent approach to the game, most who played for Wallner came away with great respect for his ability. After his solar plexus recovered, Bowman came to appreciate Wallner. "Fred would talk to you and he wasn't above you," he said. "I started enjoying football again because of him and so did a lot of other players. He got the players to produce." "He was a great coach," said Bob Shemeth, "one of the greatest motivators. He brought out the best in every one of his players."

Wallner had a tremendous knowledge of the game. "Fred was the best," said longtime assistant Bill Boehle. "It was his knowledge, his experience, his intensity. My goodness, he would watch a play and tell you what every man did. He knew what all eleven guys did."

"I never knew a man who knew more about football than Fred," said DeFelice, who played two years for Weeb Ewbank. "I can't emphasize enough how much this man knew about football and every position. It didn't matter if it was quarterback, halfback, defensive back—he knew it. If you made a mistake on the field, he saw it."

Tiblom and others who came from small colleges thought Wallner, a Notre Dame grad, had a bias toward those from bigger schools. Tiblom had a stormy, difficult relationship with Wallner. In 1971, he was starting at guard when the Knights acquired Angelo Loukas, who was also a guard and had a big league background. Before Loukas' first game, Wallner came over to Tiblom in the locker room.

"He sat down next to me," Tiblom said, "put his arm around my shoulders and said, 'Charlie, we just got this guy Angelo Loukas. He was with the Bills for a couple of years and we think he's pretty good. We're going to put Angelo in your spot and start him instead of you.'" Tiblom was furious. "I told him I'd been playing good ball and hadn't done anything wrong." "And," Tiblom added, "why don't you find someone else to snap for your damn punts and extra points because I ain't doing it. I ain't even dressing if you're dropping me down to second string."

Wallner thought about that for a few seconds. "He walked away from me," Tiblom continued, "and went over and put his arm around Pierre Marchando [the Knights other guard]. 'Pierre,' he said, 'we just got this guy Angelo Loukas from Buffalo and we're going to run him at first string in your position.'"

In Savin and Wallner, the Knights had an owner with a lot of money and enthusiasm and a coach who would stop at nothing to win. All they had to do was find enough talented players who wanted to be Hartford Knights.

11

The Championship Team: The Right Place at the Right Time

There's not a lot of difference between the ability of NFL substitutes and those who just miss making the grade. During the 1987 strike, the owners resumed the schedule with replacement players, primarily men who'd been released from NFL rosters. A number of regulars, including stars like Tony Dorsett and Danny White of the Cowboys, defied the union and played with the replacements.

One would think that the stars, playing against patched-together defenses manned by rejects, would have rolled up phenomenal statistics. Yet that was not the case. The performance of the regulars was not markedly better than normal, and there were a number of unheralded performers from the sandlots that did much better. The talent differential between those that make it and those that barely miss is quite thin and, in many cases, a matter of being in the right place at the right time.

Many players go to training camp facing very long odds. Those from a small college are at a big disadvantage, since they're unknown and have never faced top flight competition. Those that aren't drafted have a second strike. Draftees usually get some bonus money, and anytime a team has money invested in a player, they will get a much longer look than a free agent in whom the team has no vested interest. One dropped pass or missed block by a free agent generally leads to a quick bus ticket out of town.

Bob Tucker, all-pro tight end for the New York Giants, is a classic example of a player who overcame very long odds to forge a solid NFL career. In 1968, he went to camp with the Boston Patriots as an undrafted free agent from Bloomsburg State College. "When you come out of a school like Bloomsburg," Tucker said, "you don't come highly recommended and you're expected to fail. You're just a body in training camp."

"When I first started I thought I had just as much opportunity to make the club as anyone but you really don't because you don't get the playing time. They give the playing time to their veteran players, their draft choices, and the free agents that come from larger schools. There are a lot of bodies around just to rest the regular players and I was one of those bodies."

"If you're from a small school," said lineman Charlie Tiblom of Central Connecticut, "it's as if you go up there with two strikes on you. If you happen to miss the ball on the first pitch you're history."

Kicker Norm Davidson from Central had a tryout with the Bears in 1972. Chicago flew in a number of free agent kickers on a Friday evening and brought them to Soldier Field on Saturday. Each tried three field goals from the ten yard line—one from the left hash mark, one from the center of the field and one from the right hash mark. They moved back in ten yard increments and took three kicks from each distance. "I was perfect on the first twelve," Davidson recalled, "and then from the 50 I missed two wide and one short. We stayed over Sunday and had breakfast and lunch and I never heard from them again. I think maybe they just wanted another five yards of distance." That was Davidson's only major league trial, foiled by three misses.

During his tenure as a quarterback for the Knights, Tom Sherman was invited to try out for the Philadelphia Eagles. "There were about thirty quarterbacks there," he recalled, "and they put us in this long line. The first kid stepped up to the line of scrimmage and they said, 'Throw a hook route.' He threw a hook route and then he went to the end of the line. He had to wait for 29 guys to throw before he got to throw again."

"Those camps were zoos," said Lou Piccone. "Hundreds of people milling all around—fat slobs, hippies, wierdos, guys on lunch break from McDonald's. So when the coaches told me to take a powder, I realized it didn't mean anything. It just meant they hadn't seen me. I wasn't on their agenda for the day."[1]

If it was hard for a kicker or quarterback to be noticed, it was even more difficult for a lineman. Joe Ginnetti, after a few years with the Bridgeport Jets and Hartford Knights, got an invitation to the 1973 training camp of the New York Jets. "I tell everybody," he said, "that my claim to fame is that Joe Namath had his hands between my legs."

When the regular season began, however, Namath's hands were between John Schmitt's legs and Ginnetti was back in Hartford. "As an offensive lineman," he said, "I think the only chance you have to make it is if you were drafted. If they've invested some money in you they're going to keep you around."

When he was in the Jets' camp, Ginnetti became friends with linebacker Rob Spicer, who he battled every day in practice. "There was a kid they'd drafted from Clemson, and Spicer would tell me I was much tougher on him than this kid was, but they had invested money in him while I was coming off

11

The Championship Team: The Right Place at the Right Time

There's not a lot of difference between the ability of NFL substitutes and those who just miss making the grade. During the 1987 strike, the owners resumed the schedule with replacement players, primarily men who'd been released from NFL rosters. A number of regulars, including stars like Tony Dorsett and Danny White of the Cowboys, defied the union and played with the replacements.

One would think that the stars, playing against patched-together defenses manned by rejects, would have rolled up phenomenal statistics. Yet that was not the case. The performance of the regulars was not markedly better than normal, and there were a number of unheralded performers from the sandlots that did much better. The talent differential between those that make it and those that barely miss is quite thin and, in many cases, a matter of being in the right place at the right time.

Many players go to training camp facing very long odds. Those from a small college are at a big disadvantage, since they're unknown and have never faced top flight competition. Those that aren't drafted have a second strike. Draftees usually get some bonus money, and anytime a team has money invested in a player, they will get a much longer look than a free agent in whom the team has no vested interest. One dropped pass or missed block by a free agent generally leads to a quick bus ticket out of town.

Bob Tucker, all-pro tight end for the New York Giants, is a classic example of a player who overcame very long odds to forge a solid NFL career. In 1968, he went to camp with the Boston Patriots as an undrafted free agent from Bloomsburg State College. "When you come out of a school like Bloomsburg," Tucker said, "you don't come highly recommended and you're expected to fail. You're just a body in training camp."

"When I first started I thought I had just as much opportunity to make the club as anyone but you really don't because you don't get the playing time. They give the playing time to their veteran players, their draft choices, and the free agents that come from larger schools. There are a lot of bodies around just to rest the regular players and I was one of those bodies."

"If you're from a small school," said lineman Charlie Tiblom of Central Connecticut, "it's as if you go up there with two strikes on you. If you happen to miss the ball on the first pitch you're history."

Kicker Norm Davidson from Central had a tryout with the Bears in 1972. Chicago flew in a number of free agent kickers on a Friday evening and brought them to Soldier Field on Saturday. Each tried three field goals from the ten yard line—one from the left hash mark, one from the center of the field and one from the right hash mark. They moved back in ten yard increments and took three kicks from each distance. "I was perfect on the first twelve," Davidson recalled, "and then from the 50 I missed two wide and one short. We stayed over Sunday and had breakfast and lunch and I never heard from them again. I think maybe they just wanted another five yards of distance." That was Davidson's only major league trial, foiled by three misses.

During his tenure as a quarterback for the Knights, Tom Sherman was invited to try out for the Philadelphia Eagles. "There were about thirty quarterbacks there," he recalled, "and they put us in this long line. The first kid stepped up to the line of scrimmage and they said, 'Throw a hook route.' He threw a hook route and then he went to the end of the line. He had to wait for 29 guys to throw before he got to throw again."

"Those camps were zoos," said Lou Piccone. "Hundreds of people milling all around—fat slobs, hippies, wierdos, guys on lunch break from McDonald's. So when the coaches told me to take a powder, I realized it didn't mean anything. It just meant they hadn't seen me. I wasn't on their agenda for the day."[1]

If it was hard for a kicker or quarterback to be noticed, it was even more difficult for a lineman. Joe Ginnetti, after a few years with the Bridgeport Jets and Hartford Knights, got an invitation to the 1973 training camp of the New York Jets. "I tell everybody," he said, "that my claim to fame is that Joe Namath had his hands between my legs."

When the regular season began, however, Namath's hands were between John Schmitt's legs and Ginnetti was back in Hartford. "As an offensive lineman," he said, "I think the only chance you have to make it is if you were drafted. If they've invested some money in you they're going to keep you around."

When he was in the Jets' camp, Ginnetti became friends with linebacker Rob Spicer, who he battled every day in practice. "There was a kid they'd drafted from Clemson, and Spicer would tell me I was much tougher on him than this kid was, but they had invested money in him while I was coming off

11. The Championship Team

three years in the minor leagues and I was 25 years old. The handwriting was on the wall."

Often the only way to make a big league roster was as a special team player. There was actually nothing special about special teams, and they were more accurately described by their other names, such as the suicide squad or the bomb squad. "They put me on the kickoff team," said linebacker Ralph Tiner, "and told me I had to be the wedge-breaker. I asked what that meant and they said that you have to run down and when you see the wedge you hurl your body into it."

Bob Stohrer recalled playing in an exhibition game for the Redskins against the Oilers. "I was on the punt team and had the outside coverage," he said. "They put two guys on you out there and they just try to beat the crap out of you. I realized my lack of speed was a detriment because I couldn't get away from them. I had two guys knocking me down. I was picking myself up trying to get away and they'd knock me down again." "You've got to get off those special teams," said Nick DeFelice. "That's where you get killed. You don't last too long on special teams."

A player who was willing and able to play well on special teams was a valued commodity. "I did it out of necessity," said Piccone. "It was a way of staying on a roster. I broke more wedges than anybody in the fucking universe. My role was high speed impact. You talk about concussions—I'm fortunate to be standing upright after all the collisions I had. My mother had a whole crew of girls who called themselves the Nifty Knitters. They'd get together to watch the games, light candles, and say prayers. I told them to keep it going. It was tough out there and I needed all the help I could get." Piccone carved out a nine year NFL career as a backup receiver, punt and kick returner, and an invaluable special team star. "I was like shit on the bottom of their shoes," he said. "They couldn't get rid of me."

Anyone who has been around football agrees that in order for a marginal player to get a shot, he has to be in precisely the right place at exactly the right time. "I was around Gil Brandt of the Cowboys a lot," said broadcaster Lou Palmer, "and I saw that the Cowboys looked for a certain type of player. If he didn't have what they were looking for they'd pass, even if the guy had a lot of talent."

"Some of it was luck," said John Dockery, who went from the Waterbury Orbits and Bridgeport Jets to the New York Jets and Pittsburgh Steelers. "Some of it was persistence and being willing to do whatever was necessary and just refusing to quit. Those trips to Waterbury and Bridgeport were character building, but who needs that? I had enough character. It got depressing."

"You just had to somehow keep your energy up and show it to the coaches.

I'm sure some of the guys said, 'Can you believe Dockery actually made it to the NFL for a few years?' Some of them are probably shaking their heads. I wasn't the best athlete on the field or the most gifted, but I played with greats like Mean Joe Greene, Franco Harris, Joe Willie, Boozer, and Snell. You get a shot of humility when you're playing next to a guy like Mel Blount of the Steelers and he's covering guys and they can't even get off the line of scrimmage. You wonder if we're playing the same position. But then you say, 'Wait a minute. I can do some of this stuff and I'm smart enough to know what's going on. I'm delighted to be here and I'm going to enjoy it.'"

Competing for a position with a star player was intimidating and sometimes debilitating. When Lee Grosscup arrived in the Giant camp, he told head coach Jim Lee Howell that he could punt. Howell told him to join another punter working out across the field. "I took a snap and kicked the ball about 45 yards," Grosscup recalled, "a pretty decent kick. Then the other guy drops the ball and I heard a sound like I'd never heard before. It was just an enormous sound and the ball shot off his foot and went out there about 65 yards. I hadn't done my homework and didn't realize Don Chandler was there and he was one of the best punters in the game. I had such an inferiority complex. When somebody out-drives you by 20 yards on the golf course you decide you need to swing harder. I thought I needed to swing my leg harder and the more I tried the less effective I became. I was never the same punter. That's why they call it the National Football League. At every position they've got somebody who's really, really good."

The notion of place and time is important even for highly skilled athletes who become stars. "I scouted Joe Montana at Notre Dame," said Sherman. "If Joe Montana gets drafted by the Oakland Raiders, he's going to get cut. But he goes to the 49ers, where they run the West Coast offense—the short stuff—the semi-rolls—the boots—the waggles. They utilize the one thing at which he was phenomenal; he had tremendous accuracy. He would throw a seven-yard slant and it could be a 12-yard gain or it could be an 85-yard touchdown because his receiver caught the ball in stride. He got into a situation where he fit the offense."

The same was true at other positions. "Running backs are a dime a dozen," said Sherman. "The kind of scheme they're running will dictate the level of success a running back will have. If you're a power runner and they want you to run east and west, you're going to have a problem. Some guys are good outside runners, while some are good between the tackles. Sometimes it just depends on being in the right place at the right time."

Sherman also talked about a conflict between a scout and a position coach as to whether a player should be drafted, and its impact on that player. "The head coach has to make a decision," he said. "Does he take the position coach's recommendation or overrule him and go with the scout? If I'm the position coach and they bring this kid in that the scouts wanted and I didn't want I'm going to prove that the other guy is better so I'm going to negative coach my guy. But if they take the guy the position coach wants they're going to stick with the kid because the coach wants him around. There's a lot of politics. You'll see a kid get cut and say, 'Wow!' and you'll see them keep a kid and you don't understand it. But that's the way it is."

"I think a lot of it," said John Land, a long-time minor leaguer who became one of the leading rushers in the World Football League, "is where you played and who you know. You had people saying, 'I know him. He played with so-and-so and he's good.' That became a way for people to get in—because of where they played and who they played with."

Attitude and personality were important, and diversity was not part of the average coach's value system. Today's coaches are more tolerant of people who are different, and with the larger number of roster spots, more willing to work with troubled athletes. "Attitude really played a role in those days," said Bob Shemeth. "Teams didn't put up with it. You either came prepared to play football or they weren't going to waste their time on you."

Sometimes the decision to keep a player or set him adrift came down to money. Grosscup was traded from the Giants to the Vikings in 1962 with a big reputation and a fairly hefty contract. He was cut in favor of rookie John McCormick. "I thought I had played better than McCormick and deserved to stay," Grosscup said. "But [Viking coach] Norm Van Brocklin didn't want to spend a few extra thousand dollars when he thought he could have a guy who was going to be just as efficient as I was backing up Fran Tarkenton."

A player who lacked speed or size was probably not going to make it. "The biggest thing you can't coach," said Sherman, "is speed, and the other thing you can't coach is height." "I was always too short," said Land. "They wouldn't consider me because I was always the shortest running back on the team. They crossed me off the list because I was too small and they didn't think I could stay healthy the whole season. But I never missed a game."

"I may have been short," said Piccone, "and I may have only weighed 185 pounds, but I was squatting 550, benching over 400, and running a 4.3 forty. I realized that the only thing they're looking for in a guy like me is speed. You've got to put it on the clock."

"When it comes to speed," said Sherman, "you have to be careful. There are guys who can run the hundred in a straight line, but if they have to deviate off the line they can't do it. You're better off with quickness. If you're a receiver with some quickness you can create separation and get open. As a defensive lineman you never run a 40-yard dash in a game. I played with Ron McDole on the

Buffalo Bills, who was not very fast but was one of the quickest linemen I've ever seen in a confined area."

Raw speed doesn't ensure success on the gridiron. During the 1960s, track stars like Frank Budd, John Carlos, Tommie Smith, and Jimmy Hines tried to make it in football without success. Likewise, mere physical strength doesn't make a great player. "I always get a kick out of it," said Tucker, "when someone says on TV, 'Look at the size of this guy. He presses 500 pounds.' Well, great, when we have a weight lifting contest I want him on my team. In the meantime, can he play football?"

"Experience is everything in the NFL," Tucker said. "It's not just how strong you are or how much weight you can lift. You need quickness and you need brains. You have to have a full bag of tools and you have to be able to outsmart and outmaneuver people. There are a lot of people who have great physical ability. They have rippling muscles and can run like the wind. But you put them in a game and they can't play. You can't find them on the field because they can't make a play. Then there are other people you hardly notice in practice. They're just another checker on the board. But you put them in a game and they make all the plays. They're making tackles. They're making interceptions. It's amazing."

But it's a lot easier to judge speed and strength, and many of the smaller and slower checkers on the board never got a chance to show they were football players.

Timing is critical to those trying to make an NFL roster. In 1968, cornerback Tom Rowland was a late cut from a Green Bay Packer team that was coming off a second consecutive Super Bowl triumph. He went to Hartford, made the ACFL all-star team, and thought he'd be back in the Green Bay camp in 1969 with a good chance to stick. The Packers had slipped badly in 1968 and many of their veterans were approaching the end of their careers. But Rowland's contract was sold to Denver, which had a plethora of defensive backs. He was quickly cut and returned to Hartford.

"In Green Bay we had great running backs," Rowland said, "so the running backs weren't going to make the team. But if you were an offensive lineman you might, because Jerry Kramer and some of the other guys were getting old. We had offensive linemen making the Packers—my god, Nick DeFelice was much better than they were—but they were just there at the right time and in the right position."

One could also be in the wrong place at the wrong time. When he was coaching in New Jersey, Nick Cutro got a call from Vince Lombardi asking if he had a punt returner the Packers could use. "I had a great punt returner, Richie Sowells," Cutro said, "but the night before he was supposed to go to Green Bay he broke his leg in Jersey City."

Tackle Dennis Fitzgibbons suffered a similar misfortune. In 1969, near the end of his second season with Hartford, he was contacted by the New York Jets. The Knights played Pottstown in the championship game on a Saturday night, and the following day, Fitzgibbons was supposed to go to New York and meet with the Jets. During the title game, however, he tore up his knee. On the day he was to have gone to New York, he was in Hartford Hospital recovering from surgery. "After that," he said, "they couldn't have cared less. I was damaged goods."

It was the second bad break for Fitzgibbons, for a year earlier he barely missed making the 49ers roster. "If John Parker hadn't been on injured reserve," Fitzgibbons said, "I would have been on the cab squad and maybe I'd have found a place out there. But you never know and that's the way it is."

"I had a couple of really good games with the Knights," recalled defensive lineman John Skladany. "After the second game [coach] Nick Cutro came up to me and said, 'a lot of teams are talking about you. You're going to end up with a good deal for yourself.' Then, with the Eagles and a couple of other teams watching, I had a game that wasn't so good and although they said they'd get back to me, I never heard from them again."

"I always felt," Skladany said, "that if I was a step quicker I would have been a really good defensive end, and if I was twenty pounds bigger and a little stronger I would have been a good tackle. If I was just a little quicker and a little bigger I think I could have made it without having to be in the right place at the right time."

Wide receiver Bob Stohrer was another "tweener." "I knew when I went to camp with Washington," he said, "that I would be a fringe player. When I ran patterns against the defensive backs I could see I didn't have the speed to make it. If I was a tight end it would have been better but I wasn't big enough to be a tight end. I think I would have had a better chance the next year [1969] when Vince Lombardi was the coach because I think I was his type of player."

Stohrer probably would have been in the Redskins camp in 1969 if he hadn't left their taxi squad the previous year to join the Knights. "I kick myself in the ass to this day," he said, "for doing it. I don't know what made me do it, but it was a stupid move because I would at least be talking to you about my experiences with the big guy—Vince Lombardi."

The lack of non-football options sometimes played a role in whether a player continued to fight for a spot in the NFL or moved on to another career. Both Tucker and Dockery, who had college degrees and marketable skills, said they probably would have quit rather than play in the minors for several years.

"If I had a different background I would have had to make it," said Don Abbey. "I always had a soft cushion to land on. I came from a wonderful, upper middle class family. Maybe I wasn't as mentally tough as I could have been."

When Cornell graduate John Sponheimer went to camp with the Kansas City Chiefs, he was astonished to learn that hardly any of his fellow rookies had finished their college degrees. "I thought it was automatic," he said. "You graduated from college and then if you didn't make it in football you went on and did something else."

When he didn't make the Chiefs roster, Sponheimer played with the Knights and Bridgeport Jets while attending law school. "If football had been the only thing in front of me," he said, "I would have worked out more after the season. If I'd lifted and ran I probably would have had a better opportunity to make it the next year, but being in law school full time, I just couldn't give the time and effort to it." Law promised a more stable future, for there are no roster limits in the legal profession and every attorney is a free agent.

Waide Robinson also pursued a post-graduate degree while playing with the Knights and Jets. "My focus wasn't totally on football," he said, "especially when I got into my second master's degree. I know I would have eventually made an NFL team, because I was very confident, but I said 'Let's get real here. Where is the need?'" He decided to pursue a career in education.

When opportunity arose, it needed to be embraced, as demonstrated by the sad case of quarterback Gary Wichard of C.W. Post. Wichard was one of the best passers in the country in 1971, throwing for 2,287 yards and 23 touchdowns. Post was a small school, but Wichard had a good arm and big league size, 6'2" and over 200 pounds. Unfortunately, when he reported for the Senior Bowl, he was well over 200 pounds, and weak from a recent bout with the flu. He'd stopped working out and hadn't thrown a football in about a month. "I didn't really know how much emphasis the scouts put on post season games," he said.[2]

"When I was with ESPN," said Lou Palmer, "I went to the Senior Bowl every year. The game itself means nothing to the scouts. All they care about are the two-a-days. They want to see the work ethic. They want to see which guys are football-oriented. The player personnel directors, the scouts, the combines—they're all gone by game time."

Scouting systems were not as extensive in 1971 as they are today, and the Senior Bowl workouts were the first time many NFL scouts had seen Wichard. They didn't like what they saw. "He looked like he weighed 300 pounds and he was throwing balloons," said Gil Brandt of the Cowboys.

Instead of being drafted in the first two rounds, as he expected, Wichard was selected by the Colts in the 16th round. Sixteenth round draft choices don't get a long look in training camp, and Wichard was released by the end of July. That fall, instead of sitting on an NFL bench, he was playing for the Long Island Chiefs of the Seaboard League. He never played a down in the NFL.

11. The Championship Team

Tony Kyasky, who played for the Knights from 1970 to 1972, was a sixth round draft choice of the New Orleans Saints, following a stellar career as a Syracuse defensive back that earned him a spot on the Playboy All-American team. He walked out of the Saints camp and never played a game in the NFL. "It's probably the biggest mistake I ever made," he said recently. "I was married, we had two children, and I sort of lost it. I just got to the point where I thought that wasn't for me anymore and I probably made a very bad mistake."

The 1968 roster of the Hartford Knights would include many players who hadn't been in the right place at the right time, who were a bit too small or too slow, or who just needed more experience. "There were three or four different groups" said Kyasky. "You had guys who were still trying to make it back to the NFL. You had guys who'd been in the NFL and just wanted to play some ball. You had guys who were never drafted but were very good, tough football players."

Each man who arrived at Colt Park to try out for the Knights had a story—an untimely injury, a clogged roster, or a coach who just didn't like him. One man who'd played in the NFL and desperately wanted to get back was wide receiver Bob Sherlag, a six-foot, 195-pounder who'd graduated from Memphis State in 1966. Sherlag was typical of the marginal receiver. He was tough, had good hands, and ran precise routes, but he lacked blazing speed.

When Sherlag graduated in 1966, he was drafted by the Buffalo Bills in the fifth round and the Philadelphia Eagles in the sixth round. He couldn't come to terms with either team, and when negotiations reached a stalemate, George Allen, the new coach of the Los Angeles Rams, became interested, and acquired him from the Eagles.

Sherlag enjoyed his time in the Los Angeles camp. "What a great organization that was," he recalled. "What a great time!" The Rams were a collection of personalities ideally suited to the free-spirited Southern California lifestyle, including Rosie Grier, Deacon Jones, Roman Gabriel, and many other veterans.

Unfortunately for Sherlag, one of the veterans with a great personality was pint-sized wide receiver Tommy McDonald, who'd gained over 1,000 yards receiving for the Rams in 1965. One night when Sherlag was in a night club with some teammates, he watched as McDonald rode through the front door on a motorcycle. Another wide receiver was Jack Snow, a second year man who'd been a star at Notre Dame and a first round draft pick. The third receiver was Bucky Pope, who as an unknown rookie from Catawba College in 1964 caught ten touchdown passes and averaged over 30 yards per reception.

Sherlag looked good in practice and got some favorable notice in the press, but soon encountered problems with an impacted tooth. "I lost about twenty pounds and couldn't catch my butt with both hands at that point," he recalled.

He was released and signed with the Atlanta Falcons, beginning their first year in the National Football League.

Sherlag got into nine games with Atlanta, catching four passes, one for a touchdown against the Bears in his hometown of Chicago. "It was a broken play," he recalled, "and [quarterback] Randy Johnson was running for his life so he had no choice but to throw it to me." If he'd had a choice, Johnson wouldn't have thrown the ball to Sherlag, for the naïve youngster had made some serious rookie mistakes.

"When I look back," said Sherlag, "I had zero political acumen. I made some comments in practice that were not good—supposedly cute comments. I would pretend to complement a receiver catching the ball. I would say things like, 'that was just a horrendous pass—way to save that trash.' Randy heard it and that was pretty much the end of our relationship. It was just dumb as a stone on my part." Sherlag didn't get into games too often, and when he did, Johnson wouldn't throw the ball to him. "At one point, the receivers coach told me we might as well be playing with ten guys when I was out there."

Sherlag was released after the season. The next summer, he drove to southern California with the intention of working his way up the coast from one NFL team to another. He eventually landed in the camp of the New Orleans Saints, just beginning their first year in the NFL.

For the second straight season, Sherlag found himself amidst the chaos of a brand new expansion team. He was cut and sat out the 1967 season. During the spring of 1968 he wrote a number of letters to NFL and AFL clubs asking for another chance, and was referred to the Knights. As an NFL veteran, Sherlag was a prime commodity, and quickly became the starting flanker.

Defensive back Bob Mirabelle, 27, was a steady minor league veteran who'd come within a whisker of making the major leagues. Mirabelle's best shot came just after his graduation from Norwich University in 1963. His college coach, Bob Priestley, knew Coach Mike Holovak of the Boston Patriots and arranged for Mirabelle to attend a tryout session. The youngster impressed Holovak with his speed and was offered a contract and an invitation to training camp.

Don Webb, one of Boston's starting defensive backs, was out for the season with an injury, seemingly opening up a spot for one of three rookies. None won the job, however, as assistant coach Fred Bruney was activated to take Webb's place. Mirabelle was released and played with the Boston Sweepers, intercepting 12 passes and making the all-league team.

After the season, Bruney retired for good and joined the Philadelphia Eagles as backfield coach. He remembered Mirabelle and convinced Eagle coach Joe Kuharich to invite him to camp. Mirabelle didn't make the Eagles' active roster, but was carried on the taxi squad for two years. "I was the constant rookie," he said. "I was a rookie with the Patriots. I was a rookie the first year with the Eagles, and I was a rookie the second year with the Eagles." While on the taxi squad, he continued to play in the minor leagues, including stints with the Charter Oaks in 1965 and 1966. He commuted from New York City, where he was national sales manager for the Benrus Watch Corporation.

When Dick Bowman graduated from Syracuse in 1963, very few people thought he'd be playing in the Atlantic Coast Football League by 1968. In the late '50s and early '60s, the Syracuse program, under Coach Ben Schwartzwalder, was perhaps the best in the east and one of the strongest in the country. The 1959 team was voted #1 in the nation by both UPI and AP, and capped an undefeated season by beating Texas in the Cotton Bowl.

Bowman played varsity ball at Syracuse from 1961 to 1963 with Heisman Trophy winner Ernie Davis and future Hall of Famer John Mackey. He was an end on both offense and defense, and was so highly regarded that Mackey, later a star tight end with the Baltimore Colts, was moved to the backfield. In his senior year, Bowman led the run-oriented Orange squad with ten pass receptions. "We didn't throw the ball a whole lot," he said. "We were a little bit like Woody Hayes and his three yards and a cloud of dust."

In 1963, after his senior year, Bowman played in the Hula Bowl, was drafted by the NFL Cardinals on the sixth round, and also invited to sign as a free agent with the Chargers. He was tempted by the thought of moving to southern California and reuniting with former linemate Walt Sweeney, the Chargers' first round pick, but decided to sign a two year no-cut contract with the Cardinals. "In my heart," he said, "I always wanted the NFL because that was the big daddy. If you were going to make it that was where you were going to make it."

Bowman reported to Lake Forest, Illinois, for training camp, and had the worst experience of his football career. Although he played both ways in college, the Cardinals immediately placed him on defense. There was no room for a tight end in St. Louis, for the Cardinals had also drafted Jackie Smith, who held down the position for the next 15 years and was inducted into the Pro Football Hall of Fame in 1994.[3] Bowman had sent one Hall of Fame tight end to the backfield, but he could not displace a second. "I was pretty good at both [offense and defense]," Bowman said, "but not great at either and I think that probably hurts you when you're in a specialized field."

The Cardinals were a team in turmoil in the 1960s. The Bidwill brothers had recently moved the club to St. Louis from Chicago, and later earned the enmity of the former city by fleeing to Phoenix in 1988. They were unpopular throughout their tenure in St. Louis, for they had little loyalty to the city and even less to their players.

The St. Louis club was also beset by racial problems that became a national scandal later in the decade. Many NFL teams had racial issues in the 1960s, and it was rumored that the Cleveland Browns considered trading Jimmy Brown to the Cardinals for John David Crow because they considered Brown a troublemaker.

Bowman had played on a Syracuse team that was close and racially cohesive. At a time when there were few African Americans in college football, Schwartzwalder had a number of black stars, including Davis, Brown, and Floyd Little. Billy Hunter, an African American, was Bowman's close friend and was in his wedding party. The Orangemen might not be considered diverse by twenty-first century standards, but they were very enlightened for the early 1960s.

Bowman never felt comfortable in the troubled Cardinal camp, and admittedly did not put forth the effort that made him a star in college. He'd put on some weight, was slow and sluggish, and played poorly. "I just don't think he had his heart into making the NFL," said a Hartford teammate, "because he certainly could have."

Bowman agreed. "If I had to be honest with myself," he said recently, "I didn't work the way I did in college. I'm not sure I wanted it so much. I can't really answer that but I know I was not comfortable in that situation. It's hard to admit because that means I was being deceitful to myself when I said I wanted to play. I thought I did, but I didn't." Bowman was cut and asked to report to the Montreal Alouettes of the Canadian Football League. He didn't want to go to Canada, but if he refused, the Cardinals could stop paying his guaranteed contract.

Bowman protested and eventually wound up playing for the Charter Oaks. After the season, the Giants wanted him to come to camp with them. The Cardinals still held Bowman's rights and said they would let Bowman play for the Giants if he repaid his bonus (more than $12,000) and the amount he had collected thus far under his contract. There was no way Bowman was going to pay that amount of money for his release, so he asked the Giants if they would do so. The Giants told the Cardinals they would pay for Bowman's release if he made the team. The Cardinals, a divisional foe of the Giants, said they wanted the money up front. The Giants refused and Bowman was stuck in limbo. The Cardinals didn't want him and the Giants couldn't have him.

Bowman never got another opportunity to play major league football. When the Giant offer fell through, he came to the realization that his dream of playing in the NFL was finished. "That's when I decided—that's it for me," he said recently. "Two years out of football in the NFL and it's very difficult to come back. Even though I was still young, I was starting to raise a family and I was having fun. I got all excited about going to New York and when it fell apart that was the end of it." Bowman became a minor league gypsy, playing for Fred Wallner with the Charter Oaks in 1964 and 1965, the Waterbury Orbits in 1966, and the New Britain Bees in 1967.

Dennis Fitzgibbons, a Syracuse player of more recent vintage, joined the Knights after the opening game of the regular season. He'd been a defensive tackle his first two years of college, but the summer before his senior season he received a letter from Coach Schwartzwalder telling him that the team needed offensive linemen and that was where he would play his final year.

Fitzgibbons wasn't happy, for he was hoping to be drafted as a defensive lineman, and didn't think it would help his chances if he played offense his senior year. "But it was a different time back then," he said. "You just shut up and did what you were asked. So I ended up playing the first four or five games at tackle." A broken leg and a knee injury later, the team found itself shorthanded on the defensive side, and Fitzgibbons finished the year at middle guard.

Despite the constant position shifts, Fitzgibbons was drafted by the San Francisco 49ers. "I got drafted because of my size," he said. The 49ers decided to try the rookie at guard, despite the fact that they had a number of established players at the position. As a neophyte guard, Fitzgibbons was a long shot to make the team, but was told he would be offered a place on the taxi squad if he was cut. When camp ended, however, he was released, and went to Canada to play for the British Columbia Lions. When he'd been in Canada for two weeks, a Canadian defensive back was injured and an American was signed to replace him. Since the number of Americans on each roster was limited, Fitzgibbons was released.

Fitzgibbons had some friends in Bridgeport who knew the Savins and suggested he go to Hartford, polish his skills, and take another shot at the NFL in 1969. He hesitated, for he'd heard some harrowing tales of life in the minors. "Would we get dressed on the bus?" he wondered. "Would we have a shower?" Fitzgibbons was convinced that the Savins ran a first class operation and agreed to join the Knights.

Fitzgibbons became a fan favorite, at least with one fan. One night he was walking to the locker room after the game when he felt a strange sensation. "The way Dillon Stadium was set up," he said, "when you went from the field to the locker room you were in the midst of the fans leaving the game. When I was walking I felt someone pinching my ass. I thought they must have just bumped up against me, but it happened again. I turned around there was a woman there, probably about 40 or so. She said she wanted to see if that was real or if it was pads. 'Is that really your ass?' she asked me. I said, 'That's my ass back there, sweetheart.'"

The left tackle was Nick DeFelice, the offensive captain and the Knights' best lineman. "Left tackle is your key position," said line coach Roger LeClerc, "because he protects the quarterback's blind side." In 1964, as a member of the Charter Oaks, DeFelice made the all-ACFL team and played a very good game against the Newark Bears, who had a loose affiliation with the New York Jets. The following summer, he was working on the roof of a house he was building in Derby when his mother hollered up that assistant coach Chuck Knox of the Jets was on the phone. DeFelice jumped off the roof, took the call, signed a contract for $9,000, and agreed to join the Jets in training camp.

DeFelice wasn't going to start for the Jets, for the tackles were huge Sherman Plunkett and eight-time Pro Bowler Winston Hill, then in the prime of a 15-year career. Their backup was Pete Perreault, who played nine years of professional football, and the camp roster included some highly touted rookies from big schools. The Jets had just signed Joe Namath to his fabled $400,000 contract and were looking for tackles that could pass block and protect Namath's fragile knees. DeFelice had an advantage over the rookies, for he had done more pass blocking in the ACFL than any of them had done in college.

DeFelice made the team as a 25-year-old rookie and played all fourteen games of Namath's rookie season. The following year, after two games, he was sent to the expansion Miami Dolphins. The Dolphins kept their younger players and wanted DeFelice to play with the Orlando Panthers of the Continental League, to keep him nearby in case the youngsters didn't work out.

Nick wasn't earning a lot of money, didn't think he had a future with the Dolphins, and wanted to return to his roots in Connecticut. He also wasn't comfortable in the big leagues. "I was a backup," DeFelice said. "and it affected my confidence. You start second guessing yourself and think, 'Can I do that?' Being a backup just ruined me. It killed me because I wanted to be on the field all the time. You start losing your confidence. You think maybe you can't do it. Maybe this league is beyond me.

Gene Gollarney (photograph from Hartford Knights program).

11. The Championship Team

You start looking over your shoulder and thinking that if you go in and make a mistake the coach is going to pull you. It's very difficult to make that transition when you're playing against the best in the world."

DeFelice signed with the Charter Oaks in 1967, and joined the Knights when they were formed the following year. "Nick was the leader of that team," said John Sponheimer. "He was probably our best lineman and he was vociferous. People liked Nick and they rallied around him."

DeFelice and Fitzgibbons were part of the best offensive line in the ACFL. They were big, talented, and worked together seamlessly—most of the time. "I remember one time I blew the play," said Fitzgibbons. "They had a trap and Ernie Colquette was pulling from right guard. I was the left tackle and I absolutely drilled him. He wound up splitting his eye and getting some stitches. He said, 'Thanks, Fitz.' But those kinds of things happened. I just added a little more character to his face."

The other guard was Gene Gollarney from Trinity College in Texas. "Gene was a terrific pulling guard," said Bowman. "Let me tell you, when he hit you, you knew it. He would take out a defensive end or a linebacker and just keep right on going. He didn't throw himself and he could just follow the play down the field."

"He was quick," added line coach Roger LeClerc, "and he was a jokester. He kept everybody loose." Gollarney is best remembered for keeping everyone loose, and for getting a little tight. "After practice," said DeFelice, "you could always count on Gene having a couple of cold beers for us."

One of Gollarney's memorable pranks occurred during a harrowing flight to Newport News. "Christ almighty," said Joe Murphy. "He almost got arrested." "The plane seemed to be in some kind of trouble," recalled Lou Palmer. "We were descending toward the airport and all of a sudden the plane starts on an upward trajectory. One of the flight attendants ran up to the cockpit to see what was going on. At that point Gollarney grabs the microphone and says, 'Hey, if there's no trouble on this flight how come the stewardess is crying?'"

Tom Rowland, an innocent Midwestern type, was one of Gollarney's favorite victims. When he said he didn't know what a "hickey" was Gollarney decided to show him. "A bunch of guys held me down," Rowland recalled, "and Gene sucked on my neck and gave me the biggest hickey I've ever seen." Rowland's parents came in to watch him play that weekend, and he wore turtlenecks for the duration of their visit. They inquired why. "Oh, it's just an East Coast thing," he told them.

On another occasion, Gollarney decided to take Rowland out to show him how a real man drank. "While I was showering after practice," Rowland said, "he had about six beers to warm up. Then we went out. I don't know how many he had, but it was a lot. I had about three and had gotten silly, but he was still going. It didn't faze him."

In 1970, Gollarney was injured and missed most of the season. Broadcaster Arnold Dean probably should have known better, but he invited him to the press box to do some spotting. Dean had a very sore throat that evening and asked the youngster tending the press box to keep feeding him hot coffee. "I figured I wouldn't sleep for a month," he recalled, "but at least it would sooth my throat and I'd be able to keep going."

All game long, Dean poured one coffee after another down his sore throat. "After a while," he said, "I'm wondering why I'm *feeling* so *good*." The reason Dean felt happy was that Gollarney was supplementing his coffee with the contents of a flask he brought into the booth. "I didn't catch on until about three quarters of the way through the game," Dean said, "and then I said, 'Geez, cut that out. You're going to get me fired.' But I don't think he stopped."

The Knights' middle linebacker was Bill Lesinski, captain of the 1963 Boston University team. Lesinski was contacted by the Jets and Packers, but he knew that at 6'1" and 215 pounds, he wasn't big enough for the NFL. Still, he loved football and wanted to continue playing, and joined the Charter Oaks in 1964. He followed Wallner to the Meriden Shamrocks in 1965 and to the Orbits in 1966. Lesinski injured his knee in 1967 and didn't expect to play in '68, but in mid–September, Wallner called him after his starter, Bob Soleau, injured an ankle. "He called me on a Tuesday," Lesinski recalled, "and said, 'Bill, I need a linebacker. I guess I always told him that if he really needed me to give me a call. It was the best thing I ever did in my life."

Another late addition to the Knights was 34-year-old veteran tight end Tom Rychlec. Rychlec had more major league experience than nearly all of the other Knights, but he'd spent the past four years playing for the Charter Oaks, the Shamrocks, and the New Britain Bees, and was nearing the end of the line. "I was mostly a blocker with the Knights," he said, "and they'd look for me on short passes over the middle. Go over the middle. Catch a pass. Get banged. No wonder my nose doesn't look right anymore."

Rychlec and DeFelice had major league experience. Bowman and Fitzgibbons had stellar careers in a big time college program. Defensive end Fran Mallick had experience as an oiler in a Pittsburgh steel mill.

Mallick's attempt to make his high school team was short-lived. "Back then," he recalled, "they didn't have the helmets with the bars in the front. Somebody cold-cocked me in the nose and I said, 'I don't need this shit.'" Mallick played basketball, and had some thoughts of going to college, but he hadn't been a serious student and his transcript reflected the lack of effort. After a couple of years of working at menial, low-paying jobs, he joined the Air Force in 1961.

11. The Championship Team

Mallick was sent to England as a re-fueler, and heard that the base football team was looking for a player. Football players only had to work half-days, so when someone asked Mallick if he had ever played he said, sure, he had played a lot of football, and he was pretty good at it. During the next three years, Mallick found out that he loved playing and that he had talent. "I got a kick out of tackling the quarterback," he said. "That was what kept me coming back. When you could do the head slap, man, you could get around the guy. The head slap was great."

"I was fast," he continued, "and I could catch running backs from behind. I could run the 40 in five flat and I was clocked at 10.7 for the hundred yard dash." More importantly, Mallick was quick. "Fran wasn't super aggressive," said Bowman, "but nobody got around him. He was just a very gifted athlete. He had more instinct than brute strength."

After three years in the service, Mallick returned to civilian life. "I wanted to re-enlist," he said, "but they wouldn't give me any money and they wouldn't give me a stripe so I said the hell with it." A promised scholarship to the University of Colorado never materialized, so Mallick returned to the Pittsburgh area and found a job in a steel mill as an oiler. He also became a football Ironman, signing with the Pittsburgh Valley Ironmen of the ACFL.

The Ironmen folded before the season was over. Mallick never got his final paychecks, but his performance had caught the attention of the hometown Steelers. A sportswriter told him that the Steelers were interested but that he would have to make an overture to them. He did, and the Steelers signed him to a 1965 contract at a salary of $9,500.

The '65 Steelers were a bad team, finishing with a 2–12 record, but they had rugged defensive linemen like Big John Baker and Ben McGee. Baker is best remembered for a hit on Giant quarterback Y.A. Tittle depicted in the iconic photo of Tittle kneeling helmetless and bloody, symbolizing the Giants' decline from glory. "Those are the two guys who taught me everything," Mallick said of Baker and McGee, "like the head slap."

Although he was a reserve and special team player, Mallick had some memorable moments in Pittsburgh, like sacking Johnny Unitas and tackling Bob Hayes, billed as the world's fastest human, on a kickoff return. "It was in the open field with no one around," he recalled. "I came back home and all my buddies were saying, 'Hey, I saw you tackle Bob Hayes.' I didn't think anything of it. It was just another tackle." Just another tackle that Mallick remembered in detail 47 years later.

Mallick was cut before the start of the 1966 season. "We really stunk," he said, "so they fired everybody—all the coaches. They brought in Bill Austin from Los Angeles and he brought players with him. I happened to be one that didn't fit in with his group."

A year earlier Mallick had been in the right place at the right time, but now he was in the wrong place at the wrong time. He was even released at the wrong time, right at the end of camp when other teams had their rosters set. Mallick knew Lowell Lander, who was also from Pittsburgh, and Lander had told him that if he ever needed a job, he should give him a call. When no NFL team signed him, Mallick called Lander and went to the Charter Oaks.

The Knights were the farm team of the Green Bay Packers, but in 1968 they received just one player, defensive back Tom Rowland, from the Packers. A few years earlier, when he was a 4'11", 95-pound freshman at Rushville High School, no one would have ever expected Tom Rowland to wind up in the training camp of the Green Bay Packers, unless it was carrying buckets of water.

When Rowland tried out for his high school team, he fibbed a bit and told the coach he was 5' and 100 pounds. He made the team and sat on the bench for three years, not getting into a single game. By his senior year, Rowland had sprouted to 5'5" and bulked up to 135 pounds, and was very fast. He played regularly on both offense and defense, but his size discouraged college scouts. With no thoughts of a football career, Rowland planned to attend Western Illinois College, major in industrial arts, and join the family plumbing and heating business.

Two things changed Rowland's plans. First, a neighbor who'd played basketball at Illinois College told him he should consider attending IC. Second, he grew six inches and gained more than fifteen pounds over the summer. Rowland visited the Illinois College campus, liked it, and decided to matriculate. When his father asked him when football practice started, Rowland was surprised because he hadn't intended to go out for the team.

To appease his father, he tried out, made the squad, and returned kickoffs for the first four games of his freshman year. Meanwhile, the IC offense was sputtering, the running backs were playing poorly, and the offensive linemen were pestering the coaches to give the fleet-footed freshman a shot. Finally, in the season's fifth game, with Illinois trailing 12–0 at halftime, the coach put Rowland in the game. "The first time I carried the ball I got 15 yards," Rowland recalled. "The second time I got 10 and on the third carry I got 7. After that I played for the next three and a half years."

It was on defense, however, that Rowland left his legacy. In 1967, he set a collegiate record (which has never been broken) by intercepting 15 passes in a season. Intercepting passes was a skill he learned while playing the trumpet. In high school, Rowland had been a member of the band, where he acquired a knack for looking at his sheet music and watching the conductor at the same time.

"It may sound a little weird," he said, "but from all that training I had to do while playing trumpet in the band, I learned to see the whole field and still

11. The Championship Team

look at the quarterback. I could watch the receiver and the quarterback and just time it right and go. After a while I got so good at it I would bait people, let them think they were open, and then close on them."

Fifteen interceptions is an impressive feat in its own right, but for Tom Rowland in 1967, it was even more remarkable. The Illinois College Blueboys played only eight games, and finished 1–6–1. "I'll bet they didn't throw 100 passes at us all season long," Rowland said. "They never had to throw because we were always behind and they were just jamming it down our throats or trying to kill the clock. I got three interceptions in my last game and they only threw seven times."

In addition to his interceptions, Rowland averaged 5.9 yards per carry, and caught the attention of Green Bay scout Pat Peppler. Unfortunately, just before Peppler arrived on campus to work him out, Rowland sprained his ankle playing basketball, and it swelled up so badly he couldn't get his shoe on.

Tom Rowland (photograph from Hartford Knights program).

"But when else am I ever going to have a chance to run for an NFL scout?" he said. Wearing a shoe one size larger than normal, he ran a 4.6 40-yard dash. Peppler couldn't believe it and had Rowland do it again and went to the starting line to make sure it was 40 yards away.

A few days later, Rowland got a certified letter from the Packers inviting him to training camp as a free agent. At rookie camp, he briefly met Fred Wallner, in town to learn the Green Bay system and meet with the Packer coaches.

One of the traditions in professional football camps is to have each rookie stand on his chair and sing their school song after the evening meal. With the top draft choices at the College All Star Game, there were only six rookies in the Packer camp, and each was required to do a great deal of singing. The vets gave each rookie a number and when that number was called, the youngster had to stand up and sing.

One night Rowland's number was called and middle linebacker Ray Nitschke, the man who epitomized the rugged NFL middle linebacker of the 1960s, told him to sing his school song. "I got up and looked at Nitschke," Rowland recalled. "He had his teeth out, and I looked at him and said, 'Oh my god, I can't say Blueboys.' I said the Illinois College … Tigers."

Nitschke and fullback Jim Grabowski had both played for the University of Illinois, and mistakenly believed that Rowland was a fellow Illini, rather than a graduate of Illinois *College*. Rowland finally gave up correcting them. "You're a good old Illini," Nitschke would say. "Yes, I am," Rowland would reply.

Two-a-day drills in the scorching summer heat caused Rowland's weight to work its way back toward the 95 pounds of his high school freshman days. After a month he was down to 153 pounds. If the coaches knew he was that light Rowland was sure they would cut him, so when the time came for the daily weigh-in he would tape two ten pound weights under his shirt. He got away with the ruse until one day assistant coach Dave Hanner spotted him walking shirtless past the scale and told him to hop on. Rowland said he would come back later, but Hanner said, no, get on the scale now.

The moment of truth had arrived. One of Rowland's roommates, who knew what he had been doing, was nearby. Rowland pretended to cut his finger and asked his friend to put pressure on it. As he did, the scale shot up to 175. The pressure was reduced and the scale went back to 155. Then it went up to 185, and Hanner was trying to figure out what was wrong. He asked for a 25-pound weight to test the scale and found it accurate. "The scale's right," he told Rowland. "Get on it again." By this time, four of his friends had formed a protective semi-circle around Rowland and were applying pressure. The scale continued gyrating wildly until Hanner finally conceded. "Oh, 175," he said. "That's not bad, coach," Rowland replied.

Despite his shenanigans, Rowland was cut from the Packer squad. Defensive back Willie Wood said he could get him a job with the Las Vegas Cowboys of the Continental League. He was ready to go when he got a call from Wallner. Rowland told him about the Las Vegas offer but Wallner said the Continental League was in trouble and going to fold and that was why Hartford had left it to join the ACFL. Rowland decided to pass up the bright lights of Las Vegas for Hartford.

One of Wallner's veterans was defensive end Bob Shemeth, who began his minor league career with the Ansonia Black Knights in 1963 and played for the Charter Oaks from 1964 to 1967. Shemeth had a good job in New York City and no thoughts of playing in the NFL. He was an under-sized defensive end at 225 pounds, and he was 28 years old. "We all had aspirations of making it up to the NFL," he said recently, "but that wasn't my main goal. I had just enjoyed playing football in high school and college and I wanted to continue to play."

11. The Championship Team

Shemeth played with a passion that belied his buttoned-down Madison Avenue appearance. With his blond hair, good looks, and promising business career, he looked like a junior executive, but when he put on his uniform, a second, more violent persona invaded his being. "I would claw the ground like a dog," he said. "I was very intense. I was relentless. I really enjoyed hitting quarterbacks."

One of the aspirants for the Knights quarterback position was Dave Bennett, who led his Springfield College team to an undefeated season his junior year and still ranks high on many Springfield all time passing lists. Bennett was also a pretty good baseball player, good enough to garner interest from a couple of major league teams. During the spring of his senior year (1967), Bennett was playing baseball against Florida State. He hit a long fly ball that was caught against the left field fence and was trotting back to the dugout when he heard the Florida State players yelling at him.

"I was thinking," Bennett recalled, "what the hell are they talking about. I don't even know who they are." The players told Bennett to come to their dugout, where Bob Schnelker, assistant coach of the Green Bay Packers, was on the phone. He wanted to come to Florida and sign Bennett, who'd just been selected by the Packers in the 11th round of the draft, and pay him a $5,000 bonus.

Bennett wasn't likely to make the Packer roster, for they had just won the first Super Bowl and would win a second the next year. Bart Starr, of course, was the starting quarterback, with veteran Zeke Bratkowski in reserve. Don Horn of San Diego State, the Packers first draft choice, and Kent Nix, who would later start for the Steelers, were also in camp. The best Bennett could hope for was the opportunity to impress another team, plus having the experience of training with the Super Bowl champions and Coach Vince Lombardi.

"I prepared myself," Bennett said. "I really worked hard because I knew Lombardi's training camp was a bear. The first day we did 81 up-downs in a row. Most of those guys, like [linemen Bob] Skoronski and [Forrest] Gregg, were lean and mean. There were no heavy guys like you see out there today. Most of them were balding and old, and they all smoked. I couldn't believe how much Lombardi smoked. He smoked the entire time on the practice field and sometimes he had two of them in his mouth at the same time. He and [assistant coach] Phil Bengston couldn't wait to light up the next cigarette. Lombardi would be up on the sled with a cigarette hanging out of his mouth. The bus would be filled with smoke coming back from practice."

The quarterbacks rode with Lombardi to early meetings in Bart Starr's car, and Lombardi asked Bennett about his family, his background, and other personal subjects. It was a great experience, but Bennett was soon cut and placed on the taxi squad. He got a high school teaching job and played for the Lowell Giants of the ACFL, where he was the quarterback and the holder for kicker Tom Dempsey.

The following year, the Baltimore Colts showed some interest, and Bennett worked out for Coach Don Shula for a couple of days. Shula wanted Bennett to play for Harrisburg, but with a good job in Springfield, Bennett didn't want to go to Pennsylvania. He signed with Hartford so he could remain close to home.

Those were the players that filled the roster of the 1968 Hartford Knights. Some hoped a year in Hartford would give them another shot at the major leagues, and some just didn't want to stop playing football. They were a talented group, for Pete Savin wanted the best team his money could buy, and his Knights would give Hartford fans a good show in 1968.

12

The Championship Season: The 1968 Hartford Knights

Most NFL training camps follow a similar pattern. A squad of between sixty and one hundred athletes gathers together in mid-July. There is a core of veterans who will almost certainly make the team and consider the entire exercise a tedious bore. There is a group of rookies and marginal players who will fight to survive and, finally, there is a batch of poor souls who serve as practice fodder for a few days or weeks before leaving to pursue other careers.

In minor league football, the process is completely different. There are very few veterans at the beginning of camp, for many of the best players from the previous year have been invited to NFL camps, while others have decided the time has come to concentrate on a long term career. The majority of the players who take part in the early drills of a minor league team won't make the final roster.

Minor league stars arrive after the NFL clubs make their cuts. "Every week," said Tom Rowland, "we had guys coming into camp who'd just been cut by NFL teams. You could be a starter one week and the next week you might not even get a play or they might cut you because some new guy came in. You had to be like a gunfighter. You had to be on your game because every week there were guys coming in trying to take your job. Nobody was guaranteed anything because you had superstars coming down who'd just been cut."

On July 7, 1968, the Hartford Knights appeared in public for the first time, conducting an open tryout at Dillon Stadium. For ninety minutes, Fred Wallner and his assistants put sixteen aspirants through their paces and invited two of them, including barefoot kicker Wasyl Desysenko, to camp. For the next few weeks, the team practiced on Sunday mornings and Tuesday, Wednesday, and Thursday evenings. Practices weren't as long as they were in NFL camps, and they weren't as grueling, but NFL players didn't have to put in a full day of work before practice. All through July and August, players came and went, and gradually the first roster of the Hartford Knights began to take shape.

The exhibition season was a smashing success, as the Hartford defense did not allow a single opponent to cross their goal line. On August 17, the Knights defeated the Richmond Roadrunners 23–0 at Holyoke, Massachusetts. During the next two weeks, they beat the Lowell Giants 27–6 and the Westchester Bulls 7–3 at Dillon Stadium, the latter win coming in dramatic fashion on a touchdown pass from Manch Wheeler to John Wardlaw late in the fourth quarter.

During their exhibition games, the Knights proved they could play defense and run the ball on offense. They had not proven that they could pass, for neither Wheeler nor Dave Bennett had been particularly proficient. With little separating the two, Wallner decided that the veteran Wheeler would start. "Being a quarterback on the Hartford Knights," said Lou Palmer, "meant handing the ball off to the right guy and then getting out of the way. They didn't pass a hell of a lot."

"Manch was a smart guy," said Bob Stohrer. "He knew what he was doing. He knew the defenses and he knew the offenses. He was in control all the time and I felt he was a good leader. He was probably not the best guy in the ACFL in terms of arm strength but he did a good job for us."

Bennett, unlike many athletes who lose a close competition for a starting job, was not bitter. "I've got no complaints," he said. "Manch played better than I did and the guys rallied around him. He did his job and we started winning. I think Fred was right in his assessment. I was ready if I was called upon."

As big league clubs made their cuts, Wallner and Joe Fenton used Pete Savin's money to build a formidable team. Among the newcomers was offensive lineman Howie Small, known to his teammates as "The Face." "He was a good, good guy," said a fellow lineman, "but he may have been one of the least attractive people you've ever seen. He had a giant lantern jaw, a huge nose, and a terrible case of acne. In the morning he'd be shaving and he'd be singing, 'I'm just a bundle of charm.' He just cracked me up. He'd say, 'I know who I am and I am what I am. I can get through this day and this is going to be just fine for me.'"

With their new players and the confidence generated by their strong showing during the exhibition season, the Knights went to Pottstown, Pennsylvania for their opening game against the Firebirds. Hartford fans who wanted to see their new team's debut could buy a package that included a bus ride to Pottstown, good seats behind the Knights' bench, a room at the Pottstown Holiday Inn, and a meal for $17.

Pottstown, approximately 40 miles northwest of Philadelphia, was named after John Potts, the eighteenth century owner of a local forge, and many of Potts' descendants still lived there in 1968. The biggest employers were Bethlehem Steel and Firestone Tire and Rubber, and the fortunes of the town rose and fell in accordance with their activity. By the 1960s, they were falling, and the population, which peaked at 26,144 in 1960, gradually declined to 21,859 by 2000.

12. The Championship Season

Pottstown was the quintessential small town, with a simple charm that helped compensate for its fading economy. Its citizens were earnest and hard-working and criminal activity was kept to a minimum by the chief of police, who bore the improbable name of Dick Tracy. In many ways Pottstown was like Ansonia.

Pottstown has had some famous residents, including tiny left-handed pitcher Bobby Shantz, winner of the 1952 American League Most Valuable Player Award, singer Daryl Hall of Hall and Oates, the popular musical group of the 1980s, and long time NFL quarterback Don Strock. Growing up in Pottstown, Strock watched King Corcoran play for the Firebirds and later said, "I learned by watching King Corcoran that you can't learn anything watching King Corcoran."[1]

The Firebird franchise came to life in January 1968, when a number of local football enthusiasts formed the Pottstown Professional Football Association, Inc. and put in a few hundred dollars each. Unfortunately, after posting the $10,000 bond required by the ACFL, the funds were nearly depleted. The syndicate somehow managed to use the bond money to pay expenses and then began raising additional capital by selling small amounts of stock in the community. Community ownership has its limitations, the foremost being the reluctance of the average citizen to subsidize the ongoing losses that are the inevitable fate of minor league football teams. The Firebirds needed a Pete Savin.

Pottstown's angel was Ed Gruber, owner of Spring City Knitting Company, the largest manufacturer of men and boy's underwear in the United States.[2] Gruber, a gruff, intimidating man, lived in a magnificent hilltop mansion and was Pottstown's most prominent citizen. He became the Firebirds' principal stockholder. The president was Bob Calvario, one of the original founders, a service station owner, former Pottstown High star, and Korean War veteran.

Gruber was an active owner and liked being on the sidelines and in the locker room. "He was very enthusiastic about the team," recalled tight end Bob Tucker. "I don't think his mission was to make money. He would get excited like Jerry Jones of Dallas gets excited. He had a passion for it."

Gruber's passion was often expressed by outbursts directed at his team, and he was not admired by the Firebirds in the same way the Knights players appreciated Savin. Gruber and his money were a necessary evil, without which Pottstown would not have had its Firebirds.

The Pottstown coach was Dave DiFilippo, a former Villanova lineman who played briefly in the NFL with the Eagles. DiFilippo, a 37-year veteran of the football wars, coached high school and college teams before serving as an assistant with the CFL champion Philadelphia Bulldogs in 1966. At a stumpy 5'10", DiFilippo was somewhat of a bulldog himself, a highly emotional motivator of men who wanted desperately to be an NFL head coach.

The Pottstown coach was not a great strategist. When Ron Waller arrived as a Pottstown assistant in 1969, he handled the offense while former Baltimore Colt Andy Nelson ran the defense. DiFilippo served as head cheerleader and psychologist. After a fiery locker room speech, he said joyously, "This is coaching! Xs and Os? You can find millions of idiots for that shit."

"Dave waved his finger and yelled and screamed," said fullback John Land. "He was a nice guy but when it came down to it he didn't make the team any better. As far as I was concerned, Waller was the guy we looked to." "Dave was a good motivator," said Bob Tucker. "You didn't go to Dave and ask him how to run a certain play or how to make a certain move, but he knew how to motivate the players."

DiFilippo once inserted Japanese quarterback Seiki Murono into a game, he said, "to get a different slant on things." "Dave was an amazing character," Murono said recently, "and he was a very good promoter." Then he laughed. "Yeah," he said, "I think I'll just leave it at that."

Pottstown became probably the most famous town in the history of minor league football, thanks to the much-acclaimed documentary Professional Football, Pottstown, Pennsylvania, produced by NFL Films that was shown on national television before the 1972 Super Bowl. For two years, producer Phil Tuckett, who'd played for the Las Vegas Cowboys, had been pestering NFL Films founder Ed Sabol to make a film about minor league football. Finally, Sabol agreed and, in order to keep travel costs to a minimum, chose Pottstown, the minor league franchise

Pottstown head coach Dave DiFilippo (right) with assistant Carmen Cavalli (photograph from Pennsylvania Firebirds program).

12. The Championship Season

closest to NFL Films headquarters in Philadelphia. Had NFL Films anticipated ESPN and located in Bristol, Connecticut, the epic film might have featured the Hartford Knights.

DiFilippo was one of the stars of the show. "Dave was a film maker's dream," said NFL Films' Steve Sabol. "Dave was like an actor playing a minor league football coach." When the crew missed filming his locker room rampage after the Firebirds only loss of the 1970 season, DiFilippo re-enacted it for them six months later in a downstairs bathroom at NFL Films.

Dave was so invested in the film that he asked Sabol for permission to suspend star defensive end Joe Blake, and then had him film the ensuing confrontation. During games, DiFilippo hammed for the camera, hectoring the referees and erupting with glee at his clever insults. He was delighted when he found out that the microphone he was using was the same one used by a more famous Italian coach, Vince Lombardi.

DeFilippo, Corcoran, and Blake were the leading men in the drama. "I didn't even know they were shooting the film," said Land, "until the season was two-thirds over. They had three people they wanted to get and focused everything on them."

Although NFL Films chose Pottstown for its proximity, they inadvertently selected a town that epitomized minor league football. Like the fans of Wheeling, the people of Pottstown rallied behind their Firebirds. "They took their game seriously," said Tucker.

Lou Palmer felt that the most enthusiastic fans in the ACFL were found in the little Pennsylvania burg. "No question," he said, "Pennsylvania sports fans are among the most rabid in the country. They may not be as sophisticated as fans in New York, Los Angeles, or Chicago, but people are generally born and raised there and they're pretty parochial. It's our boys and all that. Some of the players stayed with local people and it was a family-type thing."

"Of all the teams I played for," said Land, "and I played for a lot of teams, Pottstown had the best cheerleading folks. They supported the team. They wanted to meet the players after the game. It was *their* team. I think that was the only team I played for where the people really felt it was *their* team. The other cities you just went and played there and whether it was home or away didn't make any difference. The fans in Pottstown were loyal to the players and they identified with them."

The opening game against the Knights was DeFilippo's Pottstown coaching debut, and it wasn't a success. The Hartford defense was just as stingy as it had been during the exhibition season. Tom Rowland intercepted two passes and blocked a field goal attempt, and the Firebirds were able to score just a single touchdown. The Knights' offense, however, was also kept out of the end zone by the rugged Pottstown defenders. Two first half field goals gave Hartford a 6–0 lead, and flanker Terry Best returned a punt 76 yards for the game's only touchdown late in the third quarter.

Best was a small, fast, athletic player from East Orange, New Jersey, where he was a center fielder on the baseball team, a guard on the basketball team, and an end, linebacker, and defensive back in football. He said he'd never been timed in a 100 yard dash, but that he could run evenly with men who'd clocked times of 9.4 and 9.5.

Best didn't go to college, and played semi-pro ball with the Plainfield Merchants after his high school graduation in 1963. The following winter, he attended a basketball game featuring a number of the Newark Bears of the ACFL. There weren't enough players to field two teams, and Best was asked to fill in. Newark coach Steve Van Buren was impressed with his athletic ability and invited him to try out for the Bears.

Best played for the Bears in 1964 and joined the Charter Oaks the following year. Still only 20 years old, an age at which most athletes are still in college, Best played well for Hartford, and his speed and flashy play made him a fan favorite. He had feelers from NFL and AFL clubs, but didn't follow up on them because he didn't think he was ready.

"He was an unbelievable athlete," said Bob Stohrer, "the most talented athlete I think I've ever run into. Terry Best should have been in the NFL. He ran so easily that you didn't know when he turned on the speed. He might be running at 75 percent and all of a sudden he was at 100 percent and he's right by you."

Despite his obvious athletic ability, Best's chances of making the big time were always hurt by coaches' doubts about his size (he weighed just 165–170 pounds) and by his questionable work ethic. "His problem," said Stohrer, "was that he was a ladies' man. He was always out with girls late at night. He came to practice late or wouldn't show up for practice. He was a very nice guy, but he just had a lot of testosterone."

After Best's punt return, a combination of good Hartford defense and inept Pottstown offense preserved the Knights' win. It was not an artistic affair, as the Firebirds caused many of their own problems with a bad snap from center on a punt, several turnovers, and a 21-yard "sack" when the Pottstown quarterback, former Miami Dolphin starter George Wilson, Jr., ran into an official. After Wilson threw a touchdown pass late in the fourth quarter to close the gap to 13–7, the Firebirds executed a successful onside kick, but Rowland's second interception sealed the win.

The Knights had a victory in their first game, but it was hard to tell if the team was really good or if Pottstown was just bad. The Knights managed only

12. The Championship Season

216 yards of total offense and, had Pottstown not made so many blunders, they would have been hard-pressed to win.

The Hartford offense looked a lot better in the home opener against Lowell. Wheeler completed only nine passes, but five went for touchdowns, two each to Best and Bob Sherlag, and one to halfback Ron McCauley. The Knights led 27-0 at halftime, and the final score was 34-13. Rowland picked off two more interceptions.

The following Saturday, the Knights traveled to Harrisburg, Pennsylvania for a game against the Capitols, an affiliate of the Baltimore Colts. The Capitols were coached by former Rams running back Ron Waller, who seemed a little too flashy for the Atlantic Coast League. A collegiate star at Maryland, he'd been the NFL rookie of the year before leg injuries shortened his career.

There were several former NFL stars who coached in the minor leagues, but none of them was married to actress Marjorie Durant, heiress to the Post Cereal fortune and niece of actress Dina Merrill. Waller had been in a number of commercials, made guest appearances on shows like *77 Sunset Strip,* and appeared in *Bed Time Story* with Marlon Brando and David Niven.

The Wallers lived a little differently than the Wallners. On March 3, 1958, a full page headline in the *Los Angeles Times* announced "Detectives Guard Home of Ron Waller." Mrs. Waller had been arrested and charged with driving under the influence, and accused the arresting officer of making improper advances toward her and her female companion. Worried about retaliation, Mrs. Waller's grandmother hired a crew of private detectives to guard the Waller residence.

Waller, who had an excellent football mind ("Ron belonged in the NFL," said Bob Tucker), installed an offense that was fairly sophisticated for the ACFL, but thus far his biggest weapon had been fullback John Land. Land gained 177 yards in the Harrisburg opener and after two games was the league's leading rusher with 235 yards and a 7.6 average. Wallner devised a plan he called "Operation Land Grab" to stop him.

Operation Land Grab was a success, as the Harrisburg fullback gained just 43 yards. The Hartford defense was again dominating. Rowland intercepted yet another pass, giving him five in three games, and returned it 63 yards for a touchdown. Newly-acquired fullback Marv Hubbard scored on two short runs and McCauley threw a 59-yard halfback option pass to Sherlag for another touchdown. The 31-0 win was the Knights' third straight victory.

The rugged, 220-pound Hubbard had fashioned a stellar career at Colgate. He was drafted by the Raiders in the 11th round, spent six weeks in the Oakland camp, was released, and then spent a week with the Broncos before they released him.

It was evident when he arrived in Hartford that Hubbard was a gifted player. "The first time he was at practice," said Wheeler, "I called his play and went to hand off and he was almost by me before I got him the ball. He *exploded* off the ball and had a knack of dropping his shoulder. You never got a good shot at Marv. He would drop his shoulder and wouldn't allow you to get at his legs. He was a stud. He was 220 but he ran like he was 250. He ran like he was made out of stone."

"He was just a tenacious north-south runner," said Dave Bennett. "He had great forward body lean and he just bounced off people. And he didn't put the ball on the ground." "He never went backwards," said Tom Rowland. "He always went forward."

When he was cut by the Broncos, Hubbard wasn't sure he wanted to go to Hartford. When he arrived, he wasn't impressed by Dillon Stadium, but if he wanted to make it back to the AFL, he had to play somewhere, and Hartford was better than most minor league cities. Therefore, Hubbard moved his wife and two-year-old daughter to Vernon and assumed a starting role in the Knights' backfield.

With skills that eventually made him a three-time Pro Bowler and one of the best running backs in the NFL, what was Hubbard doing in Hartford? Despite his talent, he had some strikes against him. First, he'd played six-man football in high school, didn't attract any interest from big colleges and wound up at Colgate. Second, he'd never learned to block in college because he almost always carried the ball. Finally, he had a difficult time absorbing a Raider offensive system that was far more complex than the Colgate playbook. "I think we had two formations," he said.

Hubbard had also acquired a reputation as a troublesome underachiever with an active social life. He had supposedly been released by Denver after a conflict with another player. "He was a great player," said one teammate, "but Marv was a little cuckoo. He was a little crazy." John Madden recalled that when Hubbard was with the Raiders, he used to go drinking at Clancy's, walk next store and punch out the window of a dry cleaning establishment, and walk back to Clancy's and give the bartender $50 to cover the damage.[3] "Marv had it all," said Knights assistant Bill Boehle, "but he wasn't—let's say—playing 110 percent like Fred wanted him to."

"Marv was a little full of himself at that time," said Wheeler. "When he got there he thought he was all–World and sometimes he would run up there and think everyone was going to drop dead for him. We're on the goal line one time and I call his play. He runs up there and gets nothing. So I do it again. He gets nothing. After two plays of getting stuffed on the goal line I call timeout and go over to Fred and say, 'Give me Tommy Morris, *please*.' He sends Tommy in, I call the same damn play and Tommy went into the end zone like a hot knife through butter. So I come off the field and Marv is just screaming at me. I said, 'Marv, these guys came down here to play football. If you're going to flop like a duck at the line of scrimmage, I don't want you in there.' He never did that again. I knew he was a stud and that he had the ability to go back up. I didn't want to see him waste it."

Hubbard and Mel Meeks were easily the best running back combination in the ACFL, but they could not have had more diverse backgrounds. Hubbard was a year out of college, young, fast, and strong, and would be back in the AFL within a year. Meeks was also fast and strong, but he was not young, and at the age of 33 had no hope of landing a spot in the major leagues.

Meeks was an Okie from Muskogee who'd played guard in high school. He then enlisted in the Air Force and played football at Westover Air Force Base in Massachusetts. After he was discharged, Meeks played in the semi-pro ranks for the Holyoke Knights and Holyoke Merchants.

When the ACFL came to Springfield in 1963, Meeks joined the Acorns. After two years with Springfield, he played with Holyoke for part of the 1965 season before joining the Norfolk Neptunes. Meeks became a Charter Oak in 1967 and stayed in Hartford when the Knights were formed.

Meeks worked at the Smith and Wesson plant and lived in Springfield with his wife and three children, the oldest being an 11-year-old who played halfback and safety for the Hilltop Giants in a Springfield peewee league. Two of Meeks' sons were adopted and his natural child and one of the adopted sons were the same age and bore the same name. Eleven-year-old Rick was the one who played football while his brother, eleven-year-old Richard, did not. On Saturday nights the family watched Dad play at Dillon Stadium and on Sunday afternoons they went to see Rick.[4]

Both Hartford running backs had outstanding seasons in 1968, but Hubbard was the one pro scouts were interested in, for Meeks, at 33 (or 31, depending on the source), was too old. Yet, he had not always been 33, and why had someone with his talent never gotten a chance to play in the NFL? Some of his teammates said he was a step too slow, although many who said that had not seen him in his younger days. Others said he was a victim of the unofficial racial quota system that existed in pro football in the early '60s. The fact that he hadn't gone to college also hurt his chances.

In many curious cases of a talented player not getting a fair shot, a bad attitude or problem personality was the cause. That was not true of Meeks, a modest, serious man universally liked by his teammates. "He was very good with the rookies," said Waide Robinson, "and was a good role model for us young players. When I met him we talked for a long time about college, values, religion. He was a good guy."

"If he lacked anything," former teammate John Sponheimer said, "it's that great burst of speed that's the difference between being with the Knights and being in the NFL. The NFL guys were probably a little faster but I don't think anyone was tougher than Mel Meeks."

Or stronger. "A chiseled guy," said Bob Stohrer, "an unbelievable build. He had a physique like Superman." "I always said," recalled Elaine Savin, "that Mel Meeks was the only person I ever knew who had muscles in his face."

"As far as I was concerned he was the best player on our team," said Dick Bowman, and his teammates agreed, voting Meeks the most valuable offensive player on the '68 squad. Tom Rowland rated him a better runner than Hubbard. "Mel Meeks was as good a running back as you could find *anywhere*," he said, and by anywhere he meant the NFL.

After three games, Hartford was alone in first place in the Northern Division, with Bridgeport close behind with a 3–1 mark. The Knights' next opponent was the Richmond Roadrunners, tied with the Virginia Sailors for the top spot in the Southern Division, each with a 2–1 record. The Roadrunners were new to the ACFL but won 12 of 13 games as an independent club in 1967. They were coached by former Redskin and Giant running back Dick James, perhaps best known in New York as the man the Redskins traded for star middle linebacker Sam Huff, one of the worst trades in Giant history.

The Roadrunners' quarterback was young Al Woodall, who expected to be the captain of the 1968 Duke squad rather than playing in Richmond. In mid–July 1968, however, Woodall was suspended from the University for allegedly allowing a coed to write a paper for him. He couldn't play at Duke, and he wasn't eligible for the NFL draft, for his class hadn't graduated. His only option was minor league football, and Woodall signed with the Roadrunners to bide his time until the 1969 draft.

The Knights had beaten the Roadrunners handily in the exhibition season but, like all minor league clubs, each had made significant changes since mid–August. Coach James had activated himself, despite not having played in three years. His team had acquired several new players and had beaten the defending champion Sailors in their opening game.

The Knights lineup had also evolved. One of the keys to a successful minor league season is having enough depth to replace injured players. Most clubs were salary-conscious, and wouldn't commit much for reserve players. Savin, however, had stockpiled quality players at a number of positions. Halfback Tom Morris fractured his ankle and Hubbard took his place. Co-captain Lew Irvin dislocated his elbow, and injured players like defensive end Leroy Moore (a former Patriot), flanker John Wardlaw, and linebacker Bob Soleau (a former Steeler) were all replaced with little loss of functionality.

12. The Championship Season

12. The Championship Season 211

The game between two first place teams drew more than 11,000 fans to Dillon Stadium, and they were treated to the most exciting game of the season. The Knights held a 10–0 lead late in the first half, helped by a 49-yard Wes Bean field goal. Woodall threw a 34-yard touchdown pass to star receiver Bill Barber with twenty seconds left in the second period to close the margin to 10–7 at halftime.

There was no scoring in the third quarter, but the Roadrunners scored ten points early in the final period to give them a 17–10 lead with 3:08 left in the game. With Hartford driving for a potential tying touchdown, the Roadrunners were called for pass interference, giving the Knights possession at the five yard line. Two plays later, Wheeler hit Sherlag in the right corner of the end zone. Bean's conversion tied the score at 17 with 1:31 left. Richmond was unable to move, and the Knights got the ball on their own 49. Wheeler connected with tight end Tom Rychlec for a 26-yard gain to the Richmond 25 with nine seconds remaining, and Wallner sent Bean into the game to attempt a field goal.

Bean's 32-yard attempt sailed outside the right upright. "When I missed that 32-yarder," he said after the game, "I didn't even want to go back to the bench.... I just wanted to walk right out of the stadium."

He didn't have to do either, as for the second time in the final minutes, a

Wes Bean kicks a game-winning field goal from the hold of Benny Russell in a 10–7 win over the Jersey Jays in 1970 (photograph from Hartford Knights program).

yellow penalty flag fluttered fortuitously through the air. Richmond had been offside, giving Bean a second chance from five yards closer. On the second try the snap was high, but Wheeler reached up, grabbed it with one hand, and placed it on the ground. Bean's kick split the uprights almost perfectly. He didn't see the ball go through, but the roar of the large crowd let him know it was good. He had gone from goat to hero in less than sixty seconds.

Bean had been kicking a football since he was a young boy, but in the early 1960s, there were few kicking specialists. He played a number of positions in high school, and finally became a quarterback—a very large quarterback—at Grambling College. Bean was drafted as a linebacker by the Cincinnati Bengals in the seventh round[5] but suffered a groin injury and was released.

Bean signed with Hartford as a linebacker, but kicking was what he liked to do, for although he was 6'2" and a powerful 230 pounds, he didn't like physical contact. "It wasn't that he was afraid," said Dick Bowman, "he just didn't want to get hit. He'd say, 'No, no, no. I'm here to kick the ball.'"

His teammates thought Bean was a little eccentric, and not all that smart. "He had an NFL leg," said Lou Palmer, "but he was wacky." Bean wore outlandish outfits, bizarre even in the free-wheeling '60s. He had a heavy Creole accent that made him difficult to understand, and in the excitement of a game his speech could become nearly impossible to decipher. Gene Gollarney liked to regale his teammates with the story of Bean entering the huddle with instructions from Wallner. Bean was so excited he couldn't remember what the coach had told him. After several false starts, he said, "Coach said we must *fight, fight, fight!*"

There was no question that Bean had big league range. Wallner said he had a stronger leg than Lou Groza, the Cleveland Browns Hall of Fame kicker. "When he kicked the ball off my hold," Wheeler recalled, "it was like a cannon going off. He'd kick them 70 yards in practice. My god, he'd just *boom* the ball. He had the most powerful leg I can ever remember. He'd just drill it. And then he'd miss an extra point attempt." A lack of accuracy was Bean's Achilles heel.

In today's game, with its emphasis on specialists, Bean might have made an NFL roster as a kickoff and long field goal man, but teams of the 1960s didn't have room for a strong-legged kicker who might shank a key extra point or short field goal.

Wallner loved Bean's natural ability and believed that assistant coach Roger LeClerc could teach him to be more consistent. LeClerc had been the kicker for the Chicago Bears from 1960 through 1966, and had initially planned to join the Hartford club as a player-coach. Once he saw Bean kick the ball in practice, LeClerc decided to limit his activity to coaching. He was as excited as Wallner about Bean's potential.

The keys to consistency, LeClerc told Bean, were using the same approach

12. The Championship Season

every time and keeping one's head down. Bean had a good approach, but couldn't remember the second half of the lesson. "He kept looking up," LeClerc remembered, "to see where the ball was going before he kicked it. He never could learn to keep his head down. Evidently he wanted to see how far it went. He wasn't interested in what the direction was." Bean spent three years as the Knights' kicker and remained an enigma—a man with immense but unpolished talent.

The next test for the 4–0 Knights was a home game against the 1–3 Westchester Bulls, an affiliate of the nearby New York Giants. The Bulls had one of the strongest defenses in the league and had played well against the Knights in the exhibition season. The first half of the October 5 game followed the same pattern, with Hartford holding a 12–7 lead at intermission. In the third quarter, the Knights broke the game open by scoring 16 points in less than three minutes, including a safety by Fran Mallick, who sacked Bull quarterback Bill Creedon in the end zone.

The final score was 41–7 and the Knights accumulated over 400 yards of offense. Wheeler completed only six passes, but they accounted for 231 yards and three touchdowns. Terry Best had four receptions in the first quarter for 127 yards. Hubbard went 67 yards with a screen pass during the 23-point third quarter, and accumulated 97 yards rushing.

If the Knights were going to win their sixth straight game, they would have to defeat the Roadrunners, who had nearly beaten them in Hartford, at Richmond's City Stadium. On game night, there were approximately 9,000 fans at City Stadium, a number of whom had flown down from Hartford on an excursion sponsored by the Knights. For $49, Hartford fans got a round trip bus ride from the Knights' Bloomfield office to Bradley Field, a charter flight to Richmond, a game ticket, lunch, a tour of historic Richmond, and dinner.

The fans did not, however, get a Hartford victory. At Dillon Stadium, Hartford had come furiously from behind in the final three minutes, and in Richmond, the Roadrunners dug themselves out of an even deeper hole. "We never should have lost that game in a million years," said Dennis Fitzgibbons.

Early in the final period, the Knights, sparked by the running of Hubbard and Meeks, held a 24–6 lead. The lead could have been even greater, for the Knights had been stopped twice near the Richmond goal line. Still, it didn't seem as though that would matter. When Meeks scored the Knights' final touchdown with 10:15 left in the game, it appeared that Hartford, whose strong defense had contained Woodall and the Richmond offense for more than three quarters, had a lock on its sixth win in a row.

Shortly after Richmond received the kickoff following Meeks' touchdown, things started to unravel for the Knights. Woodall threw a dangerous pass toward the sideline intended for Bill Robinson. Rowland, who thought he had another interception, cut in front of Robinson, got in perfect position, but missed the ball. Robinson didn't miss it and carried it 70 yards for a touchdown that made the score 24–13.

"They called a flat pass," Rowland recalled. "I cut in front of the receiver and I could have walked into the end zone, but the ball tipped off my fingers and the receiver went for a touchdown. We were watching the film and Coach Wallner said, 'Looks like you thought you had that one, Rowland.' I said, 'Yeah, I should have had it.'"

Hartford still seemed to have the game well in hand, and Wheeler, with Hubbard doing most of the work, moved his club to the Richmond 40, chewing up yardage and the clock. Then, with just over five minutes left, the Knights were faced with a third down and six yards to go for a first down.

"We ran one of those five man patterns," said Wheeler. "My key is the middle linebacker. The tight end is running an arrow across the middle of the field right at the middle linebacker. The split end, Bobby Stohrer, was running a curl in the seam of the zone. I drop back and the middle linebacker drops back so I know right away I'm going to go to the weak side. I'm going to look to the weak side and the split end is going to be open on the curl. I'm looking at him and I throw the ball and the next thing I know the strong safety picks it off." Wheeler's pass was intercepted by Tim Montgomery, who returned it 65 yards for a touchdown that narrowed the margin to 24–20.

Bob Tucker explained the intricacy of pass patterns. "They draw it up on the blackboard," he said, "and you're supposed to get to certain markers. But you're running pass patterns off the defense and you have to recognize the defense, what the coverage is and where you're going to get open. Even if you think you're going to be covered, you've got to run the hell out of the pattern to make sure the guy does cover you and can't cover someone else. If you're not disciplined in running your patterns, the guy who's guarding you is going to stick his nose in somewhere else and you've got an interception."

That was exactly what happened to tight end Tom Brockmeyer. "What he had done," Wheeler said, "was that he didn't read the middle linebacker so he ran straight across the field to where the split end was running his curl and he brought the safety with him. If he sees the middle linebacker drop he's supposed to run straight up the field and hook and occupy the strong safety. So I'm not looking for the safety. I know he's not going to be over there because the tight end's running him down the field. In the film, sure enough it shows Brockmeyer running across the field and he brought the strong safety right in there."

Following the Richmond touchdown, Hartford again moved the ball deep into Roadrunner territory, but Bean missed a 37-yard field goal and Woodall got the ball back on his 20 with 2:35 left. Two completions quickly brought the ball to the Hartford 42. On the next play, Woodall was forced out of the pocket by a fierce rush and, scrambling, found halfback Charley Herman open at the Knights' 15-yard line. Herman caught the pass, avoided a Hartford defender, and went into the end zone. Bill Joyner's extra point gave the Roadrunners a 27–24 lead. Richmond had scored 21 points in less than ten minutes.

There was still 1:40 left, time enough for the Knights to mount a final challenge. On their first play from scrimmage, however, Wheeler's pass was intercepted, cementing the Richmond win and assuring Hartford's first defeat. Still, with the season half over, the Knights were comfortably in first place.

Northern Division

	Won	Lost	Tied	Pct.
Hartford	5	1	0	.833
Bridgeport	3	2	1	.600
Lowell	2	3	1	.400
Westchester	1	5	0	.167

Southern Division

	Won	Lost	Tied	Pct.
Virginia	4	2	0	.667
Richmond	3	3	0	.500
Pottstown	3	3	0	.500
Harrisburg	2	4	0	.333

The second half of the season commenced with a game at Lowell's Cawley Stadium against the Giants. Lowell's general manager was dynamic Charley Theokas, a former college player who'd been released by the Jets in 1963 and was in the nascent stage of a lengthy career as a sports executive. Theokas later became general manager of the NBA's New Jersey Nets, athletic director at Temple, an executive with the New Jersey Generals of the USFL, and commissioner of the Atlantic 10 Conference, but in 1968 he was paying his dues operating an ACFL club on a shoestring.

Hartford Courant reporter Bill Winters called Theokas to get his opinion of the upcoming game with the Knights. "We should win by two or three touchdowns," Theokas told him with tongue in cheek. Winters expressed his doubts, since Hartford was heavily favored. "See me after the game so I can tell you I was right," Theokas replied.

The Giants of late October were much different than the team the Knights defeated in exhibition play. A few weeks earlier, Theokas had acquired King Corcoran to play quarterback. The addition of the King turned the Giants from a running team to a passing team, and his presence brought excitement to the drab industrial city of Lowell. It was hard to find a lot of action in Lowell, but Corcoran always brought his own action with him.

Corcoran had a talented receiver in tight end Bob Tucker. Tucker set a number of receiving records at little Bloomsburg State College in Pennsylvania, but was not drafted by a professional team. He was given a free agent tryout by the Boston Patriots and was one of the final players released.

Tucker looked good in practice, but never played a single offensive down in exhibition games, his activity relegated to running down on punt and kickoff coverage. He was offered a position on the Boston taxi squad, but elected to take a job teaching biology at Acton-Boxborough Regional High School and make the 40 minute drive to Lowell to play with the Giants who, despite their nickname, were actually affiliated with the Patriots. "I never could figure that one out," Tucker said.

Corcoran and Tucker had to wait an extra day to play the Knights, for a driving rainstorm turned the field into a quagmire and caused a postponement from Saturday night to Sunday evening. Only about 500 fans changed their plans and came to watch Sunday's game, and the rest missed an entertaining contest pitting King Corcoran and Bob Tucker against Marv Hubbard and Mel Meeks.

Wheeler had a bad night, missing his first eight pass attempts and completing just 5 of 19 overall. "I really can't explain what goes wrong on a night like that," he said afterward. "It's just like golf. You can go out and shoot a great round one day and the next day you're hitting the ball all over the course."[6]

There are no mulligans in football, however, and it was fortunate for Wheeler that he had Meeks and Hubbard behind him. Corcoran completed 31 passes in 50 attempts for 280 yards and Tucker caught 11 of them for 142 yards. Meanwhile, Hubbard rushed for 171 yards on only 13 carries while Meeks gained 106 in 25 attempts as the Knights picked up 329 yards on the ground.

Meeks scored three touchdowns in the second quarter to give the Knights a 20–6 lead but Corcoran brought Lowell back with two touchdown passes that made the score 20–19 with 12 minutes left in the third quarter. With the Hartford offensive line opening huge holes in the Lowell defense, the Knights built their lead to 32–19. Corcoran hit Tucker with a touchdown pass that closed the gap to 32–26 with just 21 seconds left in the game. Lowell's first attempt at an onside kick failed when Joe Egresitz missed the ball completely. Egresitz connected on his second try but the Knights recovered and ran out the clock.

The win against Lowell set up two key, back-to-back games against the second place Bridgeport Jets, the first in Hartford and the second in Bridgeport. Wallner called the first game "the biggest professional football game in the history of Hartford." Colt Park was appropriated for additional parking and Pete Savin talked about the need to expand Dillon Stadium.

12. The Championship Season

Nick DeFelice (75) leads Mel Meeks (32) on the trademark Green Bay sweep as Manch Wheeler watches from behind (courtesy Nick DeFelice from Hartford Knights program).

The game had all the excitement Wallner, Savin, and the Hartford fans could have hoped for. Again, it was the Hartford ground game against the passing of their opponents. Jet quarterback John Torok passed for 194 yards while the Knights ran for 209. Bean boomed a 50-yard field goal in the second period to give Hartford a 9–7 halftime lead. The final margin of victory was Bean's second 50-yard boot in the fourth quarter. Despite a late Bridgeport touchdown, the Knights held on for a hard-fought 19–17 win.

Bean's accomplishment was even more remarkable considering the fact that linebacker Bill Lesinski, who handled the snapping chores for field goals and extra points, had a cast on the hand he had broken in the Lowell game and was unable to make long snaps. Center Wayne Krueger took over for him, but misfired on two occasions. Lesinski therefore had his cast cut off for the snaps and had it re-taped when he went back on defense. "I would take it off," he said, "get a shot of Novacaine, and play the game with the cast held on with an ace bandage. That went on for three or four weeks," he recalled, "until the hand healed a little bit. Of course, I've got a little arthritis now, but that's beside the point."

The Knights' backs were racking up some impressive statistics. After eight games, Meeks led the league with 613 yards while Hubbard, who missed the opening game, was second with 523. Meeks averaged 4.5 yards per carry and Hubbard 5.9. When Meeks or Hubbard carried the ball, the other one was clearing out linebackers and cornerbacks. "Hubbard turned into a great blocker," said Lou Palmer. "On the power sweep he was out front behind the pulling guards and if anyone got through them he cut them down." "He told me he learned how to block from Wallner," added Dennis Randall.

Hubbard and Meeks also had the benefit of running behind the best offensive line in the ACFL. "They could shout across the line of scrimmage," said Palmer, "and tell them 'power sweep right' and they couldn't stop it because it was so well executed. Watching a game with the Hartford Knights was like watching a Packer game."

"We had confidence and we all liked each other," said DeFelice, the leader of the offensive line. "There are a lot of football teams where some of the guys are nuts and stupid. You don't like them and it rips the team apart. You see it now in the NFL with guys like Terrell Owens. In Hartford, if anybody came in and didn't have the same desire to win and to be a family, they didn't last long."

The second game against Bridgeport was played in JFK Stadium which, according to the *Courant*, "makes Dillon Stadium look like a farm tenant's shack." The crowd of 11,221 included about 2,000 Knights fans that made the 60-mile trip down from Hartford. The first game had been close and Jet coach Nick Cutro insisted that his club was better than Hartford, and but for a couple of dropped passes and two missed field goals, the Jets would have won.

In the second game, however, the Knights left no doubt as to which was the superior team. "They had a great team," Cutro said recently. "I thought I had good players but when we went on the field against them, it was like, 'oh, shit.' They had the best players."

As the game progressed and their team built up a commanding lead, Hartford fans started shouting, "We're number one." Meeks scored three touchdowns, and Hubbard gained 138 yards as the Knights rolled over the Jets 37–7. Bean kicked a 44-yard field goal, and on a 54-yard attempt, rolled the ball out of bounds on the three-yard line, a rare coffin corner field goal attempt. He also missed a 15-yard field goal attempt and bounced an extra point over the crossbar.

Hartford was 8–1, the second place Jets were 4–4–1, and the Knights needed only a tie in their last three games to clinch the title. Despite the potential clinching, tickets sales for the following week's game against Harrisburg were

12. The Championship Season

slow. The cold November weather didn't help, and the crowd was only 8,000, far less than the total for earlier games.

The clincher, a methodical 26–7 Hartford win, wasn't that exciting. Safety Wes DuBois picked off three passes and Harrisburg's vaunted run defense was unable to stop Meeks and Hubbard, who gained 112 and 78 yards, respectively. With two games left, the only remaining suspense revolved around which Knight would win the rushing title. With his performance against Harrisburg, Meeks took the lead with 768 yards to Hubbard's 739. Meeks also scored two more touchdowns to bring his season total to 13.

After clinching the Northern Division title, the Knights found themselves in a position to decide the champion of the Southern Division. Virginia led Pottstown by two games, and if the Knights beat Pottstown, the Sailors would advance to the championship game. The title game, by rotation, was scheduled to take place in the stadium of the Southern Division champion, but commissioner Iacovazzi indicated that it might be played in Hartford. The Connecticut city, the commissioner said, deserved the game because they had "better fans." What he really meant was that the Knights had more fans, and more fans meant larger gate proceeds to divide among the two teams. The Sailors played at a high school field in Herndon, Virginia that held only 3,000, while Dillon accommodated more than 11,000.

ACFL officials watched the Hartford-Pottstown contest November 16, ostensibly to gauge the suitability of Dillon as a host site for the championship game. Unfortunately, the Knights drew only 5,200, one of the smallest crowds of the season. It was a meaningless game, however, and the crowd was still much larger than the Sailors' stadium was capable of seating.

With the title clinched, Wallner played his substitutes liberally. Backups Dave Bennett and Dick Faucette split time at quarterback. Faucette, a first year professional who played his college ball at the University of Dayton, had been with the Orlando Panthers of the Continental League before signing with the Knights in early October.

The Pottstown game was Faucette's first as a Knight, and he completed just 2 of 7 passes for 22 yards (one for an 11 yard touchdown to Rychlec). Hubbard leapfrogged over Meeks to take the rushing lead 832 to 810, and safety Johnny Lee returned one punt for a 72-yard touchdown and another for 55 yards.

Lee was possibly the best athlete on the Hartford squad. An all-state quarterback at Weaver High School, he had also excelled at baseball and basketball, and played professional basketball for the Hartford Capitals. "He was the best football player I ever played with," said Tom Rowland. "He covered Bob Tucker and just shut him down. He had opportunities to try out with the NFL but his wife did not want him to do that so he stayed around Hartford. He should have been in the NFL."

Faucette led the Knights to victory in their final regular season game, hitting John Wardlaw with a seven-yard pass with 47 seconds left for a 21–17 win over the Westchester Bulls. The Bulls had allowed only 2.1 yards per carry during the season, the best mark in the ACFL, and neither of the Knights' running backs was able to do much damage. Hubbard, who rushed for 65 yards, won the title with 897 yards. Meeks finished with 826. The key statistics were the passing totals, where Faucette hit 6 of 13 for 106 yards while Wheeler completed just 3 of 13 for 22 yards. Working with a backup center in practice, Wheeler had been surprised by an early snap and jammed his middle finger, and the injury prevented him from throwing the ball effectively.

The Knights incurred a number of injuries in the game against the Bulls, the most serious of which was a broken ankle suffered by guard Jack Calcaterra. Fran Mallick suffered a broken finger, but was expected to play in the championship game. Wheeler's status was uncertain. Wallner delayed his choice for several days, and then announced on Saturday that Faucette would start.

The Virginia Sailors, affiliated with the Washington Redskins, were the only ACFL team the Knights had not played during the regular season. Under Coach Bill Cox, they had won the previous two ACFL titles, and had captured the North American League championship in 1965. Cox knew Wallner well, and the two had been roommates one summer at Duke University.

Both teams were run-oriented. The Sailors' leading rusher was fullback Ray McDonald, the 1967 number one draft choice of the Redskins who, after signing a three-year $100,000 contract, had been a big bust in Washington. After a mediocre rookie year in 1967, McDonald was sent to the Sailors the following season after just one game with the Redskins. His failure with the Redskins was a great surprise, for McDonald had an outstanding career at the University of Idaho, leading the nation with 1,329 rushing yards in 1966. At 6'4" and 248 pounds, he had the size of an offensive lineman and the speed of a college sprinter. People compared him to Jimmy Brown.

Before drafting McDonald, the Redskins investigated rumors that he was gay. Gays in the mid–1960s were considered to be criminals and sexual deviants. "A homosexual at that time," said former Packer guard Jerry Kramer, "was a 'fag' or a 'queer' and a whole variety of names that were all derogatory and all meant to be. It would have been awfully hard for [McDonald] to play at a high level without a lot of grief."[7] The Detroit Lions had asked linebacker and Idaho grad Wayne Walker to check into the rumors, and decided not to select McDonald.

McDonald *was* gay, and the Redskin players found out quickly. Star quarterback Sonny Jurgensen abused the rookie openly, calling him a "fag" and riding him mercilessly. McDonald was not the only gay player on the Redskins, but he was apparently the only one whose orientation was public knowledge. Star tight end Jerry Smith, who played with Washington from 1965 until 1977 and died of AIDs in 1986, was gay, although he never acknowledged it during his playing career. In 1969, Dave Kopay, the first NFL player to admit his homosexuality (several years after he retired), joined the Redskins and engaged in a romantic relationship with Smith.

McDonald was back in the Redskin training camp in 1969, after Vince Lombardi had taken over as head coach. Lombardi had a gay brother, and was surprisingly liberal on the matter of sexual preference. He reportedly told his assistants that he wanted McDonald to be given a fair chance to make the squad, telling them, "And if I hear one of you people make references to his manhood, you'll be out of here before your ass hits the ground." Kopay said he believed Lombardi knew of his sexual orientation and of the relationship between him and Smith.[8]

McDonald did not make the Redskin team in 1969 and was sent back to the Redskins ACFL affiliate, then based in Roanoke. His general manager was former baseball star Jimmy Piersall, whose attitudes were more in line with prevailing mores. Once, when McDonald broke a long run, Piersall shouted from the press box, "Go, go, go, Ray! Go, go, go! If you score, I'll get you a young kid."

The Sailors' kicker was 25-year-old Curt Knight, a former Coast Guard Academy player who, like Bean, had a powerful but erratic leg. "He's really exciting in his inconsistency," said Sailor assistant coach Stan Springer. "He has kicked ten field goals for us, a couple of them 48 and 49 yards, but in close he might put it under the crossbar." *Courant* sports editor Bill Lee responded, "[W]ait until they get a load of Hartford's Wes Bean." Unlike Bean, Knight gained consistency with experience, and was the Washington kicker from 1969 through 1973, playing in Super Bowl VII.

The two teams were evenly matched, and the championship game was well-played and tightly contested. Early in the first quarter, the Sailors got close to the Knights' end zone and tried to run it in with a sweep to Tom Rowland's side of the field. The pulling linemen wiped out everyone but Rowland, who made a great open field tackle on the two. The Sailors had to settle for a nine-yard field goal by Knight.

A few minutes later, Meeks broke a 65-yard run from his own 28-yard line. Faucette then hit Rychlec with a pass in the corner of the end zone. "I managed to break free," Rychlec said, "and bing-bang, there it was, six points." A short Bean field goal gave the Knights a 10–3 lead, and the teams traded touchdowns to make the score Hartford 17 Virginia 10 at halftime. Meeks had gained 114 yards and the Knights had 138 yards rushing.

The 1968 ACFL Champion Hartford Knights. Players only—first row (left to right): Bill Lesinski, Tom Morris, Nick DeFelice, Lew Irvin, Ron McCauley, Terry Best, Leroy Moore, Mel Meeks, Jack Calcaterra, Coach Fred Wallner. Second row (left to right): Bruce Williams, Dick Bowman, Wes Bean, Johnny Lee, Otis Thomas, Fran Mallick, Ken Luciani, Len Griffin. Third row (left to right): Dave Bennett, Dennis Fitzgibbons, Gene Jackson, John Naponic, Bob Sherlag, Howard Small, Tom Rowland, Dick Faucette. Fourth row (left to right): Bob Stohrer, Wes Dubois, Marv Hubbard, Bob Shemeth, Bob Mirabelle, Bob Risley, Bob Soleau, Tom Rychlec. Fifth row (left to right): Unidentified, Ernie Colquette, Manch Wheeler, Tom Brockmeyer, Gene Gollarney, Dick Carlson.

The only scoring in the third quarter was a four-yard run by Hubbard, after which Bean missed the conversion. Midway through the fourth period, Hubbard's fumble deep in Hartford territory gave the Sailors a reprieve, and quarterback Danny Talbott took advantage of the turnover by throwing a touchdown pass to close the deficit to six points.

Following the score, the Virginia defense held and the Sailors had the ball on the Hartford 49 with just over three minutes left in the game, needing a touchdown and an extra point to give them the lead. Mallick, playing with a cast on his broken finger, put a hard rush on Talbott. He knocked the ball loose, and linebacker Gene Jackson picked it up and raced 45 yards for the score that clinched the game and brought Hartford its first professional football championship. "That's one of the highlights I'll never forget," Mallick said recently.

The 30–17 victory was typical of the Knights' season. Meeks gained 184 yards and Hubbard 71, as the offensive line repeatedly opened holes in the Vir-

12. The Championship Season

ginia defensive front. Faucette passed only when he had to, completing just 3 in 9 attempts, but didn't commit any turnovers. The defense came through with a big play when the game was on the line. Each Knight collected a $450 check for their winners' share from the record gate proceeds of $50,004.

Faucette, who hadn't seen action until the eleventh week of the season, played the entire game. As Bill Lee pointed out, it was the year of the substitute quarterback. John Unitas was hurt and Earl Morrall was leading the Baltimore Colts to the Super Bowl. Frank Champi came off the Harvard bench to direct the Crimson to a miraculous 29–29 tie against unbeaten Yale. Sophomore Joe Theismann replaced injured All-American Terry Hanratty to lead Notre Dame to an upset of O.J. Simpson and the Southern California Trojans. Why shouldn't Dick Faucette quarterback Hartford to the ACFL championship?

13

The 1969 Hartford Knights

The Knights' affiliation with the Packers had contributed little to the 1968 championship. When the partnership was established, the Packers were back-to-back Super Bowl champions and the Knights were a fledgling organization that had yet to play its first game. By the end of the year, the Knights were ACFL champions and the Packers, who finished the season with a 6–7–1 mark, had commenced a long stretch of mediocrity.

"We didn't get an awful lot out of the Packers," said Manch Wheeler, who retired to serve as general manager in 1969. "We ran their offense, and all of a sudden I realized what Bart Starr was doing. But as far as helping us out with personnel, not so much."

In July 1969, the Knights announced that the affiliation with Green Bay had ended and a new one with the Buffalo Bills had begun. There were a number of connections between Hartford and Buffalo. Bills owner Ralph Wilson was a friend of Pete Savin's, and Fred Wallner and Buffalo head coach John Rauch had been assistants on the Tulane staff in 1962.

Prospects for personnel assistance from the Bills appeared to be better than they had been with the Packers. Rauch hinted that the Knights might receive whichever of Buffalo's two young quarterbacks, heralded rookie James Harris of Grambling or little used third year man Benny Russell of Louisville, failed to make his squad. The Knights needed a quarterback, since Wheeler had retired and Dick Faucette announced he would not play for personal reasons (although he did appear later in the season with the Long Island Bulls).

Several other members of the championship team did not return. Marv Hubbard was in training camp with the Oakland Raiders. Bill Lesinski took a full time job coaching high school football. Terry Best, who had missed many practice sessions, was not invited back. Veteran lineman Leroy "Sweetpea" Moore, who'd spent six years in the AFL, had been unable to recover from a knee injury and decided to retire just short of his thirty-fourth birthday. Defen-

13. The 1969 Hartford Knights

sive captain Lou Irvin re-injured his elbow and retired. Linebacker Bob Soleau, whose family had a history of heart trouble, had a couple of scares he believed were the precursor to serious coronary problems. He retired at the age of 28 and became a Knight assistant coach.

Wallner, who needed a quarterback, got two good ones. The Bills decided very early in camp they had no room for Benny Russell, and the Knights also signed Hank Washington of West Texas State, who'd been in camp with the New York Giants and played with the Westchester Bulls the past two years.

Before Harris was drafted by the Bills, many thought Washington would be the first black quarterback to play regularly in the NFL. Not only did he have one of the strongest arms in football, he had the bearing and persona of a football hero, a tall, well-built, handsome man with a beautiful wife and a young son. "He was smart," said Waide Robinson, "down to earth and a good leader. He was great with kids."

Hank Washington (photograph from Hartford Knights program).

In two years at West Texas State, Washington threw for 3,510 yards and 26 touchdowns. Teaming with running back Mercury Morris his senior year, he was fourth in the nation in total offense, fifth in passing. and played in the North-South Classic and the Senior Bowl.

Like Wes Bean, Washington was a raw talent in need of polishing. At 6'3" and 210 pounds, he had a classic pro build. And he clearly had a major league arm. "I guess he can throw the ball as far as anyone ever has," said Giant coach Allie Sherman. "When it comes to timing and technique, I'd have to say he's quite a way out." "He could throw the hell out of the ball," said Dave Bennett. "He had a gun. But he wasn't as accurate as he needed to be to make the big time."

When Nick DeFelice said Washington could throw the ball 100 yards, I dismissed it as hyperbole—until I read an article by a respected researcher that said he could throw 90–95 yards in the air. "Washington had a great arm," said Bob Stohrer, "but he threw the ball too hard. He'd be about eight yards away from you and he'd throw the ball so hard you couldn't even see it, let alone catch it." In college, West Texas receivers had their arms bloodied trying to catch Washington's passes in practice.

Before Washington could make it to the NFL, he needed to win the Hartford starting job over Russell. The latter had broken several of John Unitas' records at the University of Louisville, and spent 1967 on the Bills' taxi squad. He was on active duty with his National Guard unit for much of the 1968 season, but managed to get into one AFL game.

Many professional athletes had their careers derailed by military service in the 1960s, and Russell's luck was particularly bad, for 1968 was a great year to be a backup quarterback in Buffalo. Starter Jack Kemp went down with an injury before the season started, and backup Tom Flores quickly followed him to the sidelines. Then Kay Stephenson went down, as did rookie Dan Darraugh. Since Russell was on active duty, the Bills played their last four games with flanker Ed Rutkowski at quarterback.

By the start of training camp in 1969, the injured quarterbacks had recovered and Russell was ticketed for Hartford. Just before the opening game, he was named the starter. Russell didn't have Washington's arm strength, but he was Wallner's type. "Russell was consistent," said Bennett. "He didn't make mistakes."

As the summer wore on, some of the old Knights returned to the fold. Tom Rowland, Gene Jackson, and Wes Bean were re-signed after being cut by the Broncos. Bean's trial with the Broncos had been complicated by his military obligations.

Big defensive tackle John Sponheimer filled the void left by Irvin's retirement. Sponheimer, 6'5½" tall and 250 pounds, had been an all–Ivy selection at Cornell in 1967 and 1968 and received honorable mention on several All American teams. He played college basketball at a time when men under 6'6" could play center and was on the squad that sprung a major upset on a Kentucky team coached by legendary Adolph Rupp. Kentucky had stars like Pat Riley and had been to the NCAA finals the year before. "We beat them by 25 points," Sponheimer recalled, "and without my 2 points it would have been only 23."

Sponheimer's best sport was football, however, and he was drafted by the Kansas City Chiefs on the tenth round. He was surprised when he heard the news and disappointed when he saw the competition in training camp. "It was not a good team to be drafted by," he said. The two defensive tackles were Buck Buchanan, who would end up in the Pro Football Hall of Fame, and Curley

Culp, who played in six Pro Bowls. Sponheimer had been called the "Giant of the Ivy League" but in the NFL he was smaller than most of the NFL guards that were blocking him.

Despite the intense competition, Sponheimer stuck with the Chiefs deep into the exhibition season. It wasn't easy, for in addition to battling Culp and Buchanan, he was fending off the United States Army. After he graduated and lost his student deferment, Sponheimer had been given orders to report to Fort Dix on June 23. He managed to obtain a delay in order to allow him to attend the Chiefs' camp, but the induction notice hung over his head all summer. Finally, he injured an ankle in an exhibition game and lost any chance of making the squad that would win the Super Bowl that year.

Sponheimer wanted to continue his football career and knew about the Hartford Knights. He had grown up in Derby, one street away from Nick DeFelice, and DeFelice's sister had been his baby sitter. Further, Pete Savin was a fellow Cornell grad, so Sponheimer took on the role of full-time law student and part-time football player.

Center Jim Murphy joined the growing number of ex–Syracuse products on the Hartford roster. At Syracuse he had been the roommate of New York

John Sponheimer (70) performs what might have been professional football's first sack dance after dropping Bridgeport quarterback Harry Theofiledes. Knights defensive end Fran Mallick (84) is brought to his knees by the magnificence of Sponheimer's maneuver (photograph from Hartford Knights program).

Giants' coach Tom Coughlin, who he remembered, not surprisingly, as very intense. "He can't sit still," Murphy said. "He couldn't then and he can't now."

In the 1960s, most players played both offense and defense before finding a place on one platoon or the other. Murphy was put in the center position because of his poor vision. "I could see the guy on my head," he said, "but I had trouble finding the ball. I'd go for a fake."

Like so many of the Knights, Murphy was in Hartford due to some tough luck. His college eligibility ended after the 1967 season, but he still needed a few credits to graduate. He got a free agent tryout with the Eagles, who had veteran Jim Ringo at center and a big rookie named Forrest Blue (who would later start for the 49ers) in the wings. Murphy was cut and asked to play with the Pottstown Firebirds, who had a working agreement with the Eagles. "To me that sounded like they made up a name," said Murphy. "I'd never heard of anything like that. So I said no." He returned to Syracuse to finish his degree and the Eagles sent another center to Pottstown. Blue tore up his knee, his backup tore up his knee, and the center that went to Pottstown joined the Eagles.

The following year Murphy got in touch with his old friend Dennis Fitzgibbons and asked what life with the Hartford Knights was like. Fitzgibbons, who'd been hesitant to join the Knights a year earlier, told him the operation was first class, and Murphy agreed to join the team. He also convinced his brother Joe, a lineman from Central Connecticut State College, to come along.

Another addition to the Hartford squad was linebacker Wayne Lineberry, a tough, good looking southern boy from East Carolina. Lineberry had played defensive tackle in college, but at 235 pounds was too small for a professional lineman. The Bills drafted him and sent him to Hartford to learn how to play linebacker. "He was a handsome, handsome, kid," said Elaine Savin, "and he told Pete this story. He went to a fair in North Carolina and one of the attractions was that if you wrestled this man's bear to the ground you'd get $100. He wrestled the bear down but the guy said he didn't keep him down. He wasn't going to give him the $100. Wayne said to the man, 'Look, I already whupped your bear.'"

The 1969 Knights looked a lot like the previous year's club. Hubbard was gone, but Mel Meeks was back along with Tom Morris, who had been plagued by injuries the previous season. Wallner admitted that Hubbard was a better power runner, but claimed the Knights would be better off with the more versatile Morris, who could run inside and outside and catch passes. Thirty-five-year-old Tom Rychlec returned for another season, as did wide receivers John Wardlaw and Bob Stohrer.

The ACFL returned nearly intact for the 1969 season, a remarkable feat for a minor league circuit. The Lowell Giants, who failed both on the field and at the box office in 1968, moved to Quincy, Massachusetts. The Westchester

Bulls moved to Hempstead, Long Island, where they would play on the artificial turf of Hofstra University and be known as the Long Island Bulls. The Virginia Sailors moved to Roanoke, but not a single franchise folded.

As they had the previous year, the Knights won all three of their exhibition contests. The opening game of the regular season took place at Dillon Stadium against the Pottstown Firebirds. During the offseason, the Firebirds signed King Corcoran to a contract for a reported $125,000, an incredible amount for a minor leaguer at a time when a six figure salary was reserved for players like Joe Namath. Many AFL and NFL regulars earned less than $20,000.

Hartford Courant sportswriter Bill Winters was suspicious and called Pottstown to verify the information. Firebird coach Dave DiFilippo explained that the contract was for three years and included anticipated profits from a number of business ventures Corcoran invested in with funds loaned him by the team. DiFilippo did not tell Winters the amount of cash Corcoran was paid to play football in 1969, but it is safe to say that it was nowhere close to $125,000. If Corcoran's chain of Little Abner drive-in restaurants prospered, the King might be a $125,000 burger baron, but he was not a $125,000 ballplayer.

The Firebirds also obtained tight end Bob Tucker, the ACFL's leading receiver in 1968 with 65 receptions for 964 yards. Tucker had been invited to the Philadelphia training camp, but for a second season, he did not participate in a single offensive play during the exhibition game. He was placed on the Eagle taxi squad. Tucker lived in Pottstown, took the train to Philadelphia each day to practice with the Eagles, then took the train home, ate dinner, and went to practice in the evening with the Firebirds.

On their offensive line, the Firebirds had Leo Levandowski of Harvard— or so the program said. Levandowski was listed as a Harvard grad because that is what he told the public relations people when they asked. In fact, Leo had never gone to any institution of higher learning, having dropped out of St. James High during his junior year and eventually becoming a truck driver. After playing semi-pro ball for a few years with teams like Sun Village AA, Tinicum AC, and Ridley Township AA, he used a two week vacation to try out for the Philadelphia Bulldogs in 1965. He made the team, became one of the best guards in the Continental League and played for the CFL champions in 1966.

In the summer of 1968, Levandowski had an opportunity to try out with the Eagles. His employer, Scott Paper Company, wouldn't give him leave, so he quit his job. Leo could have taken a two week vacation, for that's how long it took the Eagles to cut him. Fortunately, the Firebirds signed Levandowski and found him a supervisory position with Jones Motors.

In the opening game against the Knights, Corcoran put the ball in the air

Benny Russell (photograph from Hartford Knights program).

37 times, but was unable to lead his team into the end zone, despite outgaining Hartford by more than 100 yards in total offense. The Knights' offense wasn't able to score a touchdown either, but three Wes Bean field goals, a Tom Rowland interception return for a touchdown and a safety resulted in an 18–3 win. Russell went all the way at quarterback but completed only four passes.

The win was nice, but if the Knights' offense didn't score, it was unlikely the team was going to win many games. The rushing offense that dominated the league in 1968 accounted for only 49 yards. Maybe, however, it was because the Pottstown defense was that good. "It is just possible," wrote Bill Lee, "that the 8,000 spectators Saturday night were looking down at the two best teams in the Atlantic Coast Football League."

13. The 1969 Hartford Knights

No one claimed the Long Island Bulls were one of the two best teams in the ACFL, but they held Hartford to a single touchdown on September 12 at Hempstead. Bean again kicked three field goals, safetyman Johnny Lee returned an interception 90 yards for a touchdown, and the Knights won 22–14. Again, Russell completed just four passes, but Wallner kept Washington on the bench. "I wouldn't trade [Russell] for any other quarterback in minor league football," he said.

Finally, in the third game of the season, the Knights' offense got rolling, piling up 31 points against Quincy while the Hartford defense held the Giants offense to just a field goal. Russell threw three long touchdown passes, two to Wardlaw (65 and 67 yards) and one to Stohrer (34 yards). Thus far, 6 of his 16 completions had been for touchdowns, and he averaged over 27 yards per completion. The running game finally came to life, as rookie fullback Jay Calabrese of Duke started for the first time and gained 70 yards on just 10 carries. Greg Walker, a backup halfback, gained 87 yards on 9 attempts. The emergence of powerful Calabrese and the speedy Walker gave the club four top flight backs who came at the opposition in waves behind the veteran offensive line.

Including exhibitions, Hartford had won 13 straight games, and had lost only once in two years. The Dunkel Index, a mathematically based formula that attempted to empirically measure the strength of college and professional football teams, gave the Knights a rating of 70.4. That put them ahead of every minor league club in the country, and only 24 points behind the Boston Patriots, the weakest rated AFL team.

The next game appeared to be a mismatch, for the Harrisburg Capitol-Colts had lost their first three games, scoring only 10 points in the process. On a rainy night at Dillon, the Knights rolled over the Capitol-Colts on their way to a record setting 55–14 triumph. Calabrese ran for three touchdowns and Morris for two, as Hartford rushed for 224 yards, in a performance reminiscent of the 1968 champions. Much of the scoring was set up by seven Harrisburg turnovers, including six interceptions.

The Knights' next game was as close as the previous one had been one-sided, as the 1–4 Quincy Giants took the game right down to the final gun. Sloppy special teams play nearly cost the Knights the game. Bean missed an extra point and Quincy scored a touchdown after a bad snap from punt formation, giving them a 17–16 lead midway through the fourth quarter.

With six minutes left in the game, Bean kicked a 25-yard field goal that gave the Knights a 19–17 lead, but the Giants then drove from their own 21 to the Hartford 13. Rather than try to score a touchdown, they maneuvered the ball to the center of the field for a 20-yard field goal attempt by Gustave Carlas with nine seconds left.

For a year and a half, Tommy Rowland had been making big plays for the Knights. He intercepted passes. He blocked kicks. He made key tackles. In the game against Quincy two weeks earlier, he had barely missed blocking two field goal attempts. Wallner noticed that Carlas, a soccer style kicker, usually kicked toward the right and hooked the ball back toward the center. He reasoned that putting Rowland, his best kick blocker, on the far left side of the line would gain him a few critical inches. "Coach told me I had to get to the ball," Rowland said.

Quincy snapped the ball and Carlas put his foot on it. John Sponheimer burst through the center of the line and thought he had a chance to block the kick. "I made real good penetration," he said, "got my hands up and all of a sudden Tommy Rowland flashed in front of me from the corner." Rowland leaped in the air and got his hand on the ball. "My first thought when it hit my hand was whether I got enough of the ball." He had, the ball fell harmlessly to the ground, and Hartford fans, who'd been very vocal throughout the tense evening, rushed onto the field, just as they had a year earlier when Bean's field goal beat Richmond at the final gun. "It was wild," wrote Bill Winters. It was also, including exhibitions, the Knights' 15th straight Dillon Stadium win.

The following week, the Knights took a giant step toward a second Northern Division title by defeating the Bridgeport Jets 23–14 at Kennedy Stadium. At 6–0, Hartford was three games in front of the 3–3 Jets, who were in second place. The Knights followed the Bridgeport win with two easy victories, 33–3 over Roanoke and 37–14 over winless Harrisburg.

The only excitement in the Harrisburg game came when a bench-clearing brawl erupted late in the contest. "We were beating them pretty good," recalled Sponheimer, "and I thought the game was over. I almost made a key mistake. I was running out to get into the fight, and realized I didn't have my helmet on, so I went back and got it. To this day Nick DeFelice claims the other guy started it, but knowing Nick, I'm not sure who started it."

With four games remaining in the regular season, the standings were as follows:

Northern Division		Southern Division	
Hartford	8–0	Pottstown	7–1
Bridgeport	4–4	Richmond	5–3
Long Island	3–5	Roanoke	3–5
Quincy	2–6	Harrisburg	0–8

The divisional title was clinched the next week when the Knights defeated the Long Island Bulls 16–6. For the second straight year, the ACFL championship game would take place in Hartford.

13. The 1969 Hartford Knights

With the division title under their belt, the Knights' next goal was three more wins to attain the perfect season that had eluded them in Richmond the previous year. The first came on November 7 when Wes Bean kicked a 47-yard field goal with 39 seconds left in the game to give Hartford a 17–14 victory over the Roanoke Buckskins. Including exhibitions and the championship game, they had won 27 times in 28 games, the last 20 in a row, and had never lost a game in Dillon Stadium.

Some, including Roanoke general manager Jimmy Piersall, thought the Knights weren't playing fair. Piersall was a former major league outfielder whose mental illness was the subject of the movie *Fear Strikes Out*. He'd been hired by the Buckskins to market the team during its first year in Roanoke.

Piersall said the Knights used veterans, didn't try to develop young players, paid salaries that were higher than those of other ACFL teams, and that the Knights' players did not have jobs other than that of football player. He said the team belonged in the Continental rather than the Atlantic Coast League.

The first time the Knights visited Roanoke, Piersall visited the Hartford locker room. "Look," he said, "you guys are really good and we're just starting out. I want you to really take it easy on us." Then he asked for quarterback Dave Bennett. More than a decade earlier, when Bennett was a small boy and Piersall was a baseball star, the latter came to speak in Southampton, Massachusetts. Bennett's father drove Piersall around while Bennett sat on Piersall's lap and listened to his stories. Jimmy remembered, and came in to say hello and tell Bennett that Vince Lombardi, who'd coached him in training camp, was asking for him. "That's my favorite sports story," Bennett said.

At halftime, Piersall went upstairs to prepare for an interview with Arnold Dean. "His language was awful," said Dean, "his MFs outnumbered all the other words he used. I said to Lou [Palmer], 'We can't put this guy on the air. We're going to have to record it.' So I told Piersall we were having technical problems and had to record the interview. He said, 'Yeah, OK, run the motherfucking thing.' The minute I turned the tape on he behaved perfectly and was a wonderful interview."

During the game, Piersall invited his counterpart, Knights GM Manch Wheeler, to go up on the roof where they could get a better view of the action. "He looked at me," Wheeler recalled, "and said, 'Manch, if I throw you off of here I'd get away with it because everybody knows I'm nuts.'" Wheeler beat a hasty retreat to the press box.

As expected, Piersall's accusations about the Knights prompted a fiery rebuttal from Pete Savin, who pointed out that the average age of the players on the Knight roster was 24.6 years. He also noted that former Knight Marv Hubbard was an Oakland Raider and that the Hartford payroll was within

ACFL limits. Further, Savin noted, the Knights, unlike the Buckskins, never had a significant number of NFL or AFL taxi squadders. "We're aware that some teams in the ACFL are unhappy," Savin concluded, "because we've done so well on the field.... But it's because we've worked harder; Fred has done a better job of coaching and our players care more."[1]

Savin would not need to defend himself much longer, for the victory over Roanoke marked the high water mark of the Knights' existence. They would never again dominate the ACFL as they had in their first 28 games.

The beginning of the end came against the Knights' intrastate rivals, the Bridgeport Jets. On November 15, on a chilly 36 degree evening at Dillon Stadium, the Knights were soundly beaten for the first time in their two-year history. The Jets jumped out to a 23–0 lead in the second quarter behind three field goals, a touchdown pass by Harry Theofilides, and a 92-yard scoring run by Allen Smith.

Bridgeport erased any hope of a Hartford comeback with a touchdown in the third quarter and a field goal early in the fourth period that made the score 33–7. The Knights scored two late, meaningless touchdowns to make the final score a more respectable 33–21. Russell had probably his worst game as a Knight, connecting on just 10 of 30 passes with six interceptions, including two by former Knight Bob Mirabelle. Russell had only thrown five interceptions in his first ten games, and after the Bridgeport game it was revealed that he was suffering from a sore shoulder.

Wallner was philosophical. "It was just one of those nights," he said. The title had been clinched, there was no pressure, and Wallner felt the team had not been ready. "We weren't up emotionally," he said.

The Knights had two games remaining, both against the Pottstown Firebirds. The regular season finale would take place in Pottstown and the championship game in Hartford. The Firebirds had taken the Southern Division title easily, their 9–2 record well ahead of Richmond's 6–5 mark.

The first game against Pottstown was even worse than the loss to the Jets. The Firebirds, who led 17–14 at the half, added a field goal early in the third period to increase the lead to 20–14. The Knights mounted a drive and looked as though they might take the lead but the Pottstown defense stiffened and Bean misfired on an 18-yard field goal attempt.

Then the roof fell in. King Corcoran had been knocked out of action by a shoulder separation in mid–October, but backup Benji Dial, an Eastern New Mexico grad who'd had a brief trial with the Eagles, took his place and wound up leading the ACFL in passing. After Bean's miss, Dial and his backup, Jim Haynie, led the Firebirds to four unanswered touchdowns, for an embarrassing final score of 48–14.

Pottstown defensive end Joe Blake (photograph from Pennsylvania Firebirds program).

Russell had another rough game, throwing three more interceptions while completing just nine passes. Bean was also off the mark. In addition to missing an easy field goal, he averaged just 26 yards on five punts, one of them a five-yarder that he almost missed completely.

As the game neared its end, during a meaningless extra point attempt, Pottstown defensive end Joe Blake delivered a message to Nick DeFelice. "Blake was a guy I played against all the time," DeFelice recalled. "We'd kick the shit out of each other during the game but after the game we were cordial and we'd shake hands. I kind of leaned up against him on the extra point and he *hit* me. He had a cast on his hand and he came up and ripped my chin open and almost drove my head through my helmet. I grabbed him and he laughed and said, 'I'll see you next week.'"

Blake was a talented but troubled individual who wrote poetry and once recited some lines from Keats in the locker room to inspire the Firebirds. He was an admirer of Jimi Hendrix who, like Hendrix, had a major drug problem. His intellect was creative but undisciplined, like his athletic ability, but he had the potential to make it to the NFL if he could get his personal life on track.

Unfortunately, he could not. Blake's college career had been plagued by academic problems and he'd botched an opportunity with the Saints due to a lack of effort. "Ah," said former teammate John Land, "Mr. Mess-up. Blake was a great athlete with the skills to do well but he just couldn't do it. He was always involved in something—alcohol, drugs. It messed up his whole career."

"I don't know what he was using or what he was taking," Ron Waller said years later. "He had too many distractions." Blake missed practice, was late for practice, would stay out all night, and then disappear for days at a time.

During the week before the championship game, DiFilippo tried to downplay his team's thrashing of the Knights. "We've lost 3 out of 4 to Hartford," he said at the Knights' weekly luncheon, "and the 48 points we made against the Knights Saturday night don't mean a damned thing. If the handicappers know what they're doing, they'll make us underdogs." Wallner, sitting next to him, laughed.

Hartford linebacker Mark Proskine, who was at the luncheon, said the Knights hadn't been hitting as hard since clinching the division title, but vowed things would be different Saturday. "You'll see a different Knights team this time," he said. Wallner said one of the keys was the ability of the Hartford forward wall to keep the big Firebird defensive line away from Russell.

When the Knights were winning early in the season, Wallner and Savin kept trying to tell Hartford fans that the league was much tougher than it had been in 1968. Finally, the fans believed them. "Can the Knights recapture the winning formula?" asked the *Courant's* Bill Winters. "They haven't lost a must game in their two-year history but this is perhaps the severest test they have faced."

The Knights failed the test and Bill Lee flubbed his pre-game prediction. He said Hartford defensive end Fran Mallick would be the key player. By the time Mallick was carried off the field on a stretcher in the fourth quarter, the Knights were trailing 20–0, which was the final score. Tackle Wade Key, who would later have a long career with the Eagles, dominated Mallick all night.

Mallick, who suffered a knee injury that required surgery, was not the only casualty. Russell went to the sidelines with a concussion, and offensive tackle Dennis Fitzgibbons went to the hospital for knee surgery. The defeat marked the first time the Knights had been shut out, the first time they lost a must game, and left the 8,700 fans with no doubt that Pottstown was the better team. "The Firebirds burned the Knights that cold November evening," wrote George Erhlich, "with overpowering size. The game was not as close as that twenty to nothing score."[2] The only bright spot was that total receipts of nearly $55,000 set an ACFL record.

It was a disappointing and discouraging finish to a season that began with ten straight victories and finished with three lopsided defeats. "We were all pumped up and excited," recalled cornerback Waide Robinson, "and we were on a winning spree. Then all of a sudden the bottom fell out."

"Even when we were winning," said John Sponheimer, "we won a couple of games that easily could have gone the other way. There was the Quincy game, and the game in Roanoke where we came from behind. Those were a couple of games we could have lost."

"We didn't have a very open offense," said Tom Rowland. "We were pretty predictable. We relied on the running game and they just stacked the line against us. They said if you're going to run on first and second down you're going to do it against an eight man front. And then on third down we'll drop everybody back. Back then you only had a couple of receivers to go to. You had your two wide-outs, and if they took those away and you didn't have a great tight end or couldn't throw to your running backs, you were in trouble. So the defense was on the field all day. We didn't have a great passing attack and once we got behind it was hard for us to catch up. The defense would say, 'Jesus Christ, why don't they throw deep once in a while to loosen it up,' but we really didn't do that."

Several of the Knights had good individual seasons. Tom Morris was sixth in the league in rushing with 655 yards. Bean led the ACFL in scoring with 82 points, succeeding on 17 of 31 field goal attempts. Johnny Lee led the league in kickoff returns with a 27.3 yard average and Wes Dubois was second in interceptions with nine. Perhaps most important, the Knights led the ACFL in attendance with an average of 8,177 fans for six games.

Following Russell's concussion in the championship game, Dave Bennett replaced him at quarterback, for Hank Washington was no longer with the team. On October 23, the *Courant* reported that Washington had an attack of food poisoning, was taken to the hospital, treated, and released. He reported for duty for the Roanoke game that evening, but had to leave the sideline during the third quarter after suffering from severe back and stomach pain, which the *Courant* attributed to the aftereffects of the food poisoning.

Two weeks later, Washington was still feeling poorly, and was sent to New

York University Hospital. Tests revealed a kidney obstruction that required surgery. Washington was placed on the injured reserve list and missed the rest of the season. "Hank was a big guy and threw the ball like a rocket," said Nick DeFelice. "Then, all of sudden, he couldn't throw the ball anymore. You'd see him sitting on the bench and he'd have the coat over him." Washington did not have food poisoning. He had cancer.

Hank Washington never played football again. Bennett saw him at a 1970 New Year's party and commented on how good he looked and that he appeared to have lost weight. "Yeah, right," Washington replied sarcastically. That was the last time Bennett saw him, for Washington passed away in January 1971 at the age of 25.

14

The Snow Bowl: The 1970 Hartford Knights

In the spring of 1970, Pete Savin grappled with an opponent every bit as tenacious as the Pottstown Firebirds. For two years Savin's Knights had played outstanding football but lost money, and the Hartford owner believed that part of the reason was the poor condition and limited capacity of Dillon Stadium. Savin was willing to lose money to keep the team in Hartford, but not the $100,000 he claimed to have dropped during each of the Knights first two seasons. He said he needed to draw 12,000 per game to break even, and since Dillon Stadium couldn't hold that many, it was impossible to cover expenses without expanding the stadium.

In early February, three members of the Hartford City Council introduced a motion calling for a $250,000 bond issue to fund improvements and a four thousand seat expansion of the old facility. In addition to new aluminum seats between the 20-yard lines on the east side of the stadium, the renovation would include a new concession stand, an air conditioned and heated press box, more rest rooms, and another ticket booth. Savin offered to increase the Knights' annual rental payment from $10,000 to $15,000 to help cover the cost of the bonds.

Bill Lee, a fervid supporter of the proposed $15 million Civic Center, opposed funding improvements to Dillon. "If the bond issue is not approved," he wrote, "the Knights can continue to survive in a down-at-the-heels home. They shouldn't have to live like second class citizens, but they can if they have to."[1]

The Knights, successful as they had been, were minor league. Lee wanted Hartford to be a major league city, and the proposed Civic Center, not a renovated Dillon Stadium, was the key to getting a major league franchise. New Haven and Springfield were building civic centers and Lee didn't want Hartford to be left behind. "If we don't match New Haven's progress in something," Lee wrote, "they'll be laughing in our faces instead of just smirking."[2]

Hartford Mayor Ann Uccello had her own agenda. She threatened to veto the Dillon Stadium improvements unless the City Council also approved funding for the Fuller Park housing project. When the Council Democrats accused her of acting like a spoiled child, the partisan battle was in full swing.

In mid-March, Savin called a press conference at which he announced that if the bond issue was not approved, there would be no Hartford Knights after the 1970 season. City Manager Eli Freedman replied, "I can't get excited about the Knights leaving Hartford.... We have a market here and there will always be a team in the area."[3] He fretted about the Knights' long term commitment to the city, the increased traffic flow, and why Pete Savin should have priority over competing needs such as housing, education, and the Civic Center. Freedman said Dillon was a "Rube Goldberg affair" and preferred a new regional facility serving Hartford and the surrounding towns.

A major bone of contention was the projected cost of the project. If it exceeded $250,000, the bond issue would be subject to a public referendum. Both Freedman and Uccello questioned whether the work could be completed within the projected cost guidelines, citing 950 additional parking spaces that would be required to meet zoning requirements. The city estimated the cost of the increased parking alone at $150,000.

On March 30, there was a public hearing on the proposal, attended by 150 people. Many were Knights fans who cheered any remark supporting the proposal. Savin had a sharp temper, and on this occasion the Knights' owner was combative. When one speaker said the project was a payback for campaign contributions, Savin called the accusation "garbage." When another spoke of the additional parking requirement he called it a "smokescreen." A third questioned whether the work could be done for $250,000. Savin said his firm would do the job and get a completion bond to ensure performance. It was obvious that the work would cost more than $250,000, and that Savin would absorb the overage.

The decisive meeting took place on May 18, and it was an emotional session. Three hundred people attended and strong feelings were expressed on both sides. One speaker questioned whether public funds should be used to support a private enterprise (even an unprofitable one) and concluded with, "if they lynch me tonight I hope they'll bury me in Dillon Stadium—unimproved."[4]

Two days later, City Manager Freedman declared that the entire proposal was illegal because it did not provide for additional parking. There were 700 spaces for the existing 10,000 seats, and an additional 950 would be required for the 4,000 seat expansion.

Each side sniped at the other and May dragged on, with the possibility of completing the improvements by the opening game diminishing with each pass-

14

The Snow Bowl: The 1970 Hartford Knights

In the spring of 1970, Pete Savin grappled with an opponent every bit as tenacious as the Pottstown Firebirds. For two years Savin's Knights had played outstanding football but lost money, and the Hartford owner believed that part of the reason was the poor condition and limited capacity of Dillon Stadium. Savin was willing to lose money to keep the team in Hartford, but not the $100,000 he claimed to have dropped during each of the Knights first two seasons. He said he needed to draw 12,000 per game to break even, and since Dillon Stadium couldn't hold that many, it was impossible to cover expenses without expanding the stadium.

In early February, three members of the Hartford City Council introduced a motion calling for a $250,000 bond issue to fund improvements and a four thousand seat expansion of the old facility. In addition to new aluminum seats between the 20-yard lines on the east side of the stadium, the renovation would include a new concession stand, an air conditioned and heated press box, more rest rooms, and another ticket booth. Savin offered to increase the Knights' annual rental payment from $10,000 to $15,000 to help cover the cost of the bonds.

Bill Lee, a fervid supporter of the proposed $15 million Civic Center, opposed funding improvements to Dillon. "If the bond issue is not approved," he wrote, "the Knights can continue to survive in a down-at-the-heels home. They shouldn't have to live like second class citizens, but they can if they have to."[1]

The Knights, successful as they had been, were minor league. Lee wanted Hartford to be a major league city, and the proposed Civic Center, not a renovated Dillon Stadium, was the key to getting a major league franchise. New Haven and Springfield were building civic centers and Lee didn't want Hartford to be left behind. "If we don't match New Haven's progress in something," Lee wrote, "they'll be laughing in our faces instead of just smirking."[2]

Hartford Mayor Ann Uccello had her own agenda. She threatened to veto the Dillon Stadium improvements unless the City Council also approved funding for the Fuller Park housing project. When the Council Democrats accused her of acting like a spoiled child, the partisan battle was in full swing.

In mid-March, Savin called a press conference at which he announced that if the bond issue was not approved, there would be no Hartford Knights after the 1970 season. City Manager Eli Freedman replied, "I can't get excited about the Knights leaving Hartford.... We have a market here and there will always be a team in the area."[3] He fretted about the Knights' long term commitment to the city, the increased traffic flow, and why Pete Savin should have priority over competing needs such as housing, education, and the Civic Center. Freedman said Dillon was a "Rube Goldberg affair" and preferred a new regional facility serving Hartford and the surrounding towns.

A major bone of contention was the projected cost of the project. If it exceeded $250,000, the bond issue would be subject to a public referendum. Both Freedman and Uccello questioned whether the work could be completed within the projected cost guidelines, citing 950 additional parking spaces that would be required to meet zoning requirements. The city estimated the cost of the increased parking alone at $150,000.

On March 30, there was a public hearing on the proposal, attended by 150 people. Many were Knights fans who cheered any remark supporting the proposal. Savin had a sharp temper, and on this occasion the Knights' owner was combative. When one speaker said the project was a payback for campaign contributions, Savin called the accusation "garbage." When another spoke of the additional parking requirement he called it a "smokescreen." A third questioned whether the work could be done for $250,000. Savin said his firm would do the job and get a completion bond to ensure performance. It was obvious that the work would cost more than $250,000, and that Savin would absorb the overage.

The decisive meeting took place on May 18, and it was an emotional session. Three hundred people attended and strong feelings were expressed on both sides. One speaker questioned whether public funds should be used to support a private enterprise (even an unprofitable one) and concluded with, "if they lynch me tonight I hope they'll bury me in Dillon Stadium—unimproved."[4]

Two days later, City Manager Freedman declared that the entire proposal was illegal because it did not provide for additional parking. There were 700 spaces for the existing 10,000 seats, and an additional 950 would be required for the 4,000 seat expansion.

Each side sniped at the other and May dragged on, with the possibility of completing the improvements by the opening game diminishing with each passing day. The improvements, although not Pete Savin, received support from an unlikely source—Bill Lee, who apparently had changed his mind. While Lee was not particularly interested in the Knights, he was quite concerned about his own domain—the press box. He called the Dillon Stadium press facilities laughable, and urged the city to approve the bond issue without further delay.

A few days later, Lee was defending himself against an accusation of being on Savin's payroll, a charge he denied with unnecessary vigor. "The man [who made the accusation] doesn't know," Lee wrote, "how close he came to getting punched right between the eyes.... Just in case there is any doubt any longer, I happen to think that Savin was disrespectful and arrogant in giving the City of Hartford the impression that if it didn't fix Dillon Stadium up he would take the Knights elsewhere. If he actually means that, the City would be justified in telling him to go fly a kite—take the Knights anywhere he wants to put them and good luck to the moving.... Dillon Stadium at best isn't much of a place.... But like the crooked dice game, it's the only one in town, and neither the Council nor the city's taxpayers should object to making it something more than a disgrace to Hartford. The people deserve the Hartford Knights and a better Dillon Stadium, but not necessarily on Mr. Savin's terms."[5]

Why were so many in Hartford so vehemently opposed to spending a relatively small amount of money on a public facility when the city was willing to dedicate much larger amounts to other projects? "I think it was a situation," said Lou Palmer, "where people were not in the mood to build facilities for those they feel are well-heeled enough to do it themselves."

When two groups sincerely and vehemently disagree, it's generally because each has an interpretation of the facts that is dramatically different from the other. Savin viewed the money he sank into the Knights as providing a civic benefit, so that Hartford could have a football team it could be proud of. Moreover, he was willing to have his company perform the renovation work at a loss.

Savin's detractors saw his investment as evidence he had money to burn and that there was much more behind it. Why should such a wealthy man be the beneficiary of public funding when Hartford was home to so much poverty? Did the presence of the Hartford Knights provide food or shelter for the poor? Each side believed they were doing the other party a favor and that party should be grateful.

Finally, on May 28, the City Council approved the bond issue, but Mayor Uccello exercised her veto power and the matter returned to the council. The subsequent favorable vote of 6–3 was sufficient to overturn the veto. Still, Lee speculated that Uccello and Freedman might find some legal basis for challenging the funding and stopping the project. "Be assured the issue of Dillon Stadium is not dead," he wrote on June 17. "Many questions remain to be answered."[6]

Fortunately, there were no further challenges. The improvements were begun in the middle of June, but due to the late start, were not completed until the November 7 game against Bridgeport. That evening's crowd of 8,500 was the largest of the season, but it would not have filled the old configuration, let alone the expanded version. Savin had his renovated stadium, but the process had been a painful one, a sad reminder that city government was a lukewarm ally and that Bill Lee was more interested in the major league franchise the city didn't have than the winning minor league club already in town.

For two years, Savin had insisted that the Atlantic Coast Football League was as good as the Continental League. In 1970, his Knights would have a chance to prove it, for at the end of the 1969 campaign, the expanded Continental League collapsed, and three of its franchises, including the champion Indianapolis Capitols, joined the ACFL. The Jersey Tigers were the transplanted Harrisburg Capitol-Colts and the Quincy Giants, who'd lasted just a year in the ACFL, dropped out, leaving the circuit with an unbalanced roster of eleven teams. All teams had NFL affiliations.

The revamped ACFL lined up as follows:

Northern Division: Hartford Knights, Jersey Tigers, Bridgeport Jets, Jersey Jays, and Long Island Bulls

Southern Division: Pennsylvania Firebirds, Roanoke Buckskins, Indianapolis Capitols, Norfolk Neptunes, Orlando Panthers, and Richmond Roadrunners

The Firebirds still played in Pottstown, although they had changed their name to the Pennsylvania Firebirds. King Corcoran was again the quarterback, but he no longer had Bob Tucker as a receiver. After leading the ACFL in receiving for a second season (66 catches for 1,016 yards) Tucker got a call from the Green Bay Packers.

"I spent a week out there in eight feet of snow," Tucker recalled, "and after the week they wanted to sign me." Tucker said he wanted $5,000 upfront, since he had spent time with two NFL teams and gotten nothing for his efforts. The Packers countered with $2,000 and Tucker didn't sign. After he left Green Bay the Chicago Bears called, and then the New York Giants. By the time the Giants called, the NFL season had ended. Tucker went to their office at Columbus Circle and asked for $8,000 upfront. The Giants offered $5,000 and a contract was signed.

Tucker reported to the Giants camp at C.W. Post College the following summer, and for several weeks, it was a replay of his time in the Patriots and Eagles camps. Before the exhibition against the Jets, the *New York Times* reported that either Dick Kotite or veteran Aaron Thomas would start in place of the injured Butch Wilson. A fourth tight end, Freeman White, was also under consideration for playing time. Kotite was a marginal player, Wilson was a journeyman, Thomas had been talked out of retiring just before training camp, and White was a converted linebacker. There was no mention of Bob Tucker.

Tucker didn't play against the Jets, but during the following week Wilson, expected to be the starter, was cut. The next game, against Pittsburgh, was the Steelers' first appearance in brand new Three Rivers Stadium. "We were getting our ass kicked," Tucker recalled, "and I remember [coach] Alex Webster telling [offensive coordinator] Joe Walton, 'Get these guys off the field, put the scrubs in, run the ball and let's get the hell out of here.'" Tucker entered the game and blocked savagely for the Giant running backs during the final quarter.

The next day, the players apprehensively watched the film of their sorry performance. "When they show the film," Tucker said, "they don't just bruise your feelings—they lacerate them. If you're playing bad they point it out and run the film back and forth a couple of times. Especially when you lose like we did it's pretty brutal. We come to the fourth quarter and we're running the ball and I come off the ball and knock a guy down. They point it out and say this is the way you should block and, by the way, who the hell is this? Everybody is getting beat up all over the place and I'm in no position to stand up and say, 'It's me!' so I'm just sitting in the back of the room. Somebody said, 'That's Bob Tucker' and they said that was a hell of a job. It happened two or three more times where I did a great job of knocking people around and putting them on their backs."

Walton came up to Tucker after the film session and said that Webster was so angry about the Giants' poor performance that he had ordered a scrimmage and that Tucker would alternate at tight end. "I want you to pick up where you left off," he told him.

The following week, Walton told Tucker he was starting in the exhibition against the Eagles at Princeton's Palmer Stadium. "I was so elated," Tucker said, "and I think it was the most fear I ever had in my life. When they announced my name, I remember thinking, 'Please, god, don't let me trip over the lines.' But I made it out there and here we go. They kick off and we had third down and something. Tarkenton throws me a pass and we get a first down. We move down the field and he throws me a pass for a touchdown. We hold, the Eagles punt, Tarkenton throws me a pass and I go about 50 yards for a touchdown, and from that point I was the tight end for the next eight years."

In his first season with the Giants, Tucker caught 40 passes, and the following year, 1971, he led the NFC with 59 catches. He had three straight seasons with more than 50 receptions and finished his 11-year career with 422 catches and 27 touchdowns. For a tight end, he was unusually effective in the open field after the catch. "The thing I liked to do was run with the football," he said.

"That was the fun of the game for me—to be able to run. I think I was an angry runner. I wasn't running to run over people, but I would do that if I couldn't do anything else. I would give someone a shot if I could."

Bob Tucker is one of the ACFL success stories, one of the very few minor league players who went on to a long and successful NFL career. The most poignant element of his story is not that he became a success, but that despite the talent that made him an NFL star, and two tremendous years in Lowell and Pottstown, he almost didn't make it at all. Had the Giants played better in the first three quarters against the Steelers, he might have been back in Pottstown, or possibly teaching biology fulltime. There were other Bob Tuckers in the ACFL for whom the stars did not align, and who never made it to the NFL, for even for players with major league ability, the road from the minor leagues to the NFL was a very treacherous one.

Fred Wallner returned for a third season as skipper of the Knights, and many of the stars from the previous two years came with him. Benny Russell remained the starting quarterback, surviving a challenge from former Penn State star Tom Sherman.

Sherman was a "name" player who'd quarterbacked the Nittany Lions for three seasons and was a member of Joe Paterno's first team in 1966. In the 1967 Gator Bowl, he threw two touchdown passes and kicked a field goal, accounting for all of his team's points in a 17–17 tie with Florida State.

Sherman was not drafted, but made the Boston Patriot squad as a free agent in 1968. He split duties with Mike Taliaferro, started seven games, and was the leading passer for a bad Boston team that finished 4–10. The next year Clive Rush, an assistant with the Jets, became the head coach of the Patriots. He'd coached Taliaferro in New York and wanted him as his starter in Boston. Sherman played four games, was let go, and finished the year in Buffalo. The next summer, the Bills cut him and he went back to Pennsylvania to take a teaching job. Before the school year began, however, Sherman received a call from Wallner asking if he wanted to play for Hartford.

Veteran Tom Morris and 35-year-old Mel Meeks returned to the Hartford backfield and receiver Bob Stohrer signed up for a third tour of duty, as did kicker Wes Bean. The opening night roster contained a number of other familiar names, such as Nick DeFelice, Fran Mallick, Dennis Fitzgibbons, and Tom Rowland.

One of the Knights' new players was defensive end Denver Samples. When Samples flew to Hartford, Savin sent his wife to pick him up at the airport. His name was Samples, Pete told Elaine, but he couldn't remember if he was Denver Samples arriving from Dallas or Dallas Samples arriving from Denver. "I found him," Elaine recalled, "and said, 'Hello, Mr. Samples.'" "I'm Denver," Samples replied, and the mystery was solved.

The roster did not, however, include John Wardlaw, Otis Thomas, or Johnny Lee, each of whom had been with the Knights since their inception. Wardlaw and Thomas were cut on August 28. Their release was a surprise, since Thomas had been an all league linebacker and Wardlaw was a starting wide receiver.

The *Courant* reported that Thomas had earned himself a place in Wallner's doghouse by reporting to camp 30 pounds overweight. Thomas claimed to be puzzled by that statement, saying Wallner told him at the end of the previous season that at 205 pounds he was too small to play linebacker. "Now I'm too big at 224,"[7] he said.

Some people thought that Wardlaw and Thomas had been released because they were African Americans. Lee, a defensive stalwart who'd been an ACFL all star in 1969, abruptly quit the team in protest. "I cannot maintain any relationship," he said, "with an organization whose policies and acts are such that I must sacrifice my dignity as a black man."[8] He said he was not angry with Wallner or Savin, and had quit in sadness rather than rage. Lee, the only black player who spoke publicly about the issue, was very involved in the Hartford community and quite sensitive to racial issues. "He tended to be a leader in that mindset," said Joe Murphy, who taught with Lee in the Hartford school system. "He was a leader in the thought process that things should be different in many ways."

Wallner and Savin issued statements in rebuttal of Lee's charges. Wallner's read: "I have coached football for many years and players of all races and creeds. This is the first time that such an accusation was ever made regarding my integrity and coaching philosophy. I do not intend to dignify these untruths with a reply."[9]

Savin's statement was much stronger. He indicated that the reaction of the players was due to personal animosity and had no basis in fact. "We have never discriminated, nor shall we ever discriminate," he said, "against a black player. We also will not discriminate against a player because he is white. Our job is to put on a very professional football show; to represent our city properly and win games. We intend to keep doing that job."[10]

The history of integration in professional football was very different from that of major league baseball. In the latter, African Americans were banned until the breakthrough appearance of Jackie Robinson with the Brooklyn Dodgers in 1947. During the period when blacks were kept out of organized baseball, there were a number of African Americans who played in the NFL. Between 1920 and 1933, thirteen African Americans, including future opera star Paul Robeson, appeared in NFL games. Fritz Pollard served as coach of the Akron Pros in 1921 and the Hammond Pros in 1925. Lineman Duke Slater, perhaps the best black player, was named to seven all-pro teams. Beginning with the 1934 season, however, the NFL barred blacks from its rosters. Some attributed the ban to George Marshall, the owner of the Redskins who had no blacks on his team as late as 1961.

In 1946, a year before Robinson played for the Dodgers, the Cleveland Rams received permission to relocate to Los Angeles, where they planned to play in the immense Coliseum. The Coliseum was a publicly owned facility, and the City of Los Angeles informed the Rams they couldn't use it if they had a segregated team. The club therefore signed UCLA star Kenny Washington, who'd been playing for the Hollywood Bears of the Pacific Coast League, and Woody Strode.

The Rams had been coerced into integrating, and other teams were slow to follow suit. The All American Football Conference, formed in 1946 as a rival to the NFL, was new, innovative, hungrier for talent, and therefore more active in signing blacks. Throughout the rest of the 1940s and during the 1950s there was a slow but gradual increase in the number of black players.

When the American Football League was formed in 1960, several blacks who had been rejected by the NFL, such as star receiver Art Powell, were signed by the new league. Powell had taken a stand against segregated accommodations as a member of the Eagles, was branded a troublemaker, and quickly released. The New York Titans of the new AFL signed him and he became a star.

By the end of the 1960s, blacks played a major role in professional football. Still, the acceptance of blacks playing against whites was not universal. "When we went down and played in Richmond and Norfolk," said quarterback Dave Bennett, "there was still tension in the air."

The people of the United States were gaining mobility during the early 1960s, with the expansion of the interstate highway system and the growing acceptance of air travel. Still, many Americans rarely ventured beyond their own region, and those who grew up in the north were shocked to learn of the racial customs that still prevailed in the south.

In 1964, Nick Cutro took his Jersey team to Atlanta and stopped at a restaurant for the pre-game meal. "These guys can't go in here," the owner told Cutro. "You've got black players." "What do you mean?" Cutro asked. "We've got a contract to eat here." The owner told Cutro to pull the bus around to the rear of the building and have the black players grab brooms and walk in through the back pretending they were there to clean the restaurant. They could eat in the back room.

"I ain't going to do that," Cutro answered. He offered an extra ten dollars if the entire team could eat together. For ten dollars, rules could be bent, and the players, black and white, entered the restaurant. "He took them in the back way," Cutro recalled, "over the boxes, over the garbage and we all ate dinner. The steak was pretty good, as I remember."

14. The Snow Bowl

Al Shanen of the Stamford Golden Bears recalled taking his team down to Baltimore in the early '60s. Before the game, the bus stopped at a restaurant for the pre-game meal, but when the players disembarked, they discovered some natives had other ideas. "A bunch of guys came out of the bar," Shanen recalled, "started banging on the bus, using the N-word, and telling us to get the hell out of there."

The players got back on the bus, played the game without eating, and began wondering if they would ever eat. Shanen asked the opposing coach where he might feed his Golden Bears. "You've got Negroes on your team," the coach replied, "you're not going to be able to go anywhere."

One of Shanen's black players came up to him and said he knew of a place they could go, and that the bus should follow a friend of his. "We got on our Greyhound bus," Shanen said, "and little did we know that Greyhound was the symbol of the Freedom Riders. We were kids from the east side of Stamford and didn't know anything about that nonsense. So we followed, and it was obvious we were going into the bowels of the ghetto. The guys were getting a little nervous."

Finally, the team arrived at their destination, a black night club, where they ate, drank, and danced until the early morning hours. When Shanen asked for a bill, the owner came out. "Forget it," he said. "It's on me. This is the first time any white people have ever been in my place, and it'll be the last time any white person's gonna come into my place. It's on the house." "We always felt," said Shanen, "that the Stamford Golden Bears were the first team to integrate Baltimore."

Members of racially integrated football teams worked together toward a common goal and spent a great deal of time together at practice and in the locker room. White players discovered that blacks shared their goals of wanting to find a spot in the NFL, establishing careers in other fields, paying their household bills, raising educated, responsible children, and occasionally having a good time on the town.

Even white men who might be considered somewhat racist generally got along well with their black teammates. "Surprisingly, it was really very good," said Waide Robinson of the relationship between blacks and whites on the Knights. Robinson was an African American cornerback who played on the 1969 team. He was educated, articulate, quiet, and likeable. "I associated with everybody," he said, "but I was quite close to a lot of the white players. I don't recall a racial situation when I was there."

"It was a great lesson for me," said Tom Rowland, "coming from a small town in west central Illinois. In college we only had one minority on the team. Then for a couple of years with the Knights I was the only white player in the defensive backfield. It was a great thing for me to meet so many kids who were minorities and become friends with them. I probably had more friends who were minorities than who were Caucasians. It was a life lesson for me to live like that instead of telling the redneck jokes and all the other stuff you were brought up doing. It really helped me in my coaching and with my life."

Unfortunately, I have been unable to locate any of the principals in the 1970 incident. Wardlaw, Wallner, and Savin are dead. Otis Thomas and Johnny Lee are such common names that it is difficult to find them. None of the other players said that they recalled the incident. Perhaps some were merely reluctant to share controversial thoughts with a relative stranger, but it is also possible that the players were so engrossed in their own efforts to make the team that they were oblivious to the incident. "I always kept my nose out of issues," said Bob Stohrer, "and just went out there to do my job the best I could."

While there was little recollection of the incident, there was universal denial that Fred Wallner was a racist. "I think some of it was a personality conflict," ventured John Sponheimer. "I don't think Fred was racist, but if you rubbed him the wrong way he could be a little thick at times."

"I just wouldn't believe that of Fred Wallner," said Dennis Fitzgibbons. "I wouldn't believe that about any coach because you do anything to win. You may not like somebody. You may not like their politics or their religion. You may be biased as hell. But when you're out on the field it's just about winning."

"I can tell you right now," said Stohrer, "that Pete Savin would never allow anything like that to happen for that reason." Other players were equally adamant.

There are no other known incidents in which Wallner was accused of racial discrimination. He was, however, dictatorial and did not take well to anyone challenging his authority. In the late '60s and early '70s, African American athletes became much more assertive and often resentful of authority figures, and it is possible that Wallner saw that as an affront to his prerogatives as head coach. He may have responded to that challenge without consciously viewing it as racism.

Linebacker Ken Blasser inadvertently shed some light on the incident with the story of his release by Wallner when the latter was defensive coordinator for Montreal in the Canadian League. During an exhibition game, Blasser got caught inside and allowed a back to get around his end. Wallner pulled him and kept him on the bench for the remainder of the evening. When the team got off the plane in Montreal, Blasser said, "Hey, coach, I made one mistake and you never put me back in." "He just glared at me," Blasser remembered, "and the next day he cut me. He said, 'Don't you *ever* question anything I do!'"

Blasser is white. Had he been black, Wallner might have been accused of

14. The Snow Bowl 249

racism, for his behavior toward Blasser was arbitrary and unfair. Given Wallner's history of intense, inflexible behavior, and the absence of any other racial incidents, the most likely conclusion is that Wallner's release of Wardlaw and Thomas was not based upon ability, but was probably not based, at least consciously, on racism. "I didn't see Fred as racist," said Pete Quackenbush. "I saw Fred as a guy you just didn't question."

After Wardlaw's football career ended, he became the director of the Hartford Housing Authority, and worked with Elaine Savin on the Bellevue Square project. He was also very friendly with Pete Savin in his later years, which leads to the conclusion that he didn't blame Savin for his release.

Another possibility is that the decision was based upon finances. By 1970, attendance was dropping, and salaries were lower than they had been in prior years. Salaries were a closely guarded secret, but as two of the Knights' better players, it's certainly possible that Wardlaw and Thomas were earning significantly more than their replacements.

The Knights opened the 1970 season against Indianapolis. The Capitols had been the 1969 Continental League champions, and meeting them gave the Knights an opportunity to see if they were as good as the teams from the supposedly superior circuit. On that night they weren't, dropping a 13–6 decision, stymied by an aggressive defense and four interceptions, two each by Russell and Sherman.

Despite the fact that neither offense was explosive that evening, the crowd at Dillon Stadium nearly witnessed some fireworks. Early in the game, Howie Holcomb of the *Hartford Times* received a call from his office inquiring whether he had evacuated the press box. Since Holcomb had answered the phone, it was clear that he was still there, and asked why he wouldn't be. The caller explained that someone had phoned the stadium and said that a bomb had been planted on the premises.

A couple of minutes later, the 5,500 fans were asked to vacate the stands and move to the center of the field, where they were joined by players, coaches, and most of the reporters. "I remember talking with the kids and giving chin straps away," said Fran Mallick. "It was great."

Holcomb decided to wait it out in the press box, where Arnold Dean and Lou Palmer remained on the air. "Who cares about us," Dean said. "They felt they had to have something on the air." "I'm being Joe Hero," Holcomb recalled. "The bomb was supposed to go off at 9:38 and at about 9:37. I said, 'Well, maybe I *will* get out of here.'" Meanwhile, the police conducted a thorough search of the stadium and assured themselves that the call had been a prank. After a 29-minute delay, the fans returned to their seats.

Despite the loss, Wallner thought his team played hard and lauded the way they had "overcome" the racial controversy of the previous week. "I don't feel the ball club lost this game," he said. "Outside interference did."[11]

The 1970 Knights were good, but they were not as dominant as they had been the two previous years. "[F]ollowing two virtually all-winning seasons," wrote Arnold Dean, "the Knights have suddenly become human. I wish I had a ticket for everyone who has asked me this year 'What is wrong with the Knights?'"[12]

Sometimes they played very well, as in a 27–0 win over the Jersey Jays in the second game of the year. But then there were games like a 37–28 defeat at Bridgeport and a 25–16 loss to Orlando in late October that dropped the Knights' record to 4–4 and put them two games behind the Jets with only four games left.

The trip to Orlando was the longest the Knights had ever taken, and it was eventful. The chartered plane was scheduled to leave Bradley at 9:30 and arrive in Orlando shortly after noon, leaving plenty of time to prepare for the game. However, the airline had not accounted for the fact that football players and their equipment weighed more than the typical passenger, and just before takeoff realized they could not get to Florida on a single load of fuel.

There were two refueling stops along the way, and the one in Roanoke was a difficult landing. "We almost bit it there," said Sherman. The Knights finally arrived in Orlando at 4:00, and found a television crew on hand to greet them. That was unusual, since Atlantic Coast football didn't usually rate a lot of media coverage. Holcomb asked a reporter why he was there. "We heard you might be overloaded," the man replied, "and might crash, so we came out to cover the landing."

Regulations require that flight crews have a minimum interval between flights, and since the Knights had arrived late, they could not leave until about one in the morning, making for a very late arrival in Hartford. The major international airport now in Orlando had yet to be built, and the players and coaches had to stand around outside until the flight was boarded.

After week 9, when the Knights lost a heartbreaker to the previously winless Long Island Bulls, it appeared that their chances of a third consecutive division title were nil. After trailing the Bulls 17–3, Hartford rallied and, with just 2:31 left, took a 20–17 lead when Bean connected on a 10-yard field goal.

In the final two minutes, two former Knights came back to haunt their old team. First, Dick Faucette connected on a 46-yard pass that brought the Bulls to the Hartford 20. Then, with 36 seconds remaining, Faucette hit John Wardlaw in the end zone. The 24–20 defeat dropped the Knights to 4–5. The only ray of hope was that the Jets had been upset by the Jersey Tigers, leaving the Knights with a slim mathematical chance. The odds were long, however, for not

14. The Snow Bowl

only would they have to catch Bridgeport, they would have to leap over the two teams from Jersey.

Northern Division		Southern Division	
Bridgeport	6–3	Pennsylvania	7–0
Jersey Tigers	4–3	Norfolk	5–3
Jersey Jays	4–4	Roanoke	5–3
Hartford	4–5	Orlando	4–5
Long Island	1–6	Indianapolis	3–5
		Richmond	1–7

In the eleven team league, teams played an uneven number of games, which made the standings a bit more difficult to comprehend. It was possible that the race could end in a four way tie, and there were a myriad of potential outcomes, but it was clear that in order to finish first the Knights had to win their final three games and get a great deal of help.

For the first week, the Knights controlled their own destiny, since they played the Jets at Dillon Stadium, whose new seats were available for occupancy for the first time. Bill Lee, perhaps feeling guilty about the beating he had given Savin in the spring, boosted the Knights in his column and urged the fans to come out and support them. "[T]his 1970 campaign," he wrote, "has not been the disaster it seems on paper." He pointed out that a number of the Knights' losses had been close games and still harbored the hope that the club could pull off the "Little Miracle of Cottage Grove Road [site of the club's office]."[13]

With every game a sudden death situation, the Knights defense rose to the occasion and limited Bridgeport quarterback Harry Theofilides, who'd tormented them in the past, to just 157 yards and a single touchdown. Meanwhile, Benny Russell passed for 267 yards and two touchdowns. Hartford's 17–7 victory kept their slim hopes alive.

Not all of the news from Dillon Stadium was good. Wes Bean converted only one of six field goal attempts and, even worse, Mel Meeks, after gaining 64 yards rushing in the first half, dislocated his elbow and was finished for the season.

The Jersey teams split, the Tigers winning to move into first place, and the Jays losing to drop them to 4–5.

Jersey Tigers	5–3
Bridgeport	6–4
Hartford	5–5
Jersey Jays	4–5

In order for the Knights to tie for the division lead, they had to win their final two games, the Tigers needed to lose two, and the Jets had to lose one. On

Friday night, November 13, the Knights played Long Island, who had upset them two weeks earlier, and the Jets played the Jays. On Saturday, the Tigers visited Roanoke.

The Knights-Bulls game was a sloppy affair played in a steady rain before just 3,500 hardy fans. At the end of the third quarter the Bulls led 7–0, as neither team was able to mount an offensive attack in the muck. Finally, midway through the fourth quarter, Russell led a 57-yard drive keyed by three completions to Bob Stohrer, the final one for nine yards and the tying touchdown.

Stohrer, a former Charter Oak in his third season with the Knights, was the club's best receiver in 1970, with 40 catches for 599 yards, good statistics on a running team and a good average per catch for a man without exceptional speed.

Faucette threw an interception on Long Island's next possession and, aided by a personal foul call against the Bulls, Hartford moved the ball to the Long Island 23. With 21 seconds remaining, Bean drilled the ball between the uprights from 30 yards out and the Knights had a narrow escape.

Meanwhile, the Jays beat the Jets 28–24 to put the Knights and Jets into a tie at 6–5. The following night, rain came to Roanoke, and in a game very similar to that played by the Knights and Bulls, the Buckskins beat the Tigers 10–7 on a field goal with 10 seconds remaining in the game. All four contenders were now bunched tightly:

Jersey Tigers	5–4
Hartford	6–5
Bridgeport	6–5
Jersey Jays	5–5

With the very real possibility of a tie, Commissioner Iacovazzi thought it was necessary to remind everyone of the ACFL rule for deciding the winner. The first test was the head-to-head results versus the other team or teams involved in the tie. The second was the point differential in the games between the tied teams, the third would be to eliminate the team that had most recently been in a championship playoff, and the fourth was a coin flip. There was no provision for a playoff.

When the Jets learned of the tie-breaking procedure, they were livid. They had beaten the Knights by nine points in their first meeting, and the Knights won by ten in the second, giving the latter a razor thin margin in the point totals. Jet owner Frank D'Addario said that had his team known about the point differential component of the rule, they might have played each Hartford game differently.

One of the areas of contention was whether all teams had been aware of the procedure and, if so, when they became aware. Iacovazzi said he mailed a

Dependable Bob Stohrer was the Knights' best receiver in 1970 (courtesy Bob Stohrer).

notice to each team in early October. D'Addario said he didn't get it, and the owners of the Orlando, Indianapolis, and Norfolk teams also said they never received anything and were not aware of the rule. In the face of the denials, the commissioner admitted he hadn't sent the notice until November 11, but said that teams should have been aware of the process without his reminder.

Iacovazzi said he was not completely opposed to a playoff, although if there was a three way tie, there was no chance of a round robin affair. At first Savin said he was willing to stage a playoff game, but then changed his mind. D'Addario threatened legal action if the title was decided on point margins.

On November 20, the Knights assured themselves of the division title by defeating the Tigers 24–17. Although Bridgeport won its final game, the best any team could do was tie the Knights, who were ahead on all of the tie breakers. At a meeting of ACFL owners at the Newark Airport, they reaffirmed the existing procedure, leaving D'Addario with only the option of testing it in court.

On December 2, after much soul searching, the Bridgeport owner decided to abide by the league's ruling, leaving the Knights free to meet the Pennsylvania Firebirds for the ACFL title on December 12 at Dillon Stadium. It was the third straight year the championship would be decided in Hartford, which now, with nearly 14,000 seats, promised a much better payday than Pottstown's small stadium.

The Southern Division winner had been scheduled to host the title match, but no one other than diehard Pottstown fans were very excited about that. The previous year, each Firebird had earned about $700 for winning the championship in Hartford, and estimated that even if the Pottstown stadium were sold out, the take would be only about $400 a man.[14] With the expanded capacity of Dillon Stadium, players hoped the winners' share might approach $1,000, big money for those who made a $150 to $200 a game. The players were all in favor of shifting the game, Firebird owner Ed Gruber wanted to move it, Hartford supported it, and it was left to Gruber to placate his followers. He offered free bus transportation to Hartford for any fans who wanted to make the trip.

The defending champion Firebirds had easily been the best team in the ACFL in 1970, cruising to an 11–1 record that put them four games in front of their closest competitors in the Southern Division. Running back Claude Watts led the league with 1,072 rushing yards (the first 1,000 yard rusher in the history of the ACFL) and teammate John Land was fourth with 548. Corcoran was the ACFL's leading passer and threw for 24 touchdowns. His favorite target was former Pittsburgh Steeler end Don Alley, who caught 16 of them. The Firebirds had the league's most potent offense, averaging 352 yards per game (compared to 278 per game for Hartford) and its stingiest defense, yielding just 192 total yards per game (compared to 260 for Hartford).

Late in the season, Coach DiFilippo announced that he had suspended Corcoran for disobeying his orders. The story was a hoax. Corcoran had pulled a hamstring badly in the next to last game against Norfolk, and there was no way he could have played in the finale. DiFilippo, not wanting Hartford to know how badly his quarterback was hurt, came up with the idea of suspending him to hide the injury. Given Corcoran's reputation, everyone was willing to believe

14. The Snow Bowl

that he had done something to deserve a suspension. If the King's hamstring healed before Saturday, December 12, the mysterious suspension would be lifted.

In 1968 and 1969, the championship game had taken place in late November. It was often cold at night in December, so the 1970 title game would be played in the afternoon, the first time the Knights had ever played during the day. Unfortunately, a major storm was predicted for Friday evening, and by the time the Firebirds' bus crossed the Connecticut line that morning, snow had begun to fall.

DiFilippo insisted on holding an afternoon practice session at Colt Park in swirling snow. By the time practice ended, the roads were so treacherous the Firebirds were barely able to get to their Wethersfield hotel. Writer Jay Acton, traveling with the team, pulled out of the parking lot, went into a spin and decided to leave his car at Colt Park. The weather was so bad Corcoran stayed in his room watching a movie, depriving the women of Hartford of his irresistible charm. "I must be getting old," he said. "No one would believe I didn't have some escapade planned for tonight."[15]

By Saturday morning, the snow had drifted as high as two feet and was still coming down. "God Almighty," recalled Dennis Fitzgibbons, "it was just a mess." Despite the dreadful conditions, the two teams decided to play. "It was the only day we could play," said Manch Wheeler. "Pottstown couldn't stay over."

There was another consideration. The New York Giants, for the first time in several years, were in contention for a division title, and their game against the Cardinals was being televised in Hartford on Sunday. So was the Patriots game, and Savin and Gruber were worried that, with snow still on the ground, football fans would stay home and watch the NFL telecasts. "They really shouldn't have played the game," said Arnold Dean, "but the post-season party was going to be held that night and Pete was damn sure going to hold it—and he was going to win that game first."

Before the game, Dean sat in the press box wondering how he was going to describe what he couldn't see. "You couldn't see anything," he recalled. "You couldn't see the yardage markers or anything else. There was just too much snow." Dean's young son was in the stands with a friend. His father told him he could go to the game but that there was no room in the press box and he would have to sit in the snow-covered bleachers. With the bravado of a twelve-year-old, young Dean readily agreed. "Don't worry about us," he told his father.

The game was an endurance contest. "We've had a lot of snowy games on the frozen tundras of the NFL," said Steve Sabol, recording the game for NFL Films, "but none were (sic) more dramatic than that day in Hartford." "The game in Hartford," said Jay Acton, "was like something out of King Arthur in medieval England. They could have played it on horses that day."

But how would the horses be shod? "Pete went out to a sporting goods store," recalled Tom Rowland, "and bought all kinds of shoes. We tried soccer shoes. We tried sneakers. We had our regular football shoes, but the field was frozen. We couldn't stand up."

The Pottstown players found a shoe strategy that worked. "I'd never played in the snow before," said John Land, "so it was a first for me. But we were committed to the idea that we had to win, because we had such a big rivalry with Hartford." Someone suggested unscrewing the spikes from the bottom of their shoes, leaving the exposed studs, which were like nails and could penetrate the ice and snow, as well as flesh and anything else in their path.

"The idea just evolved," said Land. "Somebody suggested it and Dave supported it. I'm pretty sure they knew it was illegal, but what referees are going to look at the bottoms of your feet in the snow to see if you've got cleats on? I didn't do it because I didn't want to get caught. As a running back I'm on the ground being tackled more than anybody else, so I decided not to do it."

The center of the field had been covered, but when the tarp was removed it was as if there had been no cover at all. Wheeler bought plastic streamers and nailed them to the ground along the boundaries of the field, and maintenance workers swept mounds of snow off the bleachers. Savin set his bulldozers to work clearing the field, and by game time the snow was piled twelve feet deep behind the end zones.

"We also got a little truck with a plow on it," said Wheeler, "but unfortunately the driver was drunk. He worked for Pete at Jet Lines and was a great guy, but when he got there he was in his cups pretty good. I finally got him off the field. I said, 'You're going to wreck the place. Get the hell out of here.'"

There was no way Corcoran's hamstring could function properly on a frozen field, and his "suspension" remained intact. Before the Firebirds boarded their bus at 9:00 o'clock Friday morning, DiFilippo said that backup Jim Haynie would start.[16] This was not as serious a blow as one might think, for Haynie was much better than the typical backup, having been drafted by the Vikings after graduating from West Chester State in 1968. He was cut and immediately signed by the Firebirds. A day after he signed, Haynie received a call from the Green Bay Packers asking if he wanted to play for the Hartford Knights, but it was too late. Haynie had been with the Firebirds for three years, knew the system, and knew the Hartford Knights.

Despite the snowy, blustery conditions, Haynie put the ball in the air. His receivers, especially unheralded Ron Holliday, a little 5'10", 175-pound split end, broke free time after time. Holliday hauled in eight passes for nearly 200 yards. "He was the only one who wasn't slipping," said Rowland. "He's running around and I'm thinking, 'Geez, I'm a good defensive back and I can't stay with this guy. What the hell's going on?' Finally, I tackle him and roll over and look at his shoes. He had ice picks on his shoes! He had unscrewed his spikes and all he had were studs on the bottom of his shoes."

"That's like playing on nails," said Nick DeFelice. "They should have made them take their shoes off and play in their goddamn bare feet. Their receivers were going out and making cuts and our guys were falling all over the place. The same thing with the defensive ends. They're coming in and making all kinds of cuts and we're sliding. I changed my shoes. I tried sneakers. I tried coach's shoes. I tried cleats."

"Dillon Stadium was really just frozen sand," said Fitzgibbons. "We offensive lineman had a god-awful time keeping our feet. And you'd get stepped on and you'd get cut." "I remember looking down at my legs many times," said Dick Bowman, "and seeing rivers of blood coming down. That's crazy. You're trying to hurt people."

After a scoreless first quarter, the Firebirds scored 16 points in the second to take a commanding halftime lead. While the teams went to their dressing rooms to try to warm up, Dean gave his listeners an analysis of the first half. "The wind was blowing, it was really cold, and the snow was in your face," he said, "and I saw my son and his friend looking longingly up at the press box (the new improved, heated press box)." If the Firebirds could wear nails on their feet, Dean could bend the rules just a little and let a couple of frozen urchins sit in the press box. He waved them in.

Also in the stands was Elaine Savin, who sat on the cold metal bleachers, but had the benefit of a warming agent unavailable to young Dean. She was sitting with Louise Kronholm, daughter of Democratic chieftain John Bailey, who had brought a flask. "I remember it was cold and it was fun," Elaine said. Unfortunately, Pete and his Knights were not enjoying the afternoon as much as his wife.

Sherman replaced Russell to start the second half but was no more successful. By the time the game was over, the stands were nearly empty and the Firebirds were 31–0 victors and champions of the Atlantic Coast Football League for the second year in a row. The anticipated big payday had not materialized, for although 5,100 fans (roughly 1,500 of which had come from Pottstown) braved the storm, less than half of Dillon Stadium was filled. Ed Gruber offered to give each Firebird a game check rather than the reduced payout, and in the name of brotherhood the players voted to pool the checks and divide them equally.[17]

Holliday was awarded a trophy as the most valuable offensive player and middle linebacker Steve Zegalia, who'd had a key second quarter interception and batted down several other passes, was voted the most valuable defensive player. Haynie, under horrible conditions, had completed 18 of 37 passes for 352 yards, throwing for two touchdowns and running for a third. Russell and Sherman combined for just 13 completions in 40 attempts for 133 yards. The Hartford running game had been equally ineffective, as Sherman was the team's leading rusher with just 24 yards.

In the locker room, DiFilippo accepted the trophy and declared, "If the Lord were to take me the next day, I think it would have been OK, because how many come this way ... how many people go through life and never become champions?" He led the team in the Lord's Prayer and announced that Joe Blake had been voted the Firebird's defensive player of the year. "I'd like to become a master of something," Blake said, "if only of myself."

In 1968, the Knights had been the champions and losers of just one game. The next year, they'd dominated the league until the last three weeks. In 1970, they'd barely squeaked into the playoffs on a disputed tiebreaker. In tandem with the declining results came lower attendance.

On September 30, the *Courant* ran a story headlined "Lack of Fans Puzzles Knights" in which Savin offered possible explanations and solutions. He thought about playing on Friday night rather than Saturday. He wondered if the advent of *Monday Night Football* on ABC made for too long a sports weekend. Perhaps women's liberation had taken hold and the ladies weren't letting their men watch as many sporting events. Whatever the reason, the Knights' attendance was down about 25 percent. After three years and a bitter fight, Savin had finally been able to expand the capacity at Dillon Stadium, but now he couldn't fill the seats.

The Knights weren't the only team with attendance woes in 1970. Bridgeport drew well, attracting 12,242 for an early October game against the Knights, but other teams were suffering. In late October, when the Knights were scheduled to play the Orlando Panthers, the latter club announced that it was out of money.

"For all intents and purposes," said Coach Paul Massey, "we are broke."[18] He said the team needed attendance of 7,000 per game to break even and had thus far averaged just 5,200. Annual expenses were budgeted at $240,000 and the initial capital contributed to the club was $90,000. "[We] felt we could certainly make $150,000 through gate receipts. We haven't."[19]

The Orlando players voted to play the Knights and rely upon gate receipts for compensation. If the gate was enough to pay their full salaries, they would be paid as usual. If not, they would get a pro rata share of receipts. Miraculously, Orlando managed to play its full complement of games.

Richmond was a second troubled franchise. In late October, their game with the Firebirds was postponed because the Richmond squad was too "injury riddled." When the Roadrunners' coach, J.D. Roberts, was elevated to the head job in New Orleans, there was a question as to whether the club would be able to finish the season. Yet, like Orlando, Richmond limped across the finish line, with a 2–10 record.

Even though all clubs completed their schedules, the outlook for 1971 was questionable. The consolidation of the ACFL with the CFL had proven that the combination of two weak links does not create one strong chain. After nine years, the ACFL faced its greatest crisis.

15

Hi Ho, Hi Ho, to Bridgeport We Go: The 1968–70 Bridgeport Jets

Driving south on Connecticut Route 8 from Waterbury, one is welcomed to Bridgeport by a pale green inverted "U" on the left side of the road with the letters "HI" on the left vertical and "HO" on the right. Anyone from Bridgeport can tell you that Hi-Ho is the symbol for D'Addario Industries, a large and venerable construction company owned by a prominent local family.

In 1968, the company's president, F. Francis D'Addario, purchased the struggling Waterbury Orbits and relocated them to his beloved city. Then, as now, the color of D'Addario's welcome was green, in the form of money sorely needed by the staggering Waterbury franchise.

Absentee ownership had hindered the Orbits' efforts to establish a loyal fan base. The owners had few local connections, and Mayor Palumbo's welcoming attitude was not enough to make the venture a financial success. After a second year of losses, the Orbits went in search of a more lucrative base of operations and inquired in Stamford, Hartford, and New Haven without success. Finally, in February, they found a city that had both a local owner with capital and an attractive new stadium. The Waterbury Orbits became the Bridgeport Jets and would play their home games in four-year-old, 13,660-seat Kennedy Stadium.

Frank D'Addario had money, he had a company that could provide jobs for his players, he had the connections to put the Jets in Kennedy Stadium, and he had the right attitude for the owner of a minor league team. D'Addario said he would be thrilled if he could break even and pledged to donate any profits to a charitable scholarship fund. "He loved sports," said his sister Joan Benedetto, "he loved children, and he loved the city of Bridgeport. He wanted to bring entertainment to the city. There were some people who said he was just in it to make a profit, but unfortunately there was no profit."

15. Hi-Ho, Hi Ho, to Bridgeport We Go

The Jets were a family enterprise. Frank ran the show, Joan was his office assistant, and son David served as ball boy. D'Addario employees volunteered their time on game nights as ushers and security guards.

D'Addario was a dynamic man with a contagious optimism, always bursting with new ideas and schemes. "My brother's philosophy," said Joan, "was that whenever you felt sorry for yourself, you should go to the hospital, take a walk through the emergency room, and look at all the little children. When he walked in to the office in the morning, you never knew what was going to happen, what brilliant idea he might have. He'd say, '*Joan*,' and when I heard that tone of voice I'd say, 'My God, what is he going to get us into now?'"

Like Pete Savin, D'Addario had the wherewithal to absorb losses. Like Savin, he was wildly enthusiastic about his team. Like Savin, D'Addario had parties at his house where he could show off his players to his business associates. In terms of personality, however, the two men were quite different. Savin was urbane and cosmopolitan, while D'Addario had more of a common touch.

"My father could talk to a working man on a construction site and they would love him," said his son David, "or he could talk to the governor of a state." "Frank was a guy who loved to be with the ballplayers," said Joe Ginnetti, who played for both Bridgeport and Hartford. "He'd ride with us on the bus trips, sit in the back of the bus, drink beer, and play cards with us." Savin usually rode to the games in his luxury automobile.

"Frank was a character, a little Napoleon type of guy," said Roger Milici, who played for the Jets for three years. "He was like a kid in a candy shop with his football team. He'd fight you and nickel and dime you over a contract and then he'd take you out for a hundred dollar dinner."

Milici was only partly correct. D'Addario was short like Napoleon, and like the French general was always looking for new worlds to conquer. But Frank D'Addario was much nicer to his opponents than Napoleon had been. "His attitude," David said, "was that we can kick the shit out of each other from 9 to 5, but at 5:01, I'm your friend. A lot of his best friends were also our competitors."

In 1927, Frank D'Addario's immigrant father, armed with a fourth grade education, a pick, a shovel, and a wheelbarrow, started a construction company. He dug foundations by hand and slowly built his business into one of the largest in the area. "My father broke all the stone," said Mrs. Benedetto, "and my mother got up early every morning to heat water to put in the radiator to get the truck started." The company was awarded a contract to dig the foundation for a new post office, but D'Addario's machine operator walked off the job when he was refused a five cent per hour raise. "My father went to the school," Joan recalled, "pulled my brother out and he had to get on the machine and dig the cellar.

Now all our children have choices. We didn't have choices. We were told what to do and we did it."

"My father showed up for his high school graduation picture in coveralls," said David. "He had a suit and tie on underneath, and after they took the picture, he put the coveralls back on and went back to work operating a cable shovel."

In 1951, the senior D'Addario died unexpectedly, and 28-year-old Frank inherited the family business. "The only time I ever saw him down," said Joan, "was when our father died and he had to take over the business. He was very apprehensive."

The business prospered and, a few years later, Frank adopted the name Hi-Ho for himself and his company. "People would always butcher our name," said David. "They'd call us DiAddoria or Danarrio. So my mother said, 'Frank, why don't you just put Hi-Ho in front of it and then they have to say Hi-Ho D'Addario like the nursery rhyme. A lot of people were friends with my father for 20 or 30 years and didn't even know his real name. They just called him Hi-Ho."[1]

Frank was born with deformed legs, and had to wear braces as a boy. He was never able to excel at athletics, but loved sports and always wanted to own a professional franchise. He made a bid when CBS put the New York Yankees up for sale in 1972. He tried to get the NFL to grant him an expansion team that would play in the Carrier Dome in Syracuse. He wanted to buy the Pittsburgh Condors of the American Basketball Association and move them to New Haven.

D'Addario was therefore thrilled to bring professional football to Bridgeport in 1968. Probably the only person more excited was six-year-old David. David wasn't the oldest son, but he was the one most interested in sports, and was able to spend the next seven years as a ball boy, shagging punts in practice, picking up dirty uniforms and jock straps, running out on the field to bring back the tee after a kickoff, and going on all the road trips. On the return home, he usually slept in the luggage rack, cushioned by a couple of Hi-Ho jackets.[2] "It was so cool," he said. "The trips were special. It was as if I was going to Mars." A fellow ball boy was John Fabrizi, who later became mayor of Bridgeport.

David D'Addario was not only young; he was small for his age. "I was the owner's son," he said, "so everyone was always concerned about my safety. Watch David! Watch David! There were times when someone came toward the sidelines and one of the players would just pick me up like a rag doll and swing me out of the way."

The old Orbit owners retained a minority interest in the club, and Nick Cutro came along as coach. Unfortunately for Cutro, his nemesis Milt Rosner remained the general manager. The affiliation with the New York Jets remained in place, and D'Addario adopted the Jet name for his club. The press almost always referred to the team as the Hi-Ho Jets.

Many of the old Orbits came to Bridgeport, including Milici, veteran quarterback John Torok, who'd backed up King Corcoran in Waterbury, running back Allen Smith, who'd failed to make the Chicago Bear roster, and John Dockery, the former Orbit defensive back who'd joined the Jets' taxi squad late in 1967.

Corcoran, based upon his fine season in Waterbury, was invited to the New York Jets training camp. In late July, he threw three touchdown passes in a scrimmage between the Jet rookies and the Bridgeport Jets. Corcoran was so enthused about his performance that he disappeared for a few days. According to his later report, he spent the interlude dallying with a beauty queen. A good performance in a rookie scrimmage did not generate enough capital to justify an unexcused absence, and Coach Weeb Ewbank cut the wandering playboy. It looked like a season in Bridgeport was in store for the King.

Quarterback Seiki Murono of the Long Island Bulls sets up in the pocket while Bridgeport Jet linebacker Jim Bivins (56) and defensive tackle Jim Mylinski (79) **apply pressure** (courtesy Seiki Murono).

In addition to Corcoran, Cutro acquired a second bad boy when the Jets signed linebacker Richie Connors, the former Shamrock star who'd spent a number of years in prison. In addition to playing football, Connors was tending bar in a known mob hangout. Although he had stayed out of trouble since resuming his football career, reaction to him was mixed.

Defensive back Joel Cooney of the Shamrocks said Connors was a mentor to him and an excellent instructor. Others felt differently. "How do I put this succinctly?" said a former coach. "He was kind of trouble. He wasn't very well disciplined." "He cleaned himself up and became a real good teammate," said one player. "He was very disruptive in our clubhouse," said another.

Corcoran's performance in the Bridgeport exhibition games was desultory. Torok played much better, and Cutro selected the former Arizona State star to open at quarterback. A week later, Corcoran was sold to the Boston Patriots, who assigned him to the Lowell Giants. Connors was gone shortly thereafter. He was suspended following an argument with Cutro and left to join the Westchester Bulls.

The opening game against Harrisburg at Kennedy Stadium, delayed a day by a severe rainstorm, drew an audience of 10,471, well in excess of any crowd the Orbits had drawn in Waterbury. Bridgeport Mayor Curran and new ACFL commissioner Cosmo Iacovazzi attended, and the field was gaily decorated with bunting and American flags.

The only thing missing was a Jet win. The principal villain was Harrisburg fullback John Land, a stumpy 5'9", 205-pounder who grew up in New York City, where basketball was king. Land never played high school football, but idolized Jimmy Brown, and when he matriculated to Delaware State decided that he wanted to try the sport.

"I didn't know anything," Land said. "I didn't know how to catch the ball. I didn't know how to block. I didn't know how to run with the ball. I had to learn the whole game when I got to Delaware State." Land made the team but for his first two years was primarily a blocking back. He got to carry the ball his junior and senior years, but since Delaware State rarely passed, he didn't learn to catch the ball.

Land was ignored by the NFL and AFL when he graduated. A running back from a small school who couldn't catch the ball wasn't a prize commodity, especially if he stood 5'9". Although he became a minor league star, Land had limited aspirations. He had a good job and a family in Wilmington, and the only teams he was interested in playing for were the nearby Colts and Eagles. He wasn't about to uproot his family and give up a steady job for the insecurity of a marginal NFL career and its limited financial potential.

Land gained 177 yards rushing against the Jets, including a 42-yard dash

15. Hi-Ho, Hi Ho, to Bridgeport We Go

early in the game and a 72-yard touchdown burst that put the Capitols ahead 14–13 in the third quarter. Still, despite Land's heroics, the Jets should have won. Trailing 17–13 late in the game, they drove to the Harrisburg one-yard line, where they had a first and goal situation. Running back Nick George fumbled and Harrisburg recovered and ran out the clock.

After wins against the Pottstown Firebirds and Westchester Bulls, the Jets faced Corcoran and the Giants at Kennedy Stadium. Trailing 26–16 in the fourth quarter, the Jets rallied to tie the score on a field goal by Bob Anderson, his fourth of the game, with 2:04 left. Following the ensuing kickoff, the Jet defense threw Lowell ball carriers for losses on three consecutive occasions, forcing the Giants to punt from deep in their own territory. Torok quickly completed two passes, the second to Milici on the 2-yard line.

With no timeouts remaining, the Jets lined up quickly and Torok fired the ball out of bounds to stop the clock. The officials ruled that the clock should not stop, for the ball had not been marked ready for play before the Jets snapped it.

With the seconds ticking away, the field goal team raced frantically onto the field and Anderson put the ball through the uprights with no time showing on the clock. "It was an angle shot," said Anderson, "a real tight angle. But it went right square through there."

Before the play, however, the officials had called a penalty on center Roger Hayes for moving the ball prior to the snap. "The ball was wet," said Anderson. "He just moved it a little to try to get a grip on it." As the players milled around the field in confusion, the officials declared the game over and the final result a 26–26 tie. The Jets lodged a protest with Commissioner Iacovazzi.

A few days later, after consultation with ACFL Chief of Officials William Dioguardi, Iacovazzi upheld the protest and ruled that if the game had a bearing on the division title it would be replayed in its entirety on November 27.

After seven games, the Jets were within striking distance of the first place Hartford Knights.

Northern Division

Hartford	6	1	0
Bridgeport	4	2	1
Lowell	2	4	1
Westchester	2	5	0

Torok was tied for the league lead in passing, Dick Janes was the leading interceptor with nine, and Anderson was first in scoring with 58 points, including a league best 14 field goals.

Anderson grew up in Westboro, Massachusetts, where he played baseball and other sports and, for fun, kicked a football in the local cemetery. When his family moved to Chatfield, Minnesota for his senior year, he decided to try out for the football team with the hope of winning a college scholarship. He didn't kick any field goals, and made only 6 of 11 extra point attempts.

Communication was slower and obfuscation much easier in the 1960s, and Anderson wrote to a number of college coaches, telling them he'd made 10 of 10 extra points and kicked a 60-yard field goal. "It was just like when you play cards," he said. "When you don't have too good a hand, you have to bluff."

Most schools wanted verification of the facts from his high school coach, which was problematic, but University of Iowa coach Jerry Burns invited him to enroll and try out for the team. If he performed well, Burns said, he could get a scholarship.

Anderson, 5'10" and a chubby 190 pounds, was not a gifted athlete, but he was dedicated and determined. He kicked a couple of hundred balls a day, sometimes toward a goal post, and other times at an imaginary target. He kicked outside in the winter and practiced all summer.

In the mid–1960s, virtually all kickers played other positions, but all Anderson could do was kick—and kick—and kick. As if being a kicking specialist wasn't enough to set Anderson apart, he took on a unique persona. He got an antiquated helmet and painted "Herky the Hawkeye" on one side and "Rose Bowl or Bust" on the other. He requested uniform number 007 in honor of James Bond.

Anderson's kicking for the freshman team was impressive, and it appeared that a scholarship was a real possibility. One day during practice, Burns decided to test his kicker's coolness under pressure. He had the center intentionally snap the ball past the holder directly to Anderson, who caught it and, without missing a beat, drop kicked it through the uprights. Shortly afterward, he got his scholarship.

Before Anderson's sophomore season, a 26-year-old assistant coach named George Seifert joined the Iowa staff. Seifert, who would later lead the San Francisco 49ers to a Super Bowl title, was assigned to coach Anderson, who had been completely self-taught. The first thing Seifert did was tell him to do 50 sit-ups. Anderson couldn't imagine what sit-ups had to do with kicking, but did about 20 before asking Seifert if he could kick. Seifert said he could and Anderson challenged him to a competition. If Seifert could beat him, Anderson said, he would train the way Seifert wanted him to.

Anderson had a drill in which he put the ball down on the end line in one corner of the end zone, kicked it over the goal posts, and hit the end line in the other corner. After watching him do that a few times, Seifert told him to stick to his own methods.

15. Hi-Ho, Hi Ho, to Bridgeport We Go

Anderson became the Hawkeyes' regular kicker his sophomore year, but rarely got to kick, for Iowa didn't score many touchdowns and seldom got close enough to attempt a field goal. He led the Hawkeyes in scoring his sophomore and junior years with 28 and 24 points, respectively. During his career, he never missed an extra point, kicking 32 in succession, but making only 32 touchdowns in three years led to some difficult seasons in Iowa City. After Iowa lost every Big Ten game in Anderson's sophomore season, he crossed "Rose Bowl" off his helmet and left "Bust." Anderson set a number of school records that year, including most field goals in a game (2), most in a season (6) and most points by kicking in a season (28).

The highlight of Anderson's college career was a game-winning field goal with 39 seconds left to beat Indiana and snap a 16-game Big Ten losing streak. Such heroics endeared him to the fans, for he was a lot like them, a man with limited athletic ability who had one finely-honed talent. Anderson was a self-described "Walter Mitty."

The press loved Anderson because he was a loquacious youngster who was always good for a quote or ten. Why did he kick in a cemetery? "The people there don't put much of a rush on you," he replied. When he wore number 007 he called himself "Goldfoot." After he was the subject of an article in *Sport* magazine, Coach Burns asked him if he would mention him during one of his many interviews so people wouldn't forget him.

Anderson didn't get any NFL offers, and went to the Bridgeport tryout camp, where he was placed in competition with about ten other kickers. "Most of them could kick farther than I could," he said, "but they weren't accurate."

Anderson made the team and was a good ACFL kicker, reliable from short and medium range. He kicked line drives and tried for extra distance by keeping the ball as low as possible, only a few feet higher than the crossbar and barely above the arms of onrushing linemen. Anderson became as popular with the Bridgeport fans as he had been in Iowa. "When he waddles on and off the field," wrote Pete Nevins, "it's as if he's George Plimpton made good."[3]

The Jets' fate would be decided in back-to-back games against the Knights on successive weekends, October 26 at Hartford and November 1 in Bridgeport. Before the first game, the *Post-Telegram* predicted, "The deciding factor could be the foot of either the Knights' Wes Bean or the Jets' Bob Anderson."[4]

Bean set an ACFL record by connecting on two 50-yard field goals that provided the final Hartford margin of 19–17. During the first half, Don Hubert replaced Torok as Anderson's holder and the usually reliable Jet kicker missed from 32 and 38 yards. With Torok holding once more in the second half, Anderson connected on a 38-yarder, but it was not enough.

A week later the Knights demolished the Jets' title hopes with a convincing

37–7 win that clinched a tie for the division title with three games remaining. The Knight defense totally stymied the usually potent Bridgeport offense, holding them to just one first down in the first half and only 22 rushing yards for the entire game. The only good news for the Jets was a home crowd of more than 11,000.

Home attendance was the highlight of D'Addario's first season in the ACFL. The Jets set a league record by drawing 61,201 fans for six home dates. The Knights, also in their first year and heralded for their terrific fan support, drew just over 50,000. Another new club, the Richmond Roadrunners, was third in attendance and, bolstered by new cities, the ACFL established an all-time record of 282,550. The single game high of 13,247 was achieved at Kennedy Stadium on October 18 against Pottstown.

The Jets finished their initial campaign with a record of 6–5–1 and held off Westchester for second place in the Northern Division. Torok just missed winning the passing title, being nosed out by Richmond's Al Woodall on the final weekend. Janes easily led the league in interceptions with 12, and he, along with Milici, tackle Tom Hunt, and guard Eli Strand, were named to the all–ACFL squad.

Less than two months after the Bridgeport season ended, the parent Jets upset the Baltimore Colts in Super Bowl III. Running across the Orange Bowl turf wearing #43 for the Jets was John Dockery, just a few weeks removed from the Hi-Ho Jets. Dockery had to work hard to make it to the NFL, for he was not big and lacked blinding speed. His long suit was versatility. "I was the backup quarterback," he said, "the backup kicker, I played wide receiver and defensive back, and I delivered water to the coaches when they needed it."

In 1967, Dockery practiced with the Jets but was not signed. When Bridgeport's 1968 season ended, he was signed for the final three games of New York's schedule. With an NFL spot secured, he dropped his plans for a graduate degree in city planning. "I'm just fine about that," he said recently. "There probably would have been some ugly buildings around New York City."

The Jets' season was extended for three additional weeks and Dockery picked up a full $15,000 Super Bowl winners' share. With his salary and playoff money, he estimated he earned about $25,000 for six weeks' work.

"It was unreal," Dockery said. "It was like a fantasy. We're playing the Baltimore Colts with all those legends on the other side of the field. I don't think it registered for months. It was a stroke of luck. There were a thousand guys who could have been in my spot, but for some reason I was the guy who was chosen to be there. My feet didn't touch the ground as I was running out on the field. I kept thinking it was a dream I was going to wake up from. And to win the game on top of it was just beyond belief."

Meanwhile, Nick DeFelice watched the game on television after finishing his season with the Hartford Knights. "After I left the Jets," he said, "Sherman

15. Hi-Ho, Hi Ho, to Bridgeport We Go

Plunkett retired and Dave Herman took his place. Dave did a hell of a job, but that would have been me if I had stayed up there another year."

Many of the Bridgeport Jets, especially those on the taxi squad, thought they might get Super Bowl rings, but none was forthcoming. "The Jets haven't won a Super Bowl since 1968," said Anderson. "Maybe it was the curse of not giving rings to the Bridgeport Jets."

Less than a month after the end of the season, D'Addario fired Nick Cutro. The biggest problem with Cutro was that he lived in New Jersey and only came to Bridgeport for practices and games. Further jeopardizing Cutro's status was his continuing adversarial relationship with Milt Rosner. "I had that guy in my back pocket all the time," Cutro said, "complaining that I didn't know what I was doing. I had to listen to somebody who didn't know anything about football. He knew baseball." D'Addario and Rosner agreed that their next coach would be required to live in the Bridgeport area during the season.

In mid–March, the Jets hired Ray Mathews as head coach. Reports on minor league teams often described new arrivals as former star players, generally without justification. Mathews, however, really was a star, both at Clemson University and in the NFL. He spent nine years with the Steelers, beginning in 1951, and finished his career with the expansion Dallas Cowboys in 1960. He was the first game captain in the storied history of the Cowboys.

Mathews' statistics show the versatility of players of the 1950s. During his ten years in the league, he rushed for 1,057 yards, caught 233 passes for almost 4,000 yards, completed 19 of 51 passes for 350 yards, returned 61 punts and 42 kickoffs, intercepted two passes, kicked an extra point and registered a safety.

After retiring from active play, Mathews coached and scouted in the NFL and the Canadian League. In 1966, he served as coach of the ACFL's Rhode Island Steelers and in 1968 was offensive backfield coach for Otto Graham's Washington Redskins. Graham was fired at the end of the season and replaced by Vince Lombardi, who dismissed all of Graham's assistants.

Mathews, only 40 years old and in good shape, was a handsome man who looked and acted like a football coach. "I remember him being feared," said David D'Addario. "He had a hard handshake, a stern eye and there was no bullshit. If he liked you he'd let you know and if he didn't like you, you were in trouble. Everybody was scared of him. He expected a lot from us, even the ball boys, because we were Bridgeport Jets. He was demanding and he expected excellence." "He was a very moody guy," said Roger Milici. "I never really knew how to read him." "Ray was a quiet guy," added Lou Piccone. "There wasn't anything dynamic about him. He was a man of few words."

In early September D'Addario acquired the interests of his New Haven partners and became the sole owner. Having complete local ownership and a coach who lived in Bridgeport could only help attendance. A further boost could be provided by a marquee name on the playing field.

Signing a superstar was beyond the grasp of most minor league franchises. The best players wanted to play in the best league and to be paid like top players. In 1969, the Orlando Panthers of the Continental League thought they had a chance to sign Heisman Trophy winner O.J. Simpson, who had reached an impasse with the Buffalo Bills. Panther President Elmer Cook said Simpson's agent had contacted CFL President Jim Dunn and said he would sign for a contract with a total value of $400,000. Cook couldn't afford that kind of money, but he went to the Florida Citrus Commission and pitched them on the publicity a superstar named O.J. playing in Orlando could generate for their product. It was a long shot, but Cook was an optimist.

There were no Heisman Trophy winners named "Hi-Ho," but there was a local hero with a national reputation who might be available to the Jets at an affordable price. He was former Yale quarterback Brian Dowling, an exceptional young man who had been a winner all his life. At St. Ignatius High School in Ohio, his team lost just one of 36 football games in four years, a game Dowling missed with a broken collarbone and bruised kidney.

Recruited by more than 100 colleges, Dowling turned down athletic scholarships from a number of football powers and elected to attend Yale. His other top choice had been Ohio State, but Dowling's father suggested, "Why not go first class," a remark fortunately made beyond striking distance of volatile Buckeye coach Woody Hayes.

In 1965, Dowling quarterbacked the Yale freshman team to a 6–0 mark and entered his sophomore season as perhaps the most heralded newcomer in the long, glorious history of Yale football. He and classmate Calvin Hill led the team to victory in the opening game, but the next week, on a muddy field, Dowling injured his knee and missed the rest of the season.

Prior to his junior season, Dowling broke his hand in practice and missed the first three games. The Bulldogs won every game after his return, including a dramatic 24–20 victory over Harvard on his 66-yard touchdown pass in the final minutes.

Dowling's senior season was the first in which he enjoyed good health all year. Under his leadership, Yale won its first eight games, many by convincing margins. His statistics were impressive and would have been even more glittering had he not been removed early from many games in which Yale held overwhelming leads. All Dowling needed to cap a sensational career was a victory over an underdog Harvard team in his final game.

The 1968 Yale–Harvard game is perhaps the most storied in the history of the long and legendary rivalry. With Yale on the brink of victory, Harvard

15. Hi-Ho, Hi Ho, to Bridgeport We Go

rallied behind second string quarterback Frank Champi to salvage a 29–29 tie. While the deadlock was a bitter disappointment for Yale, it was not a defeat, and Dowling finished his eight-year high school and college career without a loss in any game he had completed.

Football was only one of Dowling's talents. He played baseball and basketball at Yale, and was also an accomplished tennis player and musician. Further, he had the persona of the classic campus hero. "Brian was one of the most humble people you would ever meet," said Jet center Joe Ginnetti. Frank Deford wrote in *Sports Illustrated* twenty years after the end of Dowling's Yale career, "If your mother met him, no matter how old Brian Dowling happened to be, she would say, 'My, what a nice boy.'"[5]

The late 1960s were a time of transition for America, and also for the Ivy League. In 1968, Yale was still an all-male institution, although the arrival of women was just a couple of years away. On a campus with growing unrest, Dowling was the icon of a fading generation, the last gleaming flash of a departing era, the inspiration for B.D., the helmet-wearing traditionalist among the hippies of the Doonesbury comic strip.

Dowling finished ninth in the 1968 Heisman Trophy voting, a remarkable showing for an Ivy Leaguer, and was drafted by the Minnesota Vikings on the 11th round. Could Dowling bring his Yale magic to the NFL? Dan Jenkins wrote in *Sports Illustrated* that he was a quarterback who "runs just fast enough to get away from people, who throws just well enough to complete the big ones and who has this winning electricity about him."[6]

Carmen Cozza, his coach at Yale, described Dowling as "neither a great passer nor a great runner, but a born winner."[7] Being a winner was laudable, but NFL players needed to be outstanding in one facet of the game. "The NFL is no place for a 'flutterball' quarterback,"[8] wrote Dennis Randall.

"Brian was just a terrific college athlete," said Dockery. "But if you don't have speed, or if you don't have a great arm, or if you can't do one thing especially well, then you're not going to be there. The generalist usually doesn't survive." They usually wound up coaching, or playing in the Atlantic Coast League.

Dowling was used mostly as a running back in the Viking camp and was cut on September 5. Four days later, the Jets scheduled a press conference, promising "an announcement of major importance."[9] The content of the announcement was an open secret, for ever since Dowling's release there had been rumors that he would join the Jets. Just three days earlier, D'Addario had signed former Yale tight end Bruce Weinstein, Dowling's favorite target and a Dolphin draftee. Thus, when the press assembled at the Stratfield Hotel, it came as no surprise when D'Addario announced the signing of Dowling and presented him and Weinstein to the large group of media representatives.

Dowling immediately became the number one quarterback, for Torok had retired when his employer transferred him to its Phoenix office and Tom Tyler, who'd started in the 1969 opener, was traded to the Quincy Giants as soon as Dowling was signed.

An unusually large crowd attended Dowling's first practice and 15,000 watched him make his debut at Roanoke. It was not a success. Dowling entered the game early in the second quarter and led the Jets on a long drive that ended when he threw an interception near the Roanoke goal line. A second interception soon followed, and the only bright spot in the 22–10 loss was Dowling's six-yard scramble for a touchdown in the fourth quarter. He completed just 10 of 27 passes, but his mere appearance on the field created excitement, and his nimble scrambling style brought the crowd to its feet on numerous occasions.

The game was a sloppy one, with numerous turnovers and 134 yards in penalties against the Jets. Bill Carroll of the *Post-Telegram* wrote that the officials "should have been wearing Roanoke uniforms."[10] Carroll was not an unbiased observer, however, for he also served as public relations director for the Jets.

With a full week of practice under his belt, Dowling made his home debut on September 19. Attendance was a disappointing 9,268, a smaller crowd than the Jets had been drawing without Dowling, and the result of the game was even more disappointing.

The Richmond Roadrunners dominated the game and left the field with a 32–0 win. After an undefeated career in high school and college, Dowling was 0–2 in professional football. The *Post-Telegram* stated that "Dowling, the one-time Ivy League golden boy who is finding life in the ACFL much less enjoyable than his collegiate career ever was, made his Bridgeport debut last night and not too many fans went away awed by his performance."[11]

Although Dowling completed 17 of 34 passes, most were short throws and three were intercepted. He gained just 127 yards on the 17 completions. "He was a great athlete," said Ginnetti, "but he didn't have a good arm—a great arm that could really zip the ball."

After three games the Jets had scored just one touchdown. Dowling's charisma and leadership abilities were not resulting in any scoring or, perhaps even more important, in increased attendance. Since he didn't appear to be the answer, the Jets acquired quarterback Harry Theofiledes.

Theofiledes was a great two-way performer at Waynesburg College, setting passing and total offense records as a quarterback and earning Little All American status as a safety. Despite his college accolades, Theofiledes was a long shot to make the NFL, for he was from a small school and stood just 5'9", too short to be a prototypical quarterback.

15. Hi-Ho, Hi Ho, to Bridgeport We Go

Theofiledes, however, had connections. His college coach, Mike Scarry, had been the center for Redskin head coach Otto Graham when both played for the Browns. In 1966, when Theofiledes graduated, Graham asked Scarry to become an assistant coach. "I've got a kid that played quarterback for me," Scarry told Graham. "Let him come down as a free agent. It won't cost you anything."

Theofiledes showed enough to earn a spot on the taxi squad, and for the next two years played with the Virginia Sailors of the ACFL, leading them to the league championship in 1967. He went to his third Redskin camp in 1968 facing steep odds. Sonny Jurgensen and his backup, Jim Ninowski, were in front of him, and the third quarterback, UCLA's Gary Beban, was the 1967 Heisman Trophy winner. Beban was Washington's number one draft choice and, while no one expected him to unseat Jurgensen, everyone assumed he would make the team.

The problem with Beban was that, like Dowling, he was a collegiate star who didn't have much of an arm. "He came in with all this hoopla," recalled Theofiledes, "but he really couldn't throw that good a pass." The players said Beban threw an option pass, because one had the option of catching either end of the ball as it tumbled toward them.

The Redskins had a lot of money invested in Beban, and weren't about to cut him. They tried him at quarterback, halfback, wide receiver, and finally on defense, but he didn't stand out at any position. Meanwhile, the unheralded, undrafted Theofiledes made the team as the third quarterback. He got into five games and played well in limited appearances, completing 12 of 20 passes and throwing for two touchdowns. He rallied the Skins to a win over Detroit by leading them to two touchdowns late in the game.

Washington was 5-9 in 1968 and Graham was fired, replaced by Vince Lombardi, who was emerging from a restless year in semi-retirement as the Packer general manager. During the spring, Theofiledes paid a visit to Lombardi's Washington office and said that if Lombardi didn't plan to give him a legitimate shot to make the team in 1969, he would like to be released in order to have a shot at catching on somewhere else.

"I knew it was ballsy on my part," Theofiledes said, "but I figured, what did I have to lose?" Lombardi assured the youngster that he would get a fair shot, and he made the opening day roster. Shortly afterward, however, the Redskins signed long time Cleveland Browns quarterback Frank Ryan, and Lombardi told Theofiledes he was going to demote him to the taxi squad.

"Being as stubborn as I was," Theofiledes recalled, "I said, 'Coach, he can't outrun me. He's got a weaker arm. I'm younger. I'm faster. I don't care how many years he's been in the league. He's over the hill.'"

Lombardi wasn't buying. "My gut feeling is to stay with Ryan," he said. It was the taxi squad or nothing, and Theofiledes chose nothing. "I was hurt," he said recently, "and I was disappointed. The next day the news made all the papers and there was a big article about me. All the sportswriters liked me because I was a scrambler and I made things exciting. Everybody said Lombardi was making a big mistake." Mistake or not, Lombardi was the boss and Theofiledes an ex–Redskin. Mathews, who'd been the Washington backfield coach in 1968, called him and asked him to join the Bridgeport Jets.

Theofiledes may have been small in stature, but he had a big arm. When he showed up at his first Jet practice, center Ginnetti wondered, "Who the hell is this guy?" "He took the snap from me," Ginnetti recalled, "dropped back to pass and threw the ball 60 yards down the field. I couldn't believe it. He had a rifle for an arm."

"He could run like the wind and he was very elusive," said Milici. "He reminded me of Fran Tarkenton. You couldn't pin him down that easily. You could never stop running your pattern because you never knew if he was going to get loose." Mathews announced that Theofiledes would be the number one quarterback and that Dowling would be used primarily as a running back and flanker.

The new quarterback was an immediate success, leading the Jets to victory in his debut by running 22 yards for the winning touchdown against the Long Island Bulls. Theofiledes' second game was even better. He engineered a 42–7 win over the Richmond team that had beaten the Jets 32–0 just two weeks earlier. The offense that couldn't score during the first three weeks of the season had racked up 61 points in two games. Against Richmond, Theofiledes completed 25 of 34 passes for 343 yards and four touchdowns. The final touchdown was a pass to Dowling and 13 of the completions were to Milici, which set an ACFL record.

"Joe Ginnetti always busted my balls about that," said Milici. "He said I caught 13 passes for 32 yards. We were big into quick outs. Everything was a quick out and then we'd do variations off it. The majority of those passes were quick outs, quick ups or fake a quick out and slant."

Theofiledes liked to step on the accelerator. "What made him good," said Hartford defensive back Tom Rowland, "was that their offense was not predictable. Harry would throw on first down. He'd throw on second down. If he ever got ahead of you, he was going to throw on *every* play. He wouldn't sit on the lead, which is what most people would do. What made the Jets good was that they were throwing when you wouldn't think they'd be throwing."

Rowland thought Theofiledes was the toughest ACFL quarterback to defend against and Manch Wheeler considered him the best in the league. "He had a good arm and he was smart," Wheeler said. "Harry could run. He had good mobility and he could move around in the pocket and make things happen."

As Dowling adapted to his new position, the *Post-Telegram* compared him to Dockery. Like Dockery, he was an Ivy Leaguer, and, like Dockery, he needed to demonstrate his versatility by learning skills he had not had to develop at Yale. If he could play quarterback, flanker back, and maybe running back or defensive back, he would be a valuable man on an NFL club. Dowling could also punt, and in mid-October he took over the Bridgeport punting duties from Bruce Haak.

Haak was a medical student who took an unusual route to the Jets. He was a punter in high school, but did not play football during his first three years at Purdue. One week during his senior year, the Boilermaker punter attempted to run on fourth down and incurred the wrath of head coach Jack Mollenkopf. The following Monday, Haak asked for a tryout, kicked well, and was told that he would punt the following Saturday.

A couple of days later, however, Haak received a letter from the University of Pennsylvania Medical School asking him to appear for an interview on Saturday. He called his father and suggested they ask Penn to postpone the interview, but his father insisted he go and Haak's college football career was over before it began.

After enrolling in Yale Medical School, Haak contacted the Bridgeport Jets and asked for a tryout. He didn't have a car, so he convinced a very attractive nurse with a red convertible to drive him to Bridgeport. The nurse drove right onto the field, Haak hopped out, and kicked well enough to be signed to a contract on the spot.

Later that summer, Haak was driving through Central Park with a friend, who had a sudden brainstorm. The friend would call Jet coach Weeb Ewbank, tell him he was Haak's agent, and ask for a tryout. Remarkably, the Jets agreed and Haak headed for the New York training camp at Hofstra University. "This was right after the Jets won the Super Bowl," he said, "and the entire world down there was looking for Joe Namath and the Jets."

When Haak alighted from the train and said he was looking for a ride to the Jets camp, he set off a chain reaction. The cab driver commandeered a police escort, put a reporter in the back seat with Haak, and headed to Hofstra. "I couldn't tell them I was just a nobody," Haak recalled, "so they took me to the Jets dormitory. When I got out the kids all wanted my autograph and I couldn't tell them either so I just went along." Haak had lunch with the team and went out and punted at practice. Coach Ewbank told him to go to Bridgeport and stay ready.

Haak had an unusual style of kicking, wearing only a sock on his right foot.

"I could feel the ball better," he said. Of course, it also made it more difficult to get off the field quickly. Once, he had a punt blocked, had his helmet ripped off and suffered an ugly laceration on his scalp that had to be stitched up at halftime. "The first punt of the second half I had the ball kicked before it even got to me," he said.

Despite the fact that he kicked reasonably well, Haak was a specialist, and with Dowling taking over the punting, Mathews was able to save the $50 a game they were paying Haak.

With Theofiledes at the helm, Allen Smith and big Roy Kirksey at running back, and Milici and Weinstein receiving, the Jets had an exciting offense. The excitement, however, did not result in a championship. There were high points like Theofiledes' one-yard bootleg run with 33 seconds left that gave the Jets a 24–17 win over Harrisburg. The low points included Kirksey's three fumbles in a 34–17 loss to Pottstown.

Near the end of the season, the *Post-Telegram* summarized the mystery of the 1969 team as follows: "The Jets have some outstanding individual stars, but they have been unable to 'put everything together' this year. While they have been in contention until the final quarter in almost every game they have played, the Hi-Ho team has been unable to win consistently.... Running backs Allen Smith and Roy Kirksey have both shown some outstanding running ability at times, but both have also suffered from 'fumbleitis' in key situations."[12]

The 1969 Northern Division race was over early. The Hartford Knights won their first ten games and clinched the title after nine games. In the season's eleventh week, with first place safely tucked away, the Knights hosted the Jets and watched their two-season, 20-game winning streak come to an end. Bridgeport defenders picked off six Benny Russell passes and the Knights were never really in the game. They trailed 23–0 lead before getting on the scoreboard, and the final score was 33–21. Allen Smith scored twice, once on an electrifying 92-yard run, to increase his season total to 11 touchdowns.

Frank D'Addario was not in Hartford to see the stunning upset. He was home in bed feeling awful. "He was deathly ill," remembered his son David. "We were listening to the game on the radio and it was very exciting. Then the phone started ringing off the hook. People were saying, 'Frank, you have to come up here because we're going to win this thing.' He got dressed, took a few swigs of cough medicine and got somebody to drive him to Hartford and they had a big, hooting party. It was a *huge* win." The following week, the Jets ended their season with a solid 31–0 victory over Quincy, finishing with a 7–5 record, good for second place in the Northern Division.

The next season got off to an unusual start, for during the summer of 1970, NFL players went on strike. Virtually all veteran players stayed away, save for a few exceptions like Steeler running back Rocky Bleier. Bleier, trying to make a comeback after being wounded in Vietnam, was given permission by the union to cross the line.

Other veterans stayed away either as a matter of principle or self preservation. Later, guard Pat Matson of the Cincinnati Bengals expressed the unspoken feeling of many. "I think you'd find," Matson said, "that if we had gone to camp by ourselves, once the season finally started we'd be hit by a number of crippling injuries. There are a lot of people in pro football who know how to make injuries happen, if you know what I mean."[13]

Most of the bodies populating NFL camps in July belonged to rookies and free agents, men who would normally be on ACFL rosters. Among them were Dick Faucette, quarterback of Hartford's 1968 champions, who had a trial with the Cowboys, former Knight Bob Sherlag, who was invited to the Packer camp, and Harry Theofilides, who reported the New York Jets facilities in Hempstead, Long Island.

Theofilides was not a rookie, since he'd played with the Redskins in 1968. He was therefore crossing the picket line and risking the enmity of veteran players, but at 26 it was perhaps his last chance. Theofiledes showed enough so that when the strike ended during the first week of August, the Jets kept him around. He wasn't going to take away Namath's job, but he might oust ancient Babe Parilli or Al Woodall, the former Richmond Roadrunner who'd become the Jets' second string quarterback.

On August 23, Theofilides got his big chance when the Jets played the Giants at the Yale Bowl. The Giant-Jet contest was a big deal, for AFL and NFL teams had not yet played against each other in the regular season. More than 70,000 fans filled the Yale Bowl and watched the Giants take a commanding 28–3 lead. At that point, Theofiledes told one of the coaches that if they didn't put him in the game, he was going home.

Theofiledes entered the game in the fourth quarter and led the theretofore moribund Jet offense on three touchdown drives. On each succeeding drive, Jet fans cheered louder and louder for the scrambling little quarterback. Although the Jets lost 28–24, Theofilides' performance thrust him into the thick of the backup quarterback battle. Woodall and Parilli had been ineffective against the Giants and threw four interceptions between them.

Theofiledes' opportunity with New York created great anxiety in Bridgeport, for while Weeb Ewbank had four good quarterbacks, Ray Mathews had none. In 1970, rather than practice three or four times each week, the Jets housed their players at the University of Bridgeport and held practice three times every day, at 10:00, 3:00, and 7:00. But with the NFL labor battle continuing through early August, the only quarterback at the University of Bridgeport was Fred Salvati, a safety who'd played quarterback in college.

The most impressive newcomer in the Bridgeport camp was running back Darrick Warner, who'd set many records and garnered numerous honors during his career at the University of Bridgeport. During his senior season, he gained nearly 1,500 yards rushing, scored 17 touchdowns, and was named player of the year by the Eastern College Athletic Conference.

Even with Warner in the backfield, the Jets were not going to accomplish much with only Salvati to hand off to him. Therefore D'Addario signed veteran minor leaguer and former New York Giant quarterback Tom Kennedy on the eve of Bridgeport's first exhibition game.

The opener was much more than a routine exhibition, for the Orlando roster included a 27-year-old, 5'8", 122-pound blond named Patricia Palinkas, who intended to become the first woman to play in a professional football game. There are now football leagues for women; in fact, women had played against each other as early as 1926 when the Frankford Yellow Jackets featured women's games as halftime entertainment. But never had a woman taken part in a game against men.

A casual perusal of contemporary newspapers highlights the sexist, condescending tone with which any attempt by women to invade a male bastion was treated by the media. Women were to be admired for their beauty, not their accomplishments, and it was rare that an article about a woman failed to note her physical attributes. There were "comely chemists" and "leggy lawyers" who were always a grave but welcome distraction to their male colleagues.

When women competed in athletics, the focus was often on issues of dubious relevance. In 1970, just before Ms. Palinkas made her debut, the Amateur Athletic Union grappled with the controversial issue of banning padded bras for female runners, on the basis that a little enhancement allowed a woman to break the tape a millisecond faster than her un-augmented competitors. "Some of our flat-chested girls," said AAU secretary Marea Hartman, "have not been too pleased with some of the photo-finish decisions that have gone against them."[14]

In the summer of 1971, Jan Coelho of Florida's Hollywood Hills High School decided to try out for the football team. The Associated Press article describing Ms. Coelho's one-day quest was politically incorrect from stem to stern. The headline "Shapely Miss's Go at Football a Complete Bust" set the tone. "Jan Coelho went back to baking brownies Tuesday," the report began, before describing the "pretty brunette six footer ... a well-packed 157-pounder" and her admission that the rigors of high school football were far too great for a mere girl.[15]

Pat Palinkas was made of sterner stuff. Just a few years earlier, she had been

15. Hi-Ho, Hi Ho, to Bridgeport We Go

Pat Palinkas, the first woman to play professional football against men (courtesy Steve and Pat Palinkas).

Patricia Barzi, a University of Northern Illinois alumna who was in Germany teaching the children of American servicemen. She met a soldier named Steve Palinkas and they fell in love and were married—three times. First, they went to Basel, Switzerland and had a ceremony there. Then they returned to Germany and had a church wedding at the base chapel. "It was a very nice wedding at the officers' club," Pat recalled. "I rode from the church to the officers' club in a tank." Neither set of parents was able to attend the ceremonies in Germany or Switzerland, so when the couple returned to the States, the families gave them another reception in New Jersey. "I don't know if they believed we were really married," Pat said, "and my in-laws gave us a wonderful reception to confirm the fact that we were married, so we got married three times. If we get divorced, it will have to be three times."

The Palinkas, married beyond a shadow of a doubt, set up house in Florida and Pat got a job teaching school. Steve, whose college football career at the University of Tampa had been ended by injury, wanted to become an NFL kicker. He attended a few tryouts without success, and after one such outing the Atlanta Falcons suggested that, since he lived in Tampa, he play for the nearby Orlando Panthers to get some experience. In preparation for his tryout with the Panthers, Steve spent time practicing at the local high school field, with his wife serving as holder.

Steve went to Orlando and was terrible. "The guy they had holding the ball," he said, "I don't think he had ever done it before." Steve told the Panthers he could do much better if I had his own holder. "The holder is my wife," he said.

Steve and Pat returned and, as Steve had promised, he did much better. The Panthers had a photographer present and snapped a few pictures. The novelty of a woman on the field was a guaranteed gate attraction, something the financially strapped Panthers sorely needed. They signed both Steve and Pat, held a press conference and, in view of the fact that Pat would make history, announced that she would wear a microphone during her first game.

On August 15, the couple made their debut at the Tangerine Bowl against the Jets before a crowd of 12,440, a terrific showing for a preseason game. Since Pat was the only woman on the Panther squad, dressing facilities presented a problem. "They kind of pushed me off to the side and told me to close my eyes," she recalled. She also remembered being very nervous. The trainer asked Pat if she wanted a pill to calm her jitters. She demurred, but the doctor convinced her to take a valium tablet.

There were only three seconds left in the first half when the Palinkas made their first appearance, to attempt an extra point. Eight-year-old David D'Addario was standing on the sideline near Ray Mathews when the Jets' captain came over. He heard a strange conversation. "What do you want us to do?" Mathews was asked. "There's a woman on the field." "Crush her," Mathews replied.

Linebacker Wally Florence didn't need any encouragement. He was a tough kid from New Jersey who loved to intimidate people, on the field or off. "Before the game," said Joe Ginnetti, "Wally said, 'I'm going right after her. She's making a mockery of our game.'" "He was all pissed off," Roger Milici said. "He was going to hit her every chance he got."

The Panthers broke their huddle and Pat kneeled down seven yards behind the line of scrimmage, looked back at Steve, and said the three words Walter Cronkite, when reporting the story for CBS News, said might never again be heard on a football field. "You ready, honey?" Pat asked. Steve was ready, but Pat wasn't. The snap came back true but Pat, nervous, fumbled it. She tried to pick the ball up and set it up for the kick, but Florence burst through and blasted her straight on with a shot that snapped her head back. "Today," said Steve, "he would have gotten a fifteen-yard penalty because it was helmet-to-helmet. They showed the film and Pat's head went way back after the guy hit her. It was kind of cool."

The vicious shot jarred the ball loose. "My dear husband played the game the right way," Pat said. "He went after the ball while Wally went after me." The Panthers fell on the ball, the play was dead and so, many thought, was Pat Palinkas.

Fortunately, Pat was not injured, and got up and ran off the field. "I have to attribute it to that little half a valium pill," she said. "I just kind of went with the roll." "Sorry, team," Pat said when she returned to the sideline. She went to the locker room for the halftime break, took an aspirin for a slight headache, and came back out for the second half, which proved much better than the first. Two extra point attempts were held and kicked perfectly, and there was no more physical contact. The crowd loved it and roared its approval after each successful attempt.

After the game, which Orlando won 26–7, reporters asked Florence about his hard hit. "I tried to break her neck," he said. "I don't know what she's trying to prove. I'm out here trying to make a living and she's out there prancing around making folly with a man's game." Ray Mathews supported Florence. "I told the team to play as if she was a man," he said. "As far as I was concerned, I thought Florence's hit was a hell of a hit. To my estimation, this whole thing degrades football."[16]

Commissioner Iacovazzi said a few days after the game that he was reviewing Mrs. Palinkas' contract and consulting with league attorneys. "I hope she won't play during the season," he said. "I just don't feel it's right for a woman to be on the football field. It's just like putting her in a blast furnace."[17] He said he was concerned that Orlando was using the situation only to draw crowds which, considering the persistent financial difficulties of the ACFL, and the Panthers in particular, was probably not a bad idea.

While Iacovazzi had his doubts about letting Palinkas play in regular season games, he had no qualms about putting her in the blast furnace for exhibition games, as long as it put a few thousand more people in the stands. The following week, Pat held for two successful extra points in a 23–14 loss to the Norfolk Neptunes at Norfolk. The Neptunes estimated that they drew about 2,000 more fans than expected for an exhibition.

The Norfolk game was the last of Pat Palinkas' professional football career.

Steve, who'd injured his leg, was cut, and Pat was suspended for missing too many practices. In fact, she missed nearly all of them, for her role as the first professional woman football player had earned her national notoriety. Her story made the *New York Times* and other national publications, and she was making the rounds of television talk shows.

Pat appeared on *The Tonight Show*, *The Merv Griffin Show*, and *What's My Line?* and CBS aired a segment on the national evening news. She was on a talk show with Detroit Lion defensive tackle Alex Karras, whose antipathy toward male kickers was well known. What would he say about a woman? Pat did a couple of commercials and even had her own radio show in Tampa, in which she picked the winners of upcoming games. "I didn't do badly," she said recently, before Steve interjected to say that he provided considerable help.

Nineteen Seventy was the first year of *Monday Night Football* and, prior to the season, Pat was brought to New York for an interview with Keith Jackson and Howard Cosell, two members of the broadcast crew for the Monday telecasts. "They were worried to death," said Steve, "that women would not allow their husbands to watch Monday Night Football after watching all day Sunday, so they brought Pat in to help out with that."

With her busy schedule there was little time for football practice. There was little time for school either, but fortunately Pat's principal was a football fan and generous in granting time off for television appearances.

There was talk that Palinkas would return to the Panthers, but she never did. Orlando offered to send her to Hartford to play against the Knights if the home team paid for her travel expenses. Pete Savin was never afraid to spend money, but he took his football very seriously. His daughters were members of the Knights' cheerleading squad, and that was the only place on a football field their father thought women should be allowed. "We don't pay for opposing players—man or woman—to come to Hartford," he said. "I have too much respect for the game to use a gimmick like that just to add to the gate." So ended the football career of Pat Palinkas, who returned to her life as a Tampa teacher, a vocation she pursued until her recent retirement.

Meanwhile, the Jets began the regular season with Kennedy at quarterback. In their opener, they beat the Jersey Tigers, one of the new ACFL clubs, 16–14 on a pass from Kennedy to Warner with 28 seconds left.

During the week following the Jersey game, Theofiledes and Dowling were cut by the Jets and Patriots, respectively. A reporter asked Mathews about the possibility of signing Dowling. "He won't be back," the coach said curtly. Theofiledes was another matter. Bridgeport wanted him badly, but he had to clear waivers and, after the promise he'd shown in the Jets camp, there was a possibility that some NFL club would claim him.

15. Hi-Ho, Hi Ho, to Bridgeport We Go

The week after his great performance against the Giants, Theofiledes was given a start against the Vikings. A few days earlier, the veteran Parilli had decided to retire, removing one obstacle. Woodall, who played very little as a rookie in 1969, had done so poorly against the Giants that it appeared Theofiledes might have a chance to unseat him from the backup position. Ewbank said he wanted to see how the youngster adjusted to the pressure of starting, and minimized Theofiledes' performance against the Giants by stating that it was easier to come on in a relief role than to start.

The Viking game was a disaster. Theofiledes played the first quarter, completing just two of nine passes, with one interception. As Dave Anderson wrote in the *New York Times*, "One was intercepted and six more nearly were intercepted as the Viking defensive backs appeared to be his primary receivers."[18]

Theofiledes returned in the third quarter, fumbled on the Jets' three-yard line and threw another interception that was returned for a touchdown. His chances to make the roster were not helped when Woodall came in and threw a long touchdown pass, one of the few bright spots in a 52–21 defeat. "It was my time to shine," said Theofiledes recently, "but it was just one of those games. Sometimes you have a bad game. Our backs weren't picking up the blitzers and I was running for my life. I just couldn't get things going. And of course it was on national television."

If Theo and Woodall came out even, it was almost certain that Woodall would prevail, for he was a 6'4" "prospect" from Duke while Theo was a 5'9" minor leaguer from a small school. Ewbank spoke of how Theofiledes had to set up a yard deeper than normal and remarked, "There have only been two little quarterbacks who were really good—Frankie Albert and Eddie LeBaron, and he's not either one."[19]

"I remember Harry as a good athlete with a good arm," said Dockery, "but diminutive—small. He had trouble seeing over the line and that was a problem." "If you're throwing the ball down the field," said offensive lineman Charlie Tiblom, "height doesn't matter that much because by the time the ball leaves your hand it's at a 45 degree angle. But if you're throwing over the middle, then you run the risk of getting it blocked."

"I was always fighting my height," Theofiledes said. "They always said I was too small. I don't care if you're 6'2". You're still going to get a pass knocked down when the linemen come in with their hands up. Of course, when I got a pass knocked down they said I was too small. If a Namath gets a pass knocked down they say the lineman made a great defensive play. It's just perception. A lot of times you're throwing between the lanes. When the guys are rushing in you move around the pocket and look for an open receiver."

In addition to his height, Theofiledes faced a second obstacle, for he was a mobile quarterback in a stationary age. "They wanted you to be a pocket passer," he said of the Redskins. "They had Sonny Jurgensen and before him they had Norm Snead. They used to just drop back and sit in the pocket. They never scrambled because they couldn't run. When I scrambled they told me to sit in the pocket, but if nobody's open I'm not just going to stand there and go down. But the name of the game was to sit there and be a pocket passer."

Theofiledes did not play in the next exhibition game. Namath and Woodall split the quarterback duties, with the latter performing very poorly. Apparently it didn't matter, for Theofiledes was cut the next day. Later in the month, Bill Carroll commented on the unfairness of Theo's treatment, writing of "Weeb Ewbank, who somehow thinks that a man must be a physical giant to play quarterback. It's a good thing for Ewbank [who stood just 5'8"] that owners don't think the same thing about coaches."[20]

Theofiledes cleared waivers and signed with Bridgeport. With the star quarterback back in harness, Kennedy's days were numbered, for very few clubs could afford to carry two top quarterbacks. During the Jets' second game, which they lost to the Norfolk Neptunes, Kennedy started and was relieved late in the game by Theofiledes. It was clear that there was one too many Jet quarterbacks.

Just a couple of days later, there were no Jet quarterbacks. When the team reported for practice, neither Kennedy nor Theofiledes was present, and there was an air of mystery surrounding their absence. Kennedy, accurately deciphering the handwriting on the wall, had gone back to California and retired, and Theofiledes had gone home to Pennsylvania to iron out some personal issues. Salvati ran the offense through its paces.

Theofiledes returned from Pennsylvania and led the Jets on a winning streak. They beat Nick Cutro's Jersey Jays 14–9, coming from behind and thwarting a Jay drive at the six-yard line in the fourth quarter. They beat the winless Long Island Bulls handily to give them a 3–1 mark going into their first game with Hartford, which was tied for first with an identical 3–1 mark.

Before the Hartford game, the Jets solved a season-long kicking problem. Bob Anderson, who'd been the regular kicker for two years, was suspended for "not playing up to his ability." "No, no, that's not what happened," Anderson said recently. He'd suffered a mild concussion in an exhibition game after being hit from the blind side. "I came to the sideline and they said, 'can you see one finger, two fingers?' I couldn't see anything." Still, he went out to try a field goal shortly afterward and missed it. "I looked down to kick," he said, "and thought, I don't have enough feet to kick all the balls I see in front of me."

Mathews told Anderson that if he couldn't kick any better than that the fans were going to boo him. Most players say they don't hear the crowd, but Anderson felt connected to the fans. "That was like a death shot," he said of

15. Hi-Ho, Hi Ho, to Bridgeport We Go

Mathews' remark. "It may sound stupid but that meant more to me than the game itself. I was playing because I loved the game. The fans are going to boo me? The people who made it so great for me are going to boo me? The biggest fear for me was that I wasn't going to be able to do my best for the people who'd shown me so much love." He left a note for Mathews and never returned.

Lou Szuc kicked in exhibitions and was found wanting. Then came former Bull Carlos Mont' Alverne, who misfired on 20- and 13-yard attempts against the Jays. The fourth kicker of the season, and the best, was left-footed Paul Weidl, who'd also kicked for the Bulls.

For the second consecutive time, the Jets beat the Knights, this time by a 37–28 score, a nine point margin that would acquire overwhelming significance in a few weeks. Theofiledes threw for two touchdowns and Warner ran for two more. By the end of the evening, the 4–1 Jets were a game ahead of the Knights, the first time in their three-year history that anyone other than the Knights had led the Northern Division.

On October 9, the Jets lost to the undefeated Firebirds. The Jets staged a furious rally from a 30–9 deficit to close the gap to 30–26 and had the ball with less than two minutes to go. Theofiledes, under a strong rush, threw an interception and the Firebirds held on to win.

The following week, Bridgeport hosted the Orlando Panthers, minus Pat Palinkas, although her absence didn't stop the *Post-Telegram* from publishing a photo of her emerging from a pool clad in a white bikini. Wally Florence was no longer playing for the Jets, and was working as the deputy director for Action for Bridgeport Community Development.[21]

The Jets easily defeated the Panthers 31–7 before a Kennedy Stadium crowd of 8,642, nearly 4,000 less than had watched the Orlando exhibition when Pat made her debut. After a win the following week over the Long Island Bulls, the Jets held a two game lead with just four games to play.

Bridgeport	6	2	.750	—
Jersey Tigers	3	3	.500	2
Hartford	4	4	.500	2
Jersey Jays	4	4	.500	2
Long Island	0	6	.000	5

If the Jets could just split their last four games, they had an excellent chance of winning the division title. They couldn't do it, mainly because in their next game, against the Jersey Tigers, Theofiledes suffered a shoulder injury that would hamper him for the rest of his career. "They blitzed," he remembered, "and the halfback didn't pick it up. When he hit me he pinned my arms and we both landed on my shoulder. The shoulder wasn't broken but I busted all the bursa sacs."

Theofiledes kept playing, but he wasn't the same quarterback he'd been for the past two years. "I had to get cortisone shots before every game because it was so painful. I couldn't even lift my arm to comb my hair. But the cortisone shots helped get fluid into the joint. I did that for two or three years. It was painful to keep playing."

The Jets lost to the Tigers 35–26, setting up a key rematch with the Knights, who teetered on the verge of elimination. The Knights won by a 17–7 margin, throwing the Northern Division race into a state of confusion. Weidl missed a number of field goal attempts, including one from 44 yards that hit the upright and bounced back on the field. An inch to one side and it would have bounced through.

By winning their final two games, the Jets could have controlled their own destiny, but they lost their next game to the Jersey Jets, as Theofiledes continued to struggle with his sore shoulder. Finally, after it was too late, the Jets came through with a fourth quarter rally that resulted in a 17–9 win over Richmond in the finale. With the Knights and Jets tied for first with 7–5 records, the division title was decided in Hartford's favor in the manner described in detail in Chapter 14.

Commissioner Iacovazzi awarded the title to Hartford on the basis of the Knight's one point differential in the two games between the Knights and Jets. Had Weidl's field goal that hit the upright bounced through rather than caroming back, the Jets would have been champions. After threatening legal action, D'Addario acquiesced in the decision and, for the third consecutive year, the Jets finished second in their division with a 7–5 mark.

Darrick Warner finished sixth among ACFL rushers with 531 yards. Throughout the season the *Post-Telegram* touted the youngster as the leading candidate for the rookie of the year award, despite the fact that it did not appear that the league had ever awarded such an honor. On October 4, October 23, November 5, November 19 and November 20, the newspaper proclaimed that Warner was almost certain to win rookie of the year honors. Undaunted when the league, as usual, didn't name a rookie of the year, the *Post-Telegram* referred to Warner the following August as "last season's unofficial 'Rookie of the Year.'"[22]

The bizarre end to the 1970 season left a bitter taste. In July 1971, Al Young twice wrote in the *Post-Telegram* of the team's "second place" finish the previous year, using quotation marks on both occasions to indicate his sarcasm.[23] The Jets had come close, but Pete Savin had one championship and Hi-Ho D'Addario had none.

16

A Four-Team ACFL: The 1971 Hartford Knights and Bridgeport Jets

In 1970, the ACFL had been too big and too geographically dispersed. Air travel to Orlando and Indianapolis was an unmanageable burden for teams that were thinly stretched to begin with, and the New Jersey teams that couldn't make it in the Continental League weren't like to prosper under a different organization. During the months between the 1970 and 1971 season, several ACFL teams ceased operations.

After the smoke cleared, the league was left with just two Connecticut teams, the Knights and Jets, and two from Virginia, the Norfolk Neptunes and the Roanoke Buckskins. Each club would play the other four times, twice at home and twice on the road, to make up the league's 12-game schedule. Logistics were not ideal, for each of the four trips the Knights would make to Virginia was an eleven to twelve hour bus ride.

"A four team league," wrote Bill Lee, "may not seem like much at first glance, but if you examine the facts for a moment it takes on the appearance of a blessing in disguise."[24] Lee pointed out that the teams would be stronger and that head-to-head matchups were spaced at reasonable intervals so that fans would not tire of watching the same players week after week. "There are no weak sisters,"[25] added Commissioner Cosmo Iacovazzi, also attempting to put a happy face on a last gasp.

Fred Wallner, back for his fourth season with the Knights, boasted of the increased level of talent. "Many of the starters from past seasons," he said, "now have difficulty making the team." Wallner said the 1971 Knights were the best team he had ever coached. "We don't fool around with bad attitudes anymore," he said. "We get rid of trouble makers before they can hurt us."[26] Pete Savin declared that it was his "honest belief" that ACFL clubs could make a strong showing against some teams from the NFL.

The *Courant* pointed out that 1970 ACFL attendance was a record 429,553. The increase was attributable, of course, to the greater number of teams, and the *Courant* failed to explain why, if there was such an interest in ACFL football, only four teams remained from the eleven that began the 1970 campaign. The key to the survival of a minor league team was a deep pocket, and Pete Savin, Frank D'Addario, and Ed Gruber had more to do with their team's continuing existence than King Corcoran, Harry Theofiledes, or Tom Sherman.

Fortunately, two of the survivors were the Knights' natural rivals. The intrastate battle with the Jets would be renewed, and many of the Pennsylvania Firebirds had screwed their spikes back on and moved to Norfolk to play with the Neptunes. The Norfolk head coach was Ron Waller, former Firebird assistant, who brought along quarterbacks Corcoran and Jim Haynie and star running backs Claude Watts and John Land.

Benny Russell retired, but backup Tom Sherman was more than qualified to step into the starting role. At 6 feet even and 190 pounds, Sherman wasn't that big, and he didn't have a rocket for an arm. But he was a tough, smart quarterback, not quite good enough for the NFL, but a perfect fit for the Hartford Knights.

"I think Tom was probably the first guy," said fullback Don Abbey, "that I was exposed to who was a real student of the game. He did his homework all the time—spent the whole week studying."

Unlike Hank Washington, the strong armed quarterback who lacked finesse, Sherman knew how to throw a catchable pass. "Tom had an easy football to catch," said Abbey. "A lot of guys threw a real hard ball, but Tom was the easiest quarterback for me to catch because it was so soft when it hit your hands."

Quarterbacks must also be leaders, and virtually everyone who played with Sherman described him as the man they looked to in the huddle. "He didn't have to be a hoot n' holler guy," said Abbey, "and he wasn't. He was a leader." "Tommy Sherman acted like a quarterback," said Pete Anderson. "He was soft-spoken and did most of his talking on the field. He had a good presence."

"Tommy was very confident," said Joe Ginnetti. "He was very sure of himself and you always felt confident when he was handling the ball. He always found a way to win. Jimmy Corcoran was a legend, but Tommy Sherman was a much better quarterback."

"He was as tough as they come," added Charlie Tiblom. "He'd get hit—his helmet would be sideways and he'd just get up with blood coming out and he wouldn't say a thing. He'd get back in the huddle and call the next play."

Sherman is a likeable man with a dry, self-deprecating sense of humor. He described the predicament of Tom Moore, his quarterback coach when he played with the New York Stars of the WFL. "Tom had it pretty hard," Sherman said.

"He went from me to Terry Bradshaw, and then when he became offensive coordinator of the Colts he had Peyton Manning. So his career really went downhill after he coached me."

Tom Morris, an original Knight, would start at running back along with Abbey, a teammate of Sherman at Penn State. Abbey was a member of Joe Paterno's first class of recruits, and the two did not hit it off. "Joe just didn't like me and I didn't like Joe very much," Abbey said recently. "I came from a fairly affluent family and was a Rockefeller compared to most of the guys Joe recruited from the coal regions of Pennsylvania. I think Joe had a real issue with the fact that I drove a nicer car than he did and he thought my father had spoiled me. I'd gotten into Princeton but decided to take an athletic scholarship to Penn State. I don't know why he couldn't have respected me for that." Then Abbey laughed. "Or maybe he just didn't like me because I had a big mouth, which I did."

Abbey was a powerful runner, but by his senior year he was primarily a blocker for Lydell Mitchell and Franco Harris, and did his job so well that he was named to the All American blocking team. "That was thanks to Bear Bryant," Abbey said. "Bear called me the best blocking back in college football."

Paterno never called Abbey the best anything. "Joe was very authoritative," Abbey said. "Back then he was a screaming, yelling guy. In fairness to Joe, he was trying to find his game, too. He was kind of from the Vince Lombardi mold. Vince would scream and yell and everything but Vince always came in the locker room and gave you the molasses after he gave you the vinegar all day. Joe never gave the sweet part of it. He just always ragged you. And I *hated* it. I *hated* it."

Following his senior season, Abbey was drafted in the seventh round by the Dallas Cowboys, but decided to forgo professional football, threatening to sue the Cowboys over the negotiations. He went to the University of Connecticut Medical School instead and signed with the Knights, but injured a knee and did not play in 1970.

After a year out of football, Abbey found he really missed the game. The following summer he decided to go to Canada and try out for the Montreal Alouettes, but was cut late in camp. "I got in a fight with the captain of the team," he said, "who was a Canadian." Only a limited number of Americans were allowed on each roster, and the Alouettes were not about to use up one of those spots on Abbey. "I should have been a better politician and maybe I would have stayed around," he said.

Montreal's loss was Hartford's gain, for a couple of other players cut by Montreal came to the Knights, and convinced Abbey to do the same. "He came in," said linebacker Mark Proskine, "and thought he was a big shot. He came out of the backfield in practice one night and I just knocked his head off. He was a good-looking guy and kind of full of himself, so I welcomed him to the Hartford Knights."

When I asked Abbey about the incident he laughed. "I don't remember it," he said, "but if it happened it must have been a cheap shot. And," he added, "I don't remember Proskine being all-league [as Abbey was]."

Abbey stepped into the Hartford lineup and became one of the most feared runners in the league. "He was a real strong, physical player," said Sherman. "He was a straight-liner and hard to tackle because he was so strong in the legs." "The guy was so big," said Tiblom, "and so fast. His shoulders were wide and he had big legs. He was about 6'2" and he could hit. When he hit you he let you know it. He could guarantee some yards."

"I remember him dragging two, three, or four guys five or six yards down the field," added Norm Davidson. "He was a moose." By the end of the season, Abbey was nearly as big as a moose. "My final game," he said, "I played fullback at 287."

The Knights also signed another "name" player, All American linebacker Bob Olson of Notre Dame. Olson had been the defensive co-captain of the Irish for two seasons, led the team in tackles for three straight years, and set a career record with 304 tackles. He was voted the outstanding defensive player of the 1970 Cotton Bowl and drafted in the fifth round by the Boston Patriots.

During Boston's third exhibition game, while running down on kickoff coverage, Olson was hit on his blind side. The resulting knee injury ended his 1970 season. Olson was unable to regain his mobility following surgery, and was released early in the Patriots' 1971 camp. "His knee injury has merely delayed his major league career," Wallner said. "Olson only needs experience to become a great NFL player."[27]

Olson had two handicaps. He had a damaged knee, and he was a bit short for a professional linebacker. "He was built like a fire hydrant," said Joe Ginnetti, "but was quick at getting to the hole. I could block him because he was shorter and a bit smaller than me but he was very quick to the hole." "If he was three inches taller," said Norm Davidson, "he might have been in the NFL."

"Olson could hit as hard as anybody," said Tiblom. "One day we were running half speed drills with the forearm dummies, and he went full speed like he was in a game. I hit the bag and was just getting out of the way of the back when he came in, filled the hole, lowered down, lifted me up, and knocked me completely on my ass." On another occasion, Tiblom and Olson had a major altercation during practice when Tiblom objected to Olson's aggressiveness.

Another prominent new Knight was cornerback Marv Pettaway, a dynamic 5'7" 160 pounder who was a breakaway threat on kick returns. Pettaway, a Los Angeles City College product, played with the Las Vegas Cowboys of the Continental League for two years, and was named MVP of the Western Division in

1969. He joined the Orlando Panthers in 1970 and led the league in interceptions and punt returns.

"Marv Pettaway was the most electric and exciting football player I've ever seen," said Davidson. "I had never seen anybody who could stop as fast as he could stop and change direction. He was just electric to watch. Even though he was your teammate, you wanted to see every kickoff and every punt return because there was no telling when he would break one. He was very, very exciting and I think his size made him even more exciting." As proof of his dynamic persona, Pettaway wore number zero.

"He was one of the best football players I've ever seen," said Tiblom. "He was one of the best basketball players I'd ever seen. He was so fast and quick it was ungodly. I don't understand why he didn't make it in the pros."

Pettaway was also somewhat of a character. Elaine Savin remembered the time he approached her husband and said he might need to borrow some money. He had "something in the fire" but if that didn't work out he would be back. "He came back two days later and told Pete he was going to need the loan because he hadn't won the lottery. That was his other plan."

Joining Pettaway in the defensive backfield was Bill Fisher, a fast man with good size (6'4" and 205 pounds) who'd been bouncing around the minor leagues for a few years. Fisher, a graduate of Cal State-Northridge, was a unique individual within the world of football. During his time with the Jersey Tigers, his teammates nicknamed him "J.C." because of his beard and shoulder length hair.

Fisher had signed with Denver as a free agent in 1969, the same year Tom Rowland spent time in the Bronco camp. Rowland and Fisher learned the same lesson. Denver brought armies of players to camp, and released most of them after a cursory look. When the Broncos cut him loose, Fisher hooked up with the Las Vegas Cowboys of the Continental League. In addition to his football duties, Fisher, who had a degree in journalism, wrote press releases and worked on the game program.

Fisher was a California boy whose interests included writing poetry and spending time on the beach, and Las Vegas was not his type of city. "He looked like a California kid," said linebacker Ken Blasser, "with the long hair and the beads around the collar."

When the Continental League folded, Fisher signed with the Orlando Panthers, but before the season started, he was traded to Jersey, where he had a good year. Jersey coach Ken Carpenter had a connection in Houston and recommended that the Oilers sign Fisher and invite him to camp. That summer was Fisher's best chance to make an NFL roster. He survived one cut after another, but just before the regular season began, the Oilers traded for a veteran safety and Fisher was released.

Fisher had an interesting welcome to Hartford. When he arrived, the Knights placed him temporarily in an old three story house in the suburbs. At that time, an escaped convict from Massachusetts, whose description matched Fisher's, was believed to be in the area. One of the neighbors saw Fisher entering the home, called the police, and when Fisher stepped out for a bite to eat, he was confronted by about ten FBI plainclothesmen pointing guns in his face. "Scared the hell out of me," Fisher said, but he managed to convince the officers he was not the man they were seeking.[28]

With so many regular season games against ACFL opponents, the Knights did not want to bring any of them to Hartford for exhibitions, and therefore planned to prepare for the season with two games against the Twin City Chiefs of the Eastern League. The Twin cities were Fitchburg and Leonminster, Massachusetts, towns reminiscent of the ACFL franchises of the arly '60s.

The Chiefs were no match for the Knights, and didn't even give them a good workout. After Hartford won the first game 66–7, the second game was cancelled. The score was not even indicative of the disparity between the two clubs, for Wallner eased off the accelerator when he saw how helpless the Chiefs were against his offense, which gained the remarkable total of 512 yards on the ground. Tom Morris had 134 yards on just six carries. "We thought they were a better team," Wallner said afterward.[29]

The Knights started the regular season by defeating Roanoke 24–7, in what Wallner deemed "the best opening game performance ever."[30] Pettaway lived up to his billing, recovering a fumble and running a punt back 57 yards in a twisting, elusive scamper. The following week's home opener was less successful, as the Knights lost to Bridgeport 21–15, before 7,400 fans at Dillon Stadium.

The Knights played a sloppy game against the Jets. Sherman threw two interceptions, there were three lost fumbles, and new kicker Kevin Watts missed two field goals and two extra points. Where was Wes Bean, who'd missed so many extra points during the past three years? He was in a Bridgeport uniform, and kicked three without a miss.

In each of their first three years in the ACFL, Bridgeport lost five games and finished in second place. In 1971 they got out of that rut, but not in the manner Frank D'Addario hoped they would. After the disappointing finish to the 1970 season, Hi Ho had high hopes for 1971. In May, Harry Theofiledes signed with the Edmonton Eskimos of the Canadian League, but his shoulder was still troubling him, he had recently married, and he wanted to return to the States. By July, he was back in Bridgeport for a third season.

Unfortunately, most of the offensive line did not return, which made for a long, difficult season for the veteran quarterback. Guard Roy Kirksey earned a spot on the New York Jet roster and Harvey Palmore quit, as did a number of other veterans, in the wake of a contract dispute in early August.

D'Addario announced that no player would be allowed to take part in scrimmages or practices until they signed a contract. That did not seem particularly problematic, but in light of the financial troubles that had led to the demise of so many teams, those contracts were for less money than in previous seasons. The prospect of lower paychecks led to the departure of veterans like Palmore, Dick Janes, Waide Robinson, and punter Bill Staake. Only all-star center Joe Ginnetti returned on the offensive line. Staake's exit left Ray Mathews without a punter, a weakness that would plague the Jets all season.

Despite the personnel shortages, the Jets got off to a good start, and after four games were tied with the Norfolk Neptunes for first place with a 3–1 mark. Two of the wins were at the expense of the Knights, exciting games that were not decided until the final moments.

The Knights had defeated the Neptunes, featuring so many former Firebirds, 44–13 on September 11. The defense intercepted four Corcoran passes, two by Marv Pettaway. After the game, Wallner said he was "tickled pink." "This is the first time in a while," he said, "that we could match up with them physically."[31]

One of the Hartford touchdowns was an 82-yard pass from Sherman to Dwight Tucker, who was a first cousin of O.J. Simpson.[32] Tucker was a typical ACFL player— a man with a great talent (a 4.4 clocking in the 40-yard dash) and a few shortcomings (a tendency to drop passes being the most problematic), who was trying to learn a new position.

The Norfolk game also marked the debut of kicker Norm Davidson, a former Central Connecticut soccer-style booter who kicked three short field goals and was perfect on five extra point attempts. Davidson weighed only about 150 pounds, and didn't have the spectacular range of Wes Bean, but he didn't misfire on extra points and was consistent at medium distance.

Davidson was an all-around athlete who was a baseball player and all–American swimmer at Central. He'd played soccer in high school but Central didn't have a soccer team. Davidson became friends with a number of football players, and was in the stands for the final game of his sophomore season. On that day Central lost to Southern Connecticut, partly because their kicker missed three field goals.

Davidson thought he could do better and went to see coach Bill Loika, who gave him a bag of old footballs, told him to practice all summer and come back and try out in the fall. Davidson came from a big family, and was always able to recruit a brother or sister to hold for him and shag the balls. He practiced diligently and made the team for his junior season.

During Davidson's first year, he didn't make a field goal until the final game, when his two placements provided the winning margin in a victory that snapped a 14-game losing streak against arch-rival Southern Connecticut. His senior year, he made eight field goals, a single season school record (his total of ten career field goals was also a record). Davidson didn't have a lot of football experience, but thought that if he could show something with the Knights he might eventually get a shot at the NFL.

During the second loss to Bridgeport, the injury bug that would plague the Knights all season hit for the first time. Pettaway left the game with a charley horse, linebacker Mark Proskine broke his hand, and Bob Olson suffered a possible shoulder separation. Fortunately, replacements were available, for by that time NFL teams were making their final cuts. The Knights added five players, including former Penn State linebacker Jim Kates, a 12th round pick of the Bills in 1970, and offensive tackle John Koehler, a third round draft choice of the Denver Broncos.

The Knights began a long winning streak with a victory over the Roanoke Buckskins. As in 1968, they were propelled by a strong ground attack and a stingy defense. The steady veteran Morris gained 145 yards against the Buckskins and took over the league lead from Abbey with 423 yards and a flashy 6.0 average per carry. Davidson, not known for long distance field goals, booted a 48-yarder. In three games he'd connected on six field goals and eleven extra points without a miss. For the fifth time in as many games, the defense held the opposition to less than 100 yards rushing. Kates, playing with just two days of practice, was outstanding.

On October 2, the Knights ventured to Norfolk to take on the Neptunes, who were in first place with a 4–1 record. The Knights were a game behind at 3–2. The Oyster Bowl was drenched from the effects of Hurricane Ginger, which dumped six inches of rain on Norfolk over three days. Neither team could get traction in the mud, so the Knights relied on play action passes and straight ahead running. The Hartford defense held Corcoran to four completions and the Neptune offense to just 99 yards overall. Norfolk's only score in a 17–6 loss came on a 95-yard kickoff return.

Although Davidson missed two field goals on the muddy turf, he managed to kick a 41-yarder. The Knights had the best kicking tandem in the ACFL, with Davison and newly-signed punter Terry Swanson, a 27-year-old who played for the Patriots for two seasons and spent part of another with the Bengals. Swanson had played at the University of Massachusetts with Hartford safety Bob Ellis, and told Ellis he'd be interested in playing for the Knights. "Just a great recruiting job," said Wallner.[33]

After the win at Norfolk, the Knights and Neptunes were tied for first place, with Bridgeport a game behind. Roanoke (1–5) was out of the race. The Knights beat the hapless Buckskins 16–0 the next week, again playing in a rain drenched Virginia city, this time in front of just 200 hardy souls. The Knights slogged manfully through the mud, riding three Davidson field goals and 207 rushing yards to victory. Abbey now led the league with 538 yards and Morris was second with 470. It was like 1968 with Meeks and Hubbard.

Morris was a steady runner in his fourth season with the Knights, one of the few remaining veterans from the 1968 squad. "He was strong and well built," said John Sponheimer. "Not a speed burner but a real tough nut." Morris had no NFL aspirations, and had a good job at Hartford Hospital.

While the Knights were in the midst of a winning streak, the Jets were moving in the opposite direction. Bridgeport's fifth game was a battle for first place against the Neptunes, with each team entering the game with a 3-1 mark. The Jets led 10–7 midway through the third period before the roof fell in on the game and, as it turned out, the season. During the last 23 minutes, the Neptunes scored 23 points while the Jets scored none.

Norfolk's Ron Waller was an innovative coach, and Ray Mathews believed some of his inventions were on the nether side of ACFL rules. Waller was fond of an "end around" play in which a wide receiver went in motion prior to the snap, took a handoff and swept the opposite end. Mathews claimed that the end lined up on the line of scrimmage and was therefore illegally in motion, for only backs could move before the ball was snapped. He said he noticed the play on game films and had alerted the officials in advance, but they allowed Norfolk to run the play without calling a penalty.

The Neptunes employed the play twice against the Jets and gained substantial yardage each time. Mathews did not say why, since he knew the Neptunes ran the play, he did not use the end's motion as a key and stop it, nor did he say how two non-scoring plays caused a twenty point defeat. Moreover, he filed his protest with somewhat less than clean hands, for many at the game said both teams exceeded roster limits by dressing extra taxi squadders from the Jets and Eagles.

Waller said that if Iacovazzi ruled against him, he would withdraw the Neptunes from the ACFL. Mathews said he filed the protest "just to see what type of league this really is,"[34] but he needn't have asked. The ACFL was a struggling league, one that couldn't afford to lose a franchise, and bickering was not the best way to promote its welfare. Iacovazzi said a review of the game film confirmed Mathews' claim, but he didn't think the missed calls had an impact on the final result. He suspended all six officials but allowed the result to stand.

The following week, the Jets lost in the final minutes to Roanoke, the Buckskins' first win of the year. At 3–3, the Jets were just a game behind Norfolk and

Hartford, but halfway through the season, several weaknesses had become obvious. First, the Jets could not run the ball. They'd averaged just 58 yards per game on the ground, last in the league and well behind the Knights' league leading 178 yards a game. The inexperienced offensive line was not opening holes, forcing Theofiledes to rely on his arm. His mobility compensated for the pass blocking deficiencies but, knowing the Jets had to throw the ball, opposing defenses dropped off and intercepted Theofiledes much too frequently.

Kicking was another weak point. Wes Bean began the season in Bridgeport, after being released by the New York Jets. Bean had never been a terribly accurate kicker, and he was worse than ever in 1971. He missed several field goal attempts in a 10–7 overtime loss in the opening game, five of six in another and abruptly quit, leaving the field goal chores to left-footed soccer stylist Lou Szuc.

Bean's replacement by Szuc opened up a roster spot, for ACFL clubs were allowed a 34th player who could only serve as a kicking specialist. The designated player wore a special jersey with KS on it and could not play another position.

Szuc was adequate, but the Bridgeport punters were not. Bean had punted as poorly as he kicked field goals. After he left, Mathews tried a number of others, none of whom was successful and many of whom contributed directly to losses. In a game against Norfolk, the Jets averaged a pathetic 22 yards on five first half punts, which repeatedly provided the Neptunes with excellent field position.

Against Hartford, Mathews tried Rick Washington, who got off a 16-yard boot, Szuc, who fumbled a snap and was tackled for a loss, and Jeff Steinberger, whose punt went all of 18 yards. The following week, one of Steinberger's punts went just 9 yards, leading to the first Norfolk touchdown. "Bridgeport's poor punting," opined the *Post-Telegram*, "has been one of the prime factors in the late season swoon."[35]

On their third try of the season, the Knights finally beat the Jets, in front of the largest crowd of the season (9,300) at Dillon Stadium. The Knights piled up 251 yards on the ground, the defense sacked Theofiledes four times, and the final score was 37–21.

The battle for the league lead between the Knights and Neptunes, each with 6–2 records, drew an even larger crowd (9,800) the following week. The two teams put on a good show. After Davidson kicked a 42-yard field goal in the first quarter, Norfolk lineman Otis Sistrunk recovered Abbey's fumble, which led to a Norfolk touchdown.[36]

Sistrunk was the most dominant and feared lineman in the ACFL, and would later have a seven-year career with the Oakland Raiders. "Sistrunk was big, fast, and strong, real strong," said Charlie Tiblom, "and he was *mean*."

"I played against Sistrunk for three years," said Jim Murphy, "and he had a cast on his arm for three years. It turned out he never had a broken arm. He just used that cast to beat the hell out of you." "I lined up against him on the punt team," said Ken Blasser. "Instead of letting me try to block him, he just swung and hit me in the side of the head. I went up the field sideways. The next time we lined up I put my hands up like a boxer."

Joe Ginnetti had another plan, one that was equally ineffective. "We would double team Sistrunk," he said, "and I would end up pass blocking him. I'd try to chop his legs out from under him, which was legal back then. He got a little tired of me doing that and blindsided me on a punt. He hit me so hard I walked back to the other team's bench. I didn't chop block him after that."

With Hartford trailing 12–9, Norfolk's Ron Holliday, who'd tormented the Knights in the Snow Bowl the previous December, carried on a reverse and had the ball shaken loose on his own 20 yard line. Hartford safety Tony Stawartz scooped the ball up and ran it in for the winning touchdown.

The Knights defense, which held the Neptunes to a single first down in the second half, sealed the victory with two fourth quarter interceptions, one by Stawartz. Wallner called the 16–12 win "the best overall hitting and defensive game I have ever seen in Atlantic Coast Football play."[37] The Neptunes backfield tandem of John Land and Claude Watts had been held to just 57 yards.

The Knights gained sole possession of first place with a 7–2 mark, one game ahead of the Neptunes and, with three wins over Norfolk, control of the tie-breaker. It appeared that Norfolk, son of the Firebirds, and Hartford would meet in the ACFL title game.

The Knights solidified their hold on first place by stomping Bridgeport 41–7 and beating the last place Buckskins 19–7. After a 3–1 start, the Jets lost seven of their last eight games. For the season, the team averaged a pathetic 51 rushing yards per game while yielding 159, the worst run defense in the league. The passing offense gained more yards than any other team, but the yardage was the product of a non-existent running game and the fact that the Jets were always behind. Theofiledes led the league in passing yards with 2,151 but also in interceptions with 26, nine more than his nearest competitor.

As the Jets staggered toward the finish line, disquieting rumors began floating around Bridgeport. In late October, previewing a game against the Knights, Bill Carroll, who worked for the Jets as well as the *Post-Telegram*, titled his article "Jets-Knights Game Could Be Last Ever." Although D'Addario had not announced a decision on 1972, Carroll wrote "it is widely believed that the Jets will not operate next year."[38]

During his first two years, D'Addario had lost money, but the losses were mitigated by subsidies from the New York Jets totaling $35,000 in 1968 and $45,000 in 1969. When the NFL distanced itself from the minor leagues in 1970, the subsidy disappeared and D'Addario was forced to carry the salary budget (estimated at $100,000 annually) and his other operating expenses without assistance. Carroll estimated that D'Addario lost $150,000 during his first three years and was facing another sizable deficit in 1971.

D'Addario always knew he needed corporate support and worked mightily to get it. "He went to all the suppliers in his rolodex," said his son David, "and put a lot of pressure on people to buy box seats. They put the arm on everybody—their bankers, their suppliers, their customers. I remember my father saying, 'Dammit, I'm buying liquid asphalt from him. You make damn sure he puts an ad in the program and buys some box seats.'"

But by the end of the 1971 season, according to Carroll, Hi Ho had reached the end of the road. "Frank has decided he has had enough," Carroll said. "He has become disillusioned with the league and has not received good response from the major league teams this season. No one else wants to pay the bills for this team and this is the last game in Bridgeport...."[39] So it seems that unless some kind of miracle happens the Bridgeport football fan will not have an Atlantic Coast Football League team to cheer for next season."[40]

Pete Savin denied the rumors. "I talked with Frank D'Addario before the game," he said, "and he gave no indication of giving up the team."[41] A couple of days later, Bruce Berlet of the *Courant* spoke with D'Addario, who said, "I will just have to re-evaluate the situation when the season is over."[42]

In 1968, the Jets led the league with 61,201 admissions, but by 1971, attendance had dropped in half. The opening game was played in a rainstorm and attracted less than 1,000. One of D'Addario's initiatives to raise revenue had been a game between the rookies of the New York Jets and the Hi-Ho Jets, played at Kennedy Stadium on July 31. The game was a good one, and New York brought a number of veterans to supplement the rookies. Unfortunately, the weather was not good, and instead of a capacity crowd, the teams drew 8,300, which netted only about $5,000.

The final home game, against the Knights, drew 6,500, a little better than average but not enough to encourage D'Addario if he still had an open mind. His team didn't provide those who did attend with a very good show, losing a one-sided 41–7 game. Theofiledes and backup Les Obie threw five interceptions which, combined with the Jets' poor punting, left the club in consistently poor field position.

After the loss to the Knights, the Jets had two games remaining, one in each of the Virginia cities. They played respectably in Norfolk, losing 31–28, but completely fell apart in the finale at Roanoke. Practices the week before the Roanoke game had been desultory, and only 21 players showed up for the final session. Mathews said, "I doubt whether they'll be a team here next season."[43]

The Jets played like a team on death row, losing 53–14 to the 1–10 Buckskins. "The Bridgeport Jets saved their worst performance in history for their last," Carroll wrote.[44] The only Jet touchdowns came on a 95-yard kickoff return by Dock Mosley (his second TD return of the season) and a 35-yard return of an intercepted pass by captain Jim Quinn. Otherwise, it was the same old story of short punts, turnovers, and an impotent running attack. The Jets 4–8 record was the worst in their history, as was home attendance, and all factors pointed toward confirmation of Carroll's hypothesis that the Jets would not play in 1972.

Hartford and Norfolk, clearly the two best teams in the league, would face off for the ACFL championship on November 20, and for the fourth consecutive year the title game would take place at Dillon Stadium. It had originally been scheduled for Norfolk, but there was a high school championship game in Foreman Field on November 19, and if the weather was unfavorable, the game would be postponed until the following day. Norfolk's new civic center was to have its grand opening the same weekend, and Commissioner Iacovazzi thought the conflict would depress the crowd for a Hartford-Norfolk match.

The Knights lost the regular season finale to the Neptunes and, more importantly, suffered a number of key injuries that crippled the team for the championship contest. In the Roanoke game that preceded the finale, linebacker Jim Kates had suffered a broken leg and tight end Dan Andrews sprained his ankle badly. Fullback Pete Jilleba hyper-extended his elbow and guard Angelo Loukas injured his knee.

In the final game of the regular season, end Jay Dixon left with a leg injury. Pete Anderson hurt his shoulder. By the end of the evening, veteran offensive tackle Dennis Fitzgibbons was playing defense. Bob Olson was carried off the field on a stretcher with damaged knee cartilage, and had surgery the next day, putting a premature end to what had been a very promising career. "I was in the game that ended his career," said Ken Blasser. "He was in a pileup and he let out a deathly scream. I'll never forget it because I never heard a guy scream so painfully. It was awful."

With nearly half the roster in sick bay, the Knights' prospects looked bleak. Wallner, in the time-honored coaching tradition, refused to use the injuries as an alibi. "We know what we have to do," he said a few days before the championship game. "We'll just regroup when we get the doctor's report Tuesday, and work like hell to get some of the new fellas ready."[45]

With all three Hartford starting linebackers out of action, the Knights signed former University of Connecticut player Ralph Tiner, just out of the service, and Pete Quackenbush, who played with the club the previous two seasons. Offensive players worked on defense and vice versa.

There were simply too many "new fellas" to compete with the seasoned old Firebirds. The Knights made a valiant effort, and as most expected the game was a hard-hitting affair. As few expected, it was filled with mistakes. The two teams combined for a remarkable 236 yards in penalties, 144 by Norfolk.

Once again, Ron Holliday proved the Knights' undoing. He caught a touchdown pass from Corcoran early in the second period that gave the Neptunes a 7–3 advantage. Marv Pettaway returned the ensuing kickoff 98 yards to put the Knights ahead 10–7, but Corcoran and Holliday hooked up again from 44 yards and Norfolk led 14–10 at intermission. Davidson's field goal on the second play of the fourth quarter brought his club to within a single point, but three Hartford fumbles led to a Norfolk touchdown and a field goal, which made the final score 24–13.

The Norfolk defense kept the Knights bottled up all night, as they managed just 143 yards in total offense. "It was a sound beating," said Sherman. He was constantly under pressure and managed to complete just nine passes in 26 attempts. "We just weren't able to handle those four guys," Wallner said after the game. Those four guys were Sistrunk, ("We didn't have anybody who could even get in his way," said Sherman), Roger Anderson, who spent three and a half years with the New York Giants, former Eagle tackle Bill Stetz, and minor league veteran Tom Davis.

Stetz was an interesting blend of peace-loving hippie and maniacal football player. "If there had been a bouncer at Woodstock," said Steve Sabol, "he would have looked like Bill Stetz." Stetz had long hair, lived in a commune outside of Pottstown, and operated a head shop. "Fred Wallner always said he looked like a girl," recalled Bob Shemeth, "but, boy, every time we played them he was a one-man wrecking crew. He was probably the toughest fellow I ever played against."

Stetz played two games for the Eagles in 1967, but was better suited for the more tolerant world of the minor leagues, where he could wear his hair long and be himself. He said he was generally against violence, but not in a football game, for the controlled violence of football provided a way for players to unwind and relieve their tension.

They're more understanding now," Stetz told NFL Films in 2000. "They let anyone play. What was so bad about us? Why couldn't I play with long hair? Why couldn't Joe [Blake] play? He could have gone to drug counseling."

When summarizing the season, Wallner sounded like Hartford Knights opponents from 1968 and 1969. He said that Norfolk had destroyed the competitive balance of the league. "Not to sound like a poor loser," he said, "but if minor league football is to be balanced, there has to be a change down there."[46]

Although they lost the championship game for the third season in a row, it had been a good season for the Knights. Wallner was named ACFL coach of the year. Davidson led the league in scoring with 85 points and was named rookie of the year. He didn't miss an extra point all season and added 20 field goals. Abbey finished second in rushing to Norfolk veteran Claude Watts with 754 yards and Morris was third with 707 yards. Swanson led the league in punting with a 41.6 yard average and Pettaway led in kickoff returns. Nine Knights were named to the all star team.

As was always the case with minor leagues, the biggest question following the season was: what next? The four team league, with its repetitive matchups and long bus rides between Virginia and Connecticut, had not been viable. The Jets were talking of folding their tent. If the ACFL couldn't add teams, it probably wouldn't operate in 1972, and the prospect of adding financially solvent teams was slim.

17

A Perfect Season in an Imperfect League: The 1972 Hartford Knights

In 1970 there had been too many teams in the Atlantic Coast Football League, and in 1971 too few. In 1972 there were none. When the ACFL contracted to four teams, the intention had been to eventually add franchises. After a meeting of the owners on the morning of the 1971 championship game, Commissioner Iacovazzi indicated that eight cities, four of which appeared to be viable, were interested in joining the ACFL. In May 1972, the *Post-Telegram* reported, "Don't be surprised if the Bridgeport Jets are back in business this fall. Rumors have a four-team league again, with Bridgeport, Hartford, Boston, and Westchester competing."[1] On the last day of May, however, Iacovazzi announced that the ACFL would not operate in 1972.

Although his league had deserted him, Pete Savin had no intention of missing a year of football, and entered his Knights in the Seaboard Professional Football League, an eight-team circuit comprised of franchises in smaller cities and towns in Pennsylvania, Maryland, New York, and Virginia.

The Seaboard Football League was formed in 1971, with five teams from the Interstate Football League, two from the Mason-Dixon Football League, and one independent team. Controversy arose during the SFL's maiden season when some clubs, in violation of league rules, began paying their players. Some paid twenty dollars a game and others twenty for a win and ten for a loss. At a league meeting, when the non-paying teams protested, a nasty shouting match ensued that created a bitter division between the owners.

Prior to the 1972 season, the Frederick Falcons, citing the violations of the salary rule, the heavy travel expenses created by a geographically dispersed circuit, and the $13,000 they'd lost in 1971, left the Seaboard League to return to the Interstate League. The Carroll County Chargers followed suit. Red Hipp, owner of the Hagerstown Bears, claimed the rules had not been violated to any greater extent than they had been in the IFL. "I think they're afraid they couldn't compete," he said of the Falcons.[2]

In 1972, there would be no more under the table payments. The league's name was changed to the Seaboard Professional Football League and several new teams were added. Among them were the Long Island Chiefs, undefeated champions of the Eastern Football League in 1971, the Portsmouth Bucs, and the Hartford Knights. The Ridley Township Knights moved from Eddystone to Aston, Pennsylvania, where they would have better facilities. "We've got to be now recognized," said Hipp, "as the strongest minor football league in the country."[3]

The teams lined up as follows for the 1972 season:

Northern Division	Southern Division
Hartford	Hagerstown
Chambersburg	Aston
Northumberland	Conshohocken
Long Island	Portsmouth

Most of the Seaboard League cities were unfamiliar to Hartford fans. The defending league champions, the Northumberland Coal Crackers, played in Kulpmont, a town of about 4,000 residents located in east central Pennsylvania. Before the Knights' first visit, a reporter asked Pete Savin where Kulpmont was. "It's located somewhere near…" Savin replied and trailed off, looking around for help. He laughed and said he would stick close to coach Nick Cutro, who'd been there before.

Not a lot had happened in Kulpmont, and it didn't have many famous sons. The most prominent former residents Wikipedia could rustle up were Sam Brazinsky, who played five games in the AAFC in 1946, Joe Baksi, a heavyweight boxing contender in the 1940s, and Eleanor Bach, a New York astrologer known as "Mother of the Asteroids." About a month into the 1972 season, the Coal Crackers also became former residents, searching for a decent field and a fan base.

Not much was rockin' in Conshohocken, a Philadelphia suburb known locally as Conshy, which had a population of about 10,000. The name was derived from the Lenape Indian phrase "Gueno-sheiki-hacking" meaning "pleasant valley."[4] After the Knights played there, they thought that the Lenape phrase for "third rate field covered with broken glass," whatever that might be, was a better appellation. "It was like a cow field," said Norm Davidson. "It was the worst field I ever played on. There were divots and bumps and almost no grass. I remember the guys complaining about the dirt because it was so hard to land on."

Kulpmont and Conshohocken had probably the worst fields in the SPFL, while the New York Chiefs played on the artificial turf of Hofstra University, undoubtedly the best stadium in the league. Still, turf was in its early days and had some shortcomings. "I didn't like it," said quarterback Seiki Murono, "because we'd be forever getting brush burns and once you got one, it stayed with you the entire season. The turf didn't give like dirt did, so there was a greater tendency to turn your ankle and get abrasions on your arms and legs that were quite painful and slow to heal."

The Aston Knights had relocated from Eddystone to Sun Valley High and thus upgraded to a facility that had two locker rooms. No longer did they have to bus opposing teams to Ridley Park or Widener College to use the showers. They had a public address system at Sun Valley, better lighting, and rest rooms for the fans. Even so, the "stadium" had a capacity of just 4,000, and an "upgrade" to a high school field spoke to the caliber of SPFL facilities.

For the first time in their history, the Knights would not be led by Fred Wallner, who took an assistant coaching job with the Montreal Alouettes of the Canadian League. The new Hartford coach was Nick Cutro, formerly of the Jersey Giants and Jets, Waterbury Orbits, and Bridgeport Jets, and almost a polar opposite of Wallner.

Wallner was intense, deadly serious, and a disciple of conservative football. His manner with the press was cooperative but guarded and predictable. "Wallner had all the clichés," said the *Hartford Times'* Howie Holcomb. "We put our pants on one leg at a time like everybody else and we play them one game at a time. He was a very nice guy but you never knew too much about Fred Wallner. He never really told you anything."

Cutro was an altogether different breed of cat. "He was like an Italian Buddy Hackett," said Holcomb. "He was short and round and funny and every other remark he made was a wisecrack. And he'd tell you anything." "Nick was just a happy-go-lucky little round Italian who told jokes all the time," said Bruce Berlet of the *Courant*. "He was a kick," said Arnold Dean, "a lot of fun. We had a good time with him."

Cutro was full of entertaining stories, like the one about the Jersey game films. "On Monday nights," he said, "we used to show the film in the locker room. My brother-in-law Carmine was the cameraman." One week Cutro told Carmine to splice a picture of a topless Marilyn Monroe into the film. That happened to be the night one of the priests Cutro had known while coaching at St. Mary's came to visit. "He's sitting in the audience," said Cutro, "and all of a sudden on the screen comes Marilyn Monroe posing with her tits out. He said, 'Is this part of practice?' I said, 'Yeah, it's part of their motivation.'"

And what about the tale of the disappearing player? Just before the opening game in Jersey one year, Cutro was approached by his equipment manager who told him one of the players had received a phone call informing him his wife had been killed in an auto accident in South Carolina. Cutro arranged for the police to rush him to the airport, and didn't hear from him for two weeks. "Then," he said, "I get a call from—guess who— his wife. I said, 'Son of a bitch, here's this kid I trusted and instead of being in South Carolina, he's still in Jersey City fooling around.' But that's the kind of kids I had to deal with."

Once when he was coaching in Hartford, Cutro was stopped by the police for speeding. As the officer was writing the ticket, Cutro engaged him in conversation and asked how his radar device worked. The officer showed it to him and the coach promptly used it to clock one of his players driving by over the limit.

Holcomb remembered the evening following Hartford's victory over Hagerstown in the Seaboard League semifinals. The Knights stayed at a Holiday Inn that had a lively lounge, and Holcomb and Berlet were having a drink and watching a conga line wind its way through the room. "Sure as God made little apples," Holcomb told Berlet, "Nick Cutro is in that conga line somewhere."

"I was wrong," Holcomb said. "He wasn't in the line. He was leading it." Eventually, last call came and the reporters and assistant coaches went over to say good night. "Where are you guys going?" Cutro asked. To bed, they told him. Ridiculous, said Cutro, they were going to have breakfast. He convinced the manager to cook steak and eggs for the entire Knights entourage at two o'clock in the morning.

Cutro's free-wheeling coaching philosophy matched his personality. "Wallner's idea of offense," said Holcomb, "was power left, power right and throw the bomb. When Cutro got here he's running naked reverses and all this other stuff."

"Not to sound egotistical," Cutro told Berlet, "but I feel I can score on someone whenever I want, given the right personnel."[5] Cutro always compared building a team to making a pot of minestrone soup—taking a little bit of everything and mixing it together into something really good.

The players had respected Wallner, but they really liked Cutro and his relaxed style. "Nick would listen to you," said Bob Miranda. "You could go up to him on the sideline and tell him what you thought might work. He'd say, 'Yeah, yeah, yeah, get outta here.' But then a few minutes later he'd call the play."

"I'd say to them," Cutro recalled, "I know you're disappointed that you're not with the big team, but you're here. And since you're here you might as well put out one hundred percent and you might be back up next week. I didn't bullshit them because a lot of the guys did go up."

"Nick was the kind of coach," said Tim Miller, "who could motivate you and make you want to play for him. One time he said to me, 'I wish you were

Italian. You're not the biggest guy in the world but you give me one hundred percent. I wish you were Italian.'" Cutro wrote to Miller's hometown paper in Emporia, Kansas, stating that he was the best offensive lineman on the team, something Miller never forgot.

As entertaining and beloved as he was, few who played for both Knight coaches believed Cutro knew as much about football as Wallner. "I don't think Nick had half the knowledge Fred had, and I don't mean to knock Nick," said Bill Boehle, who served as an assistant to both. "I just thought so much of Fred." Cutro was a good coach and a great guy. Wallner, many thought, was an eccentric football genius.

Cutro said he could score at any time if he had the right personnel, and in 1972 he certainly had the proper ingredients for his minestrone soup. Veteran quarterback Tom Sherman returned for a third season, and Marv Pettaway, the Knights' most exciting defender and the ACFL's leading kick returner, came back for a second year, as did kicker Norm Davidson, the 1971 ACFL Rookie of the Year. From the defunct Bridgeport Jets, the Knights added wide receiver Don Shanklin, who'd been the ACFL's leading receiver.

The Seaboard League season started the first weekend of August, just about the time the NFL was beginning its exhibition season, and only their very early cuts were available to SPFL teams. Still, the Knights had been able to add two very good players. The first was defensive end Harry Gooden, a fourth round draft choice of the San Diego Chargers who'd been a small college All-American at Alcorn A&M.

July 20 was very early for a fourth round draft choice to arrive in a Seaboard League camp, but Gooden was 6'6" and 225 and there was no way he could play defensive end in the NFL. He'd gone up to Canada but had been released by the Hamilton Tiger Cats before the start of their season. Gooden joined the Knights to put on some weight, add a little muscle and get some experience.[6] One of the experiences the Alabaman didn't like was the cold weather. "I'm so cold my eyeballs are freezing," he said while warming up for a November game.

"Harry was a fierce football player," said Miller, "probably the best we had on defense, and he had a great attitude." "He had big arms," said Charlie Tiblom, "and there wasn't an ounce of fat on him. You couldn't block him. Why he never made it in the NFL I'll never know."

The second outstanding newcomer was running back Cecil Bowens, a powerful 6'3", 230-pounder from the University of Kentucky. Bowens played two years of college football before leaving school and trying out with the Montreal Alouettes. He was released and joined the Knights in time for the opening game against the Portsmouth (Virginia) Bucs.

The opening game set the tone for the 1972 season. "We didn't really know

17. A Perfect Season in an Imperfect League

what we were getting into," said linebacker Ralph Tiner. "We took this long bus trip down to Portsmouth, and they had about 60 guys on their team, all hootin' and hollerin' while they warmed up. I said, 'Whoa, we're in for a game.'"

It wasn't much of a game. The Knights decimated the Bucs 52–7, holding them to minus 28 yards of total offense. Cornerback Herb Marshall intercepted three passes, which was equal to the number Portsmouth quarterbacks completed to their own receivers. Overall, Hartford had five interceptions and six sacks. Bowens ran for three touchdowns. The only Portsmouth score came on a fumble recovery in the Hartford end zone.

Cutro and Savin were ecstatic. Savin said he thought Bowens was a better runner than Marv Hubbard, Mel Meeks, or anyone else the Knights ever had. Cutro said his club was better than any of the old ACFL teams. The unanswered question was whether the Knights were really that good or the rest of the Seaboard League was that bad. Perhaps the answer would be unveiled the following week during the home opener against the Long Island Chiefs.

The Chiefs had some talent, including quarterback Seiki Murono, the CFL and ACFL veteran who'd thrown 25 touchdown passes in 1971. They were further strengthened by the addition of several players who'd been cut loose by the New York Jets. Still, the Chiefs proved as helpless against the Knights as the Bucs had been, losing by an identical 52–7 score. Bowens scored two more touchdowns and backup quarterback Frank DiMaggio threw for two scores. Long Island displayed much more offense than Portsmouth, with 322 total yards, but much of it came long after the issue had been decided.

The only sobering note from the Chiefs' game was an injury to kicker Norm Davidson, the result of what the Knights thought was a cheap shot on a kickoff. Long before the New Orleans Saints were accused of putting bounties on opposing players, money was placed on the heads of players, even minor leaguers. "We actually had a bounty system in Bridgeport," said Tom Rowland, "but they weren't bounties in the sense that we were really trying to hurt somebody. You'd get $25 if you had an interception or recovered a fumble or took the quarterback out."

Bob Anderson, the kicker for the Bridgeport Jets, heard that there was a reward for anyone on the Pottstown squad that took him out of the game. "Make sure you get off the field quick," the coaches told him. "After I kicked the ball," Anderson remembered, "there was a guy about six-foot-eight throwing rolling blocks at me, and I don't think I was that much of a threat to make a tackle. I'm running for the sideline saying, 'Holy mackerel, what a way to go.' The guy kept chasing me, Hi Ho was over there yelling at me and I'm running as fast as I can for the sideline." Finally, Anderson got behind one of his teammates and sprinted to safety.

"There were guys," Davidson said, "who would just try to hurt you. You could definitely get some cheap shots in the minor leagues. When I got out of college I weighed maybe 150 pounds, and these guys were nasty. One time a guy sort of circled behind me and came at my knee from the side. Another time I was going down the field, not really paying attention, and a guy hit me so hard I thought my contact lenses had been knocked out. I must have flown five feet through the air." After a couple of incidents, the Knights assigned defensive back Bryan White as Davidson's bodyguard.

After the game, in contrast to the prior week, the Knights were more apologetic than ecstatic. "We don't like to win like this," said Hartford publicity man George Ducharme, "but you can't tell ballplayers not to play."[7]

"Some teams can be expected to be weak," said Cutro, "but it is up to them to do the coaching and recruiting necessary to become a winner."[8] He pointed out that when he was coaching in the ACFL, the Knights had also dominated the opposition. There was big difference, however, for when the Knights were winning in the ACFL, the games were usually close and exciting. A 52–7 win was not exciting, especially if it happened every week. "And I can tell you," said Howie Holcomb, "the scores were a lot closer than the games really were."

"This is great for the Knights and winning championships," one Hartford fan said after the game, "but terrible for the league."[9] "The Hartford Knights," wrote Berlet, "are apparently more than the Seaboard Professional Football League can handle."[10]

One-sided games provided the opportunity for a little fun. Fullback Bob Miranda noticed that DiMaggio always seemed to call his own number when the Knights got close to the end zone. One night, Cutro sent in a goal line play calling for Miranda to carry the ball. Sure enough, DiMaggio audibled to a bootleg. When the teams lined up, Miranda yelled, "Bootleg! Bootleg!" and DiMaggio was swarmed under before he got to the goal line. He came back to the huddle furious, and did the same thing on the next play. Again, Miranda started yelling, "Bootleg! Bootleg!" DiMaggio called time out. "I just lost it," Miranda said. "I was just laughing too hard."

Miranda was an interesting individual. He grew up in Connecticut, was recruited by nearly all the top universities, and chose the University of South Carolina because of the persuasive talents of a charismatic young assistant named Lou Holtz. A year later, by the time Miranda was eligible for varsity play, Holtz had moved on to the head job at William and Mary. "I lost my sponsor," Miranda said. He had a decent but not great career for the Gamecocks, but it was in an English class, not on the football field, that he found his true calling.

Miranda didn't want to be in the English class, and when his teacher told him she wanted him to perform in a play, he said no. The teacher said she would fail him if he refused, and the athletic department said they would have the teacher fired if she failed Miranda. "I felt really bad about it," Miranda said, "so I agreed to be in the play, which was *Rosencrantz and Guildenstern Are Dead*." He loved the experience, and also the fact that the drama department consisted of 38 females and 2 males, neither of whom was interested in the 38 females.

While playing with the Knights, Miranda studied acting and began to get some work. He appeared in ads in the Knights program. "Later on," said Ralph Tiner, "I was learning to ride a motorcycle. They showed us a safety film, where they had a bad guy playing a punk trying to do all kinds of things, like throwing nails in the road. He'd throw an oil slick on the road and they'd show us how to avoid it, stuff like that. The punk was Bobby Miranda."

As a handsome, muscular Italian, Miranda was able to carve out a niche as a Hollywood gangster, and has appeared in dozens of films and television shows with Sean Connery, Al Pacino, Whoopi Goldberg, Robert Blake, and many others.

The rest of the 1972 season was a series of overwhelming Hartford victories and a lengthy debate concerning the lack of competitiveness within the Seaboard League. The Knights beat Northumberland 58–7 and Portsmouth 58–0. Chambersburg fell by a 47–0 margin, as the Knights intercepted more passes (6) than the Cardinals completed (4).

In 16 games, including two playoff contests, the Knights outscored their opponents 625–123, posted five shutouts, and held their opponent to seven points or less on ten occasions. The closest call was a 30–24 victory over Long Island on an 88-yard kickoff return by Marv Pettaway on the first play of overtime.

After the Knights' fourth win, against Aston, Savin said the competition was becoming tougher, a claim belied by the results. The play had indeed been spirited, and DiMaggio and Aston safety Bruce Udovich were ejected for fighting. Still, a 39–13 score showed little indication that the Aston club was as skilled as it was tough. "They were a rough, hard-nosed crew," said Hagerstown coach Hugh Wyatt, "and to tell the truth, something of an affront to most of the other teams in the league, because while the rest of us were striving to create an image of 'minor league' football ... the [Aston] Knights' operation was barely a step up from sandlot."[11] Aston took a casual approach to practice and, because they couldn't afford a bus, car-pooled to road games.

Aston did, however, have a couple of very talented players. One was a 19-year-old defensive lineman listed on the roster as Jim Jones, whose alma mater was, according to the program, Poland University. His real name was Joe Klecko, and he had not attended the mythical Poland University, or any other college, having played just one year of high school ball. At the time he played for Aston,

Klecko was driving a tractor trailer for $6.22 an hour, pretty good money in 1972.

Klecko had a vague idea of going to college at some point, and used an alias to preserve his amateur standing. He also said he was never paid. A couple of years later, Klecko was awarded a scholarship to Temple and went on to a long, distinguished career with the New York Jets.[12]

The other future NFL player on the Aston roster was wide receiver Vince Papale, subject of the movie *Invincible,* starring Mark Wahlberg. Papale attended St. Joseph's College, which didn't have a football team, but he captained the track team and was a versatile decathlete. In 1972, Papale was 26 and playing his first season of organized football. He was serving as an assistant coach at Interboro High School and playing with Aston on weekends.[13]

After the 58–0 win over Portsmouth, Cutro said he needed to hold a scrimmage because his club hadn't even gotten a good workout. "We may have scored 58 points last week (against Northumberland) but we had to work for them. This time we just sent the offense on the field and scored at will."[14] The Knights had scored 10 of the 11 times they'd had the ball and averaged 14 yards per rush. The Bucs, quarterbacked by Les Obie, who joined the club just four hours before game time, managed just 36 yards of total offense.

In addition to the dearth of competition, the Knights were surprised by the amateurish fashion in which Seaboard League teams operated. Many of them had difficulty getting their players to attend practice, and rules were often treated in cavalier fashion. When Aston was accused of dressing more players than were allowed on a roster, coach Phil Pompilli replied, "I don't know how many dressed, 39, 40, maybe 41. If you want me to commit myself, I'll say 39."[15]

Opposing coaches acknowledged the Knights' superiority, but held differing opinions on its impact.

"I think [the Knights] belong in the Seaboard League and it's up to the rest of the league to emulate Hartford," said Hagerstown coach Hugh Wyatt.[16] "They have the kind of ball club that the Coal Crackers used to have," added Northumberland coach Frank Wapinsky. "If the Seaboard League intends to get any NFL affiliations, they need high-caliber teams like Hartford."[17]

Coach Tom Carr of the Chambersburg Cardinals, a former assistant with the Pottstown Firebirds, felt otherwise. "I think Hartford is too strong for our league," he said, "and they don't belong in our league."[18] Portsmouth coach Emory Davis agreed. "There is definitely an imbalance here," he said. "There has to be something done to rectify this imbalance."[19]

Carr's remark elicited an angry reply from Savin. "That gives me a big laugh and annoys me," he said. "I hope the Knights run Chambersburg right out of the ballpark this weekend." The Hartford owner noted that several Chambersburg players had been members of the Pottstown and Norfolk championship clubs and wondered why they now felt so overmatched. "We are not going to be forced out of the Seaboard League or any other league," Savin said. "The teams that feel they cannot compete should get out of football themselves."[20] Cutro expressed similar sentiments. "They have all the horses," he said after the Knights beat the Cardinals and their ex–Pottstown stars. "If you are a man you will stand up on your own two feet."[21]

The Knights' season in the Seaboard League, with its substandard facilities and lack of serious competition, was clearly a step down from the ACFL. "We were still getting to do what we wanted to do," said Tom Sherman. "We were playing football. If we didn't want to play we wouldn't have put up with the stuff we put up with. It was more fun in the earlier years, but it is what it is and you just go out there and do the best you can." "The Seaboard League was bad," said Holcomb. "But it was either the Seaboard League or nothing, because there was nothing else around. So they put up with it."

Bill Lee, never a big fan of Pete Savin and his Knights, came down hard on the Seaboard League. He watched the Knights defeat Chambersburg 47–0 and wrote, "it was a bad scene.... Nick Cutro has to fight like an all out collegian to keep the score down.... The result was a conclusive evidence of what has long been suspected—that the Hartford Knights involuntarily have found themselves in a bush league."

After lauding some of the Knights' individual performances, Lee moaned, "But oh that league. Already franchises have been moved since the season's start and one city last Saturday night had to cancel a scheduled game for lack of funds. It's a pity there isn't another strong minor league in which a team as sound as the Hartford Knights could be put to a test."[22]

"We have the best minor league football team in the country," Savin countered. "Yet the fans stay home. What do they want, a loser? Is the Big Eight Conference bush league because Oklahoma and Nebraska have been running up scores?"[23]

The Big Eight Conference didn't have a place like Kulpmont. "We drove past the field," said Sherman, "went down this alleyway and stopped in front of a garage. That was the locker room. We dressed on the second floor of the garage. There was no shower and no bathroom."

When Howie Holcomb arrived at the field, he found center Jim Murphy fuming. "He was usually a very mild-mannered guy," Holcomb said, "but you could see sparks coming out of his ears, eyes, and everything else. He said, 'If you don't write something about this blankety-blank field I'll never speak to you again.'

"I said, 'What's the matter? What are you talking about?' He said, 'This is terrible. There's broken glass everywhere.' The goal posts were made of plumbers' pipe maybe an inch in diameter. It was just terrible." "Sometimes," said Miranda, "we'd be down on our hands and knees on the field before the game trying to pick up pieces of broken glass and whatever other debris we found."

"The fields were bad," said Cutro. "One field we played on in Pennsylvania was like coal dust. If you got tackled it burned the skin off you. Then it started raining and the field got black. Everybody's uniform was the color of dirty coal."

As a kicker, however, Davidson found the barren Conshohocken field to his liking. "You didn't have any grass sticking up on the bottom of the ball. It was nice to be able to see the bottom of the ball." For years, Savin had wanted Dillon Stadium to be one of the best facilities in the league, and now it was—by default.

Bruce Berlet of the *Courant* missed the glory days of the early Knights, when the crowds were big and the team was flying to road games. Berlet, a 1970 graduate of the University of Connecticut, was just a year out of college when he began covering the Knights. He was in the vanguard of the young generation of reporters, with a mustache and longish hair that set him apart from his middle-aged contemporaries.

His second year on the beat was the season the Knights played in the Seaboard League, and the glamour of sports reporting quickly wore thin in places like Conshohocken and Kulpmont, and during the ten hour bus ride to Portsmouth. At one stretch the Knights played four road games in a row, including eight hour treks to Chambersburg and Hagerstown. On the return ride from Aston, the bus broke down and the team didn't get back to Hartford until eight o'clock Sunday morning.

Long bus rides were a part of minor league life. Being on a bus for eight hours is tedious, but for large football players, it was nearly unbearable. "One night," recalled Dennis Fitzgibbons, "we're coming back from Norfolk and Bruce Williams is next to me. So you've got about 600 pounds in a bus seat. It was like a ride from hell. Every hour and a half or two hours we'd switch. For two hours I get the window and sit all scrunched up and he's kind of bent over sitting in the middle of the aisle. Then we switch and he's stuck against the window."

The best thing about the trip back was that there was usually beer on board, stored in ice-filled garbage cans in the aisle. "They'd have like three trash barrels full of ice and beer," recalled one of the Knights, "and the guys would be yelling, 'Pass back the muscle relaxers.' There were pills being popped after the game and there were always boxes of Kentucky Fried Chicken." The magic combination of beer, muscle relaxers, and fried chicken made the victories sweeter and the losses more tolerable.

On one beer-fueled return trip from New Jersey, the Bridgeport Jets told the driver they needed to make a rest stop. The driver said he wasn't allowed to do that, but they finally persuaded him to stop along the side of the road. "Otherwise you're going to find out what Noah's Ark was like," Cutro warned. While the players were on the grass filtering their beer, a police car pulled up, and everyone expected trouble. When the officer saw 35 burly players attending to their business, however, he decided that discretion was the better part of valor, flipped his light on, and sped off to another, less threatening call.

To those who traveled with the Knights in 1972, one game stands out. "Somehow or another," said Elaine Savin, "it's Conshohocken, Pennsylvania I remember most." Almost everyone remembered the night in Conshohocken, for it was unlike any other evening in the history of the Hartford Knights.

The start of the game was delayed about an hour and a half because of severe thunder and lightning. "There was *horrendous, horrendous* rain and lightning," Berlet recalled. "It was about 9:00 or 9:30 before they even kicked off and there were about fifty people in the stands—wives and girlfriends." The stands held more Hartford rooters than Conshohocken fans. One was drinking heavily and cheering lustily for the Knights until he lost his balance and tumbled out of the bleachers into the mud.

Tim Miller's mother and aunt were there. "I'll never forget that game," Miller said. "The lights went out and stopped play for a while. My aunt caught an extra point and wanted to keep the ball. They went into the stands and said, 'Ma'm, we need that ball back because we've got to play with it.' I think it was the only one they had."

At halftime, with midnight fast approaching, the teams agreed that the third and fourth quarters would be only twelve minutes long. "The water was just gushing out of the stadium into the street," Berlet recalled. "The field was like a high school field and there was a little six-foot press box. They had a metal board in there that controlled the lights on the scoreboard. I'm on the far end of the box—I think I was the only reporter there—and the guy operating the board is at the other end. A freakin' lightning bolt hits the rod up above and goes right down through the metal board. The guy's hair stands straight up on end and I thought for sure he was dead. He was really shook up but miraculously he was fine."

The next day Berlet learned he had been the official scorer, for the rain had driven most of the media away and apparently no one else kept track of the game statistics. The league office called Berlet and asked him to send them his stats, which became the official record. "I had these wet, crumpled up pieces of paper," he said, "and I put them together and sent them off to the league."

There was no lightning in Kulpmont, but there Berlet encountered another physical obstacle. "They hadn't finished the press box," he said, "and they had this ladder about 30 or 35 feet high that went in through the bottom of the press box. You had to climb up and down the ladder to get in. Heights and I don't agree."

Since the press box was only partially completed, there were no facilities from which to transmit a report. Filing a story required a trip down the ladder, a walk to the high school, and a climb back up the ladder. Berlet was supposed to file at halftime and at the end of the game. "I called my office," he said, "and told them they were getting no halftime report from me because I'm going up there once and I'm coming down once and that's it."

Berlet was the last reporter to climb the ladder to report on a Seaboard League game. Having won only one of five games and having experienced limited success at the box office, the Coal Crackers moved to Reading, Pennsylvania to finish the season. They got a less than rousing reception, being forced to move their first scheduled home game to Chambersburg when the Reading field wasn't available.

Two weeks after the Coal Crackers moved, the Portsmouth Bucs postponed a game against Conshohocken due to a lack of funds. Fortunately, a local radio station purchased the team and provided sufficient support to enable the Bucs to finish the season.

Conshohocken was not so lucky. A week after the Portsmouth postponement, Commissioner Charlie McCullough announced that the Steelers had disbanded. "They had until noon Saturday," McCullough said, "to inform me as to whether or not they would play Saturday night, and when I did not hear from them that was it."[24] He said all the Conshohocken players were free agents and that the team's remaining games would be forfeited by 1–0 scores.

On October 21 the Reading (née Northumberland) Coal Crackers were scheduled to play the Knights on a very chilly evening at Dillon Stadium. The game was to begin at 8:00 but when kickoff time came, Reading had not arrived and the start was postponed for 30 minutes. At 8:30, eighteen Reading players were on the field, with two additional carloads supposedly en route.

It was about that time that Pete Savin angrily punched the wall of the press box. The public address announcer read a statement from the Knights' owner indicating that any fan wanting their money back could get a full refund. Only 63 of the 4,000 spectators took Savin up on his offer and the rest settled down to watch another one-sided Hartford victory.

The 41–0 margin could have been greater had the Knights not let up at the end. The defensive line put only token pressure on the Reading quarterback, and the offense killed the clock. The two cars supposedly containing the remaining Coal Crackers never arrived, and the suspicion was that the players had not been paid.

17. A Perfect Season in an Imperfect League

"It was a nightmare, just simply a nightmare," Cutro said after the game. "I really didn't know what to do at first."[25] Savin called the whole affair "distasteful and obnoxious."[26] Reading, like Conshohocken, failed to survive the season and forfeited its final games.

In an effort to stage a competitive game, Savin invited the Columbus (Ohio) Bucks, 1971 champions of the Midwest Football League, to play the Knights at Hartford. The collapse of the Conshohocken franchise left the Knights with an open date on October 28, and Savin hoped the Bucks would provide the exciting game Hartford fans were looking for. The Columbus team had been 17–0–1 in 1971 and featured a number of former Ohio State players.

Nothing went wrong on the field for the 1972 Knights, but off the field, it seemed as though almost nothing went right. On the night Savin intended to show Hartford its best game of the year, it rained. The Knights beat the Bucks 30–21 in a good, hard-hitting, competitive game, the kind the Knights played in their banner years. Unfortunately, only 4,500 fans braved the weather, a number about equal to what the club had drawn for the Seaboard League mismatches.

After the first two games of the season, it was apparent that the Knights were going to be in the playoffs, which included the top two teams in each division. Their only challenger for the league title was the Chambersburg Cardinals, yet another semi-reincarnation of the Pottstown Firebirds. Chambersburg had talent and something most of the league's teams did not—an enthusiastic following. The town had a population of just 17,000, but drew 7,500 for the game against the Knights. Fans sometimes arrived two hours before game time and rooted for the home team with a fervor not seen in Dillon Stadium since 1969.

When the Knights played in Hagerstown, a contingent of Chambersburg fans were there and sent a message to the Hartford bench stating, "The Cards and the King are waiting." A local sports editor wrote, "This year's edition of the Cards has done wonders to the city. Fans are truly interested in what coach Tom Carr has assembled. People have told me at their places of work all the talk has been centered on the Cards."[27] An envious Savin said, "That is what minor league football is all about. I have never seen a town that cared so much about their team. When I walked into the ball park, I felt this is what makes it worthwhile ... on that basis we should draw 50,000 in Hartford."[28]

The Knights whipped the Cardinals soundly in their first meeting, but Chambersburg had strengthened their squad as the season progressed. From the defunct Conshohocken eleven they added quarterback Jim Haynie, the villain who'd led the Firebirds to victory in the 1970 Snow Bowl. The Cardinals needed the Knights' permission to add Haynie to the roster, and Hartford didn't hesitate. "Let them have him," said Cutro. "We want to beat their best."[29]

Just prior to the October 7 game against the Knights at Chambersburg, the Cardinals signed King Corcoran and running back Claude Watts. By the end of the season, ex–Firebirds John Land, Ron Holliday, and Tommy Davis were Cardinals.

Corcoran arrived in his usual subtle fashion. "My name," he said, "makes the Seaboard League a bona-fide minor league. I think you're going to see more and more big name players come into the Seaboard League during the next couple of years. I've broken the ice. My name makes it the top minor league in the country."

Corcoran was available because he left the Montreal Alouettes at the end of July. Fred Wallner was an assistant in Montreal and the combination of Wallner and Corcoran was a match made somewhere south of heaven. "He hated the King," Corcoran said of Wallner. He said Wallner demoted him to second string, but actually it was head coach Sam Etcheverry who demoted the King, and it was to third string. "The King never plays No. 2 anywhere," Corcoran said.

Corcoran also left Montreal because, he said, he had to return to Washington, D.C., where his son was going blind after being accidently hit with a baseball bat. Nothing more was heard of the bat incident, and Corcoran's son could see out of both eyes when he was interviewed by NFL Films in 2000, so it is likely that the story was another of Corcoran's many fabrications. He also said he was considering buying the Alouettes.[30]

With their revamped roster and the support of a rabid crowd, the Cardinals gave the Knights a battle before succumbing by a 13-7 score. Had Corcoran played as well as he always said he could, Chambersburg would have ended the Knights' winning streak, but the rusty King passed for only 52 yards and threw two interceptions. Hartford held the ball for 25 minutes in the first half and, other than the Cardinal scoring drive, allowed them only 24 yards of offense.

When the regular season ended, the Cardinals were the Knights' closest pursuer, with Hartford having inflicted their only two losses:

Northern Division			Southern Division		
Hartford	14	0	Aston	8	6
Chambersburg	12	2	Hagerstown	7	7
Long Island	10	4	Portsmouth	3	11
Reading	3	11	Conshohocken	0	14

The playoffs pitted Hartford against Hagerstown and Aston versus Chambersburg on November 11, with the two winners to meet in Hartford on November 18. The Hagerstown game was a reprise of the regular season, as the Knights coasted to a 56-14 win. "We were out of our class, that's all," said Hagerstown coach Hugh Wyatt.[31]

Chambersburg beat Aston 20-12 and prepared to meet Hartford for the

17. A Perfect Season in an Imperfect League

title. For the fourth season in a row, King Corcoran's veteran team, of which 17 had played in ACFL title games, stood between the Knights and a championship. The first three times Corcoran had prevailed.

On the fourth try, Hartford was simply too much for the King. Fullback Bob Miranda scored the first touchdown with just over two minutes left in the first quarter. After a Norm Davidson field goal, Corcoran threw an interception that was returned to the Chambersburg 14. A few plays later, Cecil Bowens ran the ball in from the one, giving the Knights a 17–0 halftime lead.

The Knights defense dominated the third quarter, holding Chambersburg to negative rushing yardage and just one pass completion. The final score was 17–7, and the only Cardinal score came on a blocked punt that was returned 45 yards for a touchdown. For the game, Hartford's stellar defenders limited Chambersburg to only seven first downs and 141 yards of total offense. Corcoran completed just 9 of 27 passes for 106 yards and suffered three interceptions.

Marvin Pettaway, named the most valuable defensive player, was carried off the field by his teammates. Miranda was named most valuable on offense. "I was just so happy," he said. "I was running around the locker room hugging and kissing everybody." "Boy, the sting of that champagne sure feels good," said Cutro. "Now if only the Lord forgives us for what we are going to do. We have earned it."[32]

For the first time in four years, the Knights had a championship. In the same year the Miami Dolphins posted the only undefeated season in the history of the NFL, the Knights achieved the perfection that had eluded them in Richmond in 1968. The players and coaches poured champagne on each other in the locker room, but it was not the same as it had been in 1968. Only 6,500 fans turned out to see the title game, and the march toward an unblemished season had been almost too easy, blemished by the poor quality of the competition.

Still, 16 wins (17 including the victory over the Columbus Bucks) are 16 wins, and a single slip or off-night could have derailed even a team like the 1972 Knights. They played the teams that were put on the field against them, and beat them all. "People are kind of putting this league down," center Joe Ginnetti said after the game, "but I've been playing football since I was 10 years old and this was the first time I was ever on an undefeated team. I think it's pretty special."

"That was a good football team," said defensive end John Skladany. "It wasn't NFL caliber but I thought we were better than the World Football League team I played with in Birmingham and certainly better than the Canadian League team I played with in Ottawa. We had good players."

There had been some fine individual performances, the most impressive of which was that of running back Cecil Bowens. The ever-optimistic Cutro predicted he would be a first round pick when he was eligible for the NFL draft in 1973. "The kid had all kinds of talent," Cutro said recently. "He was 6'3", played at about 220 and could run like a deer."

With the Knights, Bowens ran like a man among boys, and broke Marv Hubbard's Hartford rushing record set in 1968. Hubbard's team played a number of close games and he was rarely removed due to a lopsided score. Bowens was usually on the bench by the fourth quarter, which made his record even more impressive. "He was one of the big reasons we won the title," said tackle Tim Miller. "You didn't have to make much space for him. He would get through the hole real fast and then he was gone. He was a hard man to bring down." "He was a stud," added Charlie Tiblom, "a real stud."

In the opener, the big back from Kentucky carried the ball just seven times, but gained 66 yards and scored three touchdowns. The next week he gained 66 yards in nine carries and scored twice more. After four games, Bowens had 268 yards rushing, a 6.5 yard average, and nine touchdowns. As the season went on and the Knights rolled over one opponent after another, Bowens began to set records. In Game 11 he scored two touchdowns, bringing his season total to 17 and breaking the mark of 15 set by Mel Meeks in 1968.

The next week, against the Reading Coal Crackers, Bowens gained 108 yards in only 11 carries, giving him 958 yards for the season, surpassing the 897 Hubbard gained in 1968. Bowens finished the regular season with 1,007 yards, a 6.5 average, and 18 scores. "I have become convinced," said Bill Lee late in the season, "that he is one of the most exciting runners ever to play here and that he most likely has big league potential that will see fruition in the near future."[33]

Hubbard came to the Knights with a suspect attitude and deficient blocking skills. He learned to block and to give the one hundred percent effort that propelled him to the AFL. Bowens was a great talent who didn't acquire discipline and wasn't willing to put in the effort.

Cutro benched him for disciplinary reasons for the first half of the Columbus game, and hinted recently that Bowens had a substance abuse problem. "He couldn't dedicate himself to football," Cutro said. "He always had problems." Other players noted Bowens' lack of work ethic, and rather than becoming a star, he remained an enigmatic athlete with talent who never made it. He played briefly in the WFL but never made an NFL roster.

In 1973, Bowens signed with the Western Massachusetts Pioneers, and Cutro was asked why he didn't want him back with Hartford. He already had five running backs, Cutro said, and didn't want to cut into their playing time. He certainly didn't have five backs that could run better than Bowens had run in 1972, and Cutro's reluctance to take him back is telling.

A second promising running back, Alan (A-Train) Thompson, had done better. Thompson led the Wisconsin Badgers in rushing in 1971, but was sent to the Knights by the Ottawa Roughriders due primarily to a suspect attitude. By late October the Roughriders brought him back. Thompson's rushing statistics weren't close to those of Bowens, but he'd played hard and his blocking for the big Kentucky back had drawn the attention of Canadian scouts.

With Bowens running the ball, the Knights didn't need to throw often, but when they did they were effective. Sherman threw for 19 TDs and backup Frank DiMaggio threw for eight in just 48 attempts. Despite the efforts of Bob Miranda, DiMaggio also managed to score two rushing touchdowns. Norm Davidson kicked 13 field goals and 57 conversions for a total of 96 points. Former USC player Ron Drake broke Bob Stohrer's record with seven touchdown receptions.

Like the Seaboard League title, the individual statistics and records had a somewhat hollow ring. The game in which Bowens broke Hubbard's record was the one in which only 18 Corn Crackers suited up. Hubbard gained tough yards against the hard-hitting defenses of the Pottstown Firebirds and Bridgeport Jets, while Bowens, admittedly a great talent, piled up statistics against hapless Conshohocken and Portsmouth.

Despite his long-coveted title, Pete Savin was not happy. "There are too many things I did not like about the SPFL," he said at the Knights' final press conference, "for us to remain any longer. The structure was not good enough for us to continue. I bit through my tongue 100,000 times and I am not going to go through that again."[34]

"They didn't take it seriously," said Elaine Savin, "and he took it very seriously." Her husband's beloved Knights would not spend another season in the Seaboard League, or any other league so disorganized and unstable. There would be a Hartford Knights football team in 1973, Savin said, hopefully in a reincarnated Atlantic Coast League.

18

Back in the ACFL: The 1973 Hartford Knights and Bridgeport Jets

The Atlantic Coast Football League got back in business for the 1973 season. The rejuvenated ACFL was composed of six teams, divided into Northern and Southern Divisions, the former including Hartford, New England, and Western Massachusetts. The latter franchise was based in Holyoke and coached by Fred Wallner, returning to the United States after an unhappy year as defensive coordinator of the Montreal Alouettes.

The Southern Division consisted of Bridgeport, the Long Island Chiefs, and the New York Crusaders. A six team league was much better than the unworkable four team circuit of 1971, and the franchises were all located in the Northeast, which would reduce travel costs. There would be no more eight or ten hour bus trips to Virginia and no charter flights to Orlando.

The 1973 season was the worst in the history of the Hartford Knights. "I think I put that out of my mind," said Nick Cutro. "I don't remember the season at all. I just can't come up with anything." My best hope for unearthing memories of that year was center Joe Ginnetti. Ginnetti remembers everything—his teammates, his opponents, and where each of them went to college. He always seemed to have a couple of anecdotes for every subject. When I told him Cutro recalled nothing of the season he replied, "Was he the coach that year?"

Ginnetti rallied a bit and came up with a few tidbits, but for the most part he too had relegated the bad memories to a compartment of his mind from which they could not be retrieved. Perhaps it was just as well, for the Knights' 1973 season was not one to remember. It was the only year in their history that they were not in the championship game, and it was a season during which attendance continued to decline.

Pete Savin had always lost money on his football team, but in 1968 and

18. Back in the ACFL

1969 the community had been so excited about the Knights that he didn't seem to mind. By 1973, after the battle over Dillon Stadium, the embarrassment of the Seaboard League, and the diminishing crowds, Savin was beginning to lose his enthusiasm.

Life with the Knights was not as good as it had been in the glory days, for as attendance dropped, salaries and creature comforts declined. "How much money can you pour down a rat hole?" asked Dennis Fitzgibbons. "The last year or two we took bus rides instead of flying. You can take a bus for a grand or you can take a plane for fifteen."

While the Knights hit bottom, the Jets, returning after a one year hiatus, had the best season in their history. Ray Mathews returned as coach and many of the players from the 1971 season, including star flanker Donnie Shanklin, came back as well. New additions included former Knight quarterback Frank DiMaggio and wide receiver Chuck Cornell, a local hero who'd set records for receptions, receiving yards, and touchdown passes at the University of Bridgeport.

The Jets also signed Lou Piccone, a speedy 5'10", 175-pound running back/wide receiver. Piccone grew up in a tough section of southern New Jersey, but never got into serious trouble. "I was more like an alcoholic," he said. "My high school buddies and I would booze it up on weekends and then go into Philadelphia and dance our heads off. Sports were the only things that kept me from going into a complete stupor."[1]

Piccone played just half a season of high school football as a 142-pound fullback and, with his small stature and lack of experience, got no interest from major colleges. He went to West Liberty State without a scholarship and established a reputation as a fearless, daring punt returner. The primary reason was that no one had explained to him that he could make a fair catch, and he was unaware of the rule.

After he graduated, Piccone asked his coach if he thought he had the ability to keep playing. "I don't think you've got the size," he was told. Piccone went back to south Jersey and got a teaching job, but shortly thereafter received a call from George Rodack, coach of the Youngstown Hard Hats of the Middle Atlantic Football League. Rodack asked if he was interested in playing professional football. How much did it pay, Piccone asked. Fifty dollars a game if he started and thirty-five if he didn't, Rodack replied. "OK," Piccone said, "you want me to go from south Jersey to Youngstown, Ohio for fifty bucks a game? Are you nuts?" Rodack didn't give up easily. The Browns and the Steelers both scouted the Hard Hats, he replied, which piqued Piccone's interest. He said he would think about it and call Rodack back.

Piccone's father had been listening to the conversation. The senior Piccone came from a hard working immigrant family that valued education and was thrilled that his son had gone to college. Piccone told him what Rodack had said. "Jesus, son!" Mr. Piccone replied. "You've got a job. You're teaching school. You've got your education. It's time to use your brains and not your brawn. And besides, you're too small."

Piccone had been told he was too small before, and would hear it again, but not from his father, who was his hero. "Is that what you think, Pop?" he said. It was. "Well," the son replied, "we're just going to have to find out about that."

Piccone went to Youngstown, played well, and wrote to all 28 NFL teams. Only the Redskins, Eagles, and Jets replied. He went to the Redskins camp, got no interest, and then went to an Eagles tryout. He had no more success in Philadelphia, and a couple of weeks later, he received an Honorary Eagle certificate in the mail. Piccone was not honored, and in fact was so incensed he drove back to Philadelphia and demanded to see Eagles receiver coach Boyd Dowler, the former Packer star. He asked Dowler why he wasn't interested, and when he received a trite, generic answer, realized that Dowler didn't even know who he was. But he wasn't ready to give up. "I was going to go as far as I could until somebody told me to go home." But the Redskins and Eagles had already told him to go home. "I wouldn't accept it," he continued, "if they didn't know what they were talking about."

Piccone then got a call from Dick Connors, the former Shamrock and Bridgeport Jet. Connors was running a camp in Connecticut, and asked Piccone to come to the camp and work out. He did and dazzled the counselors with his speed. "I was running 4.35, 4.38, 4.41," he said, "and I became a phenom. They had never seen a white boy run that fast." Connors recommended that the Jets invite Piccone to training camp.

The Jets were just as impressed as Connors. "They put the clock on me, and then they put the clock on me again, and again. They had five guys with clocks on me." Piccone was getting some good press and looked forward to the first scrimmage. Just before the scrimmage was to start, Coach Weeb Ewbank asked to see him. He told Piccone the Jets really liked him. And then he cut him, because if the Jets signed him and he got hurt, Ewbank said, they would lose him. Piccone was livid. "Weeb had myasthenia gravis," he said, "which meant he had to tape his eyelids open. How can you take someone seriously when they've got their eyelids taped open?" And when they were cutting you because they liked you so much.

"Weeb," Piccone pleaded, "let me scrimmage. Let me show you what I can do. If you don't like what you see, let me go and I'll go home." Ewbank persisted, even after Piccone followed him around for half an hour begging for a chance. "They couldn't get me off the field," he said.

18. Back in the ACFL

Ewbank held firm and Piccone added honorary Jet status to his honorary Eagle standing. But he still wasn't ready to quit. "Where am I going to go now," he thought. "I'm in shape. I've put all this time in. I might as well play one more year." Connors hooked him up in Bridgeport.

The Knights' first disappointment, accompanied by controversy, occurred before the regular season even began, when the Las Vegas Casinos of the Southwestern Football League invited them to be their opponents in the first annual Tropicana Bowl on August 25. The Knights were at somewhat of a disadvantage, for the Casinos began their season in early summer and had already played seven games.

"Their owner thought he had the best team in the West," said Tom Sherman, "and he wanted to get what he thought was the best team in the East to come out and play them."

People did not travel as freely in the early 1970s as they do today, and Las Vegas was a long way from Kulpmont and Conshohocken, geographically and culturally. "None of us had been to Vegas," Sherman said. "They put us on a junket with these gamblers, flew us out and put us up at the Tropicana for three days. We signed for everything. You'd eat, you'd go to a show and you'd sign for everything. We could go to the bar, and we'd sign for it. We gave the waitresses phenomenal tips. We had steaks for breakfast. It was unbelievable. So anyway, we landed, went to the hotel, and stood there looking down into the pit where all the gambling was. Our jaws were hitting the floor. Everybody sprinted upstairs, we put our stuff away, and then we're back down in the pit. I'll bet it wasn't half an hour before everyone on the team was asking everybody else, 'You got any extra money?' What I remember is everybody saying, 'I'm going to make some money' and everybody ended up flat broke."

"We weren't used to that stuff," said Norm Davidson. "A lot of the guys stayed out real late, gambled a little, had some drinks and a good time was had by all. The trip was great. Some of the guys were ordering room service for breakfast, lunch, and dinner. I don't know what the bill was for that excursion, but it must have been pretty high."

The Knights had a great time and, unsurprisingly, they did not return home with a victory. "I think we got beat," said Ginnetti, "because I don't think any of us slept more than three or four hours in four days."[2]

"I don't freakin' remember what happened in the game," Sherman said. That was probably for the best, for nothing went well that evening. First, it was a miserably hot night. "I lost about 15 pounds," said Ginnetti, "and I didn't even sweat. It was so hot and so dry that it just evaporated."

The Knights lost 20–17, when Davidson's 49-yard field goal attempt hit the crossbar with 55 seconds left in the game. "I hit the ball beautifully and I thought it was through," he said. "Then all of a sudden the ball started wobbling. I think it hit a little gust of wind and it started wobbling. It lands right in the middle of the crossbar, bounces up in the air and lands back on the field side."

It was the first time Hartford had lost since the 1971 championship game, and many drew the obvious conclusion that the ambience of Las Vegas had something to do with the team's subpar performance. In a sloppy game, the Knights incurred more than a hundred yards in penalties and made a number of mental mistakes.

Once again, Bill Lee laced into Savin. "Personally, I don't feel sorry for the Hartford Knights football team," he wrote. "They were jobbed by their boss, Pete Savin.... Las Vegas is no place for a bunch of football players who have never seen the place before. Booking the game was ridiculous."[3] After taking a few more shots at the Knights' owner, Lee published a letter from Jim Jacques, who labeled himself "An Angered Fan." Jacques complained that when he went to Dillon Stadium to see the Knights' first exhibition against the Long Island Chiefs, he had been treated like a criminal. He was upset with the increased level of security and the way he was herded to his seat.

A week later, Lee published a letter from Cutro defending the Knights. The Hartford coach stated that increased security measures had been instituted in response to fans' complaints that others had indulged in self-help seat upgrades, and that unruly fans were disturbing those who wanted to watch the game in peace. "There can be no legitimate complaint," Cutro wrote, "against a policy that requires fans to sit in the seats they paid for and one which discourages distractions from play on the field." That was true, but it appeared that the marriage between the Knights and Hartford, tested so many times, was on the rocks.

The area around Dillon Stadium had always been troubled. Dave Bennett recalled the time Mel Meeks left practice to find all four tires missing from his car and a note stuck under the windshield wiper that read "thanks." The players had to round up four spare tires so that Meeks could drive home. "Shortly thereafter," Bennett said, "Pete decided to let us park inside the gates and lock us in. That was a tough area. I remember the riots. After practice we had to go around the riots to get home." "I'd get in my car," said Dick Bowman, "and people would walk over the top of it. It was a tough area."

General manager Manch Wheeler took some steps to curb the trouble at Dillon. He gave one of the burly Savin construction workers 100 free tickets and told him to take 100 youngsters, put them in the end zone stands and keep them under control. "I'd rather have them in the end zone than climbing over the fence," he said, "which they liked to do. All of a sudden, there were no kids stealing pocketbooks. They used to go under one set of stands where they could reach up, grab pocketbooks and take off. I put a cop at each end and had it all lit up under there so they couldn't get under there. Pete liked it because he didn't want the kids getting in trouble."

Meanwhile, farther south, the Bridgeport Jets had a much less eventful exhibition season than the Knights. Their first scheduled game was cancelled by the New York Crusaders because their home field had recently been re-sodded and wasn't ready. The Jets then lost 15–7 to the New England Colonials in their only pre-season game.

The opening game pitted the Knights against the Jets at Bridgeport. The good news was that the Jets drew 7,462 to Kennedy Stadium to witness their rebirth. The bad news is that the teams stunk up the joint. The Knights' Gene Muriaty had three punts blocked, leading to two touchdowns and a safety and providing nearly all of Bridgeport's points in their 19–17 win. Between the Knights and Jets, they had three blocked punts, four blocked field goals, four fumbles, and 181 yards in penalties. The Knights led 17–5 before Jet backup quarterback Les Obie threw a touchdown pass to Cornell and Luther Howard ran 16 yards with one of Muriarty's blocked punts.

After the game, a beaming D'Addario said to Cutro, "Thanks for letting us win. We really needed this." The Hartford coach was greatly embarrassed. "I didn't like anything about the way we played," he said. "Things like that just shouldn't happen."[4] Cutro promised wholesale roster changes, the first of which was the replacement of Muriaty, who averaged just 22 yards on seven punts, by former UConn punter Ralph Tiner, a 1972 Knight who had just been cut by the Eagles.

The Knights bounced back to beat Long Island 48–13 at Hempstead the following week, but like so many Hartford 1973 wins, bad news was mixed with good. Only 500 fans watched the two clubs, which did not bode well for the continued existence of the Chiefs.

The win against Long Island was the first of four in a row. The Knights fashioned a satisfying, if not artistic, 17–13 win against Fred Wallner's club, and administered a second thrashing to the Chiefs, this time by a 58–10 margin. As NFL clubs made their final cuts, the Knights also picked up some talented players, including quarterback Tony Adams of Utah State, who would back up the veteran Sherman. Adams finished second in the nation in total offense in 1972 and threw for an NCAA record 516 yards in a game against Utah. He was a 14th round choice of the Chargers.

Despite the four-game winning streak, all was not well on Cottage Grove Lane. Bruce Berlet wrote, "Hartford Knights' President Pete Savin is unhappy; head coach Nick Cutro is unhappy; and defensive tackle Willie Crittendon is unhappy."[5] Savin was displeased because the Knights, even though they were winning, were not playing well, and because his club had drawn a total of just 8,700 fans to Dillon Stadium for the first two home games. Both Savin and Cutro thought Hartford fans had come to expect a Knights win, and if the home club did not devastate the opposition, they were disappointed.

Crittendon was unhappy because of his headgear. When the massive 6'5", 295-pounder joined the Knights, the biggest problem he encountered was finding a helmet big enough for his size 8½ head. He missed several days of practice while Cutro called around the country for a hat that would fit him.

Only 3,920 watched the Knights beat the Chiefs, the second smallest crowd in the team's six year history, second only to 3,100 at a 1970 game played in a driving rainstorm. As Berlet wrote, "When the generally regarded No. 1 minor league football team in the United States has but 3,920 fans present for a home game under ideal weather conditions, something is wrong, drastically wrong."[6]

The day after Berlet's column, the Knights and all of minor league football received some crushing news. Gary Davidson, a 39-year-old attorney who had been involved with the formation of the American Basketball Association and the World Hockey League, announced the birth of the World Football League, which would begin play in the late summer of 1974 and intended to compete with the NFL. Davidson's league would later sign NFL stars like Larry Csonka and Paul Warfield, but for the most part rosters would be filled with the best players in the ACFL. Many members of the 1973 Knights would earn places on WFL rosters, and if the Knights couldn't draw in 1973, how could they survive in 1974, bereft of their top talent?

Even after the 1970 facelift, many thought Dillon Stadium was an inadequate facility, not up to the standards of Kennedy Stadium in Bridgeport, and certainly inferior to Schaefer Stadium in Foxboro, where the New England Colonials played their home games. Schaefer Stadium had a capacity of 60,999, and if Dillon Stadium looked empty with 4,000 fans, Schaefer Stadium looked utterly ridiculous with the 2,914 who attended the Knights-Colonials game on October 26, or the 1,902 who appeared when the two teams played on November 16.

Attendance was anemic throughout the ACFL, and no team could survive with crowds of two or three thousand. The minuscule crowd that watched the Knights and Chiefs at Hempstead earlier in the season had been a bad portent, for Long Island's owners did not have deep pockets. After one game, kicker Booth Lusteg, who was supposed to be paid $100 a game, received an envelope from coach Len Feldhun containing $16 in cash, a check for $60, and a bill for $24 in phone calls he'd made from his hotel room. Then the squad was cut to 28 to save on salaries. One of the remaining players called Iacovazzi, who said he would send eight players and another coach.

The bus that left Hofstra for Schaefer Stadium had just 22 Long Island players, but when they arrived in Foxboro, they met Iacovazzi's eight conscripts, and a makeshift lineup took the field and lost 44–0. The next week when the players went to board the bus for Bridgeport, they found there was no bus. "Bad credit," Feldhun muttered as he loaded them into cars for the ride to Kennedy Stadium.

Elaine Savin and Joan Benedetto recalled the financial tribulations of the ACFL in its final year. "Finally we knew the end was coming," Elaine said. "In one of the last games, Pete was paying both teams. The other team didn't have the money, but there was a game to be played and he didn't want to disappoint the people. So he paid both teams."

"Mr. D'Addario would turn around and point at me," Joan remembered. "That meant I'd have to go to the office and pull checks to pay the other players so they'd go out and play. It was really bad if they went out and beat us. At least if we won we'd feel a little better."

On October 7, Iacovazzi announced that the Chiefs were ceasing operations, but two days later, they were back in business, with funds supplied by the other ACFL clubs. The revival was short-lived, and four days after their rebirth the Chiefs were dead for good. The players were declared free agents and the remaining games were to be 1–0 losses by forfeit.

In the meantime, the Jets were off to the best start in their history. After beating the Knights, they won their next six games to clinch a tie for the division title, with five games remaining. Most of the games weren't even close. The Jets defeated Western Mass 45–13, New York 33–0 and 38–0, and Long Island 28–0. The only close calls were a 34–30 win over Long Island and a 10–7 victory over Hartford.

The Knights (along with Pottstown) had been one of the two best teams in the ACFL since 1968, but the Jets had their number. After the second 1973 win, the Jets had beaten Hartford six times in their last nine meetings. They snapped the Knights 20-game winning streak in 1969, a 17-game regular season winning streak in the 1973 opener, and a 14-game home winning streak in the 10–7 win on October 6.

The only points in the second win over Hartford came on a 70-yard punt return by Piccone and a 47-yard field goal by newly-acquired left-footed soccer style kicker Richie Szaro. Szaro was a husky 6'2", 210-pounder who was born in Poland and arrived in the United States at the age of 12. At St. Francis Prep in Brooklyn, he played six sports, including football, where he was a kicker and star running back. Szaro was, said the *Post-Telegram*, "the most heavily-recruited New York athlete since the Lew Alcindor sweepstakes."[7] Upon his graduation from high school, he was also offered a $60,000 contract by the New York Skyliners professional soccer team.

In addition to being an outstanding athlete, Szaro was an excellent student who was fluent in English, Polish, Russian, French, and German. He was recruited by all the Ivy League schools and chose Harvard. Unfortunately, during the summer following his freshman year in Cambridge, Szaro stepped on a nail and suffered an injury that ended his career as a running back.

During his three year varsity career, Szaro was strictly a kicker, and scored more points than any kicker in the long history of Harvard football. He also set a New England record with a javelin throw of over 246 feet. Szaro began the 1973 season with the Colonials, but when the Patriots sent John Smith to New England, Szaro began playing for the Jets, commuting from his Boston home.

There was soon another new kicker in Connecticut, for in mid–October, Norm Davidson suffered a leg injury. As his replacement, the Knights signed Booth Lusteg, late of the defunct Chiefs and last seen in these chronicles leaving the Waterbury Orbits waiting angrily at the altar. Lusteg inherited Marvin Pettaway's number zero.

In 1967, the year he almost played for Waterbury, Lusteg was cut by the Dolphins and Jets, joined the Dolphins taxi squad, was activated, and played in eight games. The following year (1968) he was cut again by the Dolphins and picked up by the Steelers, for whom he played the final 13 games.

The Steelers had been doormats for years until they hired Coach Chuck Noll for the 1969 season. Noll was an old school coach who didn't like anyone who was "different," and Lusteg was clearly unique. One of his training techniques was to kick a paper cup wrapped in tape. Noll thought that was ridiculous and told him to stop doing it. Then he cut him.

After a couple of months of inactivity, Lusteg talked Green Bay coach Phil Bengston into giving him a tryout. He impressed Bengston with his booming kickoffs, was signed, and played the last four games. By the beginning of the 1970 season, Lusteg was jobless once more, and by 1973, at the age of 34, he was kicking for the Long Island Chiefs. When the Chiefs folded, and Davidson got hurt, the Knights became yet another stop in Lusteg's lengthy wanderings.

The New York Crusaders lost their first seven games before finally posting a win—a 1–0 forfeit over the defunct Chiefs. After their rocky start, the Crusaders underwent a complete overhaul. They had a new owner, Edward Petrillo, and a unique coaching arrangement. When he took over ownership of the team, Petrillo fired coach Jim Furey and replaced him with a five-man co-coaching staff, four of whom, Chuck Mercein, Bill Swain, Scott Eaton, and Bobby Duhon, were former New York Giants. Each coach had equal input into game decisions. Between the first and second time they played the Jets, the Crusaders brought in 20 new players, several, including quarterback Don Gault, from the Chiefs.

Western Massachusetts, featuring ten former Knights, was gritty and tough, as would be expected of a Fred Wallner-coached team, but they didn't have the talent necessary to compete with Hartford, Bridgeport, and New England. "It's no big secret," reported the *Post-Telegram*, "that competition in the league this year is, to say the least, spotty."[8] Very early in the season, it was apparent that Bridgeport was going to win the Southern Division and that the Knights and New England Colonials would compete for the right to meet them in the title game.

On October 19, Bridgeport and New England squared off in Foxboro. Jim Bulger, signed after the collapse of the Chiefs, played most of the game at quarterback for the Jets. The Colonials took a 16–0 halftime lead as the Jets, hampered by nine penalties, could not move the ball. A second half rally fell short and the Jets suffered their first defeat by the score of 19–9.

On October 26, before the Knights visited Foxboro to take on the Colonials, the standings were as follows:

Northern Division			Southern Division		
New England	7	1	Bridgeport	7	1
Hartford	6	2	Long Island	2	6
Western Mass	1	7	New York	1	7

A win would put the Knights in first place, but they weren't up to the task, falling 31–23, largely due to the efforts of former Massachusetts star Steve Schubert. Schubert, only 5'10" and 185 pounds, had not been drafted and signed with the Colonials in order to show pro scouts he was not too small to play in the NFL. On October 26 he showed them quite a bit.

Midway through the fourth quarter, the score was tied 17–17, and New England had the ball on its own 24-yard line. Colonial quarterback Bob Ehrhardt hit Schubert over the middle and the little receiver eluded two Knight defenders and raced into the end zone with the go-ahead touchdown. Hartford fumbled the ensuing kickoff, New England recovered, and one play later, Ehrhardt hit Schubert from 34 yards out with the score that decided the game.

Schubert wound up leading the ACFL in receiving and kickoff returns, and won a job with the New England Patriots the following summer. After one season with the Pats, he signed with the Bears and spent five more years in the NFL as a backup receiver and kick returner.

With the WFL looming on the horizon and one week of anemic attendance following another, it looked as though 1973 might be Pete Savin's final chance to bring another championship to Hartford. The odds were long, with a two game deficit and just three to play. One of New England's remaining games was against Long Island, and was thus a guaranteed 1–0 win. In order for the Knights to have a chance, they would have to win their next two games, which was expected, since their opponents were the lowly New York and Western Mass teams, and, in a more difficult proposition, Bridgeport would have to defeat New England. If all those eventualities occurred, the Knights could win the division by defeating New England in the final game.

As anticipated, the Knights won their two games. On November 9, they got the help they needed when Bridgeport beat New England 37–31 in a game with a very controversial ending. The Jets might have sewed the game up earlier but for the fact that Szaro made just two of seven field goal attempts and had three blocked. With 17 seconds left, and the Colonials trailing by six, New England fullback Andy Huff carried to the four-yard line, where he lost the ball in what appeared to be the Colonials' ninth fumble of the evening. Quarterback Ehrhardt picked the ball up and carried it into the end zone for the tying touchdown.

The officials, however, ruled that Huff was down at the four and the Colonials had to run another play. Ehrhardt then hit Schubert with a pass in the left flat, but the officials ruled that Schubert, struggling to get across the goal line, was stopped a foot short as the game ended. Colonial coach Tom Yewcic chased the officials to their dressing room. "The guys had it made and were robbed," he said later. "Those were two of the worst calls I have ever seen in all my years in football."[9]

The bizarre ending gave the Knights the chance they'd been hoping for. If New England won the final game, they were the champs. If the Knights won, the two teams would be tied, but the Knights would be awarded the title by virtue of having won two of the three games between the two teams.

The final game in the history of the Hartford Knights was a very disappointing one, played before less than 2,000 fans in massive Schaefer Stadium on a cold, windy evening. "It was really cold," recalled John Skladany. "My girlfriend was there and her family was there, and I think those were all the Hartford fans." Joe Ginnetti was so thrilled to be playing in a major league stadium he took one of the stools from the locker room as a memento.

The Colonials took a 13–0 lead into the dressing room at halftime, as the Knights offense was completely impotent. They managed only six first downs, 86 yards of offense and (-1) yards passing. When Charlie Reamon ran the second half kickoff back 89 yards for a touchdown, however, it seemed that maybe the Knights had some of their old magic left.

That hope vanished quickly, as Schubert ran the ensuing kickoff back 72 yards and John Smith booted a field goal to increase the lead to 16–7. Smith was the opposite of the well-traveled Lusteg, for he had never even seen a football game, much less played in one, until he was persuaded by the New England Patriots to cross the Atlantic and try out as a kicker.

Smith played soccer in England, and thought the idea of trying to play football would be an interesting adventure. The first time he ever saw a football game of any kind was when he'd lined up the past July to kick off in the Hall of Fame exhibition against the San Francisco 49ers. Smith had kicked well in practice, but hadn't realized there would be some very large men trying to knock him down after he kicked off. Smith survived the 49ers special teams, but not the final cuts of the Patriots and Steelers.

Rather than accept an offer to play soccer for a London team, he decided to join the Colonials to see if he could learn this strange new American game. After all, he could make $5,000 a year teaching in England, $10,000 playing soccer, or the $18,000 the Patriots would eventually offer him for the 1974 season. "That's a fortune just to kick a football," he thought.[10]

The Colonials methodically built a 30–7 lead, and the final score was 30–14. "They did everything better than we did,"[11] Cutro said afterwards. Four days later, as the Knights held their final weekly press conference, Pete Savin delivered the post mortem, not only of the 1973 season but of the franchise. In 1968 and 1969, it seemed as though the Knights were setting records every week. They had home winning streaks, overall winning streaks, and regular season winning streaks.

In 1973, the Knights began setting records of a less enviable type. It seemed that each home game set a mark for low attendance. On September 29 against the Chiefs, the Knights drew just 3,920, the second smallest home crowd in history. On October 20, the Knights and Pioneers attracted an even smaller crowd of 3,800. On November 3, the Knights leapfrogged into first place on the disappointing crowd list with just 3,032. A week later, with the weather getting colder and the quality of competition suspect, only 2,800 came out to see the return of Fred Wallner. For the year, in six home games, the Knights averaged just 4,279 fans, despite a crowd of roughly 7,000 that came to see the intrastate rivalry with Bridgeport.

Other clubs did little better. Long Island had not lasted the season. New England drew less than two thousand per game in perhaps the finest facility ever used by a minor league football team. Wallner's Western Mass team was averaging less than 700 per game in Holyoke. In the home finale against Bridgeport, the "crowd" was just 57 people,[12] with fewer in the stands than on the sidelines.

The Pioneers did no better on the road. "I remember we played down at Hofstra," said former Hartford quarterback Dave Bennett, one of the many ex–Knights who joined Wallner in Holyoke. "It was freezing cold, there was a driving rain, and there were about 50 people there. The crowds dwindled because we weren't very successful."

With the dismal results of 1973 and the WFL looming on the horizon, the die appeared to be cast. "I think they could see that the league was not the same," said Arnold Dean. "The other teams were not keeping up and you could see this was not going to last. It was pretty obvious to me. But Pete Savin was going to work it until it was dead, and sure enough it was."

"It just doesn't seem feasible to stay," Savin said at the final press conference. "I have to feel pretty much convinced the acceptance is not there." He noted that the WFL would probably sign 500 players, taking the best of the ACFL talent, and reminisced of how 8,000 tickets had been sold in two days for the 1968 championship game. "[A]lthough we still lost money," he said, "the enthusiasm and support made it worthwhile."[13] Now there was little enthusiasm for the Knights and losing money wasn't fun anymore. The Hartford Knights were history and Pete Savin became just another wealthy businessman, his days of roaming the sidelines and shouting at officials over for good.

The Jets had one more game to play—the championship contest against New England. It had been a great year for Frank D'Addario's crew, who finished the regular season with an 11–1 record, an unbelievable 8½ games ahead of the second place Crusaders and their 2–9 mark. Several Jets had fine individual seasons. Szaro led the league in scoring with 72 points. Frank DiMaggio led in passing, and Chuck Cornell and Donnie Shanklin were second and third in receiving with 37 and 36 catches, respectively.

The championship game was a letdown, as approximately 10,000 fans came to Kennedy Stadium to watch their Jets take a pounding from the Colonials. The final score of 41–17 was not indicative of the one-sided nature of the game, for New England had a 41–3 lead at the end of the third period. It was a very disappointing conclusion to the best season in Bridgeport Jet history. Neither Bulger nor DiMaggio was able to move the club, and New England quarterbacks Gary Wichard and Bob Ehrhardt drove their offense through the Bridgeport defense as if it were made of paper mache.

There was no way the ACFL could continue. D'Addario put his Jets in the Seaboard League for the 1974 season, making it to the championship game but losing to the Wilkes-Barre Bullets. Then the Bridgeport Jets, like the Hartford Knights, ceased to exist. The fierce intrastate rivalry that brought fans to Dillon and Kennedy Stadiums for five years was no more. Pete Savin and Frank D'Addario confined their competition to the construction business and their players either went to the WFL or stopped playing professional football.

Was there any way a minor league could have prospered other than having an owner willing to fund losses? The only solution would seem to be that which has enabled minor league baseball to survive—a subsidy from the major leagues. Major league baseball teams pay the minor leaguers' salaries and other expenses.

The NFL wanted nothing to do with football's minor leagues, since they got all the players they needed from college football at no cost.

The talent minor league football needed to prosper came at a price they couldn't afford, and when there were no longer enough owners or civic-minded citizens to pay the bill, there was no future. When the ACFL's best players went to the WFL, the question became academic. By 1974, the golden age of Connecticut minor league football was over.

Epilogue

Retired minor league football players don't spend their days playing golf and living off their fame. They go to work, and many of those who played in the 1960s and 1970s carved out very interesting post-football careers. Below are the stories of some of those who figured prominently in the narrative or had particularly compelling lives.

Don Abbey, fullback, Hartford Knights, 1971

Abbey's 1971 season with the Knights was the last year he played football. "I was forced out of the game," he said. "My mouth got so big and I was Joe Don Looney [a talented but rebellious 1960s running back] reincarnated. People wouldn't touch me with a ten foot pole no matter what my physical attributes were. After that early retirement from the game I loved so much I had a real tough time. I just couldn't live without it in my life. I didn't understand anything when it wasn't wrapped up in my daily routine of playing football. One day everybody knows who you are and the next day you can't get a cup of coffee. It takes a lot of adjustment and I feel very thankful and fortunate that I was able to get through that rough spot and start rebuilding and re-tooling my life and get started in the business world."

A year of medical school convinced Abbey he didn't want to be a doctor. He spent a couple of years in the Navy, went back to school on the GI bill, and then entered the world of commercial real estate. "I had $2,500 and a 1972 yellow Volkswagen when I started in the business in 1977," he recalled. After learning the fundamentals of owning and operating commercial properties, he started his own business in 1990 and named it the Abbey Company. As always, Abbey followed his own path to success. While most real estate operators were trying to use other people's money to make risk-free profits, Abbey invested his own funds and personally guaranteed debt.

"I'm probably one of the largest independent operators in the country," he said recently, "and I don't have partners for most of my properties, so everything is owned 100 percent by me. Once again, my obstinance got me to this point because the rest of the market was saying, 'Don't take a risk. Form a joint venture with an equity source. They give you the money and get the majority of the return but you don't take any risk.' I'd rather risk everything and get 100 percent of the return. I think a lot of the qualities I had as a successful football player made me a very successful businessman."

"There are guys who don't achieve what they think they should athletically, and they go and find another canvas to paint on. They overachieve because they're making up for what they thought they should have done on the athletic field. My athletic frustration has allowed me to become perhaps the exact opposite in the business world."

Abbey turned out to be a pretty good judge of risk and return, and accumulated a very impressive portfolio of properties. A few years ago, he was invited back to Penn State and toured around the campus by an eager group of fund raisers. When they sat down to lunch, they asked Abbey if he would like to consider a gift. He would. How much? "$8.5 million," Abbey replied. That was wonderful. Where would like his money to go—the football program, the endowment of an academic chair? No, said Abbey, as the fund raisers' hearts dropped like rocks, he would like the money to go to his old fraternity, Beta Theta Pi, to renovate the fraternity house and support the chapter's Man of Principle Program.

The Beta Theta Pi house in State College, Pennsylvania, is perhaps the best appointed fraternity lodge in America, and Abbey is an avid fund raiser for the Man of Principle Program, which encourages young men to succeed in life through hard work and accepting responsibility. "I believe it's the only thing I can point to," Abbey said, "as an alternative for people who don't want to go to college fat, dumb, and drunk. I didn't put this together. It's been going on across the country for about ten years and I discovered it a couple of years ago. It's a unique thing and I think it's a very important thing for our society."

As a young man, Don Abbey's bullheaded nature often got him into trouble and put a premature end to a promising football career. In middle age, it enabled him to excel in the business world and use his stubbornness to leave a legacy for a future generation.

Mike Adanti, center, Ansonia Black Knights, 1963

Adanti served as mayor of Ansonia from 1973 to 1977, and was a teacher for several years before becoming an assistant dean at Southern Connecticut State University. In 1984, he was named president of the university and served in that capacity for 19 years, during which time the school experienced tremendous

growth. After retiring in 2003, he was serving as CEO of the Monetary Funding Group when he was killed in 2005 as the result of an automobile accident during a vacation in Italy.

Wes Bean, kicker, Hartford Knights, 1968–1970, Bridgeport Jets, 1971

Bean, who never got an opportunity to kick in the NFL, passed away in October 2000 at the age of 54. At the time of his death he was employed by SNL Distribution Company. Honorary pallbearers at his funeral included legendary Grambling coach Eddie Robinson, Sr., and his son, Eddie Robinson, Jr.[1]

Dave Bennett, quarterback, Hartford Knights, 1968–1971

When the Knights joined the Seaboard League, Bennett decided not to play, due to the fact that the travel would interfere with his teaching job. When Fred Wallner returned from Canada to coach the Western Massachusetts Pioneers in 1973, he asked Bennett to join him. When the ACFL folded after the season, Bennett's career as an active football player ended.

While he was playing, Bennett taught at Holyoke Trade School and was an assistant coach at Holyoke High. He got his first opportunity as a head coach at West Springfield High, and then went to California for a few years. He returned to Massachusetts and won back to back Division I "super bowls" in 1983 and 1984. After going back to California for seven years, he returned to Massachusetts once more and served as offensive coordinator at Western New England College.

Joe Blake, defensive end, Richmond Roadrunners, 1968, Pottstown Firebirds, 1969–70

Blake was arrested for using heroin while in Pottstown, and began showing signs of increasing instability. He had a tryout with the WFL in 1974, but his body had deteriorated and he wasn't nearly the player he had been in Pottstown. "He was in bad shape," said former teammate John Land. "He looked like the typical homeless person." Land believed Blake died at Norristown State Hospital, an institution for the mentally ill.

Dick Bowman, defensive end, Hartford Charter Oaks, 1964–1965, Waterbury Orbits, 1966, New Britain Bees, 1967, Hartford Knights, 1968–1969

Bowman's first job while playing minor league football was as an advertising salesman for the G. Fox department store. He was not happy in retailing, and

Manch Wheeler suggested that Pete Savin might find him a job with Roger Sherman Rigging. Bowman accepted Savin's offer and remained in the business for the rest of his career, eventually working for Marino Crane in Middletown, Connecticut. He passed away in January 2013 after a lengthy illness.

Wayne Coleman, defensive tackle, Waterbury Orbits, 1966

Coleman did not realize his dream of a professional boxing career but, in 1970, he made his wrestling debut as a tag team partner of Dr. Jerry Graham and soon became known as Billy Graham, in tribute to the famous evangelist. He was one of the famous Graham "brothers" who included Jerry, Billy, Eddie, and Crazy Luke. Billy Graham joined the World Wrestling Federation in 1975, and defeated Bruno Sammartino for the WWF championship two years later.

Billy Graham was a bad guy, wrestling under the management of Ernie Roth, a diminutive man better known as the Grand Wizard of Wrestling. The Grand Wizard was a bizarre character who wore a turban and freaky looking sunglasses and handled most of the villains on the circuit.

"Superstar" Billy Graham was one of the foremost "heels" in professional wrestling, fighting all the good guys, and beating a lot of them, before having his career ended by a series of injuries in 1987. After his retirement from the ring, Graham experienced a number of severe health problems, which he attributed to extensive steroid use. His claims instigated a bitter feud with wrestling impresario Vince McMahon, who was fighting allegations that his association encouraged the use of steroids. After more than ten years, the rift was mended and Graham was inducted into the WWE Hall of Fame.

Sam Coppola, quarterback, Stamford Golden Bears, 1962

Coppola quarterbacked the Westchester Crusaders in 1963 and the Milford Rockets in 1965 and 1966 before retiring from active play at the age of 36. He continued with his many business pursuits, including real estate, Stamford Tile, and Stamford Marble and Granite. Coppola was an incurable entrepreneur who also attempted, unsuccessfully, to start a credit card brand and a franchise called Burger Circus. In the early 1980s, he moved to Hilton Head and opened a restaurant called Ice Cream Circus, which he operated for four years before selling it and moving back to Stamford to care for his elderly mother and disabled brother. He continued to run the tile business, and opened a Stamford nightclub called Paces, which played Frank Sinatra and Tony Bennett standards. The market for Sinatra and Bennett was waning by the 1980s, and the motif was changed to disco. In the late 1990s, Coppola sold most of his businesses and retired to Florida. He passed away in 2013.

Jim "King" Corcoran, quarterback, Wilmington Capitals, 1966, Waterbury Orbit, 1967, Lowell Giants, 1968, Pottstown/Pennsylvania Firebirds, 1969–1970, Norfolk Neptunes, 1971, Chambersburg Cardinals, 1972

Corcoran played for the Flint Sabres of the Midwest Football League in 1973. The following year the World Football League was formed, and the head coach of the WFL's Philadelphia Bell was Ron Waller. Waller signed the King and a number of other former Pottstown players, including running backs John Land and Claude Watts. Corcoran led the WFL in pass attempts, completions, touchdowns, and interceptions and was second in passing yards.

The WFL collapsed midway through the 1975 season, which Corcoran spent mainly as a backup. It was the King's last season, and he retired at the age of 31. The WFL was gone, the NFL was busy absorbing younger WFL refugees, and the minor leagues were not what they had been in the '60s. No minor league club was offering $125,000 contracts, not even bogus ones like Corcoran signed in 1969.

The King engaged in a multitude of activities over the succeeding decades. At one point he had a string of horses and played polo, although by that time he'd gained weight and was quite a load for the small ponies. He tried acting, but said he "couldn't take all the fags out there." Corcoran had a short stint as a lounge singer, dabbled in real estate, and engaged in some business activities that landed him in jail for fraud, theft, and tax evasion.

In 2000, when expanding and updating Professional Football, Pottstown, Pennysylvania, NFL Films found Corcoran in Las Vegas. He had taken on the persona of a Native American, and wore his long, dark hair tied back in a ponytail. Corcoran said he was $1/16$ or $1/32$ Lakota Indian and tried to cash in on the casino boom, taking the name Little Running Bear. He told people he was born on a reservation in Montana and orphaned at nine.

By that time, Corcoran looked and acted like an old, fat, sad Elvis, still surrounding himself with beautiful young women and acting as boastful as ever. He continued to refer to himself as The King, but it was a hollow charade. He'd never grown up and acquired a real personality and character apart from his contrived role.

Corcoran's son was interviewed at length for the film and said he was tired of the lies and con games and wanted nothing to do with his father. Corcoran told people his son was a Chippendale dancer and had appeared in *Young Guns*, neither of which was true. The last time he'd seen his son, Corcoran told him a number of Bruce Willis stories and said he was going to be in a movie with Willis.

Corcoran died of a massive heart attack in 2009, at the age of 65.[2] One obituary prompted a letter from his daughter, who said she hadn't seen her father in 22 years. Kelly Corcoran Hone was a mental health counselor and believed that her father's "larger than life personality" was really an underlying mental health condition. As a final epitaph, she wrote, "The show is over."

Frank ("Hi Ho") D'Addario, owner, Bridgeport Jets

Frank D'Addario died in 1986 at the age of 63 in the crash of his company plane, which had just taken off from Meigs Field in Chicago. His son David, then just 24, took over management of the family business, and has run it ever since.

Nick DeFelice, offensive tackle, Ansonia Black Knights, 1962–1963, Hartford Charter Oaks 1964 and 1967, Hartford Knights, 1968–1970

DeFelice held a multitude of jobs during his football career, principally teaching and selling. He was a salesman in the metal industry when he teamed up with two friends to form TAD Sales, which marketed injection molding products. When TAD ceased operations, DeFelice started Oxford Industries, where he is currently CEO. Oxford acts as the sales organization for a number of large companies, including some in the Fortune 500. DeFelice also owns a plastics manufacturing company in partnership with his son, a firm that makes a number of products for military and industrial applications.

Dave DiFilippo, coach, Pottstown Firebirds, 1968–1970

After the 1970 championship, with no more worlds to conquer in minor league football, DiFilippo resigned as Pottstown's coach to devote his full attention to finding a job in the NFL. He mailed brochures to every team in the league but never landed a position. DiFilippo died unexpectedly of a heart attack in 1983.

John Dockery, defensive back, Waterbury Orbits, 1967, Bridgeport Jets, 1968

Dockery played for the Jets from 1969 to 1971 and for the Steelers in 1972 and 1973. Following his retirement as an active player, he became a broadcaster, serving as co-host of *Sports Extra* with Bill Mazur on New York's WNYW, as a college football analyst for ABC, and as an NFL analyst for CBS. For many years, Dockery was a commentator on Westwood Radio's "Monday Night Football" broadcasts. He has operated a football camp with Joe

Namath for more than 40 years, and currently serves as CEO of Cambridge Corporate Services.

Joe Fenton, general manager, Hartford Knights, 1968

Fenton's one year stint as general manager of the Knights was his only involvement with professional football. He resigned in February 1969 with the stated intention of establishing himself in business in Perth, Australia, but in subsequent years his career took a much different path. Fenton discovered yoga, studied under Swami Satchidananda, and became a yogi and president of Integral Yoga Center of Pennsylvania. He assumed the name Sudharman and taught in colleges, hospitals, and churches throughout the United States and Europe. Sudharman played a key role in the establishment of Satchidananda Ashram-Yogaville, a 600-acre retreat in Buckingham, Virginia. He died at the age of 70 on July 5, 2010.[3]

Bill Fisher, defensive back, Hartford Knights, 1971

After leaving the Knights, Fisher had a tryout with the British Columbia Lions of the Canadian League. Late in camp, he received an offer of a teaching job in California, took it, and did not play football in 1972. The following year, he played for his old coach Ken Carpenter with the Indianapolis Capitols of the Midwest Football League.

In 1974, Fisher formed his own team, the Conejo Oaks, which joined the new California Football League. Fisher was owner, general manager, publicity director, and starting safety, and was quite successful in the latter two roles. Since he worked part time for a local newspaper, he had no trouble getting his press releases published. As safety, he intercepted nearly 30 passes over a two-year period. The Oaks finished second in 1974 and won the league championship the following season, while drawing about 5,000 a game.

Fisher sold his interest in the Oaks after the 1975 season, and dabbled in football for the next few years, playing a little, doing a little coaching, and handling public relations. Beginning in 1979, he concentrated on teaching English and theater. In 1990, Fisher co-founded the California Shakespeare Company, Southern California's only year-round producer of Shakespearean material. He has directed over 50 productions, and is involved in all aspects of the performance, including light design, set design, and costume design.[4]

Dennis Fitzgibbons, offensive tackle, Hartford Knights, 1968–1971

Fitzgibbons spent 35 years with the Hartford Insurance Group, holding positions in data processing and project management, before retiring in 2007.

After his retirement he taught special education for two years in Longmeadow, Massachusetts.

Lee Grosscup, quarterback, Hartford Charter Oaks, 1965

Grosscup spent one year with NBC as an analyst for AFL games, and then joined ABC as part of their college football broadcast crew. He spent over 40 years in broadcasting, including 20 with ABC, three years working USFL games, and 15 years announcing the games of the University of California. In 1982, Grosscup made a brief appearance in the film *Best Little Whorehouse in Texas*. Movies.toptenreviews.com rated him the 139,129th best actor of all time.

Mike Haffner, running back, Hartford Charter Oaks, 1965

In 1966, Haffner played two games with the Canadian League's Edmonton Eskimos before he was cut and signed by Montreal of the Continental League. In his second year with the Beavers, the team folded with two games left, and he was signed by the Denver Broncos for the final four weeks of their season. He wasn't eligible to play, but the Broncos paid him and invited him to camp the following summer.

Haffner made the 1968 Bronco team as a wide receiver. In his first AFL game, he caught the winning touchdown pass against the Bengals and was named the league's player of the week. On Monday morning, Haffner received a phone call from Dick Conner of the *Denver Post* informing him of the honor. "Don't get a fat head," Conner said. "Most of the writers were down covering the Olympics in Mexico, the quorum was from out west, and it included a lot of Bronco fans."

Lee Grosscup (courtesy Lee Grosscup).

Haffner got off to a

great start in 1969, catching 35 passes for 563 yards and five touchdowns before injuring his knee in the ninth game of the year. Haffner's knee bothered him for the rest of his career, which ended after three games with the Bengals in 1971. He finished his four-year AFL career with 59 receptions for 991 yards and seven touchdowns.

Oliver (Pudge) Henkel, quarterback, Ansonia Black Knights, 1962–1963

Henkel left the Ansonia Black Knights late in the 1963 season, after the club signed Vinnie Drake. He graduated from Yale Law School the following spring and moved to Cleveland with his wife and young child to join the firm of Jones, Day, Reavis and Pogue. Henkel soon became active in politics and was elected to the city council. One of his old law school classmates was Gary Hart, the Colorado senator who ran George McGovern's presidential campaign in 1972. The two men remained friends, and when Hart decided to run for president in 1983, he asked Henkel to manage his campaign. The latter put his legal career on hold, and from February 1983 until Hart lost the nomination at the Democratic convention the following year, devoted all his efforts to Hart's campaign.

From 1984 through 1987, Henkel was vice president of Progressive Corporation and then spent nineteen years with the firm of Thompson, Hine. In 2006, he joined the Cleveland Clinic as Chief Government Relations Officer, retiring in 2013. In addition to his professional career, Henkel has been very active in civic affairs, and was the founding chairman of the organization that developed the Playhouse Square section of Cleveland. The Playhouse Square project involved the renovation of a number of decayed old vaudeville theaters and resulted in the creation of a theater district second only to the Lincoln Center complex in New York City. Henkel was also involved in the creation of the Gateway sports stadiums in the city and has been active in a number of philanthropic ventures.

Marv Hubbard, fullback, Hartford Knights, 1968

After leading the ACFL in rushing in 1968, Hubbard thought he would be a free agent able to peddle himself to the highest bidder. He had not had a good experience with Oakland and was eager to move on. To his dismay, Hubbard learned that he had signed two one-year contracts with the Raiders, and was bound to report to them in 1969. He went to camp, made the team, played on special teams and served as a backup to Hewritt Dixon. By 1971, Hubbard was a starter, and for four consecutive years he rushed for more than 800 yards, peaking at 1,100 in 1972. He was selected to play in the Pro Bowl in 1971, 1972 and 1973. Unfortunately, Hubbard was on the injured reserve list during the Raiders'

1976 Super Bowl championship season; the ACFL crown he won with the Knights would be his only title. Hubbard finished his pro career with the Detroit Lions in 1977, retiring with an outstanding 4.8 yard per carry rushing average.

Tom Krzemienski, end, Hartford Charter Oaks, 1965–67

After the Charter Oaks folded, Krzemienski played a few games with the Detroit Wheels in 1968, but retired after suffering a couple of concussions. After a few years of teaching, he joined Owens Illinois as director of personnel and remained with the company for 20 years.

Krzemienski had his final moment of football glory in 1977, when he went to Chicago on a Monday night to watch his old teammate Joe Namath play for the Rams against the Bears. It was Namath's last game, and he was injured late in the contest. Krzemienski went down to the sideline to check on him, and the ABC cameras caught him and Namath leaving the field together. "The next day at work," he recalled, "I didn't get any work done because everyone was calling me saying they'd seen me on TV with Namath."

John Land, running back, Wilmington Clippers, 1966–1967, Harrisburg Capitols, 1968, Pottstown Firebirds, 1969–1970, Norfolk Neptunes, 1971, Chambersburg Cardinals, 1972

After years of playing with minor league clubs, Land, at the advanced football age of 30, followed Coach Ron Waller to the Philadelphia Bell for the 1974 and 1975 seasons. In 1974, he scored the first touchdown in WFL history, was the Bell's leading rusher with 1,136 yards, and the leading receiver with 57 catches. He was the fifth leading rusher and fourth leading receiver in the short history of the league.

While his football career was winding down, Land worked as a counselor for Del Tech Community College. He later took a sales position at Xerox Corporation and eventually was elevated to a management role.

Ray McDonald, fullback, Virginia Sailors, 1968, Roanoke Buckskins, 1969–1971

McDonald was out of football by the early '70s, and returned to Texas to work in a series of menial jobs. He kept his homosexuality a secret from his family and those friends and acquaintances that were not a part of that world. A romantic relationship ended when his partner threw boiling water at McDonald, putting him in the hospital. While recuperating, he met a nurse with whom he lived for two years.

In the late 1970s, McDonald went back to Washington, studied music, and got a job as a junior high school choir director. In 1986, he was again the victim of violence when a lover stabbed him in the back with a butcher knife, puncturing a lung. He nearly died from the wound, and after four months of hospitalization, went home with a long term death sentence, for he had tested positive for the HIV virus.

McDonald spent his final years in Washington, where his professional football career had begun with such promise. His once powerful body had wasted away to 120 pounds when he died on May 4, 1993.[5]

Larry McHugh, guard, Ansonia Black Knights, 1962–1963

McHugh became Xavier High School of Middletown's first head football coach in 1963 and remained there until 1983, posting a 160-38-6 record. He was elected to the Connecticut Coaches Hall of Fame in 1984 and the National Coaches Hall of Fame in 1986. In 1983, McHugh assumed the presidency of the nearly insolvent Middlesex County Chamber of Commerce. He increased membership from 282 to 2,450, the annual budget from $100,000 to more than $2 million, and built the organization into one of most honored and respected chapters in the United States. He is also chairman of the Board of Trustees of the University of Connecticut.

Bob Miranda, fullback, Hartford Knights, 1972–1973

Miranda has had a long career as a character actor and appeared in numerous movies, including *Sister Act, Thirteen Days* (in which he played Robert Kennedy's driver), *The Untouchables, Midnight Run,* and *Eraser*. He has also appeared on the television show *Miami Vice*.

Tom Morris, halfback, Waterbury Orbits, 1966, New Britain Bees, 1967, Hartford Knights, 1968–1971

When Morris first came to Hartford, he was a teacher in the local school system. He earned a master's degree in education from the University of Hartford and taught at Rensselaer University. Morris spent many years as an administrator at Hartford Hospital before leaving to start his own business, Tera Metals, Inc. He died unexpectedly in 2000 at the age of 58.[6]

Seiki Murono, quarterback, Philadelphia Bulldogs, 1966, New York Vikings, 1967, Pottstown Firebirds, 1968, Long Island Bulls, 1969–1970, Long Island Chiefs, 1971–1972

For several years, Murono played the dual role of quarterback and banker. As he got older and the hits became more painful, he decided banking provided safer and better long-term prospects. Murono was with Chase Manhattan Bank for many years, serving in Hong Kong as Asia Pacific CEO for Wealth Management, and in Singapore as Southeast Asia consumer and private banking head. He then returned to the U.S. as private wealth management CEO for the Western United States and president of the Chase Manhattan Trust Company of California.

After taking an early retirement from Chase at the age of 50, Murono became Chairman of the Board of Millennium Bank in San Francisco and is now a partner and managing director of Boyden Global Executive Search.

Jim Murphy, center, Hartford Knights, 1969–1972

Like so many former players, Murphy had a long career in coaching. He was head coach of the club football program at the University of Hartford for five years, and served as a physical education teacher at Kosciusko Junior High School in Enfield, Connecticut. In the 1980s, Murphy took a leave of absence from teaching to build houses and small subdivisions. When the real estate industry went into a deep slump in the early 1990s, he returned to teaching and worked in Springfield for 15 years. He retired and now builds homes on Cape Cod.

Joe Murphy, defensive tackle, Hartford Knights, 1969

Joe Murphy taught distributive education and coached football at Weaver High School in Hartford before leaving to form an international manufacturing company. "I had a master's degree," he said of his teaching days, "and I qualified for food stamps." Murphy now has five factories in China and travels all over the world promoting his products.

Lou Piccone, wide receiver, Bridgeport Jets, 1973

Piccone made the New York Jets roster during the strike season of 1974. "I came into the league as a scab in 1974," he said, "and went out as an executive committee member for the union in 1983." In three years with the Jets, Piccone was primarily a kick returner, but later with the Bills, he became a clutch third down receiver. In Buffalo, Piccone also became a fan favorite because of his intense desire, his sense of humor, and his outgoing personality. Whenever he touched the ball or made a play on special teams, the chant of "Lou, Lou, Lou!" rang out in Rich Stadium.

Waide Robinson, defensive back, Hartford Knights, 1969, Bridgeport Jets, 1970

Robinson was expecting his first child before the start of the 1970 season, and his wife told him it was time to get serious about life and forget about a football career. Robinson got *very* serious about life, and earned a master's degree in traffic and safety education from Southern Connecticut State College and a doctoral degree in Educational Leadership from Virginia Tech. For 43 years he worked as a teacher, principal, and in various administrative positions in school systems in Connecticut, Virginia, Florida, and Texas. At the time of his interview he was an adjunct professor at the University of Richmond, where he was also the director of the Math and Science Investigators Program.

Tom Rowland, defensive back, Hartford Knights, 1968–1970, Bridgeport Jets, 1971

In 1973, Rowland was invited to camp by the New York Jets. Just before he was to leave for New York, however, Illinois College offered him a teaching and coaching job. It was a wrenching decision. "If I go to camp with the Jets and don't make it," he said, "I've got *nothing*." Playing in the NFL was a dream, but the salary was only $12,000—*if* he made the team. IC offered him $10,000 a year and tenure if he got his master's degree in three years.

Rowland decided to return to his alma mater, and during the next three summers he earned a master's degree in health. He remained at Illinois College for 33 years, serving as assistant football coach for many seasons, the last few on a very bad team with a long winless streak. After the first game of 1998, the head coach was fired and Rowland was asked to take over. "You don't understand how bad this team is," he told the college president. "I'm not going to do it." The president didn't accept "no" and after the third request, Rowland gave in. The team lost its remaining nine games to finish 0–10, but improved to 2–7 the next year and then finished 6–4 two years in a row. After five years, Rowland retired, and now lives in his home state of Illinois.

Herb Savin, owner, Hartford Knights

Herb was killed, along with two others, in 1978 when his private plane crashed shortly after taking off from Brainerd Field en route to Newburgh, New York. He was 52 at the time and serving as president of Balf Construction and Savin Brothers Construction.

Pete Savin, owner, Hartford Knights

After the Knights ceased operations in 1973, Pete Savin was never again involved in the active management of a professional sports franchise, although he served as a director of the Hartford Capitols basketball team and of the New England Whalers hockey franchise. In 1982, he was elected to the Minor Pro Football League Hall of Fame.

In 1977, Savin had a massive heart attack and suffered from poor health until his death in 1998 at the age of 69. "It destroyed a good part of his heart," said his widow Elaine. "He was in bad health and a lot of pain, but he never complained. He just carried on." Pete soldiered on and did what he had done all his life: operated the family construction businesses, served in many charitable and philanthropic endeavors, and was active in his synagogue. He received numerous honors for his contributions to the Hartford community.

Bob Shemeth, defensive end, Ansonia Black Knights, 1963, Hartford Charter Oaks, 1964–1967, Hartford Knights, 1968

Shemeth worked for Clairol in Manhattan while he played professional football, but by the time he stopped playing, he'd had had enough of Madison Avenue. He moved to Florida, where a friend suggested he consider becoming a police officer. Shemeth decided to join a program that enabled him to shadow a police officer as an observer. He loved the experience, took the exam, went to the police academy, and wound up spending twenty years on the Fort Lauderdale police force. "Next to playing football," he said, "that was the most interesting occupation I had." To call Shemeth's police career interesting is an understatement. For eleven years he was in what police call "deep cover." "I was undercover with motorcycle gangs and organized crime," he said. "In the beginning it was a marijuana adventure era and it escalated into the cocaine cowboys."

In 1993, Shemeth retired from the police department, moved to Vermont, and bought a horse farm. For over 20 years, he has operated Kimberly Farms, offering boarding, riding lessons, and summer camps.

John Sponheimer, defensive tackle, Hartford Knights, 1969, Bridgeport Jets, 1970

Sponheimer finished law school shortly after ending his active football career, and is a partner in the firm of Hoyle and Sponheimer. His office in Ansonia, Connecticut, is just down the street from Nolan Field. Sponheimer has also served as an assistant coach for Ansonia High School for more than 40 years. His son Brendan was a defensive lineman for Yale and son Brian was a three year letterman at Harvard.

Bob Stohrer, end, Hartford Charter Oaks, 1966–1967, Hartford Knights 1968–1970

Stohrer left football in 1971 and opened a Shell station on Long Beach Island, New Jersey. The station was successful and he began adding complementary products. A towing company grew from one to ten trucks, and in 1983 Stohrer purchased a building and opened a Goodyear Tire store. In 2003, he opened a second store in the nearby town of Barnegat. Stohrer recently sold both stores and is looking forward to spending his retirement with his wife of nearly 50 years.

Ralph Tiner, linebacker, Hartford Knights, 1971–1973

Shortly after his football career ended, Tiner earned a master's degree in marine biology from the University of Connecticut. Upon graduation, he was hired by the state of South Carolina to conduct environmental impact reviews. In 1977, he joined the U.S. Fish and Wildlife Service and returned to New England to initiate and manage the service's National Wetlands Inventory for 13 northeastern states. He became the agency's leading wetland scientist and is an internationally recognized authority on wetlands.

Tiner is also a prolific author, producing over 250 publications, including textbooks, field guides, and articles. His book *In Search of Swampland* was recognized as the best science book for high school students by the American Association for the Advancement of Science. Tiner is also an adjunct professor at the University of Massachusetts.

Fred Wallner, coach, Hartford Charter Oaks, 1964–1965, Meriden Shamrocks, 1965, Waterbury Orbits, 1966, New Britain Bees, 1967, Hartford Knights, 1968–1971, Western Massachusetts Pioneers, 1973

After his coaching career ended, Wallner worked as an financial advisor, and died in 1999 at the age of 71.

John Wardlaw, wide receiver, Hartford Charter Oaks, 1965, Waterbury Orbits, 1966, New Britain Bees, 1967, Hartford Knights, 1968–1969, Long Island Bulls, 1970

Wardlaw retired from football after the 1970 season. Within a few years, he was deeply involved in social work in Hartford, and in 1977, much to his surprise, was asked to become the director of the Hartford Housing Authority. He did not have a degree in public administration and had no background in real estate management.

Wardlaw could have treated his position as a sinecure, keeping his head down and accumulating pension time. Instead, he attacked the job with a passion. "Few people thought as long and hard about public housing as Mr. Wardlaw did," the *Hartford Courant* wrote shortly after his death. Wardlaw wanted to make public housing the first step up a ladder of progress, not a dead end filled with drug dealers and felons. He believed in the biblical prophecy of helping those who helped themselves, and was relentless in waging war on criminal activity.

With the support of his friend and ally Mayor Mike Peters, Wardlaw embarked on an aggressive campaign to end the concept of public housing as what he called "concentration camps for the poor" and "incubators for social ills." Throughout his tenure as director, Wardlaw was a controversial figure, worshipped as a hero by many and reviled by some, including Hartford politician Elizabeth Horton Sheff, who called him "out of touch" and a wordsmith who lacked accomplishments.

During his thirty years with the Housing Authority, Wardlaw transformed the agency, and unfortunately, it transformed him. When he assumed the job in 1977 he began, at 38, to smoke cigarettes. Soon, he was smoking a lot of them, and by 2008 was suffering from an advanced case of lung cancer. He died on November 7, 2008.[7]

Manch Wheeler, quarterback, Portland Sea Dogs, 1964, Hartford Charter Oaks, 1965, Waterbury Orbits, 1966–1967, New Britain Bees, 1967, Hartford Knights, 1968, General Manager, Hartford Knights, 1969–1971

Wheeler left his general manager's position when the Knights joined the Seaboard League. As an executive with a winning team, Wheeler had enjoyed numerous perks in Hartford. He got a license plate that read "HKGM" and was tacitly allowed to park his car anywhere in the city without getting a ticket. "I could leave the motor running in the middle of Main Street and walk away," he said. The Knights hired twenty policemen for each game, and the officers were not about to jeopardize overtime pay, easy duty, and a chance to catch a ball game.

After leaving the Knights, Wheeler worked in a series of sales jobs, culminating in a position as national sales manager of Smith Gauge Company. After nine years with Smith, Wheeler had his fill of traveling and decided to return to his native Maine. For the next twenty years, he sold and appraised real estate in partnership with his brother-in-law. He then retired—sort of. At the time of his interview Wheeler, at the age of 71, was driving a taxi around the Bangor airport.

Appendix: Scores and Records by Season

Ansonia Black Knights

Date	Location	Opponent	Score	Record
9/1/62	Herkimer, NY	Frankfort	21–13	1–0–0
9/6/62	Providence, RI	Providence	14–28	1–1–0
9/8/62	Ansonia	Providence	0–0	1–1–1
9/16/62	Stamford, CT	Stamford	27–33	1–2–1
9/22/62	Ansonia	Frankfort	7–6	2–2–1
9/30/62	Portland, ME	Portland	20–15	3–2–1
10/6/62	Paterson, NJ	Franklin	7–20	3–3–1
10/13/62	Ansonia	Stamford	30–6	4–3–1
10/27/62	Ansonia	Paterson	7–14	4–4–1
11/24/62	Portland, ME	Portland	0–13	4–5–1

Date	Location	Opponent	Score	Record
8/25/63	Ansonia	Portland	36–19	1–0–0
9/1/63	Ansonia	Providence	7–24	1–1–0
9/7/63	Herkimer, NY	Frankfort	0–19	1–2–0
9/14/63	Ansonia	Jersey City	0–19	1–3–0
9/21/63	Mount Vernon, NY	Westchester	35–33	2–3–0
9/28/63	Springfield, MA	Springfield	6–20	2–4–0
10/5/63	Ansonia	Westchester	34–20	3–4–0
10/12/63	Duquesne, PA	Pitts. Valley	7–14	3–5–0
10/19/63	Newark, NJ	Newark	20–56	3–6–0
10/26/63	Ansonia	Baltimore	26–19	4–6–0
11/2/63	Hazleton, PA	Baltimore	0–26	4–7–0
11/16/63	Ansonia	Boston	7–38	4–8–0

Stamford Golden Bears

Date	Location	Opponent	Score	Record
8/26/62	Stamford	Providence	7–10	0–1–0
9/2/62	Portland, ME	Portland	0–14	0–2–0
9/9/62	Stamford	Frankfort	14–0	1–2–0
9/16/62	Stamford	Ansonia	33–27	2–2–0
9/30/62	Providence, RI	Providence	0–49	2–3–0

351

Date	Location	Opponent	Score	Record
10/13/62	Ansonia, CT	Ansonia	6–30	2-4-0
10/27/62	Herkimer, NY	Frankfort	6–28	2-5-0
11/7/62	Paterson, NJ	Paterson	0–31	2-6-0
11/11/62	Portland, ME	Portland	6–47	2-7-0

Hartford Charter Oaks

Date	Location	Opponent	Score	Record
8/15/64	Portland, ME	Portland	27–21	1-0-0
8/22/64	Hartford	Providence	38–21	2-0-0
8/29/64	Everett, MA	Boston	16–14	3-0-0
9/5/64	Hartford	Newark	10–37	3-1-0
9/12/64	Springfield, MA	Springfield	16–6	4-1-0
9/19/64	Hartford	Westchester	28–28	4-1-1
9/25/64	Providence, RI	Providence	24–28	4-2-1
10/3/64	Mt. Vernon, NY	Westchester	2–19	4-3-1
10/10/64	Herkimer, NY	Mohawk Valley	16–7	5-3-1
10/17/64	Hartford	Springfield	7–19	5-4-1
10/24/64	Hartford	Atlanta	34–7	6-4-1
10/31/64	Hartford	Boston	28–10	7-4-1
11/7/64	Jersey City, NJ	Jersey City	14–37	7-5-1
11/14/64	Hartford	Portland	41–6	8-5-1

Date	Location	Opponent	Score	Record
8/14/65	Richmond, VA	Richmond	17–10	1-0-0
8/21/65	Hartford	Toronto	16–39	1-1-0
8/29/65	Providence, RI	Rhode Island	7–19	1-2-0
9/4/65	Hartford	Richmond	21–27	1-3-0
9/12/65	Newark, NJ	Newark	0–43	1-4-0
9/18/65	Hartford	Norfolk	6–44	1-5-0
9/26/65	Wheeling, WV	Wheeling	14–34	1-6-0
10/2/65	Hartford	Philadelphia	22–62	1-7-0
10/9/65	Fort Wayne, IN	Fort Wayne	13–49	1-8-0
10/16/65	Hartford	Charleston	6–9	1-9-0
10/23/65	Hartford	Rhode Island	20–3	2-9-0
10/30/65	Hartford	Fort Wayne	30–55	2-10-0
11/7/65	Norfolk, VA	Norfolk	14–20	2-11-0
11/13/65	Charleston, WV	Charleston	7–41	2-12-0

Date	Location	Opponent	Score	Record
8/20/66	Hartford	Philadelphia	36–31	1-0-0
8/26/66	Toronto	Toronto	14–35	1-1-0
9/3/66	Hartford	Brooklyn	24–14	2-1-0
9/11/66	Norfolk, VA	Norfolk	26–21	3-1-0
9/17/66	Hartford	Richmond	48–28	4-1-0
9/24/66	Montreal	Montreal	7–31	4-2-0
10/2/66	Hartford	Norfolk	25–31	4-3-0
10/9/66	Wheeling, WV	Wheeling	24–13	5-3-0
10/15/66	Philadelphia	Philadelphia	14–28	5-4-0
10/22/66	Hartford	Wheeling	24–13	6-4-0
10/29/66	Hartford	Toronto	14–17	6-5-0
11/5/66	Hartford	Brooklyn	6–20	6-6-0
11/12/66	Hartford	Orlando	7–40	6-7-0
11/19/66	Charleston, WV	Charleston	24–31	6-8-0

Scores and Records by Season

Date	Location	Opponent	Score	Record
8/26/67	Hartford	Wheeling	30–17	1–0–0
9/2/67	Norfolk, VA	Norfolk	21–39	1–1–0
9/9/67	Hartford	Akron	27–17	2–1–0
9/16/67	Hartford	Toronto	16–3	3–1–0
9/23/67	Hartford	Orlando	0–30	3–2–0
10/1/67	Wheeling, WV	Wheeling	10–21	3–3–0
10/7/67	Hartford	Charleston	7–24	3–4–0
10/14/67	Orlando, FL	Orlando	24–38	3–5–0
10/22/67	Montreal	Montreal	0–14	3–6–0
10/29/67	Hartford	Montreal	38–14	4–6–0
11/5/67	Charleston, WV	Charleston	17–0	5–6–0
11/11/67	Hartford	Norfolk	31–43	5–7–0

Meriden Shamrocks

Date	Location	Opponent	Score	Record
8/14/65	Meriden	Brockton	21–6	1–0–0
8/21/65	Portland, ME	Portland	0–6	1–1–0
8/28/65	Meriden	Whitman	34–8	2–1–0
9/4/65	Meriden	Portland	23–20	3–1–0
9/11/65	Meriden	South Boston	41–14	4–1–0
10/2/65	Meriden	Nashua	30–32	4–2–0
10/9/65	Nashua, NH	Nashua	33–43	4–3–0
10/17/65	Meriden	Whitman	42–20	5–3–0
10/23/65	Meriden	Milford	21–32	5–4–0
10/30/65	Brockton, MA	Brockton	55–13	6–4–0
11/6/65	Milford, CT	Milford	27–6	7–4–0

PLAYOFFS

11/13/65	Meriden	Nashua	24–12	
11/20/65	Meriden	Portland	28–6	

Date	Location	Opponent	Score	Record
8/27/66	Malden, MA	South Boston	29–0	1–0–0
9/3/66	Meriden	Milford	36–14	2–0–0
9/10/66	Meriden	Maine	36–8	3–0–0
9/24/66	Bridgeport, CT	Bridgeport	13–41	3–1–0
10/8/66	Meriden	Nashua	25–21	4–1–0
10/15/66	Nashua, NH	Nashua	13–21	4–2–0
10/29/66	Meriden	South Boston	34–6	5–2–0
11/5/66	Meriden	Portland	Forfeit Win	6–2–0

CHAMPIONSHIP GAME

11/12/66	Meriden	Nashua	19–21	

Date	Location	Opponent	Score	Record
8/17/68	Meriden	Dorchester	40–20	1–0–0
8/24/68	Meriden	Malden	68–12	2–0–0
8/31/68	Marlboro, MA	Marlboro	13–24	2–1–0
9/7/68	Meriden	Dorchester	44–12	3–1–0

Date	Location	Opponent	Score	Record
9/14/68	Portsmouth, NH	Tri-City	12–12	3–1–1
9/28/68	Meriden	Marlboro	7–12	3–2–1
10/12/68	Malden, MA	Malden	34–40	3–3–1

Waterbury Orbits

Date	Location	Opponent	Score	Record
8/20/66	Atlantic City, NJ	Atlantic City	6–14	0–1–0
8/27/66	Waterbury	New Bedford	21–7	1–1–0
9/6/66	Waterbury	Jersey City	20–45	1–2–0
9/11/66	Pawtucket, RI	Rhode Island	17–17	1–2–1
9/17/66	Scranton, PA	Scranton	20–13	2–2–1
9/24/66	Waterbury	Wilmington	28–27	3–2–1
10/2/66	Waterbury	Scranton	51–7	4–2–1
10/8/66	Harrisburg, PA	Harrisburg	35–0	5–2–1
10/15/66	Lowell, MA	Lowell	24–29	5–3–1
10/22/66	Waterbury	Lowell	20–17	6–3–1
11/5/66	Jersey City, NJ	Jersey City	24–7	7–3–1
11/12/66	Waterbury	Scranton	42–21	8–3–1

Date	Location	Opponent	Score	Record
9/2/67	Alexandria, VA	Virginia	13–38	0–1–0
9/9/67	Waterbury	Wilmington	32–21	1–1–0
9/16/67	Waterbury	Westchester	14–31	1–2–0
9/23/67	Waterbury	Lowell	14–17	1–3–0
9/30/67	Harrisburg, PA	Harrisburg	26–5	2–3–0
10/8/67	Waterbury	Virginia	14–47	2–4–0
10/14/67	Lowell, MA	Lowell	24–21	3–4–0
10/21/67	Wilmington, DE	Wilmington	14–34	3–5–0
10/28/67	Waterbury	Harrisburg	42–6	4–5–0
11/4/67	Mount Vernon, NY	Westchester	20–7	5–5–0
11/11/67	Waterbury	Lowell	54–42	6–5–0
11/18/67	Mount Vernon, NY	Westchester	14–38	6–6–0

New Britain Bees

Date	Location	Opponent	Score	Record
8/11/67	Asbury Park, NJ	New Jersey	10–7	1–0–0
8/18/67	New Britain	Bridgeport	14–3	2–0–0
8/27/67	New Britain	N. Hampshire	21–19	3–0–0
9/1/67	Monmouth, NJ	New Jersey	21–36	3–1–0
9/8/67	Bridgeport	Bridgeport	3–0	4–1–0
9/24/67	New Britain	New York	34–17	5–1–0

Hartford Knights

Date	Location	Opponent	Score	Record
9/7/68	Pottstown, PA	Pottstown	13–7	1–0–0
9/14/68	Hartford	Lowell	34–13	2–0–0
9/21/68	Harrisburg, PA	Harrisburg	31–0	3–0–0
9/28/68	Hartford	Richmond	20–17	4–0–0

Scores and Records by Season

Date	Location	Opponent	Score	Record
10/5/68	Hartford	Westchester	41–7	5–0–0
10/12/68	Richmond	Richmond	24–27	5–1–0
10/20/68	Lowell	Lowell	32–26	6–1–0
10/26/68	Hartford	Bridgeport	19–17	7–1–0
11/1/68	Bridgeport	Bridgeport	37–7	8–1–0
11/9/68	Hartford	Harrisburg	26–7	9–1–0
11/16/68	Hartford	Pottstown	35–21	10–1–0
11/23/68	Mount Vernon, NY	Westchester	21–17	11–1–0

CHAMPIONSHIP

11/30/68	Hartford	Virginia	30–17	

Date	Location	Opponent	Score	Record
9/6/69	Hartford	Pottstown	18–3	1–0–0
9/12/69	Hempstead, NY	Long Island	22–14	2–0–0
9/19/69	Quincy, MA	Quincy	31–3	3–0–0
9/27/69	Hartford	Harrisburg	55–14	4–0–0
10/4/69	Hartford	Quincy	19–17	5–0–0
10/10/69	Bridgeport, CT	Bridgeport	23–14	6–0–0
10/18/69	Hartford	Roanoke	33–3	7–0–0
10/25/69	Harrisburg, PA	Harrisburg	37–14	8–0–0
11/1/69	Hartford	Long Island	16–6	9–0–0
11/7/69	Roanoke, VA	Roanoke	17–14	10–0–0
11/15/69	Hartford	Bridgeport	21–33	10–1–0
11/22/69	Pottstown, PA	Pottstown	14–48	10–2–0

CHAMPIONSHIP

11/29/69	Hartford	Pottstown	0–20	

Date	Location	Opponent	Score	Record
9/5/70	Hartford	Indianapolis	6–13	0–1–0
9/11/70	Jersey City, NJ	Jersey Jays	27–0	1–1–0
9/19/70	Hartford	Orlando	20–17	2–1–0
9/26/70	Hartford	Jersey Jays	10–7	3–1–0
10/2/70	Bridgeport, CT	Bridgeport	28–37	3–2–0
10/10/70	Hartford	Jersey Tigers	23–12	4–2–0
10/17/70	Pottstown, PA	Pennsylvania	27–36	4–3–0
10/24/70	Orlando, FL	Orlando	16–25	4–4–0
10/30/70	Hempstead, NY	Long Island	20–24	4–5–0
11/7/70	Hartford	Bridgeport	17–7	5–5–0
11/13/70	Hartford	Long Island	10–7	6–5–0
11/20/70	Elizabeth, NJ	Jersey Tigers	24–17	7–5–0

CHAMPIONSHIP

12/12/70	Hartford	Pennsylvania	0–31	

Date	Location	Opponent	Score	Record
8/28/71	Roanoke, VA	Roanoke	24–7	1–0–0
9/4/71	Hartford	Bridgeport	15–21	1–1–0
9/11/71	Norfolk, VA	Norfolk	44–13	2–1–0
9/17/71	Bridgeport, CT	Bridgeport	24–27	2–2–0

Date	Location	Opponent	Score	Record
9/25/71	Hartford	Roanoke	27–5	3–2–0
10/2/71	Norfolk, VA	Norfolk	17–6	4–2–0
10/9/71	Roanoke, VA	Roanoke	16–0	5–2–0
10/16/71	Hartford	Bridgeport	37–21	6–2–0
10/23/71	Hartford	Norfolk	16–12	7–2–0
10/29/71	Bridgeport, CT	Bridgeport	41–7	8–2–0
11/6/71	Hartford	Roanoke	19–7	9–2–0
11/13/71	Norfolk, VA	Norfolk	0–37	9–3–0

CHAMPIONSHIP

Date	Location	Opponent	Score	Record
11/20/71	Hartford	Norfolk	13–24	

Date	Location	Opponent	Score	Record
8/5/72	Portsmouth, VA	Portsmouth	52–7	1–0–0
8/12/72	Hartford	Long Island	52–7	2–0–0
8/19/72	Hartford	Aston	39–13	3–0–0
8/26/72	Conshohocken, PA	Conshohocken	25–7	4–0–0
9/2/72	Kulpmont, PA	N'thumberl'nd	58–7	5–0–0
9/9/72	Hartford	Portsmouth	58–0	6–0–0
9/16/72	Hartford	Chambersburg	47–0	7–0–0
9/23/72	Hempstead, NY	Long Island	30–24	8–0–0
10/1/72	Hagerstown, MD	Hagerstown	28–9	9–0–0
10/7/72	Chambersburg, PA	Chambersburg	13–7	10–0–0
10/14/72	Media, PA	Aston	45–0	11–0–0
10/21/72	Hartford	Reading	41–0	12–0–0
10/28/72	Hartford	Columbus	30–21	13–0–0*
11/4/72	Hartford	Hagerstown	34–0	14–0–0

*Regularly scheduled game versus Conshohocken won by forfeit

PLAYOFFS

Date	Location	Opponent	Score	Record
11/11/72	Hagerstown	Hagerstown	56–14	
11/18/72	Hartford	Chambersburg	17–7	

Date	Location	Opponent	Score	Record
8/31/73	Bridgeport, CT	Bridgeport	17–19	0–1–0
9/8/73	Hempstead, NY	Long Island	48–13	1–1–0
9/15/73	Hartford	New England	20–10	2–1–0
9/21/73	Holyoke, MA	W. Mass.	17–13	3–1–0
9/29/73	Hartford	Long Island	58–10	4–1–0
10/6/73	Hartford	Bridgeport	7–10	4–2–0
10/13/73	Mt. Vernon, NY	New York	39–14	5–2–0
10/20/73	Hartford	W. Mass.	49–21	6–2–0
10/26/73	Foxboro, MA	New England	23–31	6–3–0
11/3/73	Hartford	New York	30–0	7–3–0
11/10/73	Hartford	W. Mass	37–7	8–3–0
11/16/73	Foxboro, MA	New England	14–30	8–4–0

Bridgeport Jets

Date	Location	Opponent	Score	Record
9/7/68	Bridgeport	Harrisburg	13–17	0–1–0
9/14/68	Pottstown, PA	Pottstown	24–0	1–1–0
9/21/68	Mount Vernon, NY	Westchester	24–14	2–1–0
9/27/68	Bridgeport	Lowell	26–26	2–1–1

Scores and Records by Season

Date	Location	Opponent	Score	Record
10/4/68	Bridgeport	Virginia	20–28	2–2–1
10/12/68	Harrisburg, PA	Harrisburg	24–16	3–2–1
10/18/68	Bridgeport	Pottstown	27–7	4–2–1
10/26/68	Hartford, CT	Hartford	17–19	4–3–1
11/1/68	Bridgeport	Hartford	7–37	4–4–1
11/9/68	Lowell, MA	Lowell	29–28	5–4–1
11/15/68	Bridgeport	Westchester	14–28	5–5–1
11/23/68	Herndon, VA	Virginia	10–7	6–5–1

Date	Location	Opponent	Score	Record
9/5/69	Bridgeport	Long Island	3–0	1–0–0
9/13/69	Roanoke, VA	Roanoke	10–22	1–1–0
9/19/69	Bridgeport	Richmond	0–32	1–2–0
9/26/69	Hempstead, NY	Long Island	19–12	2–2–0
10/4/69	Richmond, VA	Richmond	42–7	3–2–0
10/10/69	Bridgeport	Hartford	14–23	3–3–0
10/18/69	Quincy, MA	Quincy	22–14	4–3–0
10/24/69	Bridgeport	Pottstown	17–34	4–4–0
10/31/69	Harrisburg, PA	Harrisburg	14–20	4–5–0
11/8/69	Bridgeport	Harrisburg	24–17	5–5–0
11/15/69	Hartford, CT	Hartford	33–21	6–5–0
11/21/69	Bridgeport	Quincy	31–0	7–5–0

Date	Location	Opponent	Score	Record
9/4/70	Bridgeport	Jersey Tigers	16–14	1–0–0
9/12/70	Norfolk, VA	Norfolk	3–14	1–1–0
9/19/70	Jersey City, NJ	Jersey Jays	14–9	2–1–0
9/25/70	Hempstead, NY	Long Island	24–14	3–1–0
10/2/70	Bridgeport	Hartford	37–28	4–1–0
10/9/70	Bridgeport	Pennsylvania	26–30	4–2–0
10/16/70	Bridgeport	Orlando	31–7	5–2–0
10/24/70	Bridgeport	Long Island	19–13	6–2–0
10/30/70	Elizabeth, NJ	Jersey Tigers	26–35	6–3–0
11/7/70	Hartford, CT	Hartford	7–17	6–4–0
11/14/70	Bridgeport	Jersey Jays	24–28	6–5–0
11/20/70	Richmond, VA	Richmond	17–9	7–5–0

Date	Location	Opponent	Score	Record
8/27/71	Bridgeport	Norfolk	7–10	0–1–0
9/4/71	Hartford, CT	Hartford	21–15	1–1–0
9/10/71	Bridgeport	Roanoke	24–20	2–1–0
9/17/71	Bridgeport	Hartford	27–24	3–1–0
9/24/71	Norfolk, VA	Norfolk	10–30	3–2–0
10/2/71	Roanoke, VA	Roanoke	21–31	3–3–0
10/8/71	Bridgeport	Norfolk	13–34	3–4–0
10/16/71	Hartford, CT	Hartford	21–37	3–5–0
10/22/71	Bridgeport	Roanoke	3–37	3–6–0
10/29/71	Bridgeport	Hartford	7–41	3–7–0
11/6/71	Norfolk, VA	Norfolk	28–31	3–8–0
11/13/71	Roanoke, VA	Roanoke	14–53	3–9–0

Date	Location	Opponent	Score	Record
8/31/73	Bridgeport	Hartford	19–17	1–0–0
9/7/73	Bridgeport	W. Mass.	45–13	2–0–0
9/15/73	Mount Vernon, NY	New York	33–0	3–0–0
9/21/73	Bridgeport	Long Island	34–30	4–0–0
9/28/73	Bridgeport	New York	38–0	5–0–0
10/6/73	Hartford, CT	Hartford	10–7	6–0–0
10/12/73	Bridgeport	Long Island	28–0	7–0–0
10/19/73	Foxboro, MA	New England	9–19	7–1–0
10/26/73	Bridgeport	New York	24–3	8–1–0
11/3/73	Holyoke, MA	W. Mass.	44–20	9–1–0
11/9/73	Bridgeport	New England	37–31	10–1–0

CHAMPIONSHIP

Date	Location	Opponent	Score	Record
11/23/73	Bridgeport	New England	17–41	

Chapter Notes

Introduction

1. *Bridgeport Post-Telegram*, October 27, 1968.
2. Hartford Knights program, September 29, 1973, p. 14.

Chapter 1

1. *The Coffin Corner*, Vol. 4, No. 8 (1982), page 1.
2. Hartford Knights program, October 10, 1970, p. 5.
3. Most of the information on the Blues comes from *The Hartford Blues*, by John Hogrogian, in *The Coffin Corner*, Vol. 4, Nos. 8 and 9.

Chapter 2

1. *Sports Illustrated*, December 16, 1968

Chapter 3

1. *Sports Illustrated*, September 22, 1980.

Chapter 4

1. *New York Herald Tribune*, February 25, 1958.
2. *New York Times* obituary, September 1, 2002.
3. *Evening Sentinel*, August 21, 1962.
4. *Evening Sentinel*, August 3, 1962.
5. *Evening Sentinel*, August 24, 1962.
6. A summary of the history of the Steamroller can be found at http://en.wikipedia.org/wiki/Providence_Steam_Roller.
7. *Evening Sentinel*, September 21, 1962.
8. In 1964, 17 ex–Syracuse players were with the team.
9. *Evening Sentinel*, September 28, 1962.
10. *Evening Sentinel*, October 13, 1962.
11. *Evening Sentinel*, October 19, 1962.
12. *Evening Sentinel*, October 29, 1962.
13. *Evening Sentinel*, November 3, 1962.
14. *Evening Sentinel*, July 26, 1963.
15. After his military commitment was fulfilled, Bellino played briefly and ineffectively with the Boston Patriots and then returned to the ACFL as general manager of the Quincy Giants. He lasted just over a month before resigning.

Chapter 5

1. Coppola named his self-published autobiography *The Silent Quarterback*.
2. Coppola, p. 58.
3. *Stamford Advocate*, September 7, 1962.
4. *Stamford Advocate*, October 19, 1962.
5. *Stamford Advocate*, November 14, 1962.

Chapter 6

1. *Hartford Courant,* January 28, 1964.
2. *Hartford Courant*, February 7, 1964.
3. Ibid.
4. Ibid.
5. *Fitchburg Sentinel*, November 2, 1945.
6. *Hartford Courant*, February 25, 1964.
7. *Hartford Courant*, August 6, 1964.
8. *Hartford Courant*, August 10, 1964.
9. Ibid.
10. *Hartford Courant*, August 24, 1964.
11. Ibid.
12. *Hartford Courant*, September 21, 1964.

13. *Hartford Courant*, October 28, 1964.
14. Ironically, the man who presided over the integration of major league baseball was mentioned as a possible running mate for George Wallace when the latter ran for president in 1968.
15. *Hartford Courant*, April 8, 1965.
16. *Hartford Courant*, May 9, 1965.
17. *Hartford Courant*, February 28, 1965.
18. Quoted in *Hartford Courant*, February 28, 1965.
19. Ray Dozier, *The Oklahoma Football Encyclopedia*, p. 153.
20. *Hartford Courant*, August 2, 1965.
21. *Hartford Courant*, August 9, 1965.
22. *The Pittsburgh Press*, December 13, 1964.
23. Grosscup stopped drinking in 1971 and for over 40 years has been helping others with substance abuse problems.
24. *Hartford Courant*, September 8, 1965
25. *Hartford Courant*, September 9, 1965
26. Many years later, when Grosscup was a broadcaster, he interviewed Dan Henning, then head coach of the San Diego Chargers. He asked Henning what coaches had most influenced him. "You did, Lee," Henning replied, "when you were player-coach of the Hartford Charter Oaks."
27. *Hartford Courant*, September 21, 1965.
28. *Hartford Courant*, October 30, 1965.
29. Kreigel, p. 49.

Chapter 7

1. *Hartford Courant*, January 13, 1966.
2. *The Sporting News*, January 15, 1966.
3. Ibid.
4. *Hartford Courant*, January 16, 1966.
5. *Hartford Courant*, February 20, 1966.
6. *Hartford Courant*, May 3, 1966.
7. Ibid.
8. Caruso also served as public relations director for the Charter Oaks.
9. *Hartford Courant*, September 4, 1966.
10. *Hartford Courant*, September 5, 1966.
11. *Hartford Courant*, September 17, 1966.
12. *Hartford Courant*, October 14, 1966.
13. *Hartford Courant*, December 1, 1966.
14. Ibid.
15. Ibid.
16. *Hartford Courant*, December 2, 1966.
17. Ibid.
18. *Hartford Courant*, December 7, 1966.
19. *Hartford Courant*, December 30, 1966.
20. The coach of the San Jose club was future 49er head coach Bill Walsh.

21. *Hartford Courant*, August 24, 1967.
22. *Hartford Courant*, June 20, 1967.
23. *Hartford Courant*, September 19, 1967.
24. *Hartford Courant*, September 4, 1967.
25. *Hartford Courant*, July 16, 1967.
26. *Hartford Courant*, August 28, 1967.
27. *Hartford Courant*, October 28, 1967.
28. *Hartford Courant*, October 29, 1967.
29. *Hartford Courant*, November 7, 1967.
30. *Hartford Courant*, November 13, 1967.

Chapter 8

1. *Morning Record*, September 8, 1965.
2. *Morning Record*, October 4, 1965.
3. *Morning Record*, November 9, 1965.
4. Boehle had finished his season with the Charter Oaks, but Hartford owner Don Brewer claimed he was still under contract and threatened to sue if Boehle played for the Shamrocks. Boehle ignored him and played anyway.
5. *Morning Record*, September 10, 1966.
6. *Morning Record*, September 21, 1966.
7. *Morning Record*, September 22, 1966.
8. *Morning Record*, November 12, 1966.
9. *New Britain Herald*, July 31, 1967.
10. *New Britain Herald*, August 14, 1967.
11. *New Britain Herald*, September 20, 1967.
12. The information on Ginzo Murono came from an interview with Seiki Murono and "Testimony of Mr. Ginzo Murono provided to the Commission on Wartime Relocation and Internment of Civilians Act, November 23, 1981."
13. *New Britain Herald*, September 16, 1967.
14. *New Britain Herald*, October 7, 1967.
15. *Morning Record*, September 16, 1968.
16. *Morning Record*, October, 13, 1969.
17. *Hartford Courant*, October 29, 1970.

Chapter 9

1. *Waterbury Republican*, March 22, 1966.
2. *Waterbury Republican*, April 10, 1966.
3. *Waterbury Republican*, April 13, 1966.
4. *Waterbury Republican*, June 5, 1966.
5. *Waterbury Republican*, June 26, 1966.
6. *Waterbury Republican*, June 15, 1966.
7. *Waterbury Republican*, September 4, 1966.
8. Biographical data for Cutro can be found at shipraiders.com.
9. *Waterbury Republican*, August 24, 1967.

10. http://www.baltimoreorgan.com/organ/index.php?option=com_content&view=article&id=449:king-corcoran&catid=19.

11. After Corcoran's death, Al Goldstein wrote an article that erroneously gave Corcoran credit for beating Staubach, which elicited an angry reply from Petry that read, in part, "I was the QB that year from the 2nd play of the first game to the end of the season. If you were there Alan you must have been drunk or loosing [sic] your mind." baltimoreorgan.com

12. *Waterbury Republican*, September 6, 1967.

13. *Waterbury Republican*, December 23, 1967.

14. Ibid.

15. *Waterbury Republican*, September 9, 1967.

16. *Waterbury Republican*, August 6, 1967.

17. Much of the information on Lusteg's background is taken from his autobiography, *Kick Rejection ... and Win*.

18. *Waterbury Republican*, October 10, 1967.

19. *Waterbury Republican*, October 13, 1967.

20. *Waterbury Republican*, November 10, 1967.

21. *Hartford Courant*, August 25, 1965.

22. *Waterbury Republican*, November 15, 1967.

23. *Waterbury Republican*, January 10, 1968.

24. *Waterbury Republican*, February 9, 1968.

Chapter 10

1. *Hartford Courant*, October 31, 1968.

2. Perhaps Hartford should not have been so upset that New Haven was forging ahead, for the latter city's coliseum was imploded in 2007. Hartford's Civic Center is still standing, while city and state officials decide its fate. The retail component of the development prospered for a while and then faded, and the opening of the Connecticut Convention Center created competition the aging Civic Center (now known as the XL Center) could not survive.

3. *Hartford Courant*, January 15, 1968.

4. *Hartford Courant*, March 19, 1968.

Chapter 11

1. *Sports Illustrated*, September 22, 1980.

2. Brandt and Wichard's quotes are from the *Bridgeport Post-Telegram*, February 4, 1972.

3. Unfortunately, the enduring image of Smith is that of him dropping a sure touchdown pass in the 1979 Super Bowl, his final professional game.

Chapter 12

1. *Sports Illustrated*, January 11, 1982.

2. Ironically, according to author Jay Acton, who spent the entire 1970 season with the Firebirds, Dave DeFilippo, the coach employed by underwear mogul Gruber, made a point of never wearing underwear.

3. John Madden, *Hey, Wait a Minute, I Wrote a Book*, division of Random House, New York: Villard, 1984, pp. 162–3.

4. Much of the background information on Meeks was obtained from an undated article in The *Hartford Times* by Dennis Randall, who was kind enough to provide me with a copy.

5. Cincinnati was in its first year in the AFL and received multiple picks. Bean was actually the 21st player selected by the Bengals.

6. Quoted in undated article from the *Hartford Times*.

7. *Idaho Statesman*, December 20, 2007.

8. www.profootballtalk.nbcsports.com/2013/05/03/vince-lombardi-accepted-gay-players-on-his-team.

Chapter 13

1. *Hartford Courant*, November 12, 1969.

2. Program for 1970 championship game, p. 5.

Chapter 14

1. *Hartford Courant*, February 8, 1970.
2. *Hartford Courant*, February 21, 1970.
3. *Hartford Courant*, March 17, 1970.
4. *Hartford Courant*, May 19, 1970.
5. *Hartford Courant*, June 2, 1970.
6. *Hartford Courant*, June 17, 1970.
7. *Hartford Courant*, September 5, 1970.
8. Ibid.
9. Ibid.
10. Ibid.
11. *Hartford Courant*, September 7, 1970.
12. Knights Program, November 7, 1970, p. 5.
13. *Hartford Courant*, November 7, 1970.
14. Acton, p. 207.
15. Acton, p. 242
16. The championship game is covered in Acton pp. 239–250.

17. Acton, p. 243.
18. *Bridgeport Post-Telegram*, October 23, 1970.
19. Ibid.

Chapter 15

1. D'Addario's real first name was Fiore, which means flower in Italian. In an effort to Americanize himself, he always referred to himself as F. Frank D'Addario.
2. Apparently the luggage rack was where ballboys slept, for Ansonia general manager Frank Berlinger's son Bob also dozed there on his way home.
3. *Bridgeport Post-Telegram*, October 6, 1968. George Plimpton was a writer who spent the 1963 training season with the Detroit Lions disguised as an erstwhile quarterback. Plimpton's final product was *Paper Lion*, one of a series of writings based upon Plimpton's succession of Walter Mitty episodes.
4. *Bridgeport Post-Telegram*, October 26, 1968.
5. *Sports Illustrated*, September 5, 1988.
6. *Sports Illustrated*, December 4, 1967.
7. *Bridgeport Post-Telegram*, June 9, 1969.
8. Knights program, September 27, 1969, p. 5.
9. *Bridgeport Post-Telegram*, September 9, 1969.
10. *Bridgeport Post-Telegram*, September 14, 1969.
11. *Bridgeport Post-Telegram*, September 20, 1969.
12. *Bridgeport Post-Telegram*, November 6, 1969.
13. *Hartford Courant*, August 1, 1970.
14. *Bridgeport Post-Telegram*, June 18, 1970. Apparently Pat Palinkas didn't need a padded bra, for the media eagerly informed the public that she measured 35–25–34.
15. *Bridgeport Post-Telegram*, August 18, 1971.
16. *New York Times*, August 17 and 20, 1970.
17. *Bridgeport Post-Telegram*, August 18, 1970.
18. *New York Times*, August 31, 1970.
19. *New York Times*, September 5, 1970.
20. *Bridgeport Post-Telegram*, September 28, 1970.
21. Later in the season, Florence joined the Hartford Knights and played against the Jets, before the Knights released him for poor attendance at practice.

22. *Bridgeport Post-Telegram*, August 27, 1971.
23. *Bridgeport Post-Telegram*, July 20 and 31, 1971.

Chapter 16

1. *Hartford Courant*, July 4, 1971.
2. *Hartford Courant*, June 18, 1971.
3. *Hartford Courant*, October 23, 1971.
4. *Hartford Courant*, July 29, 1971.
5. Information on Bill Fisher was obtained primarily from "Shakespeare in Cleats: The Story of Bill Fisher, from Minor League Vagabond to Shakespeare Aficionado" by Ace Hendricks in *The Coffin Corner*: Vol. 27, No. 2 (2005).
6. *Hartford Courant*, August 16, 1971.
7. *Hartford Courant*, August 30, 1971.
8. *Hartford Courant*, September 13, 1971.
9. After Simpson was acquitted of murder, Tucker wrote an apparently unpublished manuscript called "The O.J. I Know."
10. *Hartford Courant*, October 4, 1971.
11. *Bridgeport Post-Telegram*, September 29, 1971.
12. *Bridgeport Post-Telegram*, November 6, 1971.
13. Sistrunk is perhaps best known for the remark of Monday Night Football commentator Alex Karras who, noting Sistrunk's shaved head, a style extremely rare at the time, said that Otis was a graduate of the University of Mars.
14. *Hartford Courant*, October 25, 1971.
15. *Bridgeport Post-Telegram*, October 28, 1971.
16. *Hartford Courant*, October 31, 1971.
17. *Bridgeport Post-Telegram*, October 28, 1971.
18. *Hartford Courant*, October 31, 1971.
19. *Hartford Courant*, November 3, 1971.
20. *Bridgeport Post-Telegram*, November 11, 1971.
21. *Bridgeport Post-Telegram*, November 14, 1971.
22. *Hartford Courant*, November 15, 1971.
23. *Hartford Courant*, November 22, 1971.

Chapter 17

1. *Bridgeport Post-Telegram*, May 21, 1972.
2. *Morning Herald* (Hagerstown, MD), March 16, 1972.
3. *The Daily Mail* (Hagerstown, MD) July 24, 1972.

4. http://en.wikipedia.org/wiki/Conshohocken,_Pennsylvania.
5. *Hartford Courant*, July 14, 1972.
6. Gooden had an outstanding season for the Knights, put on 27 pounds and was in demand when the year ended.
7. *The Morning Herald*, September 11, 1972.
8. *Hartford Courant*, August 14, 1972.
9. Ibid.
10. Ibid.
11. Unlabeled internet post from Hugh Wyatt.
12. *The Miami News*, November 22, 1978.
13. Disney took extreme liberties when creating the movie about Papale's life. In the movie, he is depicted as someone plucked from the streets of Philadelphia with no football experience. In fact, he played two years of Seaboard League football and two years in the World Football League. He also failed to score a touchdown against the Giants in real life, as he did on screen.
14. *Hartford Courant*, September 11, 1972.
15. *The Morning Herald*, September 18, 1972.
16. *The Morning Herald*, September 11, 1972.
17. Ibid.
18. Ibid.
19. Ibid.
20. *Hartford Courant*, September 14, 1972.
21. *Hartford Courant*, October 12, 1972.
22. *Hartford Courant*, September 19, 1972.
23. *Hartford Courant*, October 13, 1972.
24. *Hartford Courant*, September 25, 1972.
25. *Hartford Courant*, October 23, 1972.
26. *Hartford Courant*, October 26, 1972.
27. Quoted in *Hartford Courant*, October 9, 1972.
28. *Hartford Courant*, October 12 and 13, 1972.
29. *Hartford Courant*, September 16, 1972.
30. Quotes on Corcoran's leaving Canada and joining Chambersburg are from the *Bridgeport Post-Telegram*, November 3, 1972, and *The News* (Frederick, MD) July 29, 1972.
31. *The Daily Mail*, November 13, 1972.
32. *Hartford Courant*, November 20, 1972.
33. *Hartford Courant*, October 31, 1972.
34. *Hartford Courant*, November 23, 1972.

Chapter 18

1. *Sports Illustrated*, September 22, 1980.
2. Marvin Pettaway was on the Casinos' roster, but he didn't play against his former teammates. "He had gotten in trouble," said Elaine Savin, "not with the law but with his lady friend. So he didn't play."
3. *Hartford Courant*, August 29, 1973.
4. *Hartford Courant*, September 5, 1973.
5. *Hartford Courant*, September 26, 1973.
6. *Hartford Courant*, October 1, 1973.
7. *Bridgeport Post-Telegram*, November 7, 1973.
8. *Bridgeport Post-Telegram*, October 26, 1973.
9. *Hartford Courant*, November 16, 1973.
10. http://sports.espn.go.com/boston/nfl/news/story?id=4584811.
11. *Hartford Courant*, November 17, 1973.
12. Gill, p. 20.
13. *Hartford Courant*, November 21, 1973.

Epilogue

1. www.afrigeneas.com/obituaries/la/bean_wesley.html.
2. An excellent profile of Corcoran is "It's Good to be the King" by George Bozeka, *The Coffin Corner*, July/August 2011.
3. http://dailyitem.com/obituaries/x302724526/Sudharman-70-New-Berlin
4. Information on Bill Fisher was obtained primarily from "Shakespeare in Cleats: The Story of Bill Fisher, from Minor League Vagabond to Shakespeare Aficionado" by Ace Hendricks in *The Coffin Corner*: Vol. 27, No. 2 (2005).
5. Most of the information on McDonald's life is taken from *The Idaho Statesman*, December 30, 2007.
6. *Hartford Courant*, September 13, 2000
7. Much of the information on Wardlaw's tenure with the Hartford Housing Authority was gathered from articles in the *Hartford Courant* dated November 11 and 12, 2008. Wardlaw's obituary indicated he was 71 at the time of his death in 2008, suggesting that he may have shaved a couple of years off his age for football, since his football records list his year of birth as 1939.

Bibliography

Books

Acton, Jay. *The Forgettables: The Bittersweet Portrait of a Minor League Football Team in the Heart of America*. New York: Thomas Y. Crowell, 1973.

Coppola, Sam, and Rock Osbourne. *Silent Quarterback*. Stamford: Milliemarble Sales, 2010.

Dozier, Ray. *The Oklahoma Football Encyclopedia*. New York: Sports, 2006.

Gill, Bob with Steven M. Brainerd, and Tod Maher. *Minor League Football, 1960–1985: Standings, Roster and Statistics*. Jefferson, NC: McFarland, 2002.

Kriegel, Mark. *Namath: A Biography*. New York: Penguin, 2004.

Lusteg, G. Booth. *Kick Rejection ... and Win*. Baltimore: Publish America, 2001.

Madden, John. *Hey, Wait a Minute, I Wrote a Book*. New York: Villard, 1984.

Meriden Public Library under the direction of Meriden's Bicentennial Committee. *Meriden at 200: A Half-Century of Change*. Meriden, 2006.

Newspapers

Bridgeport Herald
Bridgeport Post-Telegram
Chicago Tribune
The Daily Iowan
The Daily Mail (Hagerstown, MD)
The Evening Sentinel
Fitchburg Sentinel
The Gazette (Iowa City, IA)
Hartford Courant
Hartford Times
Idaho Statesman
Lowell Sun
Miami News
Morning Herald (Hagerstown, MD)
The Morning Record (Meriden, CT)
New Britain Herald
New York Herald Tribune
New York Times
The News (Frederick, MD)
Newsday (Long Island)
Pittsburgh Press
The Sporting News
Stamford Advocate
Washington Post
Washington Times
Waterbury Republican

Interviews

Personal interviews were conducted with the following individuals:

Don Abbey
Pete Anderson
Joan Benedetto
Dave Bennett
Bruce Berlet
Bob Berlinger
Ken Blasser
Bill Boehle
Dick Bowman
Joel Cooney
Nick Cutro
David D'Addario
Norm Davidson

Arnold Dean
Nick DeFelice
John Dockery
Dennis Fitzgibbons
Joe Ginnetti
Lee Grosscup
Bruce Haak
Mike Haffner
Oliver Henkel
Tom Hermanowski
Howard Holcomb
Harry Katzman
Bob Kelso
Joe Klimas
Tom Krzemienski
Tony Kyasky
John Land
Roger LeClerc
Bill Lesinski
Fran Mallick
Rich Marazzi
Larry McHugh
Roger Milici
Tim Miller
Bob Mirabelle
Bob Miranda
Mike Mosolf
Seiki Murono
Jim Murphy
Joe Murphy
Pat Palinkas
Lou Palmer
Lou Piccone
Tony Pontillo
Mark Proskine
Pete Quackenbush
Dennis Randall
Bill Richter
Waide Robinson
Tom Rowland
Sandy Rubera
Tom Rychlec
Elaine Savin
Al Shanen
Bob Shemeth
Bob Sherlag
Tom Sherman
John Skladany
John Skubel
John Sponheimer
Bob Stohrer
Harry Theofiledes
Charlie Tiblom
Ralph Tiner
Bob Tucker
Manch Wheeler

Other

Ansonia History Collection at the Ansonia Public Library.
Atlantic Coast Football League 1971 Directory and Schedule.
Hartford Knights, Hartford Charter Oaks, Jersey Jays, Pennsylvania Firebirds, Long Island Bulls, Jersey Tigers, Bridgeport Jets, and Waterbury Orbits game programs.
minorleaguebaseball.com.
pottstownfirebirds.com.
Testimony of Mr. Ginzo Murono Provided to the Commission on Wartime Relocation and Internment of Civilians Act.
University of Iowa game program.

Periodicals and Articles

The All-American Blockers by Bernie McCarthy (library.la84.org).
Bozeka, George. "It's Good to Be the King." *The Coffin Corner*,* Vol. 33, No. 4.
Gill, Bob. "Don Jonas: Best Little Quarterback You Never Heard Of." *The Coffin Corner*,* Vol. 16, No. 3.
Hendricks, Ace. "Shakespeare in Cleats: The Story of Bill Fisher, from Minor League Vagabond to Shakespeare Aficionado." *The Coffin Corner*,* Vol. 27, No. 2.
Hogrogian, John. "The Hartford Blues." *The Coffin Corner*,* Vol. 4, Nos. 8 and 9.
Maxymuk, John. "He Was a Contender: Hank Washington." *The Coffin Corner*,* Vol. 30, No. 5.
Rozendaal, Neal. "Remembering Duke Slater." *The Coffin Corner*,* Vol. 34, No. 6.
Sport.
Sports Illustrated.
Street and Smith's Official 1966 College Football Yearbook.

**The Coffin Corner* is a publication produced by the Professional Football Researchers' Association.

Index

Abbey, Don 3, 5, 24–6, 28, 36, 175–6, 185, 288–9, 294–6, 302, 335
Acton, Jay 361
Adams, Bob 48
Adams, Tony 325
Adanti, Mike 336
Adley, Dan 139
Akron Vulcans 110, 113, 115
Albert, Frankie 283
Allard, Don 75
Allen, George 111, 187
Allen, Mel 99
Alley, Don 254
Altieri, Tom 175
Altobello, Mayor Henry 117
Amato, Bruno 64, 65
Anderson, Bob 265–7, 269, 284–5, 307
Anderson, Dave 283
Anderson, Pete 26, 28, 37, 173, 288, 299
Anderson, Roger 300
Andrews, Dan 299
Andrews, Mike 155
Ansonia Black Knights 5, 21–2, 30, 38–61, 67, 70, 198, 351
Antwine, Houston 84
Aston Knights 303–4
Astoria Regalmen 62
Atlanta Spartans 78
Atlantic City Senators 141, 143
Austin, Bill 195
Avco Lycoming 163

Babacas, Socrates 82
Babbidge, Homer D., Jr. 165–6
Bach, Eleanor 303
Bailey, John 8
Baker, John 195
Baksi, Joe 303
Balducci, Rich 136
Baltimore Broncos 58–9
Barber, Bill 211
Barbuto, James 115
Barron, Ted 56, 59, 154
Barron, William 21

Barrows, Bob 74
Bauman, George 127
Bayonne High School 146
Bean, Wes 211–4, 217–8, 221–2, 225–6, 230–2, 235, 237, 244, 251–2, 266, 292–3, 296, 337, 361
Beban, Gary 273
Beck, Frank 49, 77
Beddoes, Dick 81
Behunick, Dennis (Whitey) 62
Bell, Bert 19
Bell, Walter 127
Bellino, Joe 56, 359
Benedetto, Joan 11, 260–1, 327
Bengston, Phil 199, 328
Bennett, Dave 26, 199–200, 202, 208, 219, 222, 225–6, 233, 237–8, 246, 324, 331, 337
Berlet, Bruce 170, 304–5, 308, 312–4, 325–6
Berlinger, Bob 60, 362
Berlinger, Frank 41–2, 45–48, 51–3, 57–9, 61, 362
Best, Terry 113, 206, 207, 213, 222, 224
Bialosuknia, Wes 16
Bidwill, Bill 189
Bidwill, Charles 189
Billingsley, Beau 135
Bivins, Jim 263
Blackney, Harry 113
Blake, Joe 205, 235–6, 258, 300
Blake, Robert 309
Blakely, Bob 103, 106
Blasser, Ken 27, 149, 175, 248–9, 291, 297, 299
Bledsoe, Gene 147
Bleier, Rocky 277
Blue, Forrest 228
Bodley, Hal 151–2
Boehle, Bill 73, 77, 87, 124, 129, 140, 177, 208, 306, 360
Booker, Lorenzo 4
Boozer, Emerson 156–7, 182
Bork, George 75
Boston Patriots 17, 143, 231
Boston Sweepers 54, 56, 59, 65, 69, 75, 78–9, 154, 188

Index

Bowen Field (New Haven) 139, 145
Bowens, Cecil 306, 317–9
Bowman, Dick 6, 12, 29, 34, 82, 123–4, 128, 140, 169, 172–3, 176–7, 189–91, 193–5, 210, 212, 222, 257, 324, 337
Boyle Stadium 65, 66
Braddock, Jim 140
Bradshaw, Terry 289
Brando, Marlon 207
Brandt, Gil 181, 186
Bratkowski, Zeke 199
Brazinski, Sam 303
Brennan, Bob 135
Brewer, Bill 71
Brewer, Don 70–73, 78, 81–2, 85, 89–90, 98, 103, 107–109, 111–2, 114, 121, 123, 169, 360
Brewer, Ned 70–1
Bridgeport Jets 22, 216, 218, 232, 234, 251, 260–301, 320–33, 356–358
Bridgeport Rockets 128–9, 131
Brockmeyer, Tom 214, 222
Brockton Pros 123–4
Brodhead, Bob 20, 82, 102, 131
Brooklyn Dodgers 100, 103–4, 106, 109, 110, 112
Brooklyn Lions 16
Broulillet, Arthur 165
Brown, Bill 56
Brown, Jimmy 190
Bruney, Fred 188
Bryant, Paul (Bear) 289
Bucci, Joe 58, 73
Buchanan, Buck 226–7
Buckman, Neal 50, 53
Budd, Frank 184
Buffalo Bills 224
Bulger, Jim 329
Bulkeley, Morgan 14
Burnett, Billy 158
Burnett, Bobby 157
Burnett, Tommy 157–8
Burns, Jerry 266–7
Burton, Cliff 125
Burton, Leon 20
Butts, Wally 87

Calabrese, Jay 231
Calabrese, Tom 78–9
Calcaterra, Jack 220, 222
Calhoun, Jim 16
Calvario, Bob 203
Cantina Ristorante 5–6
Carlas, Gustave 232
Carlin, Vidal 113
Carlos, John 184
Carlson, Dick 222
Carpenter, Ken 111–2, 291, 341
Carr, Tom 310, 315
Carroll, Bill 272, 284, 297–9
Carroll County Chargers 302
Caruso, Mickey 101, 360

Casey, Gene 42, 48, 53, 118, 124, 126, 134, 135
Castiglione, Joe 135
Cavalli, Carmen 131, 204
Ceppa Field 119, 122
Chamberlain, Wilt 41
Chambersburg Cardinals 315, 317
Champi, Frank 223, 271
Champion, Cornell 114
Chandler, Albert (Happy) 80–1, 96–98
Chandler, Don 182
Charleston Rockets 93, 97–99, 106, 110, 111, 114
Chlebek, Ed 20–1
Christy, Earl 147
Clancy, Gil 140
Clarkin Field 15
Cloutier, Dave 83
Coelho, Jan 278
Coleman, Herb 140
Coleman, Wayne 140, 338
Colquette, Ernie 78, 193, 222
Columbus Bucks 315
Committee for Non-Violent Action (CNVA) 162
Conejo Oaks 341
Conerly, Charley 84, 95, 99
Connecticut Bearcats 1–2
Connecticut Giants 43
Conner, Dick 342
Connery, Sean 309
Connors, Dick 119–21, 125, 127, 136, 264, 322–3
Conshohocken Steelers 303, 313
Continental League 21–2, 79, 80, 81, 96–9, 110, 112, 169, 242
Conzelman, Jimmy 46
Cook, Elmer 270
Cooney, Joel 134, 264
Coppola, Sam 48, 64–5, 67–8, 122, 338, 359
Corcoran, Jim (King) 12, 147–51, 156, 203, 205, 215, 217, 229, 234, 242, 254–6, 263–5, 288, 29–4, 303, 315–7, 339–40, 361, 364
Cornell, Chuck 321, 325
Corrigan, Thomas 70
Cosell, Howard 282
Coughlin, Tom 228
Counts, Johnny 30, 63, 67–9
Cox, Bill 220
Cozza, Carmen 271
Creedon, Bill 213
Cretella, Salvatore 116
Crittendon 325–6
Cronkite, Walter 280
Crow, John David 190
Crow, Wayne 106
Crowley, Jim 15
Csonka, Larry 326
Culp, Curley 226
Curko, Stan 153
Curran, Mayor Hugh 264

Index

Cutro, Nick 33, 35, 145–7, 149, 151–3, 155, 159, 184–5, 218, 246, 262, 264, 269, 284, 303–8, 310, 311–3, 315, 317–8, 320, 324–6, 331, 360
Czuckery, William 163–4

D'Addario, David 261–2, 269, 276, 280, 298
Daddario, Emilio 8
D'Addario, Frank (Hi-Ho) 11, 22, 252–4, 260–3, 268–9, 271, 276, 278, 286, 288, 292–3, 297–8, 307, 325, 327, 332, 340, 362
Darraugh, Dan 226
Daugherty, Duffy 91
Davidson, Gary 326
Davidson, Norm 6, 180, 290–1, 293–6, 300, 303, 306–8, 312, 319, 323, 328
Davis, Al 92, 94
Davis, Emory 310
Davis, Ernie 189–90
Davis, Tom 300, 316
Dawson, Jim 88
Dean, Arnold v, 6, 10, 169–71, 173, 194, 233, 249–50, 255, 257, 304, 332
Dee, Bob 84
DeFelice, Nick 5, 6, 9, 11, 28, 30, 31, 43–4, 47–8, 51, 53, 58, 73, 89, 172, 176–77, 181, 184, 191–4, 217, 222, 225, 227, 232, 235, 238, 244, 257, 268, 340
DeFillippo, Lou 64
Dell Isola, John 103, 107
Delpo, Duke 141
Dempsey, Gov. John 139, 163
Dempsey, Tom 152–3
Dennis, Sonny 76
Desysenko, Wasyl 201
Detroit Wheels 344
Dial, Benji 105, 234
DiFilippo, Dave 203–5, 229, 236, 254–6, 258, 340, 361
DiGravio, Ron 113, 124
DiLeo, Jake 66
Dillon Stadium v, vi, 2, 3, 5, 70–74, 77, 78, 89, 95, 103, 114–5, 168–9, 191, 201, 208, 211, 216, 218, 232–3, 239–41, 249, 251, 254, 257–8, 296, 299, 312, 314–5, 321, 324, 326
DiMaggio, Frank 307–9, 319, 321, 332
Dioguardi, William 265
Dixon, Hewitt 343
Dixon, Jay 299
Dockery, John 30, 147, 150, 155–6, 181–2, 185, 268, 271, 275, 283, 340
Dodd, Christopher 163
Dodd, Thomas 163
Dolbin, Jack 9–10
Dooley, Mayor Kenneth 126
Dorsett, Tony 179
Dow Chemical Company 165
Dowler, Boyd 322
Dowling, Brian 270–2, 274–5, 282
Downer, Clifford 42
Doyle, Joseph 39

Drake, Ron 319
Drake, Vinnie 40, 44, 57–61
Drumm, Lt. Clarence 54
DuBois, Wes 219, 222, 237
Ducharme, George 308
Dugan, Fred 65, 67
Duhon, Bobby 328
Dunlevy, Bob 105
Dunn, Jim 270
DuPont, Edward 151
Durant, Marjorie 207
Dziadik, Bob 48

Easterly, Dick 49
Eastern Football League 134
Eaton, Scott 328
Egresitz, Joe 216
Ehrhardt, Bob 329, 332
Ehrlich, George 237
Eisenhauer, Larry 84
Eldon B. Keith Field 123
Ellis, Bob 294
Ellis, Roger 105
Erickson, Keith 102
Etcheverry, Sam 316
Ewbank, Weeb 146–7, 153, 156–7, 177, 263, 275, 277, 283–4, 322–3

Fabrizi, John 262
Fallon, Gary 49
Fassell, Jim 4
Faucette, Dick 219–24, 250, 252, 277
Feldhun, Les 326
Fenton, the Rev. Arnold 40
Fenton, Joe 174, 202, 341
Finklehoff, Fred 99
Fisher, Bill 34, 291–2, 341, 362–3
Fitzgibbons, Dennis 10, 33, 149, 175–6, 185, 191, 193–94, 213, 222, 228, 237, 244, 248, 255, 257, 299, 312, 321, 341–2
Fletcher, Ron 82–3
Florence, Wally 280–1, 285, 362
Flores, Tom 226
Flushing Vets 62
Fort Wayne Warriors 98–100
Franchina, Joseph 66
Frankford Yellow Jackets 16
Frankfort Falcons 45, 48–9, 67
Franklin Miners 62, 119
Frederick Falcons 302
Freedman, Eli 240–1
Freiheit, Al 77, 127–30
Fuccillo, Chuck 56, 59
Furey, Jim 328

Gabriel, Jim 53–5, 135–6
Gabriel, Roman 187
Gaiters, Bobby 101, 107, 112
Gant, Edward 165
Gardner, Mitchell 127
Garrett, Jim 156

Index

Gault, Don 328
Gehrig, Lou 14
Gelish, Carole Ann 141
Gengras, Clayton 141
Genovese, Joe 127
Gentile, John 82
George, Nick 265
Geraghty, John 79
Giardi, Gus 124
Ginnetti, Joe vi, 30, 144, 156, 180, 261, 274, 280, 288, 290, 293, 297, 317, 320, 323, 330
Glacken, Scotty 150
Gladstone, Louis 163
Glynn, Mayor William 71
Goeke, Jerry 127
Gogolak, Pete 47, 154
Goldberg, Frank 102
Goldberg, Whoopi 309
Goldstein, Al 361
Gollarney, Gene 6, 192–4, 212, 222
Gooden, Harry 306, 363
Gordon, Israel "Babe" 139
Grabowski, Jim 198
Graham, "Superstar" Billy 338
Graham, Otto 269, 273
Granatelli, Tom 77, 98–9
Grange, Red 128
Greco, Ralph 47
Green, Vic 99
Greene, "Mean Joe" 182
Gregg, Forrest 199
Gresco, Joe 135
Grier, Rosie 187
Griffin, Len 222
Griffing, Glynn 140
Grosscup, Lee 9, 26–28, 84–8, 90–5, 101–2, 182–3, 342, 360
Groza, Lou 212
Gruber, Ed 203, 254–5, 257, 288, 361
Gunaldo, Don 145

Haak, Bruce 275–6
Haffner, Mike 87–8, 92–5, 102, 342
Hagerstown Bears 303
Hagler, Mike 131
Hall, Daryl 203
Hamden Hall Country Day School 172
Hanner, Dave 198
Hanratty, Terry 223
Harris, Franco 182, 289
Harris, James 224, 225
Harrisburg Capitols (also known as Capitol-Colts) 49, 143, 158–9, 207, 219, 231–2, 242, 265
Harrison, Don 159
Hart, Gary 343
Hartford Blues 14–16
Hartford Charter Oaks 22, 30, 70–115, 121, 169, 352–3
Hartford Chiefs 14

Hartford Civic Center 166–7, 239–40, 361
Hartford Colonials 3–4
Hartford Dark Blues 13–4
Hartford Knights v, vi, 3, 5, 8–11, 13, 17–8, 22, 37, 43, 72–3, 164, 167–8, 178, 180, 187, 200–202, 205, 211, 217–8, 222, 224, 227–8, 230, 239–242, 256, 265, 268, 276, 287–8, 300, 302–3, 308, 311, 313, 319–20, 324–5, 330, 332, 335, 337, 340–1, 343, 345–350, 354–6, 359, 362, 366
Hartford Whalers 14
Hartman, Marea 278
Hayes, Bob 195
Hayes, Roger 265
Hayes, Woody 270
Haynie, Jim 234, 256, 258, 288
Henkel, Oliver (Pudge) 42, 46, 50–1, 54, 55, 57–8, 61, 166, 343
Hennessey, Clint 42
Henning, Dan 82, 91, 360
Henry, Chick 57–9, 73–5, 78, 118
Herman, Charley 215
Herman, Dave 269
Hill, Calvin 270
Hill, Winston 192
Hilton, Baron 96
Hines, Jimmy 184
Hipp, Red 302–3
Hirsch, Elroy 88
Hoffman, Abbie 161
Hogrogian, John 13
Holcomb, Howard 170–1, 173, 249–50, 304–5, 308, 311
Holland, Lou 92
Holliday, Ron 256–7, 297, 300, 316
Holovak, Mike 65, 188
Holtz, Lou 308
Holyoke Bombers 82, 89
Hone, Kelly Corcoran 340
Horn, Don 199
Howard, Luther 325
Howell, Jim Lee 182
Hubbard, Marv 4, 9, 207, 216, 222, 224, 233, 307, 318, 343
Hubert, Don 267
Huff, Andy 330
Huff, Sam 210
Humphrey, Hubert 163
Humphreys, David 38
Hunt, Jim 84
Hunt, Lamar 96
Hunt, Tom 268
Hunter, Billy 190
Hurn, Frank 110, 112, 115

Iacovazzi, Cosmo (ACFL commissioner) 219, 252–3, 264–5, 281, 286–7, 295, 299, 302, 326, 327
Iacovazzi, Cosmo (Princeton player) 156
Impellitteri, Sam 39
Impellitteri, Vincent 38

Index

Indianapolis Capitols 249
Interstate Football League 302
Irvin, Lew 210, 222, 225

Jackson, Gene 222
Jackson, Keith 282
Jackson, Red 65, 67
Jacques, Jim 324
Jagger, Mick 3
James, Dick 210
James, Jerry 131
Janes, Dick 265, 293
Jartos, Ted 131
Jenkins, Dan 271
Jersey City Giants 51, 54
Jersey City Jets 140, 142
Jersey Tigers 242
Jilleba, Pete 299
Johnson, Ann 171
Johnson, Jerry 74–9, 83, 122, 124, 127–8
Johnson, Preston 176
Johnson, Randy 188
Jonas, Don 31, 82, 90, 106
Jones, Deacon 187
Joyner, Bill 215
Jurgensen, Sonny 102, 220, 273, 284

Karras, Alex 282, 362
Kates, Jim 294, 299
Katzman, Harry (Lime) 39–41, 57, 60
Kellett, Don 51
Kelly, Thomas 117, 119, 123, 127, 134, 136
Kelso, Bob 35, 42, 49, 58–9, 118, 121–3
Kemp, Jack 84, 226
Kennedy, Tom 20, 30, 77, 82, 94, 98, 100, 106, 278, 282, 284
Kennedy Stadium 145, 218
Keough, Jack 15
Kessler, Bob 47
Key, Wade 236
Keyes, Frank 83, 89, 98, 104, 108, 111, 113–4
Kimball, Toby 16
King, Dr. Martin Luther 161
King, Rich 82–3, 89–90, 123
Kirksey, Roy 276, 292
Klecko, Joe 309–10
Klimas, Joe 24–5, 34–5, 46, 48–51, 57, 59
Klimas, Larry 59
Knight, Curt 221
Knox, Chuck 192
Koehler, John 294
Koenig, Charles 127–9, 133–4
Kopay, Dave 221
Kotite, Dick 242–3
Kraft, Robert 17
Kramer, Jerry 184, 220
Kreuger, Wayne 217
Kronholm, Louise 257
Krzemienski, Tom 91–2, 94, 107, 113, 344
Kuharich, Joe 188
Kulpmont, Pennsylvania 303, 311, 313

Kyasky, Bob 41–2
Kyasky, Tony 187

Lamberti, Jim 139
Lamonica, Daryle 84, 155
Land, John v, 32, 152, 183, 204–5, 207, 236, 254, 256, 264, 288, 297, 316, 337, 339, 344
Lander, Lowell 83, 90–1, 94–5, 100–1, 103, 106–10, 196
Landino, Joe 45, 48–51
Landry, Tom 76
Las Vegas Casinos 323
LeBaron, Eddie 83, 283
LeClerc, Roger 192–3, 212–3
Lee, Bill 71, 73–5, 81, 89–90, 91, 97, 104, 108, 112, 114, 167, 221, 223, 230, 236, 239, 241–2, 251, 287, 311, 318, 324
Lee, Greg 102
Lee, Johnny 219, 222, 231, 237, 245
Leeka, Bill 101–2
Leigh, Charley 108
Lesinski, Bill 6, 123, 194, 217, 222, 224
Levandowski, Leo 229
Lineberry, Wayne 228
Little, Floyd 190
Loika, Bill 293
Lombardi, Vince 4, 111, 133, 184, 185, 199, 205, 221, 233, 269, 273, 289
Long Island Bulls 229, 231–2, 252
Long Island Chiefs 303–4, 307, 327
Loukas, Angelo 177–8, 299
Lowell Giants 143, 152, 202, 215–6, 228, 265
Lucas, Carol Lee 91
Lucas, Curt 78
Luciani, Ken 78–9, 140, 222
Luciano, Ron 49
Lumsden, Arthur J. 167
Lusteg, Booth 75, 153–4, 326, 328, 361

MacDonald, Rod 44
Mack, Connie 14
Mackey, John 189
Madden, John 208
Mahoney, Dan 126
Maine Mustangs 125
Mainolfi, Pat 42, 58–9
Mallick, Fran 6, 103, 194–5, 213, 220, 222, 227, 236, 244, 249
Manning, Peyton 289
Marazzi, Rich 40, 42, 60
Marchando, Pierre 177, 178
Marlboro Shamrocks 135
Marsh, Larry 32, 118, 122, 125, 127–8, 133–6
Marshall, George 246
Marshall, Herb 307
Mason-Dixon Football League 302
Massey, Paul 258
Matcheski, John 117, 124, 127, 134, 136
Mathews, Ray 236, 274, 276–7, 280–2, 284–5, 293, 295, 321
Mathis, Bill 156–7

372   Index

Matson, Pat 277
Mautino, Fred 49
McCann, Ernie 15
McCauley, Ron 89, 207, 222
McCormick, John 183
McCown, Josh 4
McCullough, Charlie 314
McDole, Ron 183
McDonald, Ray 220–1, 344–5, 363
McDonald, Tommy 88, 187
McGee, Ben 195
McGrath, James 165
McHugh, Joe 52, 59
McHugh, Larry 25, 34–5, 42, 44, 47–8, 52–3, 59, 345
McMahon, Vince 338
McMullan, John 35
McNamara, Robert 149
Meade, Bill 67
Meeks, Mel 4, 25, 77, 209–10, 216–7, 222, 228, 244, 251, 307, 318, 324
Mendez, Mario 79
Mercein, Chuck 328
Meriden, Connecticut 116–7
Meriden Falcons 55, 135–6
Meriden Shamrocks 32, 89, 90, 118–127, 353–4
Merrill, Dina 207
Middletown (Mansfields) 13
Milford Rockets 123, 140
Milici, Roger 32, 117, 140–1, 143–5, 147, 150, 156, 176, 261, 263, 268–9, 274, 276, 280
MIller, Don 15
Miller, Tim v, 26, 28, 305, 313, 318
Miller, Warren 125, 127, 130
minor league baseball 19
Minutemen 162
Mirabelle, Bob 33, 188, 222, 234
Miranda, Bob 305, 308–9, 312, 317, 319, 345
Mitchell, Chris 112
Mitchell, Lydell 289
Mollenkopf, Jack 275
Monardo, Frank 139–41, 145, 159
Monroe, Marilyn 304
Mont Alverne, Carlos 285
Montana, Joe 182
Montgomery, Tim 214
Montreal Beavers 99–100, 104, 109, 112, 114
Moore, Leroy (Sweetpea) 210, 222, 224
Moore, Tom 288
Morello, Carl 135, 153
Morgan, Bob 106
Morgan, Jerry 47, 77
Morgan, Tom 127, 134
Morrall, Earl 223
Morris, Eugene (Mercury) 225
Morris, Joe 156
Morris, Tom 128, 141, 170, 208, 210, 222, 228, 231, 237, 289, 292, 294–5, 301, 345
Mosley, Dock 299
Mosolf, Mike 27, 76, 79, 81–3, 88–9, 91, 93, 175
Moss, Perry 99

Mulligan, George 15
Mulligan, John 128–9
Munford, Chuck 107
Municipal Stadium (Waterbury) 138–9, 141, 145
Muriaty, Gene 325
Murono, Ginzo 131–2, 360
Murono, Seiki v, vi, 27, 29, 33, 131–3, 204, 263, 304, 307, 345–6, 360
Murphy, Jim 32, 166, 175, 227–8, 296, 311, 346
Murphy, Joe 33, 173, 193, 228, 245, 346
Murray, Jack 90, 108
Muzzy Field (Bristol, CT) 138
Mylinski, Jim 263

Namath, Joe 91, 149, 156, 180, 182, 192, 229, 275, 277, 283–4, 344
Naponic, John 222
Nashua Colts 121, 123–4, 126–7
Nelson, Andy 204
Nery, Ron 85, 93–4
Nevins, Pete 267
New Bedford Sweepers 126, 141–3
New Britain Bees 127–134, 354
New Britain Rock Cats 14
New England Colonials 329–332
New England Football Conference 56
New England Football League 22, 117
New Hampshire Colts 128–9
New Haven Annex Rams 62
New Haven (Elm Cities) 13–4
New Jersey Generals 128–9
New York Crusaders 328
New York Jets 268
New York Vikings 128, 131, 133–4
Newark Bears 49, 59, 77, 90, 98, 100–1, 206
Newman, John 100
NFL Films 204–5, 339
Ninowski, Jim 273
Nitschke, Ray 198
Niven, David 207
Nix, Kent 199
Nixon, Richard 163, 167
Nolan, Andrew 39
Nolan Field 45, 46, 52, 54, 141
Noll, Chuck 328
Norfolk Neptunes 115, 281, 288
North American Football League 22, 127, 134
Northumberland Coal Crackers 303; *see also* Reading Coal Crackers
Nugent, Tom 150

Obie, Les 298, 310, 325
O'Brien, Thomas 138
O'Connor, Mike 119, 123
Olderman, Murray 84
Olin-Matheson Company 165
Olivetti Underwood 164
Olson, Bob 290, 294, 299
O'Malley, Chick 144–5
Orlando Panthers 100–1, 250, 258, 280

Otto, Jim 36
Owen Steve 15
Owens, Terrell 218

Pacific League 109
Pacino, Al 309
Palinkas, Pat 278–282, 285, 362
Palinkas, Steve 279–282
Palmer, Chris 4
Palmer, Lou vi, 10, 13, 168, 170–1, 173, 175, 181, 202, 212, 218, 233, 241, 243, 249
Palmore, Harvey 293
Palomba, Mayor Frederick 138–9, 141, 145, 260
Panagoulias, Alkis 153
Papale, Vince 310, 363
Parilli, Babe 277, 283
Parker, Jim 76
Parker, John 185
Paterno, George 156
Paterno, Joe 244, 289
Paterson Miners 50–1, 53, 68
Patterson, Worthy 41
Peppler, Pat 197
Perreault, Pete 192
Peters, Mayor Mike 350
Peterson, Dale 109
Petrillo, Edward 328
Petrocelli, Rico 155
Petry, Phil 150, 361
Pettaway, Marvin 290–2, 294, 300–1, 306, 309, 317, 328, 363
Phelps, Anson 38
Philadelphia Bell 339, 344
Philadelphia Bulldogs 93, 102, 103, 105, 110
Piccone, Lou 9, 29, 31, 180–1, 183, 269, 321–3, 327, 346
Piersall, Jimmy 221, 233
Pietrosante, Nick 40
Pistorio, Salvatore 103
Pittsburgh Valley Ironmen 73, 78, 195
Pittsfield Red Sox 139
Pivec, Dave 93
Plainfield Giants 68
Plainfield Merchants 206
Plimpton, George 267, 362
Plunkett, Sherman 192, 268–9
Pollard, Fritz 245
Pompilli, Phil 310
Pontillo, Tony 42, 118, 123–6, 130, 134–6
Pope, Bucky 88, 187
Portland Mustangs 124
Portland Seahawks 49, 52–3, 67–8, 73–4, 84
Portsmouth Bucs 303, 306–7, 314
Potenza, Mike 62, 64
Potts, John 202
Pottstown Firebirds 4, 10–1, 149, 185, 202–7, 215, 219, 228–30, 232, 234–5, 237, 239, 242, 244, 254–7, 265, 268, 276, 300, 307, 310–1, 315, 319, 327, 337, 339–40, 344–5, 354–7
Powder Ridge Festival 166

Powell, Art 85, 246
Powell, Colin 38
Powell, Luther 38
Priestley, Bob 188
Professional Football League of America 21–2, 110, 169
Proskine, Mark 26, 166, 172, 236, 289, 290, 294
Providence Steamroller 15, 44–5, 47–9, 54, 56, 66–8, 75, 77, 99, 128

Quackenbush, Pete 35, 166, 249
Quigley Stadium (West Haven, CT) 139
Quincy Giants 228, 231–2, 242
Quinn, Jim 299
Quiriconi, Gino 134

Randall, Dennis 169–70, 218, 271, 361
Randall's Island 100, 104
Rather, Dan 162
Rauch, John 27, 224
Reading Coal Crackers 314–5; *see also* Northumberland Coal Crackers
Reamon, Charlie 330
Rentschler Field 4
Rhode Island Indians 94, 98
Rhode Island Steelers 141–3
Ribicoff, Abe 8, 163
Riccuiti, Renato 164
Richmond Roadrunners 3, 110, 202, 210, 258–9, 268, 272, 337
Richter, Bill 28, 30, 32, 40, 43, 47, 53, 58, 60, 118
Riley, Pat 226
Ringo, Jim 228
Risley, Bob 131, 222
Roanoke Buckskins 233
Roberts, J.D. 259
Robeson, Paul 245
Robinson, Bill 213
Robinson, Eddie 337
Robinson, Jackie 100, 245
Robinson, Waide 26, 166, 172, 186, 209, 225, 237, 247, 293, 346–7
Robustelli, Andy 62, 67, 100, 103–4, 110
Rockefeller, Jay 110
Rodack, George 321–2
Rogers, Louis 162
Rohrschneider, Hugh 74–5, 78
Rolling Stones 3
Rood, George 162
Rosen, Sol 30, 98–9, 103–4, 109–10, 113, 115
Rosentover, Joe 63, 67, 78
Rosner, Milt 139, 141, 145–6, 152, 156–7, 159, 262, 269
Rote, Kyle 98
Rote, Tobin 110, 112
Roth, Ernie (The Grand Wizard of Wrestling) 338
Rowland, Donna 8
Rowland, John 17

374 Index

Rowland, Tom 6, 8, 17, 31, 34–6, 177, 184, 193, 196–8, 201, 205–8, 210, 213–4, 219, 221–2, 226, 230, 232, 237, 244, 247, 256, 274, 291, 307, 347
Rozelle, Pete 19
Rubera, Sandy 172, 174
Rubin, Jerry 161
Rupp, Adolph 226
Rush, Clive 153, 244
Russell, Benny 25, 211, 224, 226, 230, 231, 234–7, 244, 249, 251–2, 257–8, 276, 288
Rutkowski, Ed 226
Ryan, Frank 273
Rychlec, Tom 117–8, 122, 124, 127–8, 194, 211, 219, 221–2, 228

Saban, Lou 83
Sabol, Ed 204
Sabol, Steve 205, 255, 300
St. Alphonso's Boy's Club of Port Chester 62–3
St. Louis Cardinals 189–90
St. Mary's High School (Rutherford, NJ) 146
Salvati, Fred 277–8
Samples, Denver 244
Sanders, Red 101
Santa Cruz, Linda 128
Sapienza, Rick 75–6
Sarette, Dave 121
Satchidananda, Swami 341
Savill, Al 99
Savin, Butch 168
Savin, Elaine vi, 7–9, 168, 171, 210, 228, 248, 257, 291, 313, 319, 327, 348, 363
Savin, Herb 34, 167, 347
Savin, Moses 168
Savin, Nina 8
Savin, Pete 7–9, 17, 22, 27, 20, 31–4, 70, 73, 111, 167–9, 171–5, 178, 200, 203, 210, 216, 224, 227, 233–4, 236, 239–42, 244–5, 248–9, 251, 254–6, 258, 261, 282, 286–8, 291, 298, 302–3, 307, 309–12, 314–5, 319–21, 324–7, 329, 331–2, 338, 347–8
Savin, Stacy 8
Scarry, Mike 273
Schaefer Stadium 326, 330
Schenk, C. Newton 139
Schichtle, Henry 141–2, 147
Schmidt, Joe 151
Schmitt, John 180
Schnelker, Bob 199
Schubert, Steve 329–30
Schwartzwalder, Ben 189–91
Schweickert, Bob 142, 147
Scranton Miners 142–3
Scrim, Russ 100
Seaboard Professional Football League 302–319
Seifert, George 266
Shanen, Al 30, 61–6, 68–9, 247
Shanklin, Don 306, 321, 332
Shantz, Bobby 203

Shaunessey, Bob 47
Sheff, Elizabeth Horton 350
Shemeth, Bob 32–3, 35, 57, 58, 73, 101–2, 177, 183, 198–9, 222, 300, 348
Sherlag, Bob 187–8, 207, 211, 222, 277
Sherman, Allie 119–20, 144, 173, 225
Sherman, Tom 6, 29, 34, 180, 182–3, 244, 249, 250, 257–8, 288–90, 292, 293, 300, 306–7, 311, 319, 323, 325, 338
Shippensburg College 145
Shive, Tom 153
Shockley, Bill 93–4, 103, 107, 154
Shortell, Matthew (Pop) 40
Shula, Don 200
Simpson, O.J. 223, 270, 293, 362
Sistrunk, Otis 296, 300, 362
Skladany, John 173, 185, 317, 330
Skoronski, Bob 40, 199
Skubel, John 53, 57, 65, 118, 123, 125, 127, 136
Slater, Duke 245
Small, Howie 202, 222
Smarra, Clem 114
Smith, Allen 151, 156–8, 234, 263, 276
Smith, Jackie 189, 361
Smith, Jerry 221
Smith, John 328, 330–1
Smith, Tommie 184
Smolinski, Mark 156–7
Snead, Norm 284
Snell, Matt 156–7, 182
Snow, Jack 88, 187
Snowden, Ricky 1–2, 4
Snyder, Bob 104–5
Soleau, Bob 194, 210, 222, 225
Solomon, Alan 121
Songin, Butch 52, 105–6, 129
Sonnenburg, Gus 46
South Boston Chippewas 121, 126
Southern Maine Raging Bulls 1–2
Southington Gems 55, 136–7
Sowells, Richie 184
Spahn, Warren 14
Spencer, Robin 129
Spicer, Rob 180
Spink, C.C Johnson 139
Spivey, Bill 41
Sponheimer, John 176, 186, 193, 210, 226–7, 232, 237, 248, 295, 348
Springfield Acorns 59, 73, 77–8
Staake, Bill 293
Stamford Golden Bears 21–2, 30, 48, 51, 62–69, 247, 351–2
Starr, Bart 199, 224
Staubach, Roger 15, 361
Stawartz, Tony 297
Stein, Jon 150, 155, 159
Steinberger, Jeff 296
Steiner, Henry II 171
Stephens, Harold (Hayseed) 20
Stephenson, Kay 226
Stetz, Bill 300

Index

Stevenson, Jerry 141–5, 147
Stohrer, Bob v, vi, 25, 27, 32, 34, 70, 102, 113–4, 166, 173, 176, 181, 185, 202, 206, 210, 214, 222, 226, 228, 231, 244, 248, 252–3, 319, 348–9
Strand, Eli 268
Strock, Don 203
Strode, Woddy 246
Stromberg, Mike 147
Strumpke, Bill 123
Stuhldreher, Harry 15
Sutton, Herb 127
Svare, Harland 88
Swain, Bill 328
Swanson, Terry 294, 301
Sweeney, Walt 189
Sykes, Maurice 50, 74–5, 78–9, 87, 91, 94, 101
Syracuse University 189–90
Szaro, Richie 327–8, 330, 332
Szuc, Lou 285, 296

Talbott, Danny 222
Taliaferro, Mike 244
Tarkenton, Fran 149, 243
Tarrant, John 164
Tavares, Tony 45, 48–9, 53, 118
Texas League 22
Theismann, Joe 223
Theofiledes, Harry 25, 30, 227, 234, 251, 272–4, 276–7, 282–6, 288, 292, 295, 297–8
Theokas, Charley 215
Thomas, Aaron 242
Thomas, Otis 222, 245
Thompson, Alan 319
Thorn, John 11
Thorpe, Jim 16, 128
Thrower, Willie 44
Tiblom, Charley v, 6, 33, 35, 176–8, 180, 283, 288, 290–1, 296, 306, 318
Tiner, Ralph 9, 26, 181, 299, 307, 309, 325, 349
Tittle, Y.A. 84, 99, 102, 141, 195
Tobin, Bill 31
Torok, John 101, 105, 113–4, 217, 263–4, 267–8, 272
Toronto Rifles 103, 106, 113
Tracy, Dick 203
Traficant, Jim 56–7
Tremaglio, Lennie 127
Tri-City Chargers 135
Tropicana Bowl 323
Tucker, Bob 9, 149, 179, 184–5, 204–5, 207, 214, 216, 219, 229, 242–4
Tucker, Dwight 293, 362
Tuckett, Phil 204
Tuckner, Howard 85
Turco, Dr. Vincent 8
Turner, Clyde (Bulldog) 105
Turner, Jim 155
Twin City Chiefs 292
Tyler, Tom 272

Uccello, Mayor Ann 240–1
Udovich, Bruce 309
Unitas, John 19, 195, 223, 226
United Football League: (1961) 20, 79; (2012) 3
University of Connecticut 165–6
University of Iowa 267

Valan, Mike 21, 79
Valente, Terri 4
Vallely, John 102
Van Brocklin, Norm 183
Van Buren, Steve 128, 133, 154, 206
Van Galder, Gary 47–51, 60
Van Nasse, Bob 131
Vece, Phil 117, 121
Velodrome 15
Virginia Sailors 3, 141, 155, 158, 210, 220, 229, 273, 344
Von Sonn, Andy 103, 106–7

Wahlberg, Mark 310
Wakefield Redskins 45
Walker, Doak 110, 112
Walker, Greg 231
Walker, Wayne 220
Wallace, George 162–3, 360
Wallace, Mike 162
Waller, Ron 152, 158, 203–4, 207, 236, 288, 295, 339, 344
Wallner, Carl 72
Wallner, Fred 6, 8, 17, 24, 34, 55, 72–4, 79, 87, 89–91, 107–8, 111, 121–4, 128, 140–1, 168, 170, 174–8, 191, 194, 197–8, 202, 207, 211–2, 214, 217–8, 220, 222, 224–6, 228, 231–2, 234, 236, 244–5, 248–9, 287, 290, 292–4, 297, 299–300, 304–6, 316, 320, 325, 329, 331, 337, 349
Walsh, Bill 360
Walton, Joe 243
Wapinsky, Frank 310
Ward, Jim 93
Wardlaw, John 88, 94, 134, 140, 202, 210, 220, 228, 231, 245, 248, 250, 349, 350, 363
Warfield, Paul 326
Warner, Darrick 278, 282, 285–6
Washington, Hank 8, 225–6, 231, 237–8, 288
Washington, Kenny 246
Washington, Rick 296
Washington Sharks 78
Waterbury, CT 138
Waterbury Blues 15
Waterbury Giants 138–9, 145
Waterbury Orbits 22, 138–160, 260, 354
Watts, Claude 254, 288, 297, 301, 316, 339
Watts, Kevin 292
Webb, Allan 30, 40, 44, 63, 67, 69
Webb, Cloyd 92
Webb, Don 188
Webster, Alex 243
Weidl, Paul 285–6
Weinstein, Bruce 271, 276

Werblin, Sonny 168
West Hartford Spartans 70
West Texas State University 225–6
Westchester Bulls 202, 213, 220, 229
Westchester Crusaders 55–6, 77–8
Westhaver, James 128
Westminster School 101, 112
Wheeler, Manch v, 3, 8, 31, 74, 83–4, 87, 90–1, 101, 134, 140–3, 147, 151, 168, 172, 202, 207–8, 211–7, 220, 222, 224, 233, 255–6, 274, 324, 338, 350
Wheeling Ironmen 20–1, 93, 98, 104–5, 110, 113–4
White, Bryan 308
White, Danny 179
White, Freeman 242–3
Whitman Townies 45, 122, 124
Whitmore, Jim 102
Wichard, Gary 186, 332
Wilkinson, Bud 99
Wilkinson, Tom 106
Willard, John 30, 32, 70, 108

Williams, Bruce 222, 312
Williams, Joe 89, 103
Willow Brook Park 127
Wilmington Clippers 151–2, 158
Wilson, Butch 242–3
Wilson, George, Jr. 206
Wilson, Ralph 168, 224
Winston-Muss Development Corporation 111
Winters, Bill 215, 229, 232, 236
Wismer, Harry 105
Woitkowski, Ray 105
Wojtusik, Henry 138
Wood, Gary 128
Wood, Willie 198
Woodall, Al 210, 213–5, 268, 277, 283
World Football Leage 326, 339
Wyatt, Hugh 309, 310, 316

Yewcic, Tom 330
Young, Al 286

Zegalia, Steve 257

www.ingramcontent.com/pod-product-compliance
Ingram Content Group UK Ltd.
Pitfield, Milton Keynes, MK11 3LW, UK
UKHW041921140426
5217IPUK00014B/261